2.0

AN INSIDER LOOK AT THE MOST
INFLUENTIAL GAMES OF ALL TIME

VINTAGE GAMES 2.0

AN INSIDER LOOK AT THE MOST
INFLUENTIAL GAMES OF ALL TIME

MATT BARTON

CRC Press
Taylor & Francis Group
Boca Raton London New York

CRC Press is an imprint of the
Taylor & Francis Group, an **informa** business

CRC Press
Taylor & Francis Group
6000 Broken Sound Parkway NW, Suite 300
Boca Raton, FL 33487-2742

© 2017 by Taylor & Francis Group, LLC
CRC Press is an imprint of Taylor & Francis Group, an Informa business

No claim to original U.S. Government works

Printed and bound in India by Replika Press Pvt. Ltd.

Printed on acid-free paper
Version Date: 20160511

International Standard Book Number-13: 978-1-138-89913-1 (Paperback)

Library of Congress Cataloging-in-Publication Data

Names: Barton, Matt, author.
Title: Vintage games 2.0 : an insider look at the most influential games of
all time / Matt Barton.
Description: Boca Raton, FL ; London ; New York : Taylor & Francis, 2017. |
Includes bibliographical references and index.
Identifiers: LCCN 2016006333 | ISBN 9781138899131
Subjects: LCSH: Video games--History.
Classification: LCC GV1469.3 .B37 2017 | DDC 794.8--dc23
    LC record available at https://lccn.loc.gov/2016006333

Visit the Taylor & Francis Web site at
http://www.taylorandfrancis.com

and the CRC Press Web site at
http://www.crcpress.com

Contents

Preface

We use the term *gamer* to refer to someone who plays lots of games, but it'd make more sense to have a term for people who've never played them. Statistically speaking, they're the oddballs. Today, almost everyone plays video games—not just the stereotypical basement-dwelling geek! We play them every chance we get, and, thanks to smartphones and other mobile devices, we have access to them anytime and anywhere. Games have diffused across all sectors of society, from kindergarten rooms to nursing homes.

Game designer and author Jane McGonigal opened her TED Talk with a startling figure: We spend 3 billion hours per week playing video games![1] Contrary to popular belief, it's not just boys playing them—94% of teenage girls report playing video games on a regular basis, and more than half of 30- to 49-year-olds haven't put down their controllers.[2] Those of us with an account on Steam can see at a glance how many hours we've personally spent enjoying any particular game. Mine shows that I've spent more than 750 hours playing *Sid Meier's Civilization V*, one of my personal favorites (see Figure P.1). That's nearly a month of my life, but it pales in comparison to the years I've put into *World of Warcraft*. While these figures might arouse "gamer's regret" in some people, my guess is that people spend as much time watching television or doing other things they enjoy; there's just no computer there to time it. Besides, what's the alternative—workaholism?

In short, our culture loves video games, and it's difficult to imagine what our lives would be like without them. After the "Great Video Game Crash of 1983," prognosticators were all too ready to declare that the "fad" of video games was over. Obviously, that didn't happen, and video games have only gotten bigger and better since the glorious days of *Pac-Man*, *Space Invaders*, and *Donkey Kong*. Today's best-selling games range from "Triple-A" major studio productions with budgets in the hundreds of millions, to quirky "indie" projects designed by lone hobbyists using cheap or even free development tools. Online distribution services like Apple's App Store, Microsoft's Xbox Games Store, or Steam roll out new games on a daily basis. Steam alone has more than 3700 games, far more than any one person could

---

[1] Gaming Can Make a Better World. Produced by TED Video. Performed by Jane McGonigal (2008).

[2] Lenhart, Amanda, Joseph Kahne, Ellen Middaugh, Alexandra Rankin Macgill, Chris Evans, and Jessica Vitak. Teens, Video Games, and Civics: Teens' Gaming Experiences Are Diverse and Include Significant Social Interaction and Civic Engagement. Pew Internet & American Life Project (2008).

Figure P.1   Steam tracks the number of hours you play each game.

Figure P.2   The top seven sellers on Steam as of this writing. It's a diverse mix of high production titles and indies.

play to any depth in a lifetime.[3] It would take a year just to play each one for 2 hours—barely enough time to make it through the introductions or tutorials (see Figure P.2)!

There are video games that cater to every conceivable style and taste. While violent or controversial "shooters" steal most of the mainstream media's attention, the truth is that there's an overwhelming diversity of video games. There are games designed for all ages, genders, and even for cats and dogs!

The subjects, themes, styles, interfaces, and gameplay mechanics are also incredibly varied. On the one hand, we have sophisticated computer games such as *Elite: Dangerous*, which serious fans/players play with "flight control systems" featuring elaborate joysticks, dedicated throttle controls, and integrated multi-function displays. On the other hand, we have "clicker" games such as *Cookie Clicker* for mobile devices, in which gameplay consists of, well, the name really says it all: you use your finger to click on a cookie. In

between this "casual" and "hardcore" divide is a smorgasbord of genres, usually divided into broad categories of action, adventure, multiplayer, racing, role playing, simulation, and strategy games. Under each of these headings, we could easily list dozens of subcategories, and many popular games, such as *Portal 2*, are hard to classify.

We play video games on a multitude of devices, from stunningly powerful "gaming rigs" costing thousands to smartphones, tablets, and handhelds costing hundreds (or less). Smartphones have opened up gaming to audiences who would never purchase a dedicated gaming device, but are, for whatever reason, perfectly okay with playing *Words with Friends* or *Candy Crush*. Also, the plethora of mobile options means that we can play games anywhere, at any time. Next time you whip out your iPhone for a quick round of *Angry Birds* in the bathroom, imagine if the only place you could play video games were in an arcade!

---

[3] Makuch, Eddie. "Steam Reaches 100 Million Users And 3,700 Games." *GameSpot.* September 22, 2014. http://www.gamespot.com/articles/steam-reaches-100-million-users-and-3-700-games/1100-6422489/ (accessed March 9, 2015).

Video games have become a critical part of our culture, just as important, if not more so, than film, television, sports, books, or music. In 2013, Americans alone spent more than $20.5 billion on games.[4] Yet, despite the enormous financial success and ubiquity enjoyed by the video game industry, many people (and, sadly, many parents and teachers) regard video games at best as a childish time waster and at worst a menace to society. Even active gamers may struggle to name even a few notable game designers, whereas prominent film directors or pop artists are known to everyone. Saddest of all, even some professional game designers dismiss their own past masterpieces, believing that these games are now obsolete and not worth playing anymore. Imagine if we had the same prejudice in the music industry—if The Beatles' or Jimi Hendrix's albums had been out of print for decades because they hadn't been recorded with the latest equipment!

In short, it's time we started taking video games seriously as a cultural phenomenon. To me, that means getting to know the maestros and their masterpieces—the games that have helped define the industry as we know and love it today. I want to tell the story of the video game industry by talking about the movers and shakers; the paradigm shifts— those moments when, suddenly, whatever people thought they knew about video games turned out wrong. Our best game developers were renegades, maniacs, geniuses, failures, and dreamers. Some considered themselves cultured artists; others wouldn't know a Picasso from a pepperoni pizza.

Video games have become a big business, but that doesn't mean developers are driven solely by profit. Ron Gilbert, designer of some of the biggest hits of the 80s and 90s, put it this way: "With any game I make, the goal is to make enough money that I can make another one." As we'll see, the best games were made by people who wanted to play them, not merely to sell them. At the end of the day, a game is either fun or it's not, and no amount of marketing dollars, cutting-edge tools, or high-level assets will change that. Video games are a risky business, and the game developers of today are not descended from businessmen.

Bill Loguidice and I wrote the first *Vintage Games* book back in 2009. That might seem like yesterday to some readers, but 6 years is a century in this industry. There's a whole new generation of consoles and mobile devices, exciting new VR technologies such as Oculus Rift and Microsoft HoloLens, an explosion of indie game development, and, perhaps most significant of all, the runaway success of crowdfunding. Kickstarter allowed projects such as Double Fine Adventure ($3.3 million), Obsidian Entertainment's *Project Eternity* ($4 million), and Chris Roberts' *Star Citizen* ($2.1 million) to resurrect moribund genres, bypassing publishers and appealing directly to fans for backing. Finally, Valve Corporation's Steam OS, a Linux-powered operating system optimized for gaming, will power a line of "Steam Machines" that may at last bridge the gaps between PC and console gaming. Nintendo's NX, meanwhile, may do the same for console and mobile gaming. At any rate, it'll be exciting to see how these new devices affect both PC and console markets.

---

[4] Ewalt, David M. "Americans Will Spend $20.5 Billion On Video Games In 2013." Forbes. December 19, 2013. http://www .forbes.com/sites/davidewalt/2013/12/19/americans-will-spend-20-5-billion-on-video-games-in-2013/ (accessed March 09, 2015).

If you read the first *Vintage Games*, you'll notice some big changes to the format that I think you'll appreciate. First, the chapters are no longer organized alphabetically by game title, but rather chronologically by the date of their publication. This arrangement makes it easier to tell and understand the story of video games, especially the context surrounding their development and publication. While it was convenient in the old book to flip directly to your favorite game, the new structure will make it easier to keep track of what was going on at any particular moment.

I organized the book into five sections based on sociologist Everett Rogers' Innovation Adoption Lifecycle, which he described in his book *Diffusion of Innovations*. The basic idea is that the widespread adoption of any technology follows a predictable series of stages, and we can generalize about the type of people who adopt the technology at any given stage. For example, Rogers calls the first people to embrace a new technology "the innovators."[5] According to Rogers,

> Innovators possess a type of mental ability that better enables them to cope with uncertainty and to deal with abstractions. [They] must be able to conceptualize relatively abstract information about innovations and apply this new information to his or her own situation.[6]

As we'll see, almost all of the games covered in the first part of this book were created by precisely these kinds of people, and I think it makes sense to keep these categories in mind as we proceed through the "generations" of video game history.

Many people look to historians to determine who did something first, or whether so-and-so had been "inspired" by some earlier project. The Internet is rampant with contradictory claims of this type, especially in the early days when commercial developers were attempting to sell games they'd adapted from earlier ones they'd played on mainframes. Did Bruce Artwick play *Air Fight* on PLATO before developing his *Flight Simulator* game? Was John Romero or John Carmack, credited as the fathers of the first-person shooter, really just repackaging *Maze War*, an earlier mainframe game with similar gameplay? Did *Minecraft* rip off *Infiniminer*? These are often the hardest kind of questions to answer, especially when great sums of money (and personal glory!) are at stake. Whenever possible, I've contacted the parties in question to get their story and presented my findings as objectively as possible.

A second major change to this edition is that I've updated the list of games covered, based largely on feedback I received from readers of the first book, my editors at Focal Press, and informal panels of game experts and designers. As you can imagine, one of the hardest challenges of putting together a book like this is deciding what games to cover. You or I could easily add dozens, if not hundreds, of titles to this list, and still feel that key games were missing. For obvious reasons, I can't cover everything, and even if I

---

[5] Rogers, Everett. *Diffusion of Innovations*. New York: Free Press, 2003.

[6] See footnote 5, p. 215.

could, even the e-book version of this book would weigh more than an Xbox! I sincerely hope you will forgive me if your favorite game doesn't get the attention it deserves.

Finally, I've tried to integrate as many insights as I can from the many game developers and designers I've interviewed on my Matt Chat program on YouTube. Since I began producing the show in 2009, I've had in-depth conversations with such industry luminaries as John Romero of *Doom*, Richard "Lord British" Garriott of *Ultima*, Tim Cain of *Fallout*, and Robert Woodhead of *Wizardry*—just to name a few. Often enough, they've told me fascinating behind-the-scenes information that I'm excited to share with you in this book, especially when they give us a better understanding or new perspective on a design decision or play mechanic.

I really hope that you will enjoy this book. I love video games, and the opportunity to write books about them is a privilege and a joy. However, the real reason I do this is to connect with people like you, who share my passion for video games and their history. If you want to chat with me about the book or your favorite games, please visit my website at http://mattchat.us or visit my YouTube channel at http://youtube.com/blacklily8. I can also be reached on Twitter (@mattbarton).

Acknowledgments

I would like to thank Chet Bolingbroke, Marty Goldberg, Nathan Tolbert, Adam Dayton, and Shane Stacks for their help and friendship. Special thanks to my wife, Elizabeth Barton, for scanning all those boxes and cartridges!

Part I
The Innovators

The world did not always have video games, but there have always been games. Indeed, the Dutch historian and cultural theorist Johan Huizinga argues in his book *Homo Ludens* that games and play are what make our culture and civilization possible. While even animals play—as anyone who's watched the squirrels on a college campus knows—only humans play *games*, that is, play that involves an agreed upon structure or system of rules. And we've been doing it for a very long time. Archaeologists have found board games that are at least 5000 years old, and it's likely they were around long before that. Chess dates back to 6th century India, and the Chinese invented playing cards over a thousand years ago.

The immediate predecessor of the video game is pinball and electromechanical games. The first coin-operated pinball machines were introduced by David Gottlieb in 1931, and innovations quickly followed—electricity and bumpers in 1933, flippers in 1947, and solid-state electronics in the 1970s. It's beyond this book to give you a detailed account of the evolution of pinball and the role it played in this story—I suggest you watch Brett Sullivan's excellent film *Special When Lit* (2009) for a quick overview of this fascinating story and subculture.

For our purposes, what's important to note is that pinball and similar games had already established markets and accustomed people to the idea of arcades, coin-operated gaming, and gaming culture long before Bushnell and Alcorn built their

first *Pong* machine. Indeed, Bushnell's experience working in a pinball arcade (Figure PI.1) is what inspired him to make his first coin-operated video games.

Rogers argued that "innovators" are the first to adopt technologies "not only because they become aware of the innovation somewhat sooner than others in their system, but also because they require fewer months or years to move from the knowledge stage to the decision stage."[1] They like the new ideas, are eager to learn more about them, and can deal (mentally and otherwise) with frequent failure as they struggle to master them. Furthermore, they are "perceived with suspicion and often with disrespect" by the more "sensible" and "well-behaved" members of their group (318). In the academic world of 1950s and 1960s computer labs, these innovators were called "hackers."

Today, the word *hacker* is synonymous with cybercrime or even terrorism. However, as Steven Levy points out in his marvelous book *Hackers: Heroes of*

Figure PI.1   Pinball games were around well before *Pong* showed up in the arcades, but they are still around today. Shown here is John Papadiuk's *Theatre of Magic* from 1995.

the Computer Revolution, the term originally demarcated a very different group: "They were adventurers, visionaries, risk-takers, artists ... and the ones who most clearly saw why the computer was a truly revolutionary tool."[2] The particular group of hackers that concern us, however, had a slightly different view. For them, the computer was a truly revolutionary *toy*.

Fifty years ago, the word *computer* conjured up in people's minds images of room-sized machines with banks of vacuum tubes, punch cards, and professional staff in lab coats. These computers cost millions, but your mobile phone is far more powerful. The

---

[1] Rogers, Everett. *Diffusion of Innovations*. New York: Free Press, 2003: 214.

[2] Levy, Steven. *Hackers: Heroes of the Computer Revolution*. Cambridge: O'Reilly Media, 2010.

very idea that anyone would use these behemoths just to play games was absurd and offensive. They were for serious purposes, such as scientific research, census data, and military ballistics. The rules were absolutely clear: Computers were for *serious* uses only; gaming was *strictly* prohibited.

Computers follow rules. Hackers ... not so much.

Chapter 1

Spacewar!: It's Rocket Science

One of the earliest and most influential hacks of all time is a real-time, physics-based, spaceship dogfighting video game called *Spacewar!*, which began making its way across university campuses in the early 1960s. It was designed by and for hardcore nerds—or "hackers," a term they coined and applied to themselves. The hackers never intended to create a new form of entertainment or make a ton of money. They just wanted a way to show off their elite programming skills, and *Spacewar!* was one of many ingenious "hacks" to one-up their fellows.

The story of *Spacewar!*'s creation has been told many times, most notably by Steven Levy in his excellent book *Hackers: Heroes of the Computer Revolution*, which I highly recommend to anyone interested in computer history. Levy paints a vivid picture of the unique hacker culture at the Massachusetts Institute of Technology (MIT), which was formed largely by members of MIT's Tech Model Railroad Club. These engineering students spent their time constructing elaborate and incredibly intricate model trains. When they gained access to a computer, they discovered an equally complex system to tinker with, and promptly began making all kinds of impressive programs called "hacks." Steve "Slug" Russell's hack was a full-fledged game called *Spacewar!*, which he programmed on a DEC PDP-1 at MIT. He didn't come up with the idea on his own. Credit is also owed to Russell's friends J. Martin "Shag" Graetz and Wayne Wiitanen, as well as Alan Kotok, who got help from DEC with some geometry routines (see Figure 1.1).

DEC's corporate strategy differed sharply from IBM's, which put a staff of professionals between end users and the hardware. Russell thought IBM's process was slow and boring. He hated having to put his programs on a deck of punch cards, hand them to the staff, wait for hours, and then try to make sense of the huge printout of numbers he'd get back from them. This setup might be fine for busy professionals with no interest in how the hardware actually worked. For the hackers, though, this policy was inefficient if not insulting. DEC, by contrast, let you get your hands dirty, an attitude that resonated strongly with these young engineers.

Why would members of a model railroad club care about computers? Model trains and computers have more in common than you might think. Both model train building and computer programming share a deep concern for logic systems; essentially, a computer's circuitry and software operate like the rails and switches of a railroad, guiding the processor along a series of tasks and conditions. This may not sound like much fun, but consider the appeal of systems games like *SimCity* or *Tropico*. There's just something

Figure 1.1   Steve "Slug" Russell, father of *Spacewar!*. (Photo courtesy of YMS.)

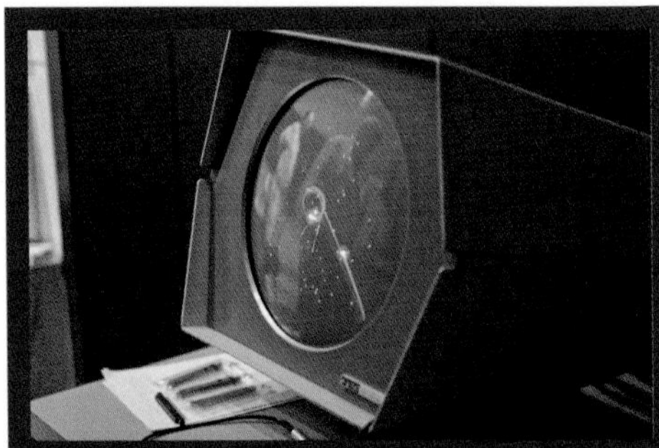

inherently satisfying about building a complex but well-ordered system of moving parts. See Figure 1.2.

A key feature of *Spacewar!* was its display. At the time, most computers relied on printers to relay information to users—there was no screen. While this technology worked for some types of games (see Chapter 4), an action-based game needed a way to present information in real time. Russell and his friends learned that MIT's DEC PDP-1 would soon be upgraded with a Type 30 Precision CRT Display and set themselves the challenge of coming up with a suitable application for it. According to Graetz, the three hackers wanted a program that would satisfy these three criteria:

1. It should demonstrate; that is, it should show off as many of the computer's resources as possible, and tax those resources to the limit.
2. Within a consistent framework, it should be interesting, which means every run should be different.
3. It should involve the onlooker in a pleasurable and active way—in short, it should be a game.[1]

What's interesting about Graetz's criteria is how well they apply to modern games. The first point in particular is vital for the "launch titles" associated with a new console; gamers will not invest in a new generation if there are no good games to clearly demonstrate its superiority over the previous one.

The setting and gameplay of *Spacewar!* were inspired by the novels of Edward E.

Figure 1.2   *Spacewar!* running on a PDP-1. (Photo courtesy of Joi Ito from Imbamura.)

---

[1]   Graetz, J.M. "The Origin of Spacewar." *Creative Computing*, August 1981: 56–67.

"Doc" Smith, especially the *Lensman* and *Skylark* series. These were classics of Golden Age science fiction, chocked full of space aliens, weird science, starship combat, and fantastic technology. Doc Smith ignited the hackers' imaginations with bold visions of the future, and they were in a situation to turn some of these fictions into science. See Figure 1.3.

"Slug" Russell worked on his project in an open and supportive environment, with some of the best engineering minds of the era supporting him. This was well before commercial software and non-

Figure 1.3 *Spacewar!* running on Norbert Landsteiner's PDP emulator.

disclosure agreements; the hackers at MIT shared their code and modified each other's programs with no fear of lawsuits. Russell's code was soon modified and expanded by a great many other programmers, including fellow Tech Model Railroader Pete Sampson, whose "expensive planetarium" hack replaced the game's random backdrop of stars with an actual star field as seen from Earth.

After nearly 2000 hours of coding, the initial version of the game was ready for play. It was an impressive hack indeed. Two players controlled one of two spaceships that circled a small star with powerful gravity. The object of the game was to destroy the opponent's ship with a missile, being careful not to get sucked into the star's gravitational field. Players could also enter hyperspace, which randomly relocated them somewhere else on the screen. This feature, of course, shows up in the much later *Defender*, which also shared similarities with much of the rest of *Spacewar!*'s control options. Players controlled the game by flipping four switches, but this cumbersome control scheme was quickly replaced with do-it-yourself game pads and joysticks.

Spacewar! was an immediate hit at MIT and spread to other universities, including Stanford—host of the first "Spacewar Olympics." The competitive nature of the game encouraged friendly rivalries complete with "trash talk," and since you couldn't play it by yourself, there was always an appetite for fresh meat. There were even reports of "Spacewar elbow." At MIT, an external display was set up to allow the crowds of people who showed up annually at MIT's Science Open House to watch timed matches. Graetz claims that in just a few short years, "Program tapes were already showing up all over the country, not only on PDP-1s but on just about any research computer that had a programmable CRT."[2,3]

Spacewar! wasn't the first video game—there are at least two that predate it, including *OXO* in 1952 and *Tennis for Two* in 1958. *OXO* was programmed by Alexander S. Douglas

---

[2] See footnote 1, p. 66.

[3] Martin Goldberg and Devin Monnens have disputed this claim, arguing that it spread much more slowly than was originally thought, and its impact was more limited to MIT and Stanford than many realize (Smith 2014).

for the Electronic Delay Storage Automatic Calculator (EDSAC) computer, which sported a dot-matrix CRT display and a rotary telephone for input. *Tennis for Two* was programmed by William Higinbotham on a Donner Model 30 analog computer, which had an oscilloscope for a display. I'll talk more about it in the next chapter.

Spacewar! was far more ambitious than either of these early games and inspired many of the countless men and women who played it to pursue careers in computer programming. After all, what made *Spacewar!* so impressive wasn't just that it was fun; it demonstrated new possibilities for computers.

However, video games were still unknown to the general public. The arcade industry was limited to pinball and other electromechanical games. One man familiar with both worlds was a University of Utah engineering student named Nolan Bushnell, who spent his summers working at Lagoon Amusement Park in Salt Lake City. There, he saw firsthand how these machines appealed to the general public. "The things I learned about getting you to spend a quarter on me in one of my midway games," said Bushnell; "I put those sales pitches in my automated box."[4]

One day after school, Bushnell's friend said he had something exciting to show him in the computer lab. At midnight, the two trekked over, and the future founder of Atari got his first glimpse of *Spacewar!*. Bushnell quickly saw that it was much more fun than the simple midway games he'd hawked as a carney. "If I could take this game and put it into the arcade at the park," thought Bushnell, "it could make a *lot* of money."[5]

Bushnell teamed up with a friend named Ted Dabney and began work on a cheap, coin-operated version of *Spacewar!*. Because microprocessors weren't yet readily available, the two had to work with bulkier and older transistor–transistor logic (TTL) digital circuits. They did, however, build a sleek futuristic cabinet for the game out of fiberglass. They fitted in a modified General Electric 15^2 black-and-white television for the display. The result was *Computer Space*, a stripped-down version of *Spacewar!*. It lacked the gravity well and the all-important two-player combat of the mainframe version. Gameplay was limited to dodging enemy fire and shooting down computer-controlled flying saucers. It paled in comparison, but Bushnell hoped the novelty of playing a video game, particularly on such an otherworldly cabinet, would compensate for these omissions—and besides, most of the public wouldn't know what they were missing. See Figure 1.4.

Calling themselves "Syzygy," Bushnell and Dabney worked long hours repairing broken pinball machines to survive as they sought out a manufacturer for Computer Space. They finally settled on Nutting Associates, a struggling manufacturer of electromechanical arcade machines. Their game rolled off the line in November of 1971. For its first test, they put a machine in a bar called The Dutch Goose, a popular hangout for Stanford University students. It seemed they had a hit on their hands; the students there were very

---

4 Seabrook, John. "Game Master." *The New Yorker.* November 6, 2006. http://www.newyorker.com/magazine/2006/11/06/game-master?currentPage=all (accessed July 7, 2015).

5 There's considerable controversy surrounding when, where, and on what computer Bushnell actually played *Spacewar!*. For a fuller account, see Marty Goldberg and Curt Vendel's book *Atari, Inc.: Business is Fun.*

excited. Nutting decided to produce 1500 of the machines.[6]

Computer Space was not the smash hit they'd expected. Apparently, the patrons of The Dutch Goose were a special breed. Even a later two-player version of *Computer Space* flopped miserably. Bushnell concluded that the game was too complicated for gamers accustomed to pinball. "The lesson was," said Bushnell, "keep it simple."

However, *Computer Space*'s failure is probably owed more to its dull gameplay than dull-witted players—as later, more successful efforts shows. One of these was Larry Rosenthal's *Space Wars*, released in 1977. Rosenthal had been a student at MIT, home of the original game, and did a better job adapting it. However, he demanded a full 50% of the profits, and only the floundering Cinematronics company was willing to accept his demands.

Rosenthal developed a special processor, which was cheap yet sophisticated enough to run the full version of *Spacewar!*, complete with the gravity well and the two-player dogfighting that made the original so fun. It also let you take damage before exploding. Players could even adjust gravity and inertia. Most importantly, it had the sharp vector graphics of the original (based on lines) instead of the raster graphics of *Computer Space* (based on dots or small blocks called pixels). To make it profitable, there was still a time limit; whoever had the most kills at the end of the match won the game. It was a great adaptation of *Spacewar!* and fared much better than *Computer Space*.

In 1978, Atari built *Orbit*, yet another raster-based adaptation of *Spacewar!*. Unlike the previous effort, however, this one at least offered two-player side-by-side play and borrowed the partial damage system of *Space Wars*. The ships in *Orbit* look like the *Enterprise* and a Klingon Bird of Prey from *Star Trek*. Like *Computer Space*, however, the game boldly went nowhere. A simplified version of this game called *Space War* was released in 1978 for the Atari VCS, but it too failed.

Atari had more luck with games inspired by, rather than based on, *Spacewar!*. They went vector skelter in 1979 with *Lunar Lander* and *Asteroids*, two stunning but difficult games. *Lunar Lander*, as the name implies, had players landing a fragile lunar module on one of several moon bases (platforms, really). The gameplay concepts introduced in

Figure 1.4 An infamous advertisement for *Computer Space*. The bizarre cabinet earned it a cameo in the film *Soylent Green*. (Scan courtesy of Critical Commons.)

---

[6] Dillon, Roberto. *The Golden Age of Video Games*. Boca Raton, FL: CRC Press, 2011: 10.

Lunar Lander would inspire the "gravity" and "thrust" games of the 1980s, including Atari's *Gravitar* in 1982.

Lyle Rains's and Ed Logg's *Asteroids* offered a terrific innovation: instead of blasting a rival space pilot, *Asteroids* had players destroying huge rocks floating in space. Whenever one of these asteroids was hit, it splintered into pieces, any one of which could collide with and destroy the player's ship. As with *Spacewar!*, players could blink into hyperspace, but they might reappear in an even more dangerous situation than before. Unlike its many attempts at a faithful *Spacewar!* clone, *Asteroids* was a huge success, and has been ported, cloned, and modified ever since.

Despite the success of *Asteroids* and *Space Wars*, enthusiasm for this style of game ebbed after Taito's *Space Invaders* in 1978. It gobbled up far more quarters than any of the old gravity-and-thrust games, which suggested that while realistic physics were extremely impressive to the engineering types who understood them, they weren't important to most gamers. Soon, games that required players to deal with complex issues of inertia and momentum were pushed to the dustier corners of the arcade.

That said, there are types of games that do benefit from accurate physics, most notably flight simulators, racing, and virtual pinball games. Clearly, all of these types of games rely on complex "physics engines" to make their gameplay feel more realistic, concepts and approaches that were pioneered in *Spacewar!*.

Spacewar!'s ultimate contribution, however, might be its virtual world. Although some argue that even a tic-tac-toe or tennis game has a virtual world, I disagree. There's a difference between a game *surface*, such as a tennis court or chessboard, and a game *world*, such as the outer space environment of *Spacewar!* or the islands of *Myst*. Though it's easy to get bogged down in theoretical discussions of "navigable space" and "habitable environments," suffice it to say that *Spacewar!* introduced the idea that computers could represent and let players explore virtual worlds (with accurate star maps, no less!), not just abstract space. You didn't just play *with* these toys; you played *in* them.

For his part, Steve "Slug" Russell's time in the video game industry was short. After MIT, he worked on Lisp for the IBM 704, studied artificial intelligence at Stanford, and eventually took a job at Nohau Corporation designing embedded systems tools. If you're lucky, you might catch him at one of the Computer History Museum's "Revolution" exhibits, standing humbly before a well-maintained DEC PDP-1. Today, he's gray haired, bespectacled, and demure. But, oh, just get him talking about the early days—or rather the very late nights—of programming *Spacewar!*, and his eyes light up, like the vector sun twinkling in the center of a Type 30 Precision CRT display.

1.1 Playing *Spacewar!* Today

Even if you don't have a working DEC PDP-1 in your basement, there are plenty of easy ways to experience this game. I recommend visiting Norbert Landsteiner's implementation at http://www.masswerk.at/spacewar/. It runs in your browser, supports gamepads, and sports a window reminiscent of the original's oscilloscope. Another option is at http://spacewar.oversigma.com/html5/. The compilers of this no-frills version claim that it is "extremely faithful" to the original, but with larger ships and some tweaks to compensate for varying machine speeds. In any case, be sure to play it with a friend. Then as now, much of the game's appeal relies on competition and social interaction.

Assuming you don't own one of the original arcade machines, *Computer Space* is more challenging to find and play. Your best bet is probably Mike "Moose" O'Malley's version, available at http://www.computerspacefan.com/NewCompSpaceSim.htm. Most other arcade spin-offs mentioned in this chapter are easily played with MAME. Instructions for downloading and configuring MAME are available at http://mamedev.org.

Chapter 2

Pong: Easy to Learn, Hard to Master

There was one key difference between the hackers of the Massachusetts Institute of Technology and Nolan Bushnell. They were in it for the science; he was in it for the money. A bold entrepreneur, Bushnell could see dollar signs where no one else did.

The disappointing reception of *Computer Space* was frustrating for Bushnell, who prided himself on the salesmanship skills he'd honed as a successful carney at Lagoon Amusement Park. "I had the highest per-caps of any amusement park in the nation," bragged Bushnell, a feat he'd accomplished by personally redesigning some of the midway games. "And they did make money."[1] So why hadn't *Computer Space*? (see Figure 2.1).

Bushnell and his partner Ted Dabney were determined to find out why. Perhaps the problem wasn't the game, but gamers. They knew about pinball and ring toss, not dogfighting in space. They needed a game that would be more familiar to average Americans—but also novel enough to draw their attention away from pinball machines. They adopted a new mantra: easy to learn; hard to master. Bushnell and Dabney's next game would be as easy to learn and hard to master as pinball.

It's worth noting that Ping Pong, or table tennis, had been steadily gaining popularity in the United States, especially after the introduction of the foam rubber paddle in 1952 (a Japanese invention). Around the time Bushnell was contemplating his next foray into video games, the official US table tennis team was invited to China to play against their champions—the first time Americans had been allowed into the country since 1949! Magazines and newspapers made a big to-do about this "Ping-Pong diplomacy." With all this talk of Ping Pong in the air, it's hardly surprising that Bushnell would have thought to make a video game out of it.

What happens next is, and probably always will be, shrouded in controversy. According to one version of events, he and Dabney hired Allan Alcorn, a recent graduate of Berkeley's electrical engineering and computer sciences program. Alcorn had no

---

[1] Geffen, Haley, and Brandon Lisy. "Atari's Co-Founder Explains Why Pong's Ball Wasn't Round." Bloomberg.com. December 04, 2014. http://www.bloomberg.com/bw/articles/2014-12-04/atari-co-founder-nolan-bushnell-on-gamings-pioneer-years (accessed March 13, 2015).

experience with video games, so Bushnell gave him a "warm-up" exercise: make a simple game with "one moving spot, two paddles, and score digits."[2] After he'd learned the fundamentals with this project, they'd move on to a more ambitious (and hopefully) more profitable version of *Computer Space* (see Figure 2.2).

However, Alcorn's game had potential of its own. The young engineer had a good feel for game mechanics, such as having the ball speed up and reflect off the paddle at an angle. Bushnell asked Alcorn to add sound effects, including a roaring crowd. Dabney wanted boos and hisses. "How do you do that with digital circuits? Ones and zeroes? I had no idea," said Alcorn.[2] Nevertheless, he found a way to make sounds: "Since I had the wire wrapped on the scope, I poked around the sync generator to find an appropriate frequency or tone. So those sounds were done in half a

Figure 2.1   *Pong* cabinet designed by Allan Alcorn. (Photo courtesy of Chris Rand.)

day. They were the sounds that were already in the machine."[3] These weren't the realistic sounds Bushnell and Dabney wanted, but they were a key factor in the game's success.

On November 29, 1972, Bushnell and his newly rebranded "Atari" company set up their first *Pong* machine in Andy Capp's Tavern in Sunnyvale, California. They'd changed the name after learning their old one, "Syzygy," was, believe it or not, already in use by another company. Overcome with anxiety that they had another *Computer Space* on their hands, they left quickly, leaving their creation to its fate.

Later that evening, the bar filled with regulars. The patrons, clad in colorful bell bottoms and wide-collared plaid shirts, stared curiously at the odd yellow and wood-grained cabinet, with its metallic dials and stylish "Pong" logo. After one, perhaps two Pabst Blue Ribbons, one brave fellow and his date walked over and plunked a quarter

---

[2]   Shea, Cam. "Al Alcorn Interview." *IGN.com.* March 10, 2008. http://www.ign.com/articles/2008/03/11/al-alcorn-interview (accessed March 13, 2015).

[3]   Kent, Steve L. *The Ultimate History of Video Games: From Pong to Pokémon and Beyond: The Story Behind the Craze that Touched Our Lives and Changed the World.* Rocklin, CA: Prima Pub., 2001: 42.

into its slot, no doubt self-conscious of all the eyes on his back and the sudden silence that had fallen over the tavern. But he was surely unaware that he and his date that night were witnessing the dawn of a new form of entertainment, a "hot" medium that would change their culture forever. Until then, they had watched passively as others performed for them on television or movie screens. Now *they* were performing the action on the screen. The game was easy to learn, but, as his date scored yet another point, the man realized it would be hard to master.

Figure 2.2   Al Alcorn, designer of *Pong*. (Photo courtesy of Alex Handy.)

Others joined them. A queue formed. The man forgot all about his Pabst Blue Ribbon.

The next day, Atari received an angry call from Andy Capp's. The machine had already broken down. No doubt groaning and cursing Alcorn, Bushnell's day brightened considerably when he discovered the cause of the problem: the machine was so full of quarters that it had jammed up. The first bug in the history of commercial gaming was an easy one to solve: Make room for more quarters!

All in all, it wasn't a bad return for a few cheap parts, some boards, and a $75 black-and-white television from a Walgreens drug store (see Figure 2.3).

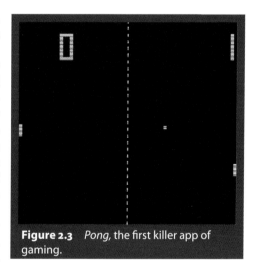

Figure 2.3   *Pong*, the first killer app of gaming.

Bushnell and Alcorn approached Bally, one of the eminent manufacturers of pinball and other electromechanical games, to produce *Pong* for them on a mass scale. Bally paid them $24,000 for the rights, but ended up canceling the agreement, even after 10 more successful demonstrations.[4] According to Dabney, the company suspected them of exaggerating the numbers on their income report.[4] Bushnell decided to try manufacturing the machines on their own, a fortuitous decision that would make Atari a household name.

---

[4] Dillon, Roberto. *The Golden Age of Video Games*. Boca Raton, FL: CRC Press, 2011: 16.

This story of *Pong* has been told many times, and it's a lot more compelling if you don't mention the precursors. Bushnell and Alcorn, much like Jobs and Wozniak (the two Steves who founded Apple), are cultural heroes who are often portrayed as mad scientist types, ingenious inventors who woke up one morning, shouted "Eureka!" and changed the world in a single stroke of brilliance. As always, though, the facts have a habit of getting in the way.

Perhaps the most controversial question is to what extent Bushnell and company were familiar with the previous games that bear an uncomfortable similarity to *Pong*. The earliest of these debuted in 1958 on a visitors' day at the Brookhaven National Laboratory (BNL) in Upton, New York. It was there that American physicist William Higinbotham and technical specialist Robert Dvorak demonstrated *Tennis for Two*, an analog computer game. Like *Spacewar!*, it used an oscilloscope for its display.

During the war, Higinbotham had witnessed the first atomic bomb test, a terrifying sight that troubled him deeply and led to a lifelong crusade against the proliferation of such weapons. However, he also liked to have fun, throwing parties and amusing his guests with wild accordion playing. More significantly for our purposes, he was completely obsessed with pinball.[5] In short, he had the training, skills, and playfulness necessary to create a video game.

Visitors' day was an annual tradition at BNL. A glorified science fair, it attracted thousands of people, who milled about a gymnasium filled with boring displays of black-and-white photographs and stationary equipment. "I knew from past visitors' days that people were not much interested in static exhibits," said Higinbotham, "so for that year I came up with an idea for a hands-on display—a video tennis game. If I had realized just how significant it was, I would have taken out a patent and the U.S. government would own it!"[6] Higinbotham wrote up plans for the game and gave them to his friend and colleague Robert "Bob" V. Dvorak, who managed to get it built in just 3 weeks—just in time for the exhibit.

Tennis for Two's graphics consisted of a moving ball that was affected by gravity—the first known use of physics in a game. Each player rotated a knob to change the angle of the ball, and pressing a button shot the ball across the court. Unlike *Pong*, *Tennis for Two* showed players a side view of a tennis court, not the top-down view. The contraption was roughly the size of a microwave oven.[5] Despite the game's popularity, it was dismantled 2 years later, and its parts were recycled for other exhibits.

Unlike Higinbotham, who never pursued any commercial interest in his invention, inventor Ralph Baer was determined to turn his idea for a "television game" into rich profits. After witnessing *Tennis for Two* in 1958,[7] Baer conceived the idea for a home

---

[5] Nowak, Peter. *Sex, Bombs, and Burgers: How War, Pornography, and Fast Food Have Shaped Modern Technology.* Toronto: Viking Canada, 2010: 127.

[6] Brookhaven National Laboratory. "Video Games—Did They Begin at Brookhaven?" *Research and Development of the U.S. Department of Energy.* January 21, 2011. http://www.osti.gov/accomplishments/videogame.html (accessed April 30, 2015).

[7] Kline, Stephen, Nick Dyer-Witheford, and Peuter G. De. *Digital Play: The Interaction of Technology, Culture, and Marketing.* Montréal: McGill-Queen's University Press, 2003: 92.

version of the game, but took 10 years to garner enough support to even build working prototypes. His first attempt was a simple game of tag featuring two glowing squares, which soon morphed into his "Brown Box" prototype. The prototype included several additional diversions, including target shooting and the pivotal paddle and ball games. After being rejected by several TV manufacturers, Baer finally signed an agreement in 1971 with Magnavox, who produced the Odyssey Home Entertainment System the following year.

The Odyssey shipped with six printed circuit game cards rather than true ROM (read-only memory) cartridges, which have their own code. The Odyssey's cards merely altered the electrical connections between components inside the console but did allow for a variety of games, including *Table Tennis,* which is the closest to *Pong* in look and design. There are, however, significant differences between the two. *Table Tennis* had no sound effects and did not keep score. Moreover, the controller had three knobs, which players used to move their square paddles up and down and left and right, and adjust the English or the angle of the ball's deflection.

Pong's controls were much simpler and arguably more intuitive. Instead of a dedicated knob or dial to control English, the designers segmented the rectangular paddles into separate zones; the angle depends on what part of the paddle is struck by the ball. Furthermore, players could move their paddles up and down, not side to side. This setup not only simplified the controls but also let players have one hand free to hold a beer (an important consideration given its location in a bar!).

Despite these differences, Baer and Magnavox took Atari to court for patent infringement, coercing the fledgling company to settle for a lump sum and other manufacturers to pay hefty licensing fees for years to come. Baer, a meticulous German engineer with an array of broad patents, was certainly not willing to stand idly by as Atari and others reaped all the rewards.

The suit led to considerable animosity between Baer and Bushnell, who admitted to seeing the game at a Magnavox showing. "I thought it was a relatively crappy product," said Bushnell, who felt (and most would agree) that Atari's version was substantially better. "Ralph [Baer] likes to claim he invented *Pong,* which he didn't. He invented Odyssey, which was a marketing failure. *Pong* happened to be successful, and so he wants to claim that. I just think it's wrong."[8] In a classic bit of turn-about-is-fair-play, Baer released the best-selling *Simon* toy in 1978, which was essentially a handheld version of Atari's *Touch Me* arcade game from 1974. There is still some debate over the true paternity of the video games industry, though most agree that Bushnell is the rightful "Father of Arcade Games" while Baer is "The Father of Consoles" (see Figure 2.4).

After settling with Magnavox, Atari set to work on its own home version of *Pong,* complete with the arcade version's automatic scoring and sound. Sears (the dominant retailer at the time) agreed in 1975 to distribute it under their own brand name, Tele-Games.

---

[8] Edwards, Benj. "VC&G Interview: Nolan Bushnell, Founder of Atari." *Vintage Computing and Gaming.* December 12, 2007. http://www.vintagecomputing.com/index.php/archives/404/vcg-interview-nolan-bushnell-founder-of-atari (accessed May 1, 2015).

Figure 2.4   Nolan Bushnell, founder of Atari. (Photo courtesy of Tech Cocktail.)

The arrangement was a huge success and vindicated Baer's vision of a viable market for video game consoles. Atari branded its own version in 1976, just as an explosion of me-too products inundated the market.

A key moment came in 1975, when chip maker General Instrument announced a low-cost "Pong-on-a-chip." This AY-3-8500 chip could play as many as six paddle-and-target games, depending on the vendor configuration. Baer was notified early on about the chip's development and contacted Coleco's president, Arnold Greenberg, to discuss the possibilities. Greenberg responded swiftly, and Coleco became the preferred vendor for the first and largest supply of chips. The lucrative deal gave them a sizable advantage with their "Telstar" *Pong* clone.

Sensing the opportunity for a quick buck, a wide range of companies rushed hundreds of new *Pong* clones into production. Several of these machines were popular and offered sophisticated features, such as Nintendo's *Color TV Game 6*, which was launched in Japan in 1977. However, demand for *Pong* was on the decline. In 1976, Fairchild introduced its Video Entertainment System (VES), a fully programmable console with interchangeable game cartridges, and Atari soon followed with its Video Computer System (VCS, also known as the Atari 2600). By 1980, *Pong* and the other fixed-game consoles of the 1970s were as obsolete as paisley ties and bell bottoms (see Figure 2.5).

Pong remains one of the most significant and influential games in the history of the industry. It was the first video game many of us ever played, and its simple, intuitive, and competitive gameplay is still quite fun today. I was personally struck by this fact upon visiting the *Game On* exhibition at Chicago's Museum of Science and Industry in 2006. This exhibit featured hundreds of playable games from all eras and across a broad spectrum of platforms. However,

Figure 2.5   Atari's *Home Pong* console. Hundreds of clones followed, saturating the market. (Photo courtesy of Evan-Amos.)

the game that attracted the most attention—from all ages, genders, and nationalities—was good ol' *Pong*. As always, what drew gamers to the classic game had less to do with technology and much more to do with the simple joys of competing with loved ones and making new friends. For that purpose, *Pong* will never be obsolete.

2.1 Playing *Pong* Today

The easiest way to play *Pong* is to play it in a browser at http://www.ponggame.org/. A more graphically sophisticated version with music can be played at the online Atari Arcade, located at https://www.atari.com/arcade#!/arcade/atari-promo. Purists may object that these are simulations, not emulations, of the arcade originals. Early arcade machines such as *Pong* were built without central processing units (CPUs) and digital code; they are analog systems of resistors and transistors. Assuming one is comfortable with this limitation, there's also the question of controls. *Pong* is arguably best played with analog dials or "spinners," not mice, gamepads, or keyboards. Unfortunately, it's a bit tricky finding spinners for modern personal computers (PCs). If you're ambitious and determined, do-it-yourself solutions and parts do exist, however.

A simpler solution is to purchase a universal serial bus (USB) adapter such as the 2600-daptor and a set of Atari or knockoff paddles. Such a device will allow you to connect the paddles to a modern PC and get you much closer to the feel of the original game's controls.

If your goal is to play one of the many *Pong* for home games, you should probably skip the emulation step and just pick up a working unit off eBay. There are literally hundreds to choose from, including Atari-, Sears-, and Coleco-branded versions for $30 or less. Some are available for little more than the price of shipping, while others, rarer and more desirable, command prices of $100 or more. It'd be fun to collect four or five units from different manufacturers to compare their look and feel.

Emulating the Magnavox Odyssey on a modern PC is a challenging endeavor, especially considering its unique controllers and the small size of the emulation community. You're probably better off just buying an actual Odyssey console from an online auction site. At the time of this writing, prices on complete systems run from $225 to $800.

Finally, *Pong* is a simple game to program yourself, and many of the programmers I've talked to over the years mention coding their own version as part of their initial training. Why not take this opportunity to have fun learning some programming skills? You can also test out your creativity in coming up with fun new variations. Good luck!

Chapter 3

Space Invaders:
The Japanese Invasion

So far, our story has focused on the United States. The earliest video games, spawned on powerful mainframe computers, made their way from universities, to arcades, and finally into the living rooms of millions of American homes. However, America's dominance of the video game industry was short lived. Much as the "British Invasion" of the mid-1960s rocked the music industry to its core, the "Japanese Invasion" of the 1980s was a turning point for both the industry and culture of gaming. Nintendo and Sega would become *The Beatles* and *The Rolling Stones* of video games, selling more systems and software than all of their American competitors combined.

The Japanese side of our story begins with a 34-year-old engineer named Tomohiro Nishikado, and a simple little shoot'em up called *Space Invaders* (see Figure 3.1).

The Japan of the 1970s was already fast on its way to becoming the technology juggernaut it is today. After Japan's defeat in World War II, its government launched initiatives and protections designed to spur rapid growth in the technology sector.[1] These maneuvers paid off handsomely, and by 1978, Casio's calculators, Sony's stereos, Toshiba's televisions, and JVC's VCRs were familiar sights on both shores.

Nishikado's interest in games and electronics goes back to his boyhood, which he spent playing Shogi, a Japanese form of chess, and tinkering with audio electronics, particularly radios and vacuum tube amplifiers.[2] A year after graduating with an engineering degree from Tokyo Denki University in 1968, Nishikado landed a job at Taito Trading Company. There, the 24-year-old worked on the company's line of electromechanical arcade games, but in 1973, the company designed their first fully electronic games, *Elepong*, a clone of Atari's *Pong*, and *Soccer*, a soccer-themed variant.

In 1975, Nishikado's game *Western Gun* was licensed by American arcade game manufacturer Midway Manufacturing Co., who had its partner Dave Nutting Associates[3]

---

[1] Uekusa, M., and H. Ide. "Industrial Policy in Japan." In The Japanese Economy: Technology, Foreign Investment and Competition Policies, by Peter Drysdale and Luke Gower, 34–58. New York: Routledge, 1999: 54.

[2] Parkin, Simon. "The Space Invader." *The New Yorker*. October 17, 2013. http://www.newyorker.com/tech/elements/the-space-invader (accessed May 5, 2015).

[3] Dave Nutting is the brother of Bill Nutting, founder of Nutting Associates, the company that manufactured Bushnell and Dabney's *Computer Space*. Dave founded Nutting Industries in 1967, which is probably best known for revolutionizing the pinball industry with hardware based on Intel's microprocessors.

Figure 3.1   Tomohiro Nishikado in 2011, the creator of *Space Invaders*. (Photo courtesy of Jordan.)

update its discrete logic–based hardware with a microprocessor—a first for the industry. Nishikado was impressed with the redesign and began training himself to use microprocessors, too.

Nishikado was also impressed with a brilliant new *Pong* variant called *Breakout*, designed by Steve Jobs and Steve Wozniak. *Breakout* offered several key innovations to the "ball and paddle" formula. Instead of two players bouncing a ball back and forth, *Breakout* had a single player bouncing a ball up and down. In between the player and the top of the screen was a row of bricks, which the player destroyed by hitting them with the ball, which would then ricochet off the brick. Nishikado felt that *Breakout* gave him a greater sense of achievement than *Pong*; somehow, clearing out all those bricks and advancing to a fresh level made the experience more psychologically rewarding. The game inspired him to try to create something even better. "I felt I could improve upon [*Breakout*] by giving the targets a more interesting shape and turning it into a shooting game"[2] (see Figure 3.2).

His first thought was turning them into airplanes, but he changed his mind after hearing about *Star Wars*, which debuted to incredible fanfare in the United States on May 25, 1977. He hadn't seen the film—it premiered in Japan on June 30, 1978, 11 days after the first *Space Invaders* machines rolled off the assembly line. However, Nishikado predicted that the timing was perfect for a sci-fi–themed game. Since he had no idea what X-Wing or TIE Fighters looked like, he thought back to the descriptions of aliens in the H.G. Wells stories he loved as a kid. He went to work trying to create a pattern of pixels that would look recognizable as aliens, ending up with three basic designs that are now iconic symbols of gamer culture.

Nishikado had certainly given himself an ambitious task. Not only was he designing a new type of game, but he was doing it with a spanking new technology—the microprocessor. The design took him more than a year to complete, but at last, *Space Invaders* was ready. It was immediately clear that it was much, much more than just another rip-off or variant of *Pong*. The player controls a laser cannon that moves left and right along the bottom of the screen. Pressing the fire button sends a bolt from the cannon, which soars upward until striking an alien or flying off screen. Only one shot can be in the air at one time; hitting the button again causes the first shot to disappear and another to launch from the cannon (see Figure 3.3).

At the top of the screen are five rows of invaders. Reminiscent of an old-fashioned typewriter, the aliens move to the extreme left and right of the screen, dropping down one row each time they reach the border. Between the cannon and the aliens are four destructible bases that serve as temporary cover from the aliens' bombs. The typical strategy is to duck in and out of cover, fire some shots, and then use the cover to avoid the bombardment. The player can also try to shoot the aliens' bombs with the cannon; doing so nullifies the bomb. The aliens speed up as their comrades are eliminated; the last few move very quickly and require great skill to hit. The game also features a flying saucer that occasionally flies across

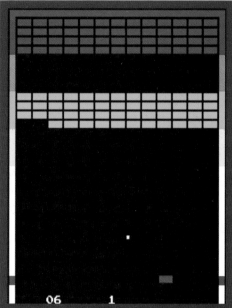

Figure 3.2 *Breakout* and *Super Breakout* (shown here) were fast and furious block-smashing paddle games that helped inspire *Space Invaders*.

the top of the screen. Hitting this target requires even greater precision (or, more often, just dumb luck).

Another flash of brilliance was the game's "high score indicator," an innovation that became a mainstay of the arcade industry. *Space Invaders* didn't offer the more elaborate high score tables with initials seen in later games—only the single highest score was recorded and displayed. Nevertheless, this component added a competitive edge to an already engrossing game. Unlike *Pong*, only one person at a time could play *Space Invaders*, and the opponents were computer-controlled aliens, not other players. However, the high score indicator allowed friends to compete with each other indirectly, and it may have even cut down on street graffiti!

Figure 3.3 Midway's *Space Invaders* arcade machine. (Photo courtesy of Jordiferrer.)

Figure 3.4   *Space Invaders* running on MAME emulator with simulated inlay and cabinet art.

The proud young engineer showed his game to his colleagues, who applauded his achievement (while they were waiting impatiently for *their* turn at the controls!). Nishikado's bosses, however, were much less enthusiastic. They complained about the speed of the game and predicted low sales. They preferred an underwater shooting game called *Blue Shark*, which they all agreed would be their big hit that year.[4] The negativity extended to the owners of arcades, who, perhaps catching wind of the company's own doubts about the game, rejected it flatly. None of them could seem to grasp the idea that there was anything fun about shooting row after row of aliens (see Figure 3.4).

Fortunately for Nishikado (and the video game industry!), a few brash pachinko parlors and bowling alleys were willing to take a risk on the game. There, amid the blaring gambling games and crashing pins, a weird, ominous, and irresistible sound joined the cacophony: "dum, dum, dum, dum ... Dum, dum, dum, dum." What on earth was that? Finally, someone's curiosity prevailed, and he plunked a hundred-yen coin into the slot. And when that was done, he put in another. And another. Word soon spread—there was a new game in town, and it was a hell of a lot more fun than *Pong*!

Nishikado is skeptical of the oft-repeated claim that the game caused a national shortage of the hundred-yen coin. But there's no denying that it was enormously successful. Indeed, many of the bowling alleys and pachinko parlors sold off the rest of their games to make room for more *Space Invaders* cabinets. Sadly, Nishikado did not receive the veneration and affection his achievement deserved. The president sent him a bonus, which Nishikado exhausted buying a modest television set for his mother.[4] Taito had a strict anonymity policy designed to keep talented employees from being lured away to work at other companies. Nishikado walked by row after row of *Space Invaders* machines and mesmerized players—but couldn't reveal to any of them that he'd had anything to do with it. However, perhaps he wouldn't have enjoyed the attention anyway—"All I could think about was how terrible it would be if a critical bug appeared," he later told

---

4 Hodgson, David. "Where Are They Now?" *Electronic Gaming Monthly*, November 2001: 36.

The New Yorker.[2,5] More sadly still is that he was promoted to Section Chief, which, though it brought a rise in status and compensation, also meant that he'd no longer be doing what he loved—designing games.

Space Invaders arrived in America via Bally Midway, who began distribution in 1979. At the time, the American video game industry was in a slump. Atari's founder, Nolan Bushnell, had sold out to Warner Communications, who promptly put a no-nonsense Harvard MBA named Ray Kassar in charge. Atari's VCS (or 2600) game console was not selling well, and no amount of advertising could seem to change that fact. Some pundits were already declaring the whole video game thing had just been a fad. *Space Invaders* soon proved them wrong: "People who had never before stuffed a quarter in a game machine couldn't destroy enough of the itchy-looking aliens," wrote a report for *InfoWorld* magazine.[6]

Kassar and his team at Atari realized at once that *Space Invaders* was the shot in the arm they needed to finally start selling their new cartridge-based console. They set a programmer named Rick Mauer to the task of porting it over, which he accomplished in four sleepless days and nights.[7] Despite the rushed production, Mauer's version was close enough to the original to please most gamers of the era, and demand for Atari's console surged upward[8] (see Figure 3.5).

Computer gamers had access to several unauthorized clones, most notably M. Hata's *Super Invader* (1979), also known as *Apple Invader*, a Japanese import for the Apple II. It was judged by *Softalk* magazine's readers as the most popular game ever in 1981,[9] and by 1982, it had sold more than 20,000 copies, tying with Richard Garriott's *Ultima*.[10] There were many other clones, including several made or published by the home computer manufacturers themselves to help market their systems: Commodore's *VIC Avenger* or just *Avenger* for its VIC-20 and 64, Tandy's *Invaders!* for the TRS-80, and Texas Instruments' *TI Invaders* for its TI-99/4A computer.

Space Invaders inspired far more than just copycats. It spawned a massive genre called the "shmup," or "shoot'em up," that eventually split into a variety of subgenres. One of the most famous and beloved of these is *Galaga*, developed by Namco of Japan in 1981 and brought to the United States by Midway. *Galaga* was based on an earlier

---

5 Allegedly, a programming bug was eventually discovered—the "Nagoya Uchi" technique. Once the aliens reach the lowest row, they can be shot with minimal risk of hitting you with their bombs. Nishikado claims that "no one would get further than level 6 or 7" without exploiting this "bug" (Hodgson, David. "Where Are They Now?" *Electronic Gaming Monthly*, November 2001: 36).

6 See footnote 7, p. 157.

7 Hubner, John, and William F. Jr. Kistner. "What Went Wrong at Atari?" InfoWorld, November 28, 1983: 151–152; 157–158.

8 For a fuller account of the story of how *Space Invaders* saved the Atari VCS, see our book Vintage Game Consoles (ISBN: 978-0415856003).

9 Tomervik, Margot Comstock. "The Most Popular Program Ever—Results." Softalk, April 1981: 13.

10 Lombardy, Dana. "Inside the Industry." *Computer Gaming World*, September 1982: 2.

Figure 3.5 *Super Invader* or *Apple Invader* was one of many unauthorized clones of the arcade game for home computers.

Namco game named *Galaxian* (1979), which introduced several key innovations. Besides vastly improved audiovisuals (it was the first arcade game in 100% RGB color), the aliens could now attack in kamikaze-style formations. The four destructible shields were gone as well, making the game substantially more difficult. *Galaga* is essentially an enhanced remake of this game, offering stat tracking and even better audiovisuals. The coolest innovation, though, is that the enemy's motherships can trap the player's ship in a tractor beam. If the player is out of ships, the game is over. Otherwise, the player can try to destroy the mothership (called a "Galaga") without hitting the trapped ship; if successful, the captured ship is released. It then attaches to the side of the player's ship and doubles its firepower!

Space Invaders–style games evolved into a plethora of styles. One of the first major innovations was scrolling. Instead of showing all the action on a single screen, games like Konami's *Scramble* (1981) and *Gradius* (1986) featured a background that moved horizontally as the game progressed. The player's ship could also move up and down as well as left and right, increasing the complexity. Namco's *Xevious* (1982) is often cited as the first vertically scrolling shooter, though it was predated by Atari's *Sky Raider* (1978). In any case, vertical scrolling became quite popular. Activision's *River Raid* (1982) for the Atari VCS is an example of an early console game of this type. Other influential shooters of the 1980s include Capcom's *1942* (1984; vertical), Toaplan's *Tiger-Heli* (1985; vertical), and Irem's *R-Type* (1988; horizontal), just to name a few (see Figure 3.6).

As the years progressed, the audiovisuals improved dramatically, along with nice features like power-ups, damage resistance, and boss fights. The genre seemed to peak in the mid to late 1990s with ambitious titles such as Konami's *Axelay* (1992, Super Nintendo), which featured both horizontal and vertical scrolling along with a bevy of impressive visual effects. The Atari ST and Commodore Amiga computers were also home to plenty of lavishly detailed shooters, particularly those from the British company Psygnosis, such as *Menace* (1988), *Blood Money* (1989), and *Agony* (1992). Game developers competed to see who could design the best-looking and best-sounding shooters. One of my personal favorites is Edgar M. Vigdal's, an unauthorized shareware game *Deluxe Galaga* for the Amiga. It manages to preserve much of what made the original game great but adds power-ups and other updates. Visit http://deluxegalaga.monroeworld.com/ for information with setup and installation.

The influence that Nishikado's *Space Invaders* has exerted over the video game industry is immense. It's rare indeed to find a single title that can lay claim to so many firsts: the first major video game import from Japan, the first to record a high score, the first Japanese game based on microprocessors, and, of course, the first "shmup," a genre that is still commercially active.

3.1 Playing *Space Invaders* Today

The Taito Corporation seems to be actively enforcing their copyrights on *Space Invaders*, making it difficult (and potentially litigious) for anyone searching for a way to play the original game in

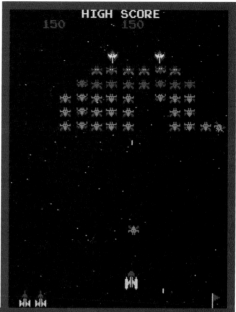

Figure 3.6 Namco's *Galaxian* (1979) was an early *Space Invaders*–inspired game with much improved audiovisuals and interesting enemies.

an emulator or browser. The best legal option I've been able to find is *Taito Legends*, a 2005 compilation that includes *Space Invaders* and 28 other Taito games, available for PC, Xbox, and PS2. If you have an iOS device, you can buy Taito's enhanced version of the game from the iTunes store. There are a great many knockoffs and unauthorized ports of *Space Invaders* available for most systems.

If you have a sizable budget and space, you might look for a vintage *Space Invaders* arcade machine, which tend to run $1500–$3000 on online auction sites. A cheaper option is the *Space Invaders TV Game*, a nice-looking device with an arcade-style joystick that plugs directly into your TV—but keep in mind that the original game had buttons for left and right movement, not a joystick.

Of course, *Space Invaders* is only the first of thousands of shoot'em ups, and many of these later games are widely available. A common sight in any reasonably sized arcade is a combination *Ms. Pac Man* and *Galaga* machine, and they aren't too expensive if you'd like to own for your personal collection (expect to spend at least $3000).

If you'd like something more modern, try searching for "SHMUP" on Steam. At the time of this writing, there are more than 106 of these games available there, covering a broad spectrum of themes and styles. Currently, the most popular SHMUP there is *Crimzon Clover World Ignition* by YOTSUBANE, a Japanese studio. It's of the "bullet hell" subgenre, meaning that the screen is plastered with vivid and colorful enemy fire that forms and swirls into mesmerizing patterns (and which you must dodge to avoid damage). It's quite enlightening to play this game immediately after a bout of *Space Invaders* or *Galaga*; you'll see at once how far the basic concept has evolved since those early days.

Finally, making your own SHMUP is a painless process thanks to all the cheap (or even free) tools designed to simplify the process. Indeed, as early as 1987, Sensible Software had released its famous *Shoot'em Up Construction Kit* for Commodore 64, Amiga, and Atari ST, which made it easy for novices to create their own scrolling games. One of the best modern tools for making SHMUPs is YoYo Games' GameMaker, especially when combined with the free GMOSSE game template. This tool reduces the complexity down to a simple drag-and-drop interface, so you can focus on building attractive and rewarding levels. Indeed, building a fun and engaging SHMUP is still a good learning exercise for anyone interested in a career in game design—see how far you can push the core mechanics Nishikado introduced back in 1978!

Chapter 4

Zork: Sticking Graphics Where the Sun Don't Shine

From the beginning, gamers, developers, and hardware makers have made a big to-do about graphics. Indeed, the very term *video game* suggests that what distinguishes them from other games is their video display. Whether that display be an oscilloscope, computer monitor, LCD screen, or an ordinary television set, good graphics are often a decisive factor in a game's success. Each new generation of consoles arrives with a flood of advertisements showing off their superior graphics and animation. Each wave brings us higher resolutions, broader color pallets, or faster frame rates, and woe be unto developers who fail to stay abreast of these changes.

It's hard to imagine the video game industry without this insatiable drive for better and better graphics. But one of the most successful companies in the history of video games couldn't have cared less. That company was Infocom. And they stuck their graphics where the sun don't shine. Here's how they did it:

> It is pitch black. You are likely to be eaten by a grue.

Zork relies totally on simple text for both output and input, which explains why it's called a "text adventure" game, though many prefer the term *interactive fiction* (IF) for the genre. Players usually assume the role of a character within the game world, who responds to commands such as "go west" or "light torch," which the player types in with a keyboard. The part of the program that tries to interpret this input is called the "parser." The game provides textual descriptions of the scene, objects in view, sounds, other characters, and other bits of information, such as the character's mood or thoughts. In short, playing *Zork* is like reading a novel as it's being written, or starring in a play without knowing one's lines.

Zork's designers describe the game as a "computerized fantasy simulation" and use terminology familiar to fans of the game *Dungeons & Dragons*: "In this type of game, the player interacts conversationally with an omniscient 'Master of the Dungeon,' who rules on each proposed action and relates the consequences."[1] Creating such a game is "as much an exercise in creative writing as in programming."[1] Like a good dungeon or

---

[1] Lebling, P.D., M.S. Blank, and T.A. Anderson. "Special Feature Zork: A Computerized Fantasy Simulation Game." *Computer* 12, no. 4 (April 1979): 51–59.

```
Taken.
    Welcome to Dungeon!

    Dungeon is a game of adventure, danger, and low cunning.  In it
you will explore some of the most amazing territory ever seen by mortal
man.  Hardened adventurers have run screaming from the terrors contained
within.

    In Dungeon, the intrepid explorer delves into the forgotten secrets
of a lost labyrinth deep in the bowels of the earth, searching for
vast treasures long hidden from prying eyes, treasures guarded by
fearsome monsters and diabolical traps!

    No DECsystem should be without one!

    Dungeon was created at the Programming Technology Division of the MIT
Laboratory for Computer Science by Tim Anderson, Marc Blank, Bruce
Daniels, and Dave Lebling.  It was inspired by the Adventure game of
Crowther and Woods, and the Dungeons and Dragons game of Gygax
and Arneson.  The original version was written in MDL (alias MUDDLE).
The current version was translated from MDL into FORTRAN IV by
a somewhat paranoid DEC engineer who prefers to remain anonymous.

    On-line information may be obtained with the commands HELP and INFO.
>
```

game master in a tabletop role-playing game, *Zork*'s writers had to rely on words to communicate with players, firing their imaginations with vivid descriptions and dialog (see Figure 4.1).

Zork is set in the subterranean ruins of an ancient empire. Your objective is to search these ruins for treasure, which you place in a trophy case for points. There are many obstacles and dangers, including a

Figure 4.1   The original mainframe version of the game was called *Dungeon*. This leaflet, found at the start of the game in a mailbox, told the story of its development.

troll, cyclops, the ever-popular grues, and an infuriating thief who'll steal your treasure. *Zork* is primarily about exploration, involving such activities as breaking into a supposedly abandoned house, rappelling down a steep cavern, and even floating across a river in an inflatable raft.

Like any good novel, *Zork* compensates for its lack of images with effective imagery, irony, and wit. However, the descriptions also contain hints for the players and help getting them into the proper mindset. After all, even though *Zork*'s parser was well regarded at the time for its versatility, it couldn't anticipate or give a proper response to every reasonable input the player might try. The challenge of designing such a game was providing just enough guidance, helping players along without spoiling the fun or leaving them hopelessly stumped.

For example, here's a description of an art gallery: "Most of the paintings have been stolen by vandals with exceptional taste. The vandals left through either the north or west exits. Fortunately, there is still one chance for you to be a vandal, for on the far wall is a painting of unparalleled beauty." Note how this description manages to convey useful information (possible exits) but also hints at a desirable outcome—you can steal the painting. A more thoughtful player might consider why the vandals left the painting behind, though, especially since it looks so valuable!

Here's another description, this time of an art studio: "The walls and floors are splattered with paints of 69 different colors. Strangely enough, nothing of value is hanging here. At the south end of the room is an open door (also covered with paint). A dark and narrow chimney leads up from a fireplace; although you might be able to get up it, it seems unlikely you could get back down." A player might never have considered trying to climb up the chimney, so the writers suggest it directly—albeit with a caveat. The number 69 here appears to be one of the countless references in the game to the Massachusetts Institute of Technology's (MIT's) hacker culture; it was routinely used by them to refer to any large quantity. *The Original Hacker's Dictionary*, based on a text file compiled by members of MIT's Artificial Intelligence lab, remarks that the number was appealing because 69 in decimal is 105 in octal, and 69 in hexadecimal is 105 in decimal. Such esoteric allusions and references litter the game and probably account for much of the game's appeal—no doubt many a proud owner of a Commodore 64, Apple II, or TRS-80 self-identified as a "hacker" and was eager to embrace this culture, pimples and all! (see Figure 4.2).

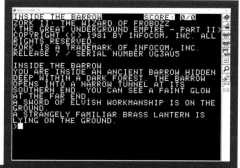

Figure 4.2 *Zork II* running on an Apple II emulator. The brass lantern became an icon of the genre.

It may surprise some readers to learn that text adventures like *Zork* are still being made and sold today, though, as Nick Montfort quips in his wonderful book *Twisty Little Passages*, it's a cottage industry that serves mostly to "amuse the initiated."[2] However, when a fresh new company named Infocom released *Zork* commercially in 1980, it was a runaway bestseller.

Infocom wasted no time following it up with popular sequels and other hit titles, many of which are also widely regarded as masterpieces, such as Steve Meretzky's *A Mind Forever Voyaging* (1985) and Brian Moriarty's *Trinity* (1986). These games appealed to a broader audience than action titles. A writer for the *New York Times* wrote in 1987 that "teen-agers, at least those with a somewhat literary bent, particularly love it, but it can prove addictive for the most serious adult spreadsheet jockey."[3] Other articles joke about frantic executives quickly clearing *Zork* off their screens whenever the boss walked by. Pundits waxed eloquently about the exciting future of the "participatory novel," especially as bestselling authors of print novels, including Douglas Adams and Michael Crichton, entered the fray.

The story of *Zork*'s development begins like that of many early computer games, that is, as a fruitful, informal collaboration by ambitious college students. Like *Spacewar!*, it was developed at MIT, but by members of MIT's Dynamic Modeling Group, not the Tech Model Railroad Club. Both teams were excited about the possibilities of computer games, and both were fueled by the adrenaline rush of hacking. However, the *Zork* team—who took to calling themselves "imps" because they *imp*lemented their ideas in code—were more excited by advances in artificial intelligence (particularly Natural Language Processing) than graphics (see Figure 4.3).

The imps were enchanted with a game called *Colossal Cave Adventure*, also known as *Adventure* or *Advent*, which began making its way around college campuses in 1976. *Colossal Cave* was truly a groundbreaking game, both in the figurative and

---

[2] Montfort, Nick. *Twisty Little Passages: An Approach to Interactive Fiction*. Cambridge: MIT Press, 2003.

[3] Shannon, L.R. "Peripherals; Adventure Continues." *New York Times*, December 22, 1987: C11.

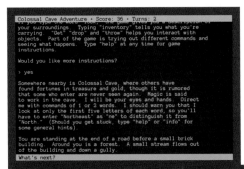

```
Colossal Cave Adventure • Score: 36 • Turns: 2
                                              a description of
your surroundings.  Typing "inventory" tells you what you're
carrying.  "Get" "drop" and "throw" helps you interact with
objects.  Part of the game is trying out different commands and
seeing what happens.  Type "help" at any time for game
instructions.

Would you like more instructions?

> yes

Somewhere nearby is Colossal Cave, where others have
found fortunes in treasure and gold, though it is rumored
that some who enter are never seen again.  Magic is said
to work in the cave.  I will be your eyes and hands.  Direct
me with commands of 1 or 2 words.  I should warn you that I
look at only the first five letters of each word, so you'll
have to enter "Northeast" as "ne" to distinguish it from
"North".  (Should you get stuck, type "help" or "info" for
some general hints).

You are standing at the end of a road before a small brick
building.  Around you is a forest.  A small stream flows out
of the building and down a gully.

What's next?
```

literal sense—the original author, Will Crowther, and his wife were dedicated cavers, and he based much of the game on an actual cave system in Kentucky. This caving connection helps explain the appeal of *Colossal Cave* and *Zork*. Both games are focused on the thrills one enjoys as a caver or urban explorer, making one's way into remote areas that may

Figure 4.3   *Colossal Cave Adventure* was an influential mainframe game that relied purely on text for output and input. Its creator was a real-life caver named Will Crowther. Shown here is an emulated version created for the *Halt and Catch Fire* television series.

have been seldom, if ever, visited before. These games are really less "interactive novels" than "interactive maps" (or "interactive worlds" to use language popularized by Cyan of Myst fame). Another fun coincidence is that the first jigsaw puzzle ever sold was of a map, and what would an adventure game be without puzzles?

The authors of the mainframe *Zork*, Tim Anderson, Marc Blank, Bruce Daniels, and Dave Lebling, began writing the program in 1977 for the DEC PDP-10 computer, the same computer used by Will Crowther and Don Woods to create *Colossal Cave Adventure*. The PDP-10 was a powerful mainframe computer that made home computers look like toys. This fact explains why so many early game programmers felt there was no money to be made in it. There just weren't enough people with access to mainframes to make it worthwhile, and the idea that a humble machine like the Apple II could run "serious" software seemed ludicrous at best. Even if a programmer was willing to work with such paltry amounts of memory and processing power, there was another issue—there were just too many different home computers on the market, and most were completely incompatible with each other. Even if you managed to adapt a game for the Apple II,

you'd have to start from scratch if you wanted another version for the TRS-80, and again for the Commodore VIC-20 (see Figure 4.4).

The clash of cultures between mainframe and home computer enthusiasts went deeper than technology. The imps were part of the "hacker ethos" at MIT. Software should be freely shared to advance the state of the art, not locked up with copyrights and proprietary code.

Figure 4.4   Dave Lebling, one of the creators of *Zork* and a cofounder of Infocom, in 2010. (Photo courtesy of Ben Collins-Sussman.)

In particular, restricting access to information purely for the sake of making a profit seemed crude; unworthy of a truly brilliant mind. The imps disagreed. According to Lebling, "*Zork* itself was written because of the hacker ethos, but the ports were good design and good business sense in a happy marriage." In any case, the official story is that Infocom was founded not to sell *Zork*, but rather simply to keep the team together after they left the lab.

The imps had a cunning plan for turning their hobby into a successful business. First off, they broke it up into three different games, though not without some modifications and additions. Second, rather than port the code to so many different platforms, Joel Berez and Marc Blank created a virtual platform called the "Z-Machine," which was programmed using a LISP-like language called ZIL. Afterward, all that was required to port the entire library to a new platform was to write a "Z-Machine Interpreter," or ZIP. Scott Cutler took on the task of creating the first ZIP, which was written for Tandy's TRS-80, and others soon followed. Although their reliance on purely text-based games would become their downfall later on, at this point, it gave them a major advantage—as a publisher, they could cheaply and easily offer their games on all the major platforms. Graphical games were much harder to port, and results were often inaccurate at best.

According to Lebling, this part of the design was in place from the start: "We designed a system tailored to writing adventure games. Instead of a one-off, even from the beginning we wrote *Zork* as collection of library and reuse-oriented code." Lebling also believes that they were the first company to make games that were larger than the computer's memory, a feature that also simplified the porting process.

The first port of *Zork* was a TRS-80 version published by Personal Software in 1980. Personal Software had recently released the first electronic spreadsheet, Visicalc, a breakthrough product whose runaway success would soon divert them from pursuing other endeavors. This version was packaged "baggie" style, placed in a Ziploc-style plastic bag with a disk and thin booklet. Infocom soon took responsibility for its own publishing and ended up producing some of the most creative and iconic game boxes and "feelies" in the history of the industry. My favorites are Michael Berlyn's *Suspended* (1982), whose box sports a creepy white face mask, and Lebling's *Starcross* (1982), which shipped in a plastic flying saucer. Sadly, Infocom stuck to fairly conservative packaging for its *Zork* games, but eventually added feelies, including one of the "Zorkmid" coins referenced in the games. On a side note, these coins have become so valuable that some have stooped to counterfeiting them!

At first, sales were sluggish—only 1500 copies were sold. However, the later Apple II release fared much better, selling more than 6000 copies.[4] As sales continued to climb, the company expanded, bringing on stellar talent such as Steve Meretzsky, who turned out some of the company's biggest hits (*Planetfall* and *Hitchhiker's Guide to the Galaxy*) despite his loathing of computers. At one point, 10 of Infocom's text adventures were

---

[4] Briceño, Hector, Wesley Chao, Andrew Glenn, Stanley Hu, Ashwin Krishnamurthy, and Bruce Tsuchida. "Down From the Top of Its Game: The Story of Infocom, Inc." 2000: 12. http://web.mit.edu/6.933/www/Fall2000/infocom/infocom-paper.pdf (accessed May 2, 2015).

in the top 20 of the Softsel Hot List of software sales.[5] By 1985, the company had raised enough capital to throw a lavish "murder mystery party" at the Consumer Electronic Show, hiring a troupe of live actors and allowing participants to indulge in some live-action role playing. Infocom had hit their peak.

Unfortunately, the company soon floundered. From the beginning, Infocom was not intended solely to develop and publish games; they felt they needed a "killer app" that would raise the vast sums that their former publisher, Personal Software, had acquired with Visicalc. They thought they had such a product in a relational database called Cornerstone (1985). Cornerstone sounded brilliant—everyone knew that database software had revolutionary potential for business, but the current offerings were far too complex for the average user. Infocom saw an opportunity, and felt that the same virtual machine strategy they used for *Zork* would work for Cornerstone.

Unfortunately, by the time copies of Cornerstone began lining up on store shelves, the IBM PC was the overwhelmingly dominant platform for business; portability was no longer an issue. Furthermore, the virtual machine setup reduced its speed, and it lacked several of the advanced features that made its rival database programs worth learning in the first place. The program was not a success, and some wit quipped that its name was apt—it sat on store shelves like a stone. Infocom had invested so heavily in the product, however, that they were unable to recover, and in 1986 the company was acquired by Activision.

What happens next is dismal, at least for fans of the pure text adventures. Activision seemed uninterested in publishing such games, preferring instead to exploit the brand's popularity in graphical adventure games. The first of these was Moriarty's *Beyond Zork: The Coconut of Quendor* in 1987. *Beyond Zork* had a crude automap and several random-ized and role-playing game elements to enhance the game's re-playability. Some fans objected to these changes, but it was generally well received. Steve Meretzky followed in 1988 with the prequel *Zork Zero*, which had in-game hints, menus, an interactive map, and a graphical version of the "Double Fanucci" card game. This game was also praised by critics and received favorable reviews (see Figure 4.5).

The last game published under the Infocom label was *Return to Zork*, a 1993 game released for Apple Macintosh and PC. Developed by Activision, *Return to Zork* is much different than the previous *Zork* games, or even the graphically enhanced games described above. *Return to Zork* has more in common with *Myst*, which was released a few months after it. The parser is gone, replaced by a purely graphical interface that is surprisingly complex and multifaceted. The game also offers live action sequences, including per-formances by Robyn Lively, star of the 1989 cult classic film *Teen Witch*. Contemporary reviewers seemed mostly pleased, though *Zork* fans remain divided. Very few of the orig-inal characters show up in the game, and there will always be the issue of whether any graphical adventure game could truly compare to the great text-only classics. Jay Kee, who reviewed the game for *Compute!* magazine, wrote that "people accustomed to the

---

[5] Suplee, Curt. "Through the Zorking Glass: Home Computer Games to Plot Your Own Adventure." *The Washington Post*, December 22, 1983: C1.

speed and flexibility of a text-only parser are going to feel handcuffed."[6]

Even without Infocom's failure with Cornerstone, the desire for graphics would likely have pushed the pure text adventure to the side anyway. On-Line Systems (later Sierra On-Line) published *Mystery House* in 1980 for the Apple II. Though its parser was severely limited

Figure 4.5 *Return to Zork* was an attempt in 1993 to reboot the series as a graphical adventure game.

compared to Infocom's, *Mystery House* had graphics (though admittedly crude). By 1984, Sierra was releasing much nicer looking games, including its bestselling *King's Quest* series. Another rival, Scott Adams' Adventure International, had also moved beyond pure text adventures and begun integrating graphics into his games. Other companies tried to please purists by allowing them to turn the graphics (really illustrations) on and off and maintaining text input, but by the 1990s, the industry was clearly moving to a parser-less, "point and click" format. By May of 1989, the once-bustling offices of Infocom, the world's leading computer game publisher, were pitch black.

Even without the lure of commercial success, hobbyists and independent designers have continued to write and publish text adventures. A good source of these games is the annual Interactive Fiction Competition, which is now in its 21st year. This contest is just one of the more visible aspects of a thriving IF community, a robust network of like-minded enthusiasts who pool their creative and technical resources to distribute text-based games as well as help newcomers play and create their own works. Emily Short's blog at http://emshort.wordpress.com is an excellent place to start if you're interested in learning more about modern IF. There is at least one active commercial publisher of IF—Howard Sherman's Malinche Entertainment, though his posted sales figures (in the hundreds of thousands) have been challenged by skeptics.

Even if text adventures like *Zork* are but a mere historical curiosity for some, there's no denying their influence on plenty of modern games. What *Zork* contributed more than anything was the idea that the computer could simulate a rich virtual world, something much, much larger and deeper than the playing fields seen in games like *Spacewar!* or *Pong*. Furthermore, the game demonstrated the literary potential of the computer. Thousands upon thousands of gamers have been charmed by the wit and elegance of *Zork*'s many descriptions, and modern IF authors have continued and expanded this rich tradition of rich, rewarding prose.

If you'd like to try your hand at making a text adventure, you're in luck. There are several extremely powerful, yet easily learned—and free—tools to help you achieve

---

[6] Kee, Jay. "Return to Zork." *Compute!*, September 1994: 94.

your goal. Three of the most popular ones are Quest, TADS, and Inform 7. Even if you have no programming background or knowledge at all, you can be up and running with one of these programs in no time, and each is supported by communities of likeminded authors.

The title of this chapter takes its name from one of Infocom's most brazen advertisements, which shows a giant, colorful brain under the headline: "We stick our graphics where the sun don't shine." The ad goes on to explain that "there's never been a computer built by man that could handle the images we produce. And, there never will be." Anyone who has ever been disappointed by a movie's adaptation of a novel will likely agree. The grues that we imagine will always seem more frightening than an artist's interpretation. No matter how much skill, talent, and money a game developer has to work with, sometimes it's just not possible to match the evocative power of a twisty little passage of text.

4.1 Playing *Zork* Today

While there are several websites that host versions of *Zork* that can be played for free in your browser, please note that the game is still being sold commercially at http://gog .com (just look for "Zork anthology"). This package (available for $5.99 or less) includes several other *Zork* games, *Planetfall*, and lots of fun and historical extras. If you'd like to try the original mainframe version, visit http://almy.us/dungeon.html to download ports for Windows, Mac, or Linux.

If you prefer an iPad or iPhone, look for *The Lost Treasures of Infocom* on iTunes. These versions include a built-in hints system, interface enhancements, and an on-screen keyboard. There are more than enough classic Infocom adventures in this collection to keep you busy for a long, long time.

If you'd like to try *Colossal Cave Adventure*, the game that inspired *Zork*, an intriguing browser-based version is hosted by AMC to publicize their show *Halt and Catch Fire*. You can play it for free at http://www.amctv.com/shows/halt-and-catch-fire /colossal-cave-adventure.

Chapter 5

MUD: Swords with Friends

The United States and Japan weren't the only countries playing and making video games in the 1970s. Indeed, one of the most influential of all video games was created by Roy Trubshaw and Richard Bartle, students at the University of Essex in Britain. Trubshaw and Bartle were avid fans of J.R.R. Tolkien's *Lord of the Rings* books, especially its richly detailed fantasy world, Middle Earth. After playing *Zork* and *Colossal Cave Adventure*, they began work on a new type of game that would essentially let players act out the role of a character within a fictional world. According to Bartle, "We wanted to give people freedom. Roy and I wanted to create a world in which people could be themselves." The result was a game called *MUD*—the most influential of all massively multiplayer online games[1] (see Figure 5.1).

The name *MUD* is an acronym for Multi-User Dungeon. The *Dungeon* part of the name was Trubshaw's idea. He'd played a FORTRAN version of *Zork*—whose name had temporarily been changed to *Dungeon* (it was later changed back after Infocom was threatened by TSR, the makers of *Dungeons & Dragons*, who felt they were infringing on their trademark). Since *Dungeon* already had a large, active community, naming their game after it seemed like a good way to tap into this audience and give everyone some idea of what to expect. Trubshaw's goal was to build a "multi-player adventure game with a programmable database."[2] Trubshaw went to work, programming the game with the MACRO-10 assembly language for the university's DEC PDP-10 mainframe (he used BCPL for a later version). After he'd achieved his goal, Trubshaw graduated and handed the code and the reins over to Bartle, who took over the project.

On the surface, *Zork* and *MUD* have much in common. They both rely purely on text for both input and output, and there are plenty of fun areas to explore and puzzles to solve. Anyone familiar with text adventures will thus feel quite at home in *MUD*. However, once you've figured out how to solve the puzzles in *Zork* or *MUD*, it's not much fun doing it again. To keep things fresh, Bartle decided to add some basic role-playing mechanics, introducing some randomness into each session.

Although Trubshaw had never played *Dungeons & Dragons*, Bartle had played it extensively for years and had even created his own role-playing systems before that. Bartle says that he was never "attempting to do a computer version of *D&D*" but did

---

[1] It's also known as *MUD1* and *Essex Mud.*

[2] Bartle, Richard. "Richard Bartle's Pages." *Richard A. Bartle's Consultancy Web Site.* June 24, 2003. http://mud.co.uk/richard/acloct87.htm (accessed May 8, 2015).

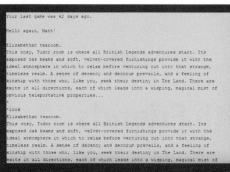

```
Your last game was 42 days ago.

Hello again, Matt!

Elizabethan tearoom.
This cosy, Tudor room is where all British Legends adventures start. Its
exposed oak beams and soft, velvet-covered furnishings provide it with the
ideal atmosphere in which to relax before venturing out into that strange,
timeless realm. A sense of decency and decorum prevails, and a feeling of
kinship with those who, like you, seek their destiny in The Land. There are
exits in all directions, each of which leads into a wisping, magical mist of
obvious teleportative properties...

*look
Elizabethan tearoom.
This cosy, Tudor room is where all British Legends adventures start. Its
exposed oak beams and soft, velvet-covered furnishings provide it with the
ideal atmosphere in which to relax before venturing out into that strange,
timeless realm. A sense of decency and decorum prevails, and a feeling of
kinship with those who, like you, seek their destiny in The Land. There are
exits in all directions, each of which leads into a wisping, magical mist of
```

borrow or adapt several conventions and mechanics from tabletop role-playing games. The most obvious is the leveling system—as you play, your character gradually gains experience and becomes more powerful, capable of taking on increasingly ferocious monsters as well as other players. If you make it all the way to the top level, you "make wiz,"

Figure 5.1   On the surface, *MUD* looked very much like *Zork* or *Colossal Cave Adventure*, but this was an online multiplayer game.

becoming a witch or wizard and earning some administrator privileges. The combat system is much simpler than that in *Dungeons & Dragons*; players merely type "kill <name of monster or character> with [weapon]," initiating a turn-based battle that lasts until victory or death.

The social dimension is what really set *MUD* apart from other games. Players who had never met each other face to face began to feel a sense of community they lacked outside the game. One of many such players was "Sue the Witch," a wiz who dialed into the game each day from a modem. Sue was respected for her extensive knowledge of the game and her fair but firm approach to enforcing the rules. According to Bartle, "She played every night for 6 hours solid, day in, day out, and her phone bill came to over 1000 pounds a month."[3] When Sue suddenly quit playing, concerned players drove a minibus down to South Wales to check on her. "It transpired that Sue was a man who had just been jailed for defrauding the Department of Transport of 60,000 pounds," said Bartle. "We normally leave that bit out of our guidelines for good wiz behavior."[3]

Soon after *MUD* went live at Essex University, word began to appear all across bulletin board systems all over the English-speaking world. The game was popular with players in the United Kingdom as well as the United States, who could access the game through the ARPANET. Unfortunately, the machine time required to host the game strained the budget of the University Computing Society. Thankfully, Bartle was able to get his university to offer a free account for external users, though only during off-peak hours (see Figure 5.2).

In an interview with me in 2015, Bartle noted that he knew of at least three other *MUD*-like programs that had been developed around the same time, though none of these developers were aware of each other's existence. The best known of these is Alan E. Klietz's *Scepter of Goth*, and *Avatar*, a game for the PLATO system. Bartle points out that the basic concepts behind all of these projects was obvious; who "came up with" the original idea

---

[3] Bartle, Richard. "Anecdotes, Set 3." *Richard A. Bartle's Counsultancy Web Site.* June 21, 2006. http://mud.co.uk/richard/anec3.htm (accessed May 8, 2015).

was much less important than who could best implement and distribute them. The fact that *MUD* was free to play, host, and build on goes a long way toward explaining its success over its rivals.

Bartle himself eventually made a commercial version of the game called *British Legends* for the proprietary online service, CompuServe. Luckily, CompuServe used the same model of mainframe that *MUD* had been written for. The game remained a popular draw until it was shut down in 1999. A 1989 review of the game in *PC Magazine* is telling: "Camaraderie and large-scale player interaction are rampant in *British Legends*—so much so that more sophisticated players may be put off by it. Scene descriptions, for example, often scroll off the screen as players communicate back and forth on topics hardly related to the adventure at all."[4]

Figure 5.2   Richard Bartle in 2011, the cocreator of *MUD*.

The popularity of MUDs increased throughout the 1980s as more Americans equipped their computers with modems and subscribed to commercial networks. Simutronics' Gemstone series debuted on GEnie in 1990 and attracted quite a large following. It was significantly more complex than *British Legends*, with a 25,000-word manual that was required reading for anyone serious about the game.

MUDs reached their peak in the 1990s, when the Internet made it possible to bypass the subscription and usage fees of services like CompuServe. One by one, the private networks shut down, but MUD fans found they had many more alternatives on the Internet than they ever had before. Indeed, the demand for MUDs was great enough that they split into different types for diverse applications. Perhaps the most popular of these was MUD Object Oriented (MOOs), which abstracted the chat and social functions from MUDs and are still used in various academic settings. Professors at St. Cloud State University in Minnesota, for instance, use them to teach English to students from other countries. James Aspnes' *TinyMUD*, which debuted in 1989, let players create and expand their own virtual world on their own, leading to a surge of creativity (and mayhem!).

Even in the late 1990s, the majority of MUDs were still entirely text or ASCII based; transmitting graphics would have taken too long given the slow dial-up modems of the era, and games programmed for UNIX, while accessible via terminal programs, were typically limited to character set graphics. A convenient workaround to this problem was to put a game's audiovisuals on a disk and then use the bandwidth merely to update

---

4   O'Brien, Bill. "CompuServe Role-Playing Games: A Respite from the Modern World." *PC Magazine*, May 30, 1989: 476.

object locations, send messages, and handle the players' input. This could all be done "behind the scenes," with the installed software serving as an intermediary between the host (the mainframe running the game) and the client (i.e., the user's personal computer). The host tracked the locations and activities taking place in the game, whereas the client provided the user with a handy graphical interface. This approach led to graphical multiplayer online games, such as LucasFilm Games' *Habitat* in 1987 and Beyond Software's *Neverwinter Nights* (1991–1997)[5] and ultimately modern massively multiplayer online role-playing games (MMORPGs) like *World of Warcraft*.

Despite all the advances in audiovisuals since the first *MUD*, there are still many players who prefer MUDs to MMORPGs. According to Top MUD Sites (http://topmud sites.com), currently the three most popular MUDs are *Aardwolf MUD*; *BatMUD*; and *Achaea, Dreams of Divine Lands*, each of which has more than 250 players online at any given moment. There's also MUDs dedicated to the works of fantasy authors Robert Jordan (*Wheel of Time MUD*), Raymond E. Feist (*Midkemia Online*), Terry Pratchett (*Discworld*), and, of course, J.R.R. Tolkien (*The Two Towers*). Most MUDs are free to play but may need player donations to keep the servers running. While it's possible to connect to most with a simple TELNET program, many offer attractive and useful custom clients.

5.1 Playing *MUD* Today

The easiest way to try out the original game is to go to http://www.british-legends.com and play it in your browser. If that doesn't work for you, you can try connecting via TELNET to british-legends.com port 27750. You can also download the WizTerm32 client program by "SirSloth the Wizard." After getting some *MUD* on your feet, track over to Top MUD Sites and look at all the different games available there (100 in all).

---

[5] Not to be confused with BioWare's *Neverwinter Nights* (2002).

Chapter 6

Rogue: Procedural Generation

The problem with text adventures like *Colossal Cave Adventure* and *Zork* is that once you've completed them, there's little reason to keep playing. Trubshaw and Bartle had tried to solve this problem by turning them into massively multiplayer games, but around the same time an American team was taking a different approach. Like *MUD*, their game would introduce role-playing game (RPG) elements to randomize the gameplay. However, they went much further than that, pioneering a concept called "procedural generation." Their game, *Rogue*, and the countless "roguelikes" to follow, created new mazes each time you played, populating them with monsters, traps, and loot according to a carefully contrived algorithm. The result was a radical new kind of adventure game that, at least in theory, you could play over and over again without getting bored.

Rogue's development, like many games originating on mainframes, was a collaborative effort among college students, who had little thought at the time of profiting from their creation: Michael Toy, Glenn Wichman, Ken Arnold, and Jon Lane. *Rogue*'s story begins with Toy and Wichman, who met at the University of California, Santa Cruz, where the 19-year-old Wichman was struggling to teach himself enough BASIC to make a text adventure game (see Figure 6.1).

Wichman had grown up playing board games and spent many happy years as a child making up his own prototypes. He became an avid fan of *Dungeons & Dragons* as a teenager and longed to design his own game like it. However, he kept running into problems keeping up with all the "boring parts," namely, the calculations, dice rolling, and other "housekeeping" duties associated with playing or being a dungeon master.[1] Wichman realized that a computer could take over many of these duties, allowing players to focus on the adventure.

Computer RPGs (CRPGs) were nothing new, but Toy and Wichman conceived of a program that could go a step further. They imagined a game that would create new dungeons each time you played it, distributing monsters, loot, and other elements according to a randomized procedure. It's important not to confuse this with a purely random process, which would have resulted in a hopeless muddle. Toy wanted to write an algorithm that would ensure that their dungeons were fully playable (see Figure 6.2).

As a game-loving college student at Berkeley, Wichman had access to arcade games like *Asteroids* and *Galaxian* but could also play *Adventure* and *Zork* on his lab's mainframe. The gulf between the arcade and the mainframe was vast indeed. Arcade

---

[1] Wichman, Glenn, interview by Matt Barton. *Matt Chat 225: Glenn Wichmann, Co-creator of Rogue* (January 26, 2014).

games had color graphics and sound, but their twitch-style gameplay was limited to short bursts of gratification. The mainframe games, by contrast, had no graphics or sound whatsoever, but significantly more memory and power—games could last weeks, if not months! Toy and Wichman dreamed of making a UNIX-based game that could have some form of graphics but were stymied by the crude terminals they used to access the mainframe. These terminals were never designed for gaming and were limited to American Standard Code

Figure 6.1   Glenn Wichman, cocreator of *Rogue*.

for Information Interchange (ASCII), a set of numerals, letters, punctuation marks, and other characters for displaying information. Unfortunately, the way each terminal handled text and cursors varied from brand to brand, another major obstacle for anyone attempting graphics.

Figure 6.2   *Rogue* running on PC. The character set graphics may look primitive, but this game can still get your blood pumping.

This is where Arnold enters the picture. Arnold had designed a "library" called Curses, short for "Cursor optimization." Curses allowed programmers like Toy and Wichman to control the way text was laid out on the screen, as well as cursor control—elements vital for any kind of graphical game. It also eliminated the compatibility issue with different brands of terminals. In short, it was exactly what Toy and Wichman needed to make *Rogue*.

Imagine trying to make a map of a dungeon using only the letters, numerals, and other symbols you can type with your keyboard. You might decide to make a wall by lining up a series of dashes or vertical bars: —|. You might then use these characters to make rooms, filling up the empty spaces with periods. Doors might be plus signs. Finally, you might use an unusual character such as @ for your hero and letters to stand for your monsters (Z for zombie, R for Rust monster, and so on). Thanks to Curses, this was a relatively straightforward process, but the algorithms were a different matter.

According to Wichman, the procedural generation "took a lot of creativity and a lot of problem solving. We were running into things that nobody we knew had ever run into before. But it was a lot of fun—we were creating something new and exciting."[1] Even with Toy's expertise and Arnold's Curses library to work with, they still had to scale back their original

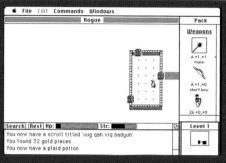

Figure 6.3   *Rogue* running on a Classic Mac emulator. This version takes advantage of the Mac's celebrated GUI.

design for the algorithm. The end result were rooms laid out like tic-tac-toe boards, with nine slots—but rooms could be made smaller than this maximum. Instead of revealing the entire map all at once, Toy and Wichman introduced what we'd call a "fog of war" mechanic today, meaning that only sections of the dungeons that the player previously explored would show on the map (see Figure 6.3).

The control scheme was as intuitive as one might expect from the era before mice and pulldown menus. Besides the basic movement keys (h, j, k, and l), players also had to remember somewhat arbitrary comments like "q" for quaff potion or "e" to eat food. Even with all these commands committed to memory, the game was very challenging. Sudden death could occur at any moment, particularly if the character wasn't yet equipped and stocked with potions and scrolls. However, starting over wasn't so bad—at least you wouldn't have to slog through the same old dungeon again on your next attempt.

Toy and Wichman's game was a hit with the nerds on campus, but it didn't get its big break until it was added to Version 4.2 of BSD UNIX, the operating system of choice on university mainframes all over the world. Ostensibly, the game was included as a way to make sure the operating system had been installed correctly, but it's just as likely the technical staff were playing it for fun. According to Wichman, *Rogue* was the most popular game on college campuses.[2] "It was interesting to see the surge of adrenaline you'd get when you'd see a T on the screen," said Wichman, reminiscing about the good old days. "That T was a troll, the first really threatening monster you'd see if you were doing well. You could watch people hitting the keys harder, thinking it would help them beat it. We'd hear screams"[1] (see Figure 6.4).

Rogue's success on the college scene seemed to bode well for a commercial release. After graduating and moving to Italy, Toy met Jon Lane, who helped him found a company called A.I. Design to adapt and publish *Rogue* for the new IBM PC. They handled the entire operation for 2 years before turning things over to Epyx, an established publisher.

[2] Wichman, Glenn. "A Brief History of Rogue." *Wichman.org.* 1997. http://www.wichman.org/roguehistory.html (accessed June 9, 2015).

Epyx was no stranger to RPGs; their *Dunjonquest: Temple of Apshai* series was one of the first commercial RPGs to hit the market, and they had even published *Sword of Fargoal* in 1982, which also featured procedurally generated dungeons. Wichman did a Macintosh port of *Rogue*, and Epyx worked with others to create versions for a wide variety of computers.

Figure 6.4   Epyx released this charming sprite-based version of *Rogue* in 1986.

Unfortunately, *Rogue* was not the hit game they'd hoped for, even with more sophisticated tile-based graphics and other niceties. The team blamed piracy, which was rampant in those days. Another issue may well have been the abundance of similar games, such as the aforementioned *Sword of Fargoal* by Jeff McCord or Daniel Lawrence's *Telengard* (1982), as well as a large number of free or cheap public domain or shareware variants like *Hack* (1982) and *Moria* (1983). Another strong possibility is that the game simply got overshadowed by *Ultima III* (1983; see Chapter 15), a superb, critically acclaimed RPG.

The most influential of the countless "roguelikes" are probably *Moria, Hack, Larn*, and *Ancient Domains of Mystery* (*ADOM*). *Moria*, as the name implies, is themed on J.R.R. Tolkien's *The Lord of the Rings*. The original version was authored by Robert Koeneke, a student at the University of Oklahoma. *Moria* had a persistent town with six shops where players could buy equipment. *Angband*, a popular and more recent roguelike, is derived from this game. *Hack*, which first debuted in 1982, was authored by Jay Fenlason and three friends. It was noted for its clever interaction with the gameworld and its creatures. Slaying and then eating a leprechaun, for instance, would teleport the character to a random location. *Hack* was the basis for the ever-popular *NetHack*, a 1987 game whose developers took advantage of the Internet. Noah Morgan's *Larn* (1986) offered a persistent starting level and a town with a bank, school, shop, and a tax office. Thomas Biskup's *ADOM*, released in 1994, was probably the most complex of the lot. It offered quests, skills, and a selection of 10 races and 20 character classes.

Although Epyx didn't have much commercial success with *Rogue*, its descendants have fared much better—indeed, the genre has become quite popular on Steam over the past few years. Subset Games' *FTL: Faster than Light* (2012), AMPLITUDE Studios' *Dungeon of the Endless* (2014), and Red Hook Studios' *Darkest Dungeon* (2015) are remarkably successful indie titles whose designs are clearly inspired by *Rogue*. The success of these titles—among at least 50 others tagged with "rogue-like"—has ushered in something of a modern-day "rogue-like renaissance" that shows little sign of slowing down.

Meanwhile, the "7-Day Rogue-like Challenge," established in 2005, is now in its 10th year. For this challenge, contestants strive to create a fully functional rogue-like game in a week. In 2015, there were 128 games completed for the challenge. Wichman himself entered back in 2007, submitting a game called *Seven Day Quest*.

An interesting question concerning rogue-likes is whether advanced graphics contribute to or distract from the essential gameplay. Some prefer ASCII or other character set graphics, but others choose games with more advanced graphics. To accommodate both preferences, many modern rogue-likes offer the choice of a graphical front-end or a more traditional character-set display. There's also a debate about how far a game can deviate from the original *Rogue*'s gameplay and still be considered a rogue-like. For instance, Mossmouth describes its game *Spelunky* (2013) as a "rogue-like platformer," though it certainly bears little resemblance to Toy and Wichman's creation. Rather, Mossmouth, like many others, apply the term to any game with some form of procedural generation.

Perhaps this tendency gives a little too much credit to *Rogue*. Like many design concepts we've encountered so far, such as online multiplayer, procedural generation was likely an inevitable concept that occurred to many different, totally unconnected people. For example, the aforementioned *Telengard* game was designed back in 1978, well before Toy and Wichman released *Rogue*, and Jeff McCord makes no mention of the game in interviews about *Sword of Fargoal*. It seems more likely that the term *rogue-like* has simply become a convenient label, perhaps because it rolls off the tongue more easily than *Telengard*-like!

Regardless, *Rogue* represents an addictive and compelling hack and slash type of experience. Unlike the majority of CRPGs, it's an easy game to pick up and play for a few minutes while waiting for a bus. The character set versions are also easy to get running on even the most limited hardware. The purists may have a good point; the lack of advanced audiovisuals does allow one to better appreciate the more abstract, mathematical nature of the genre. Indeed, perhaps the best way to think about *Rogue* is as the CRPG (or at least the "dungeon crawler") boiled down to its very essence. This approach might explain its enduring appeal after so many advances in audiovisual technology, as well as why so many talented programmers continue to explore its potential.

6.1 Playing *Rogue* Today

Playing the classic *Rogue* is as simple as visiting http://rlgallery.org/and clicking on the web app. You can also download the source code to various versions there. If you'd like to explore the traditional rogue-like genre, check out the RogueBasin at http://rogue basin.com. Modern rogue-likes with graphical front ends are plentiful on Steam; just do a search for "rogue-like."

Chapter 7

Maze War: The First First-Person Shooter?

You might assume that games evolved along a linear timeline, gradually growing in sophistication and complexity as new technologies were systematically invented or refined. However, history is a lot messier than that, and we often find that supposedly modern concepts go much further back—to obscure, thankless origins. A prime example of this is *Maze War*, which featured a first-person, three-dimensional (3D) perspective, avatars, online multiplayer, a level editor, bots, and trash-talking cheaters running through levels shooting at each other. Sound familiar? You may be surprised to learn that *Maze War* debuted in 1973—18 years before id's Software's *Catacomb 3-D*, the game widely considered the *first*, first-person shooter.

I wouldn't normally include a chapter about an obscure game like *Maze War* in a book about, well, influential games. However, the more I read about it, the more intrigued I became about how and why a game so groundbreaking in so many ways could possibly be so little known today. In my mind, *Maze War* joins PLATO, the Amiga 1000, and other groundbreaking computer technologies that were the right ideas at the wrong time. If we're going to understand what makes certain games influential, it's helpful to see what factors inhibit or even prevent it.

Like so many of the games in this chapter, *Maze War* was not a product of commercial game development. Instead, it began life at NASA's Ames Research Center, where a summer intern named Steve Colley was doing a series of 3D experiments on an Imlac PDS-1, a graphical display system. After achieving some success with a rotating cube, Colley thought it'd be fun to expand his program into a full 3D maze, shown in a first-person perspective. He then went to work creating different mazes, or, as we'd say in modern parlance, designing levels. "It was surprising how quickly you could learn them," said Colley, who couldn't wait to show off his game to his colleagues Greg Thompson and Howard Palmer.[1]

Thompson and Palmer could see the potential, but just running through the maze looking for an exit got old quickly. They decided to connect some of the Imlacs together, so that multiple players could run through the same level, chasing down and shooting at each other. The other players were represented by disembodied eyeballs—the first

---

[1] Colley, Steve. "Steve Colley's Story of the Original Maze." *DigiBarn Computer Museum*. November 7, 2004. http://www.digibarn.com/history/04-VCF7-MazeWar/stories/colley.html (accessed May 6, 2015).

avatars. They now had a fun game on their hands, but they continued refining the code and adding new features, such as the ability to peek around corners, and a level editor that let players construct their own mazes. Movement in the game was tile based rather than fluid as in modern games, a necessary concession to the graphics and networking technology of the era. It also allowed one of the

Figure 7.1   *Maze War SVG*, a modern remake of the game in Java. (Image courtesy of Chris W. Johnson.)

first "bugs" that turned out to be a feature—the delay on the serial ports meant that two people could kill each other—as if their bullets had passed one another in the hallway (see Figure 7.1).

As the game began making its way to other institutions, other innovations followed. Dave Lebling, one of *Zork*'s creators, became enamored with it. He added a computer-controlled robot, which silently prowled the corridors in search of human targets—the first "bot." Another key innovation came in 1977, when a version was made that could be played over the ARPANET (the progenitor of the Internet). Now, players from geographically distant institutions could play together online.

Like *Zork* and *Spacewar!* before it, *Maze War* attracted a large following of highly dedicated players—who were often told in no uncertain terms that they shouldn't be "wasting" precious computing resources playing games. Lebling notes: "To say that the game was an immediate hit would be an understatement. We had six or eight Imlacs, and during off-hours they were almost all playing *Maze*. People would come down from the AI Lab to play, or bring their friends in to play with them. Some of the best people recruited by the DM (Dynamic Modeling) group were originally attracted there by these midnight *Maze* sessions."[2] The competition grew so intense that some unscrupulous players resorted to cheating, which led to encrypting the game's source code.

For many years, the game didn't have a way for players to chat, but Jim Guyton, who helped adapt the game for play on Xerox's Alto systems, noted that "you could get a little extra feedback by paying close attention to the screams" up and down the hallways.[3] Later versions of *Maze War* did let players chat with each other, and as with modern online games, many players logged in simply to socialize. Bruce Damer argues that this

[2] Lebling, David. "David Lebling's Story of Maze at MIT (1974+)." *DigiBarn Computer Museum*. November 7, 2004. http://www.digibarn.com/history/04-VCF7-MazeWar/stories/lebling.html (accessed May 6, 2015).

[3] Guyton, Jim. "Jim Guyton's Story of Maze at Xerox (Alto and Star)." *DigiBarn Computer Museum*. November 7, 2004. http://www.digibarn.com/history/04-VCF7-MazeWar/stories/guyton.html (accessed May 6, 2015).

game originated the concept of being "in-world," laying the groundwork for the persistent virtual worlds of today's Massively Multiplayer Online games.[4]

Written well before the Internet and networked personal computers were ubiquitous in American homes, *Maze War*'s commercial potential was virtually nil. This changed in 1987, when a company named Macromind released a version called *MazeWars+* for the Apple Macintosh, which could be played over the Appletalk network and was even bundled with some Macintosh systems. It could support up to 30 players, but the flyer recommends limiting it to 6. During the same year, another port called *MIDI Maze* was developed for the Atari ST, which, as the name implies, used the system's built-in MIDI interface—normally used for music applications—to serve as a network. *MIDI Maze* could theoretically support up to 16 players, but again, adding more than 4 caused the game to slow down and ultimately become unplayable.

Maze War's first-person perspective proved useful for other kinds of games, especially role-playing games for early home computers. We can clearly see the influence in games like *Wizardry*, whose turn-based gameplay removed (or at least reduced) the need for fast, CPU-intensive rendering, making it suitable for play on machines like the Apple II and Commodore 64. It also allowed many gamers an early glimpse at networked action games.

Matthew Kirschenbaum of *Slate* named *Maze War* the second most influential software program (not just game) of all time, calling it the "first first-person shooter."[5] When we consider how many "firsts" the game can legitimately lay claim to, it's easy to see why—but not everyone is convinced the game is worthy of such accolades. Richard Bartle, the celebrated cocreator of *MUD* (see Chapter 5), directly questioned its influence: "We're all told of *Maze*'s firsts," he wrote in an online comment in 2007, "but merely being first is no guarantee of influence ... 3D graphics was something that was always going to happen, because it was too obvious not to."[6] Bartle's claim was lent some credence when I asked if *Maze War* had inspired John Romero and John Carmack, celebrated cofounders of id Software and fathers of the first-person shooter. According to Romero, neither he nor Carmack has ever played *Maze War*.[7] It's hardly surprising; after all, availability was limited mostly to college campuses and research centers. Unlike *Tennis for Two*, *Spacewar!*, or *Zork*, *Maze War* did not benefit from an effective transition to arcades, consoles, or home computers.

How could a game so ahead of its time remain so obscure? Everett M. Rogers' book *Diffusion of Innovations* offers some substantial insights into this question. Rogers

---

[4] Damer, Bruce. "Meeting in the Ether." *Interactions* 14, no. 5 (September 2007): 16–18.

[5] Kirschenbaum, Matthew. "The 10 Most Influential Software Programs Ever." *Slate*. July 30, 2013. http://www.slate.com/blogs/browbeat/2013/07/30/_10_most_influential_software_programs_of_all_time_from_sabre_to_minecraft.html (accessed May 6, 2015).

[6] Bartle, Richard. "Comment." *Terra Nova.* March 6, 2007. http://terranova.blogs.com/terra_nova/2007/03/march_topics.html (accessed May 6, 2015).

[7] Romero, John. *Twitter Tweet.* May 6, 2015. https://twitter.com/romero/status/596116245637824512 (accessed May 7, 2015).

posits that there are always five *perceived* attributes of an innovation that lead to their widespread adoption: relative advantage, compatibility, complexity, trialability, and observability.[8] It seems clear that, at least to those who played it, *Maze War* was technically advanced (relative advantage), fulfilled all the same psychological or social desires as other games (compatibility), and was not especially difficult to learn how to play (complexity)—though making a game like *Maze War* required fairly advanced 3D graphics programming skills.

By "trialability," Rogers is referring to the costs of simply trying out a new product or feature. For example, trying out *Pong* costs only a quarter, which was literally pocket change. Imagine, however, if the machine had demanded a dollar per play, which would have been well over $5 in today's currency. That's roughly the price of a good bottled beer or a cocktail and certainly a lot higher than what pinball gamers were accustomed to. Bushnell wisely kept the price per play low, making it painless for even the poorest bar patrons to give those dials a spin.

Maze War's trialability is more difficult to define. On the one hand, it was basically "free software" in the modern sense; anyone with access to a compatible mainframe computer could have legally downloaded and played the game for free. On the other hand, very few people owned or had access to such a machine, and not just anyone could waltz into NASA, Xerox, or MIT's computer labs and play a game! As mentioned above, there were ports available for the classic Macintosh (*MazeWars+*) and the Atari ST (*MIDI Maze*). While devotees of these vintage platforms are rightly proud of these games, they remain obscure to the broader gaming community.

Observability is where *Maze War* fails the hardest. Rogers gives a helpful example of observability: solar panels. Even if you don't have them on your roof, you may be able to see them on your neighbors' houses. Seeing solar panels on a daily basis might well put the idea in your head to look into installing them yourself—the old keepin' up with the Joneses phenomenon. It's also the principle behind product demonstrations—once you've *seen* what that new Blend-o-Chop can do, you're more likely to want one. It's clear that many people did see, play, and love *Maze War*—just not enough to hit the tipping point.

Maze War may have been the first game to introduce a great many important innovations that are now standard in modern games—but Bartle is right; just being first does not guarantee influence. I'd add that it's especially hard when you don't try to capitalize on your innovations and protect your intellectual property. Timing is also important, and *Maze War* was simply too much, too soon for an industry that still thought *Pong* was a pretty neat idea.

History is full of fabulous "what ifs," and I'll end this chapter with a good one. Lebling noted that after Infocom was founded in 1979, his company strongly considered building an arcade version of *Maze War*. It's fascinating to imagine what the industry would look like today if Infocom had successfully followed through on this plan, rather than abandoning it to focus on text adventures. The arcades of the 1980s might have

---

[8] Rogers, Everett M. *Diffusion of Innovations*. New York: Free Press, 2003, 15.

looked more like the LAN parties of the 1990s! Of course, we'll never know, and, besides, I liked those arcades just fine the way they were.

7.1 Playing *Maze War* Today

If you'd like to try out *Maze War*, you can download *Maze Wars SVG*, a recreation of the 1987 Macintosh port. Once you've set up a server (it's written in Java, so you'll need a web application server like Tomcat), you can play it with your friends using their web browsers. Surprisingly, I wasn't able to find anyone running a guest server. Forty years later, *Maze War* is still suffering from a lack of trialability!

Part II
The Early Adopters

Rogers' next category is "early adopters," a larger and more influential group than the innovators. Rogers described them with a pithy old saying: "Be not the first by which the new is tried, nor the last to lay the old aside."[1] They tend to be empathetic, imaginative people, who are open to new ideas, but prefer to wait and see awhile before committing to them. However, once they commit, they bring many others with them; people who respect their judgment enough to overcome their initial skepticism.

Perhaps no other game sums this section up the "early adopter" era better than *Pac-Man*. While *Pong* and *Space Invaders* were enormous successes, they pale in comparison to Toru Iwatani's great masterpiece. *Pac-Man* enticed people into arcades who had never been before, people who'd been willing before to sit out what they felt was just a crazy new fad. *Pac-Man* was far more than just a game; he was a cultural phenomenon, and the icon of a new generation.

Much of what we take for granted in the video game industry evolved during this period thanks to early adopters. Of particular interest is the introduction of cheap game

---

[1] Rogers, Everett M. *Diffusion of Innovations*. New York: Free Press, 2003.

consoles with slots for read-only memory (ROM) cartridges. This innovation eventually led (despite much legal wrangling) to the separation of video game hardware and software developers. Some owners complained about having to buy extra cartridges; why couldn't they just be built-in like they were in the "good old days?" But imagine what the industry would be like today without independent software houses like Electronic Arts and Bethesda! The third-party software companies churned out a huge variety of games, some of which were as good if not better than the manufacturer's own. Unfortunately, the lack of industry regulation, control, and common sense led to the "Great Videogame Crash" of 1983, in which tons of poorly conceived games and related products oversaturated the market, bringing the industry to its knees.

Early adopters also witnessed the first great console rivalries, as gamers struggled to decide among a bevy of incompatible machines each claiming to be the best. Coleco, Mattel, and others vied for Atari's clientele, making all kinds of promises that seem bizarre today. It's hard to imagine a major game console today advertising its educational value, or its potential to be expanded into a full-blown computer. Yet, at this period, the market was so young that marketing departments were willing to try anything to gain a foothold over the competition!

The home computer market was also rapidly expanding, especially after the introduction of the Commodore 64, the best-selling PC of all time. Even though it was a pain to program for and had a slow, inefficient disk drive, the C-64 was cheap, powerful, and more than just a great game machine. My grandmother ran her tax preparation business with one.

Floppy disks and earlier "datasettes" were a double-edged sword for the home computer industry. On the one hand, it did mean that the machines could be used for business and other nongaming purposes, since you clearly needed a way to save all your hard work. It also made it much easier for third parties to publish software for your machine, since disks and tapes were cheaper and more accessible than custom cartridges. On the other hand, try as they might, software publishers could not seem to prevent unscrupulous users from illegally copying and distributing their products. These early "pirates" may have made life hard for publishers, but they inadvertently boosted sales of the machines, since potential buyers might reckon on tons of "free" software to justify the purchase.

Finally, this generation was the Golden Age of the video game arcade, when hordes of teens flooded each weekend to their local mall, bowling alley, or dedicated gaming center for bout after bout of *Pac-Man*, *Donkey Kong*, *Space Invaders*, *Q*Bert*, and *Pole Position*. At this point, arcade machines offered much better audiovisuals than your humble Atari 2600 or Commodore 64, and, besides, what's the point of racking up high scores that no one will ever see?

In short, the period we're about to cover is one of the most exciting, important, and wildest eras in the history of the video game industry, with major implications for console, arcade, and computer games. It all began with a slice of pizza.

Chapter 8

Pac-Man: Gamers Just Want to Have Lunch

If the peace sign sums up the America of the 1960s, a bright yellow circle with a slice removed—Pac-Man—is a fitting icon for the 1980s. Long before the days of Master Chief, Lara Croft, Sonic, and Mario, this humble pie guy chomped out of the arcades and into public consciousness. He had something that other arcade games like *Pong* and *Space Invaders* lacked—charisma. He eventually found himself on lunch boxes, breakfast cereals, Saturday morning cartoons, toys, and pretty much anything else that could be affixed with his image and sold in a store. He even had a top-40 song written about him, appropriately titled *Pac-Man Fever* (see Figure 8.1).

Pac-Man was designed by a 25-year-old pinball fan named Toru Iwatani. After earning an electrical engineering degree from Tokai University, a small private university in Tokyo, Iwatani applied and was hired at Namco, hoping to make his own pinball games. His bosses, however, had different plans. Japan was still enthralled with Taito's *Space Invaders*, and Namco wanted a piece of the action. Iwatani, who'd never taken any classes in programming or graphics, was handed some pencils and graph paper and told to get to work. The president of Namco, Masaya Nakamura, actually thought Iwatani's lack of training was an asset: "For game designers, the knowledge acquired in school is not so helpful. I want people who think in unusual ways, whose curiosity runs away with them, fun-loving renegades."[1]

The first game Iwatani designed was called *Gee Bee*, a 1978 ball and paddle game best described as a mash-up of *Breakout* and pinball. Like *Breakout*, the goal is to knock out the rows of destructible bricks along the top and sides of the screen. The twist was that in between the paddle and the bricks were pinball bumpers and other elements. It was a clever idea, but neither this game nor a more elaborate sequel called *Bomb Bee* sold very well. Iwatani's third effort was *Cutie Q*, a similar game but with odd (dare I say cute?) little creatures. Success still eluded Iwatani. Meanwhile, Iwatani's rival designer at Namco, Kazunori Sawano, had scored Namco's first major hit—a *Space Invaders* clone called *Galaxian* (see Figure 8.2).

Finally giving up on his pinball-inspired designs, Iwatani went back to the drawing board. Perhaps chafing a bit from Sawano's roaring success with *Galaxian*, he

---

[1] Lohr, Steve. "Technology Spurs Change: High Technology Spurs Nonconformists in Japan." *New York Times*, March 8, 1983: D1.

Figure 8.1   Toru Iwatani, the creator of *Pac-Man*. (Photo courtesy of Official GDC.)

argued that violent games appealed mostly to males. But what sort of game would appeal to women? "When I imagined what women enjoy," said Iwatani, "the image of them eating cakes and desserts came to mind, so I used 'eating' as a keyword. When I did research with this keyword, I came across the image of a pizza with a slice taken out of it and had that eureka moment."[2] Iwatani was also inspired by manga and American cartoons. *Obake no Q-Taro* and *Casper the Friendly Ghost* inspired the ghosts in the game, and *Popeye the Sailor*, whose spinach-powered super strength was the impetus for the game's famous power pills.[3]

Iwatani took pains to make sure the ghosts in the game would seem cute rather than genuinely menacing. "It's an enemy, but still somewhat amicable," said Iwatani. "Even when you eat them, their eyeballs come back," decreasing the appearance of real violence.[4] Iwatani recounted later that his supervisor, who he described as a kind, elderly woman, asked him to make all the ghosts one color (red) to make them easier to identify as enemies.[5] Iwatani wisely held out, and Inky (blue), Blinky (red), Pinky (pink), and Clyde (orange) kept their colors. Sticking with his food and eating theme, Iwatani called his game *Puck-Man*—the sound "puck puck" is a Japanese convention to represent the sound of eating, similar to our "nom nom."

[2] Purchese, Robert. "Iwatani: Pac-Man was made for women." *Eurogamer.net.* May 20, 2010. http://www.eurogamer.net /articles/iwatani-pac-man-was-made-for-women (accessed May 19, 2015).

[3] Kshosfy. "Q&A: Pac-Man Creator Reflects on 30 Years of Dot-Eating." *Wired.* May 21, 2010. http://www.wired.com/2010/05 /pac-man-30-years/ (accessed May 19, 2015).

[4] Pfeffer, Helen. "Exclusive: Pac-Man Creator Speaks!" *VH1 Game Break.* June 6, 2007. http://vh1.blogs.com/vh1 _games//2007/06/exclusive_pacma.html (accessed May 19, 2015).

[5] Cifaldo, Frank. "A Real Ladies Pac-Man: How Namco's Yellow Dot Won Over Female Gamers." *1up.com.* May 25, 2011. http:// www.1up.com/features/history-pac-man (accessed May 19, 2015).

Perhaps the real brilliance of Iwatani's design was the algorithm he created to control the ghosts' movement through the maze. "It was tricky because the monster movements are quite complex," said Iwatani:

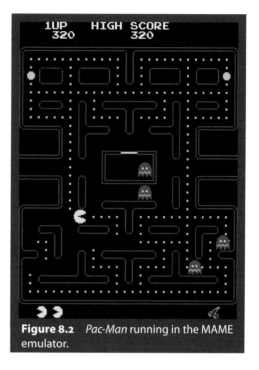

Figure 8.2 *Pac-Man* running in the MAME emulator.

> This is the heart of the game. I wanted each ghostly enemy to have a specific character and its own particular movements, so they weren't all just chasing after Pac Man in single file, which would have been tiresome and flat. One of them, the red one called Blinky, did chase directly after Pac Man. The second ghost is positioned at a point a few dots in front of Pac Man's mouth. That is his position. If Pac Man is in the center then Monster A and Monster B are equidistant from him, but each moves independently, almost "sandwiching" him. The other ghosts move more at random. That way they get closer to Pac Man in a natural way.
>
> When a human being is constantly under attack like this, he becomes discouraged. So we developed the wave-patterned attack–attack then disperse; as time goes by the ghosts regroup and attack again. Gradually the peaks and valleys in the curve of the wave become less pronounced so that the ghosts attack more frequently.[6]

A key part of relaxing the tension was a small set of cut scenes or "intermissions." These humorous sketches starred Pac-Man and Blinky, the red ghost. These brief, charming segments gave gamers a chance to relax their wrists, while also helping to establish personalities for what would otherwise have been abstract characters.

It took Iwatani and his small team 18 months to complete the game, and anxiety was running high. They knew they would face incredible competition in the arcades. How would *Pac-Man* fare against the likes of Atari's *Centipede* (1980) and *Asteroids* (1979), or Namco's own *Galaxian*?

---

[6] Lammers, Susan. *Programmers at Work: Interviews With 19 Programmers Who Shaped the Computer Industry*. Redmund, WA: Microsoft Press, 1989.

To check its appeal, they secretly placed a test unit in the lounge of a large movie theater, where couples were known to congregate after watching a movie. Iwatani hid himself nearby and nervously waited to see if all his hard work had paid off. Iwatani was delighted to see that "the women and couples were very happy about the machine, very excited," even if "the core gamers, the men, were not … But it was for people who didn't play games on a daily basis—women, children, the elderly."[3]

Sadly for Iwatani, the core group was the one that mattered. Japanese gamers were far too enamored with shoot'em up games to give *Puck-Man* a chance. One might well have expected Iwatani to shrivel up and die like his own captured *Puck-Man*. When Midway approached Namco to license some of their games for America, they were far more interested in *Galaxian* and another game called *Rally-X*. Still, they decided that *Puck-Man* was worth a shot. Before shipping it to the Americans, Namco's president Nakamura quietly changed the name to *Pac-Man* to discourage vandalism, and, no doubt, inappropriate jokes.[7]

Nakamura was right. We Americans thought *Pac-Man* was pucking awesome.

Pac-Man hit Western shores like a tsunami, flooding into arcades and then out into the wider market. Soon, every pizza parlor, supermarket, and drug store in the United States had to have one. It was all Midway could do to keep up with the demand for the quarter-munching machines, churning out a hundred thousand of them in 1980 (three times that number would be produced over the next 7 years). The machines were well worth the investment; in total, they raked in more than a billion dollars' worth of quarters in the first year alone.[8] As successful as *Space Invaders* had been just 2 years earlier, it was just a small slice of *Pac-Man* (see Figure 8.3).

"Pac-Man is the most popular video game ever," said Harold Vogel, an analyst for Merrill Lynch. "With 100,000 units out there [by November, 1981], that's an all-time record."[8] It's not hard to appreciate *Pac-Man's* appeal. As Iwatani had predicted, there were hordes of potential female gamers who'd been turned off by space, war, and tank games. But the game had a lot more going for it than simply its avoidance of any violent themes: it was extremely competitive.

While anybody could learn to play and enjoy *Pac-Man* in a matter of minutes, it was possible to master it on a level that you just couldn't say about the likes of *Pong* or *Space Invaders*. The predictable behavior of the ghosts as they chased Pac-Man could be learned and incorporated into successful strategies. These "pattern players," as they came to be known, could earn scores (and hog the machine!) far longer than a casual player. For countless gamers of the 1980s, mastering these patterns was highly rewarding, not just for the social status it might bring, but the thrills of hacking a system—in effect, outsmarting the game's designers. Pattern players were the new pinball wizards of America. Determined players could even buy books like Ken Uston's *Mastering*

---

[7] Kent, Steve L. *The Ultimate History of Video Games: From Pong to Pokémon and Beyond: the Story Behind the Craze that Touched Our Lives and Changed the World*. Rocklin, CA: Prima Pub., 2001.

[8] Katya, Goncharoff. "Video Games: A Glutton for Globs… And Quarters." *New York Times*, November 15, 1981: F21.

Pac-Man, whose introduction (written in 1982) gives us a nice insight into the "hard-core" gamer of the era:

> When the [novice] player is through, he has probably amassed a score of 600, or perhaps 1500 if he was lucky. The game has lasted perhaps one minute … Yet chances are the player will put another quarter, and another, into the machine … His ability to maneuver *Pac-Man* gradually improves and his score mounts … The player's scores

Figure 8.3 *Pac-Man* and *Puck-Man* arcade machines. (Photo courtesy of Gerard van Schip.)

may increase, to perhaps 5000 or so. He will note the "High Score" posted at the top of the screen and wonder how on earth any mortal could have scored 56,800, or 106,500, or even 249,300 … It's surprisingly easy if a methodical approach is taken. Indeed, the characteristic that attracted me to *Pac-Man* is that a predetermined plan is far more important … than physical coordination.[9]

Thus, *Pac-Man* really could appeal to everyone, from casual players drawn to the cute graphics or charming characters, to the hardcore gamer who could truly appreciate the game's complexities.

More recently, a 34-year-old kitchen manager named Billy Mitchell came to international attention after playing the first-ever "perfect" *Pac-Man* game, gaining the maximum 3,333,360 points after 6 hours of play, earning himself a Guinness World Record for his trouble.[10] Rather than following patterns, Mitchell worked out methods to manipulate the ghosts into the corners of his choice. "I chose to do it this way because I wanted to demonstrate the depths of my abilities," said Mitchell, "I wanted to raise the bar higher—to a level that no one else could match."[11] We'll have the opportunity to discuss Mitchell again when we discuss *Donkey Kong.*

A list of Bally Midway's Pac-Man licensees from May 28, 1982, reveals just how lucrative and widespread America's "Pac-Man Fever" had become in just 2 years. There are lunch boxes, watches, roller and ice skates, stadium cushions, towels, lapel pins, board

[9] Uston, Ken. *Mastering Pac-Man.* Brattleboro, VT: Echo Point Books & Media, 1981.

[10] Kahney, Leander. "July 3, 1999: Gobbling Up a Pac-Man Record." *Wired.* July 3, 2008. http://archive.wired.com/science/discoveries/news/2008/07/dayintech_0703 (accessed May 20, 2015).

[11] Trueman, Doug. "An Interview with Billy Mitchell." *GameSpot.* 2004. http://www.gamespot.com/features/vgs/universal/hist_pacman/p11_01.html (accessed June 17, 2004).

games, lamps, air fresheners, swimwear, cross-stitch patterns, drapes, soaps, cigarette lighters and cases, and even a hot air corn popper.[12] At the height of his fame, *Pac-Man* even had his own Saturday morning cartoon produced by Hanna-Barbera, which ran for two seasons between September 1982 and November 1983. I'm pretty sure that even *The Beatles* didn't get this much love. Sadly, that love didn't extend to Iwatani himself, whose bosses at Namco didn't give him a raise, bonus, or even a citation for his epic achievement. "I was just an employee," said Iwatani.[4]

Naturally, Atari and other console manufacturers were eager to cash in on America's *Pac-Man* Fever, but the crude consumer hardware of the era made a satisfactory port unlikely, even with a talented team, extra memory to work with, and a lengthy development cycle. Atari's executives must have felt the *Pac-Man* branding alone would be sufficient to sell 10 million copies of the game, because they gave Tod Frye only 6 weeks to develop the game all by himself.[13] Furthermore, they restricted him to 4K ROM rather than the more expensive (but significantly more capable) 8K bank-switched ROM.[14]

Needless to say, Frye's game was a poor substitute indeed for playing *Pac-Man* in the arcade. Even compared to other Atari 2600 games, *Pac-Man* was a disaster, with crummy audio, flickering visuals, missing cut scenes, and inaccurate gameplay. Although millions of unsuspecting or desperate Atari 2600 owners purchased the cartridge, word quickly spread, and Atari was soon overwhelmed with unsold inventory—which many blamed for crashing the industry in 1983. In any case, *Pac-Man* ports for other consoles, such as Mike Winans' for the Mattel Intellivision (a licensed Atarisoft product), and Atari's own version for their 5200 console, adhered more faithfully to the original (see Figure 8.4).

Having paid millions for the exclusive home translation rights, Atari was determined to stop competitive maze chase games from reaching market, especially on non-Atari hardware. Even though programmer Ed Averett took pains to distinguish his excellent *K.C. Munchkin!* Game for the Magnavox Odyssey2, providing four mazes, moving dots, and user-programmable playfields, Atari sued them for infringement. Magnavox's game sold briskly at first and was far superior to Atari's game for its 2600. Magnavox won in court, but grew complacent in victory. Atari's deep pockets helped them win a hard fought appeal, and *K.C. Munchkin!* was taken off shelves. Yet again, Atari had smashed its old arch-enemy Magnavox.

In 1981, Midway released *Ms. Pac-Man*, which they'd based on *Crazy Otto*, a *Pac-Man* conversion (mod) kit developed by engineers at the General Computer Corporation (GCC). Midway presented the game as a sequel to *Pac-Man*, altering its appearance to make it more in-line with the original. *Ms. Pac-Man* improved on its predecessor in several key areas. First, the character now sported a bright red bow, lipstick, and a beauty

---

[12] Bally Midway Mfg. Co. "List of Bally Midway Mfg. Co. Pac-Man Licensees." *Arcade Museum*. November 28, 1982. http://www.arcade-museum.com/manuals-videogames/P/Pacman%20Licenses%20May%201982.pdf (accessed May 20, 2015).

[13] Montfort, Nick, and Ian Bogost. *Racing the Beam: The Atari Video Computer System*. Cambridge, MA: MIT Press, 2009, 67.

[14] Montfort and Bogost's book *Racing the Beam: The Atari Video Computer System* gives an excellent account of the technical challenges faced by Frye in adapting the game.

mark. Many critics claim this change
made the game even more appealing
to females. The sequel also added new
mazes, new behavior for the ghosts, and
new intermissions concerned with the
budding relationship between Mr. and
Ms. Pac-Man. *Ms. Pac-Man* was widely
admired by fans, many of whom judged it
superior.

Figure 8.4　The wretched Atari 2600 version of *Pac-Man* was a high-profile disaster for Atari.

A popular misconception is that GCC and Midway's *Ms. Pac-Man* game was unauthorized by Namco, who took them to court over it. I'm not sure how this myth got
started, but GCC's founder Doug Macrae set us straight in 2010 during a presentation at
California Extreme. Macrae claims that not only was Namco aware of their project, they
actively supported it, with Namco's president Nakamura himself suggesting the character's distinctive bow (see Figure 8.5).

While most people still have fond memories of the original *Pac-Man*, many modern
gamers prefer the sequel. Indeed, one of the most common "retro" arcade machines in
production today is a combination *Ms. Pac-Man* and *Galaga* cabinet. Atari took more
care in porting *Ms. Pac-Man* to its 2600,
resulting in a much more polished and
playable game.

A few months after *Ms. Pac-Man*'s
debut, Midway released *Super Pac-Man*,
substantially altering the gameplay of
the original. Most noticeably, Pac-Man
no longer eats dots, but fruits and keys.
As the title suggests, Pac-Man can now
gain super powers by munching a super
pellet. In super form, Pac-Man is twice
as big and invulnerable, but cannot eat
ghosts. Despite these innovations, the
game wasn't nearly as popular as *Ms.
Pac-Man*. Bally and Midway (later Bally
Midway) released other *Pac-Man*–related
games throughout the early 1980s, including *Pac-Man Plus* (1982), a minor altera-
tion of the original that manipulates the

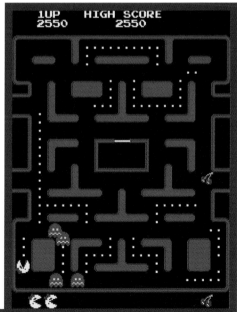

Figure 8.5　*Ms. Pac-Man* was a much-loved follow-up to the original game.

effects of power pellets, an innovative, but notoriously difficult pinball/video game hybrid named *Baby Pac-Man* (1982), and a poorly received trivia game called *Professor Pac-Man* (1983). Toward the middle of the decade, the franchise drifted into platforming. *Pac-Land* (1984) was a lackluster side-scrolling platformer that had little in common with its predecessors. Similarly, Namco's *Pac-Mania* (1987) took the maze game into an isometric perspective and featured boards that were much larger than a single screen. The key innovation here was Pac-Man's ability to jump at any time. None of these efforts could trump the charm and appeal of the original or *Ms. Pac-Man*.

Iwatani's last game was *Pac-Man Champion Edition* for the Xbox 360, which debuted in 2007 for Xbox Live Arcade. Despite its trippy, hi-definition visuals, sound, and wild new game modes, the game stays faithful to the original's concepts and timing.

Iwatani is best known for *Pac-Man*. But as we'll see in Chapter 10, it was not his only major contribution to the video game industry.

8.1 Playing *Pac-Man* Today

Unlike Taito and its *Space Invaders* game, Namco Bandai offers countless ways to legally play *Pac-Man* on just about any modern device. Just go to http://pacman.com and browse the options there for mobiles, PCs, and Macs. The various console online stores also offer the game as well as *Ms. Pac-Man* and other sequels. There are also several plug-and-play TV devices with a built-in joystick and *Pac-Man* ROM.

To honor *Pac-Man*'s 30th anniversary, Google created a fun playable Doodle featuring a *Pac-Man* theme. While the maze has been changed to advertise the company, it still feels enough like the original to whet your appetite. Better yet, you can play it for free at https://www.google.com/doodles/30th-anniversary-of-pac-man.

Chapter 9

Donkey Kong: Miyamoto's 800-Pound Gorilla

The early 1980s were the golden age of the arcades, when playing the latest games meant jamming your way into a boisterous neon arena where throngs of fickle teenagers, quarters in hand, queued up for 30 s of twitch. The stakes were high for the owners of these pop-fueled establishments, the arcade operators, who had to predict which machines would collect more quarters than dust. The International Arcade Museum website lists 244 machines manufactured in 1981 alone, and for each *Frogger*, *Galaga*, or *Defender*, there are dozens of obscure titles like Sun Electronics' *Funky Fish* and Universal's *Cosmic Avenger* (see Figure 9.1).

It's hardly surprising, then, that few of these operators paid much attention in 1980 when a new developer from Japan set up shop near Seattle. They were the American branch of a playing card company called "Nintendo," who'd jumped on the *Pong* and *Space Invader* clone bandwagon back in the 1970s. They seemed like just another Johnny-come-lately who could hardly compete with the likes of Atari, Taito, and Namco. No one could have guessed that in less than a decade, this upstart would be the most important, influential, and successful video game company the world had ever seen.

The "notoriously imperialistic" president of Nintendo, Hiroshi Yamauchi, had put his son-in-law, Minoru Arakawa, in charge of his new American branch of the operation.[1] It wasn't simply nepotism; Arakawa had gone to college in the United States and toured the country extensively in an old van. After college, he went back to Japan and got a job with a real estate developer, where he proved himself a smart and savvy manager. Despite his total lack of experience in the games industry—and over the protests of his daughter, who feared its impact on their personal life—Yamauchi made Arakawa an offer he couldn't refuse.[2]

Arakawa's first decision was to promptly order 3000 units of *Radar Scope*, which was then Nintendo's most popular game in Japan. *Radar Scope* was a mash-up of *Space Invaders* and *Galaxian* and featured an intriguing playfield with curved vectors. It had all

---

[1] Kent, Steve L. *The Ultimate History of Video Games: From Pong to Pokémon and Beyond: The Story Behind the Craze that Touched Our Lives and Changed the World*. Rocklin, CA: Prima Pub., 2001, p. 157.

[2] IGN. "Profile: Minoru Arakawa." *IGN*. June 25, 2004. http://www.ign.com/articles/2004/06/25/profile-minoru-arakawa (accessed June 2, 2015).

Figure 9.1   Shigeru Miyamoto at GDC 2007. (Photo courtesy of Vincent Diamante.)

the makings of a hit, but Arakawa was only able to sell a third of the machines he'd ordered.[1] The flyer that Arakawa's distributors had put together declared Nintendo "the most exciting name in video games," but it was empty rhetoric. By this point, *Pac-Man* fever had gripped the nation, and the shoot'em up gameplay of *Radar Scope* was hopelessly passé. Arakawa's company

Figure 9.2   Hiroshi Yamauchi, president of Nintendo from 1949 to 2005.

was on the verge of collapse—and we can only guess at the anxiety he felt about asking his stern father-in-law for a bailout. Something had to be done, though, so he made the call (see Figure 9.2).

Yamauchi, meanwhile, had been hearing about one of his employees in the art department, a scruffy, freckle-faced kid named Shigeru Miyamoto. A few years ago, he'd given the boy a job as a favor to Miyamoto's father, an old family friend, and set him to work drawing up artwork and button labels for their arcade cabinets and *Pong* consoles. He was ambitious, though, and played all the popular arcade games, desperately seeking their secret formulas.

Yamauchi's star toy and game designer, Gunpei Yokoi, had taken a liking to him, and had long conversations with him about all his fantastic ideas for sophisticated new games; with all the new technological advances coming out on an almost daily basis, the possibilities seemed endless. He talked about games based on cartoons and movies, like *King Kong* and *Popeye the Sailor Man*, with detailed backstories and epic special effects.

Yokoi had invented the Game & Watch system and would go on to design the Game Boy. He was committed to a design philosophy called "Lateral Thinking with Withered Technology," which is all about finding creative, unexplored ways to use old technology—not foolishly chasing after the cutting edge. "There is a better way," he told Miyamoto.

Yokoi told his young protégé to sit down and open his hand whenever he flipped on the lights.[3] Miyamoto did as he was instructed. "Okay, now stand up when you hear a sound … Bleep! … Bloop!" Again, Miyamoto obeyed, probably wondering if his mentor had gone senile. "Now," said Yokoi, "do both simultaneously." As Miyamoto struggled to keep up with Yokoi, laughing and trying not to trip over his chair as he leapt to his feet, it suddenly dawned on him: this was *fun*.

Something else dawned on Yokoi: his protégé was ready for his first real test, and there was a perfect storm brewing. Nintendo had an American branch in imminent peril, with a warehouse crammed with 2000 machines that nobody wanted. He told Yamauchi about the progress he'd been making with Miyamoto. "But he is an artist. He knows nothing about programming—about technology," Yamauchi must have thought. "I will guide him," promised Yokoi.

"Bring him to me," said Yamauchi.

We can only imagine the anxiety and nervousness the young Miyamoto must have felt, standing there in front of the powerful man. Many words have been used to describe Nintendo's third and greatest president, Hiroshi Yamauchi, but never "sympathetic." He was a cold, ruthless administrator, who'd had his own kin fired to remove any challenge to his absolute authority.[4] What a sight—this severe, austere man sitting at his massive desk, staring at this shaggy-haired, goofy young artist. A long, tense silence passed as Yamauchi took his measure of the man.

"Do you think you can design a video game?" he asked at last.

"Yes, Yamauchi-san!" said Miyamoto.

"Then design one," said Yamauchi. The interview was over.

If there was ever a time for Yokoi's "lateral thinking with withered technology," this was it. Yamauchi wasn't interested in new tech; he wanted a game that would run on *Radar Scope*'s hardware, which Arakawa could use to convert his unsold machines (see Figure 9.3).

Miyamoto, meanwhile, hadn't even thought about the hardware—he was going about his game design backward, thinking first about the story and characters. That sort of thing was what the professionals did last, grafting some kind of story onto a finished game. Miyamoto's story was straight out of Hollywood—a giant gorilla escapes, kidnaps a carpenter's girlfriend, and brings her up to the top of a giant construction site.[5] As the carpenter tries to make his way up the structure, the ape rolls barrels at him.

This was a fine story for any game, but it was just the first *act*. Miyamoto was just getting started! No, after the carpenter makes his way to the gorilla, the scene changes.

---

[3] Minkley, Johnny. "Nintendo's Shigeru Miyamoto." *Eurogamer.* March 3, 2010. http://www.eurogamer.net/articles/shigeru-miyamoto-interview (accessed June 3, 2015).

[4] Kohler, Chris. *Power Up: How Japanese Video Games Gave the World an Extra Life.* Indianapolis: Brady Games, 2005, p. 29.

[5] Nintendo had been pursuing a license to make a game based on *Popeye the Sailor Man,* but when that fell through, Miyamoto had to create his own characters and storyline. You can still see some vestiges of the earlier game; the Lady is similar to Olive Oyl, and Donkey Kong is like Bluto.

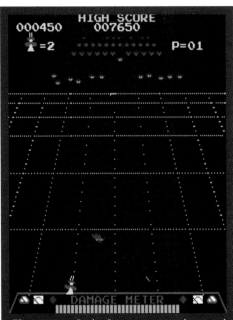

Figure 9.3 *Radar Scope* was a cool game that did well in Japan, but Americans gave it no quarter.

Now the carpenter has to dislodge a series of girders on a five-story steel structure, all the while dodging fires.

One can imagine the look on the supervisor's face when Miyamoto said, "And now, the third stage..." He was essentially asking them to make *two* different games, and now he was talking about a third one! But Miyamoto insisted on *two* more advanced stages, one based on conveyer belts, the other on elevators. In short, this game would have *four* discrete stages, with *Pac-Man*-like cut scenes in between to flesh out the story.

Miyamoto's game was controlled entirely with the joystick, but there was a problem—*Radar Scope* had a fire button! "What does the fire button do?" interrupted the technical supervisor.

Miyamoto was flummoxed. He'd forgotten all about that damn button! Sweat beaded on his freckled forehead.

Sensing his protégé's discomfort, Yokoi asked, "Miyamoto ... If you had a barrel rolling toward you, what would you do?"

"I would jump," said Miyamoto. "It's not a fire button! It's a jump button!"

"Fire button jumps," noted the supervisor. Miyamoto had been thinking all along of another "maze-chase" game like *Pac-Man*.[6] Now, that entire concept was overturned. A game with a running man who could jump called for a different perspective—a side view. The levels—they wouldn't just be separate games; they were higher levels of the building ... How high could you go? It was all starting to come together.

"What is the name of this game?" asked another.

"*Donkey Kong*," said Miyamoto.

"*Donkey Kong*?"

"Yes, you know, *Kong* means gorilla in English, and *Donkey* means stubborn. So this name is like *Stubborn Gorilla*. Don't worry; I looked it up."

"*Donkey Kong*," noted the supervisor.

---

6 Iwata, Satoru. "New Super Mario Bros: Volume 1." *Iwata Asks*. n.d. http://iwataasks.nintendo.com/interviews/#/wii /nsmb/0/0 (accessed June 3, 2015).

After hammering out the details of the gameplay, it was now time for the artwork. Miyamoto had imagined characters with lots of detail, similar to those in cartoons like *Popeye* or the manga he loved so much. He wanted faces that showed emotion and convincing body language; hair billowing in the wind. When he learned that none of this would be possible on the primitive hardware, he went back to "lateral thinking" and looked for ways he could work around the limitations. Instead of hair, he gave his carpenter a bright cap. Since he couldn't show a good looking mouth, he gave him a big mustache instead. The running animation looked better with a squat character, so he made him short and pudgy.

Miyamoto found other ways to breathe life into his game. He gave Donkey Kong a smirk, and had his lady scream "Help!" in comic-style text. A purple heart appears above the carpenter and the lady when they are reunited at the top. These were simple, relatively easy additions, but they helped tell a story.

When the prototype was ready, it was presented to Yamauchi. His approval was far more than a rubber stamp; he could easily have canned the entire project and sent Miyamoto to clean out his desk. What he saw was weird; unorthodox. Nintendo had always played it safe, sticking to clones of existing games and trying to find minor ways to stand out from the crowd. This was something new, something ... risky.

Many words have been used to describe Yamauchi, but never "coward." He picked up the phone and called Arakawa. "We are sending you *Donkey Kong*."

"Yes, Yamauchi-san," said his son-in-law.

Now, it was Nintendo of America's task to sell this game to the arcades. It wasn't an easy sell, to say the least. The name was weird, and the gameplay didn't look anything they'd seen. Arakawa's sales team tried to get Yamauchi to change the name, but that was futile. Like it or not, they were stuck with *Donkey Kong*, and now they had to translate its story into artwork for the cabinet. They called the lady "Pauline," after one of their wives, and the carpenter "Jumpman" (see Figure 9.4). However, they nicknamed him "Mario," because he looked so much like the owner of their warehouse, Mario Segale.[7]

Now, it was all up to Nintendo of America's two distributors, Ron Judy and Al Stone. Arakawa had offered them a great deal on commissions, but so far, it hadn't paid off—and now they were on the brink of bankruptcy. As predicted, owners were wary of the weird name and couldn't wrap their heads around the concept. Perhaps if Nintendo had a string of hits behind their name, they could've overcome these doubts, but the *Radar Scope* debacle loomed large. They needed more than just a clever marketing spiel and promises; they needed hard evidence that *Donkey Kong* was more than just a silly name.

Judy and Stone decided to take a page from Bushnell's playbook, and set up a couple of demonstration machines in a couple of bars in Seattle. A week later, they had their evidence. For seven straight days, players plunked in 120 quarters ($30) for a shot at

---

[7] See footnote 1, p. 159.

rescuing Pauline.[8] The managers asked for more machines.

It didn't take long for Nintendo to sell the rest of the *Radar Scope* conversions, and the orders kept coming—faster than Japan could ship them over, in fact. *Donkey Kong* was selling 4000 units a month in America and was doing just as well in Japan. Hundreds of millions of dollars poured into Nintendo's coffers. Judy and Stone were millionaires, and Nintendo really was the most exciting name in video games.

Donkey Kong soon joined the pantheon of other video games to make the

Figure 9.4   *Donkey Kong* was Miyamoto's first great triumph for Nintendo.

Saturday morning cartoon circuit, and likewise reaped the benefits of a third-party licensing. Kids could start their day with Donkey Kong cereal, dance to Buckner and Garcia's "Do the Donkey Kong" on the radio, and then go to bed in Donkey Kong pajamas. Naturally, Atari and other console makers were eager to sign an exclusive deal with Nintendo.

However, it was Eric Bromley, the designer of the ColecoVision, who sealed the lucrative deal. In typical Yamauchi fashion, the president of Nintendo demanded $200,000 upfront and $2 per cartridge, and before Bromley could protest that these figures were completely unreasonable, he threw in the kicker—get the money by midnight or the deal was off.[9] Knowing that *Donkey Kong* would give the ColecoVision the leverage it needed to compete against the Atari 2600 and the Mattel Intellivision, Bromley made the deal.

It turned out to be a smart move. For 6 months, the only way you could play *Donkey Kong* at home was to buy a ColecoVision. Coleco's profits soared, especially after they made versions for their rival systems—though not the Atari 5200, whose graphics rivaled their own console. Programmer Garry Kitchen did a wonderful job on the conversion and really showed off the power of the new console. Coleco also developed a line of popular (and, now, very collectible) "table-top" games, which looked like miniature arcade machines: *Donkey Kong*, *Pac-Man*, *Galaxian*, and *Frogger*. Nintendo would later use *Donkey Kong* to help sell its own console, the Famicom. As with *Pac-Man* and *Space Invaders*, there was no shortage of unauthorized clones, bootlegs, and rip-offs.

---

[8] See footnote 1, p. 160.

[9] Hunter, William. "The ColecoVision—The Arcade In Your Home!" *The Dot Eaters*. January 2014. http://thedoteaters .com/?bitstory=colecovision (accessed June 3, 2015).

Donkey Kong is also significant for being the target of a historical lawsuit. Universal Studios, who owned the trademarks to the *King Kong* film, sued Coleco for infringement. They hoped for a cut of the enormous profits the game was making, and Coleco caved. Not satisfied with this windfall, Universal foolishly went after Nintendo, who was more willing to fight back. Not only did Nintendo win the case, but they won $1.8 million for damages and attorney fees.[10]

In 2007, a documentary called *The King of Kong: A Fistful of Quarters* aired in theaters, returning *Donkey Kong* to public attention (see Figure 9.5). In the film, an expert player named Steve Wiebe tries to take on Billy Mitchell for the title of world's best player. While the

Figure 9.5   Billy Mitchell was one of the stars of *The King of Dong* documentary in 1997. (Photo courtesy of Florence Ivy.)

film has its critics, it does give us a peek into the fascinating subculture of modern competitive arcade gaming.

After *Donkey Kong*, Miyamoto went on to create *Popeye* in 1982, and a trio of games the following year: *Donkey Kong Jr.*, *Donkey Kong 3*, and *Mario Bros.* While all of these games were successful, none could save the American side of the industry from a terrific "video game crash," which we'll talk more about in Chapter 14. They did, however, allow Miyamoto to hone the skills he'd need to build his greatest masterpiece, *Super Mario Bros.*

In 1994, a British studio named Rare developed *Donkey Kong Country* for the SNES, with considerable input from Miyamoto. Even after a decade, Miyamoto was obsessing over details and trying to find small but effective ways to squeeze more personality out of his characters:

> I ordered them to give Donkey Kong eyebrows, but because that was something that was difficult to show in CG, I was pacified by making the area around his eyes black.

---

[10] Caruso, Norman. "Universal vs. Nintendo Case." *The Gaming Historian.* March 24, 2011. http://thegaminghistorian.com /universal-vs-nintendo-case/ (accessed June 4, 2015).

And then, I had indicated that I wanted his hair to stand up straight more, but that was also difficult, so we made it all one piece. In the end, I felt like the "dumb" feeling wasn't apparent enough, so I was the one to decide to give him a necktie.[11]

When Retro developed *Donkey Kong Country Returns* a decade later for the Wii, Miyamoto was clear about his passion for the characters: "This is my baby," Miyamoto told them. "You'd better get it right."[12] Miyamoto's paternal attitude toward the legacy of one of his oldest games is touching, but it may also reveal why his games have remained so endearing. Lesser designers worry about whether their games are cutting edge enough, or whether they'll appeal to the broadest possible demographic, or how they can attract the attention of the mass media with over-the-top violence or sex.

Miyamoto is more concerned with the necktie on an ape.

9.1 Playing *Donkey Kong* Today

The best way to play *Donkey Kong*, of course, is to track down one of the arcade machines and plunk in a quarter. There are still plenty of working machines "in the wild," and any self-respecting vintage arcade will have at least one. You can, of course, head to eBay and place a bid, but it won't be cheap; expect to spend $2000–$3000. It's easy, if also illegal, to emulate *Donkey Kong* on a modern PC with MAME and a proper joystick. Finally, Nintendo has done its own versions for most of its systems, including its Virtual Console.

---

[11] Miyamoto, Shigeru, interview by Riko Kushida. *Exclusive Interview with Donkey Kong Creator Shigeru Miyamoto* (February 2000).

[12] Parish, Jeremey. "Shigeru Miyamoto is Still Donkey Kong's Papa." *US Gamer.* June 14, 2013. http://www.usgamer.net /articles/shigeru-miyamoto-is-still-donkey-kongs-papa (accessed June 4, 2013).

Chapter 10

Pole Position: Where the Raster Hits the Road

"Prepare to qualify!" What gamer of the 1980s could forget this banner, conveyed across the screen by an Atari or Namco blimp? Certainly not any of those whose souls still carry some trace of rubber, some hint of those skid marks left there by Namco's revolutionary *Pole Position*, which arrived in American arcades in November of 1982 (see Figure 10.1).

Pole Position was designed by Toru Iwatani, and in some ways is as significant as his masterpiece *Pac-Man*. It was a major hit in North American arcades and for Atari, who'd licensed it from Namco. Atari ended up selling more than 21,000 machines and earning more than $60 million in revenue.[1] It even had its own 13-episode Saturday morning cartoon series, which ran on CBS in 1984. Unfortunately for historians, the story of its development is not nearly as well documented as *Pac-Man*'s, whose circular shadow looms large over this groundbreaking racing title.

What we do know about the game's design is that it implemented three Zilog Z8002 microprocessors, making it the first arcade game with 16-bit hardware.[2] This powerful hardware enabled graphics vastly superior to other racing games—even those released just months earlier. The animation was much smoother and more realistic, and the stereo sound effects, generated by custom Namco hardware, were varied and clear. It had a racetrack based on the existing Fuji Speedway, with a definite start and finish line (earlier games just let you play until a timer ran out). Another novel feature was a qualifying lap that determined the player's pole position for the actual race. Players who couldn't complete the lap in 73 s were disqualified and had to insert another quarter to try again.

Atari released two main cabinet styles for the *Pole Position* arcade game. One was a fairly standard upright model, with a steering wheel, gear shifter, and a pedal. However, a much cooler model was an "environmental" or semienclosed model, which let you sit inside and pretend to be in a real race car. It also had separate pedals for braking and gas. Needless to say, it would make a fantastic addition to anyone's home arcade room (see Figure 10.2)!

---

[1] Fujihara, Mary. "Atari Sales Estimates for Other Manufacturers #2." *Atari Games.* November 2, 1983. http://www.atarigames.com/index.php?option=com_content&view=article&id=49:atari-sales-estimates-for-other-manufactures-2 (accessed May 20, 2015).

[2] Defanti, Thomas A. "The Mass Impact of Videogame Technology." *Advances in Computers* 23 (1984): 93–140.

Figure 10.1   The Japanese version of *Pole Position*. The billboards were changed for the American version.

Atari rolled out *Pole Position* for its 2600 console in 1983, a highly successful adaptation by GCC. Even though the programmers were, for obvious reasons, not able to achieve anywhere close to 100% audiovisual fidelity with the arcade version, their port is highly innovative. For instance, the Atari 2600's infamous flicker was used to simulate motion on the car's tires.

Figure 10.2   This cool *Pole Position* cabinet lets you sit inside and pretend to be in a real race car. (Photo courtesy of the International Arcade Museum.)

Pole Position was far from the first arcade racing game. In fact, the first arcade racing games were introduced as early as the 1940s. Games like *Drive Mobile*, made by International Mutoscope Reel Company in 1941, operated purely on "electromechanics." While not technically "video games" (there was no video display), these games used electrical and mechanical components like relays, resisters, belts, and bells to simulate the driving experience.[3] Players controlled a small metal car by turning a steering wheel. The car hovered above a road or

map printed on a cylinder that rotated and moved side to side as the game progressed. It was the player's job to keep the car positioned above the road while avoiding any obstacles. Primitive by today's standards, these games still earned tidy profits for their owners—even though players inserted pennies rather than quarters!

Auto Test, a driving simulation released in 1959, was, as the name implies, intended more to help teach driving skills to students than entertain children. Nevertheless, it

---

[3]   Carter, Lance. *History of Racing Games.* June 13, 2007. https://historyofracinggames.wordpress.com/ (accessed May 20, 2015).

offered a nice innovation—the road was shown in a film projected onto a screen located directly in front of the player. There were many such machines produced throughout the 1960s and 1970s. Perhaps the pinnacle of this genre is Namco's *F-1*, a 1976 title imported by Atari. The "deluxe" model offered a cabinet that resembled an actual race car and was quite popular with gamers. Unfortunately for modern collectors and anyone who'd like to try these machines, their fine, complex assemblies of moving parts weren't built to last. If you'd like to see one, watch carefully during the arcade scene in George Romero's zombie flick, *Dawn of the Dead*.

The first true racing video game in arcades was Atari's *Gran Trak 10* (1974). The cabinet featured a steering wheel, accelerator and brake pedals, and even a gear shift. The graphics consisted of a fixed screen, with the player's car shown from a top-down perspective. Since there were no other cars, the game was really only a race against time—the challenge was staying within the pylons and avoiding oil slicks. Atari's *Indy 800* was a particularly ambitious 1975 game that allowed eight players simultaneously. The players' wheels surrounded a screen housed in a central pit. It was also the first video game to use full color, boasting an enormous 25″ display. There were even mirrors that let bystanders watch the race!

The Japanese got into the top-down racing craze in the mid-1970s as well. A great example is Taito's *Speed Race*, which made its way in 1974 to US arcades via Midway, who rebranded it as *Racer*. Its claims to fame were vertical scrolling and great collision detection. This model would prove quite influential. We can definitely see its influence in Atari's 1975 game *Highway*, the first racing video game to feature a sit-in cabinet like the old electromechanicals.

In passing, I should mention Exidy's infamous *Death Race* (1976), a top-down game that aroused controversy for its gameplay, which consisted of running over people (later called "gremlins") to earn points. An otherwise forgettable game, *Death Race* somehow managed to attract the attention of the mainstream media, who always seemed eager to tarnish the neophyte industry. Phil Brooks, Exidy's general manager, downplayed the violence: "It's like laughing at ourselves. None of us drive all that well. It's poking fun at our driving ability."[4] The National Safety Council was not amused, calling it "sick, sick, sick" and calling for a ban on the game. Imagine what they would have thought of *Grand Theft Auto*!

Atari used some of its leftover cabinets from *Highway* for Night Driver, released in 1976. *Night Driver* was a hodgepodge of old and new technology. Superficially, it resembled the older electromechanical games, which offered a scrolling road rather than a fixed view. Atari's game was black and white, and the car was merely a plastic overlay glued to the bottom of the screen. The "night driving" aspect of the game was really just a justification for its primitive graphics, which consisted of rectangular reflectors demarcating a winding road. The challenge came from taking sharp turns at high speeds; there were no other cars. Despite these limitations, the game deserves some respect for offering some

---

[4] Blumenthal, Ralph. "'Death Race' Game Gains Favor, But Not With the Safety Council." *New York Times*, December 28, 1976: 12.

semblance of the first-person perspective that would become such an integral part of later racing games.

The next big step came in 1981 with Sega's *Turbo*. Like *Night Driver*, *Turbo* offered a first-person perspective of the road. Besides the obvious addition of color and other cars to compete against, it also offered a third-person ("above and behind") view of the player's vehicle on the screen. The objects alongside the road (buildings, trees, and so on) scaled and whizzed by as the race progressed. However, the game isn't won by reaching a finish line, but only by staying on the road and passing 30 other cars before a time limit ran out.

As this brief history shows, by the time *Pole Position* appeared on the scene in 1982, gamers had come to expect some sort of racing game at every major arcade. However, its super graphics, sounds, and physics let it blaze past the competition like a Formula One against a Model T. Atari had really lucked out by securing the rights to *Pole Position*, which no one expected to be the best-selling arcade game of the year. Namco had given Bally/Midway first dibs on which of two new

Figure 10.3 The standard arcade cabinet for *Pole Position*. It was still fun, even if driving while standing felt a little strange. (Photo courtesy of the International Arcade Museum.)

games it would license for manufacture in the United States. The company foolishly chose *Mappy*, a cutesy jump and run game that received nowhere near the success of *Pole Position*. Atari later licensed *Pole Position* for its own platforms as well as others (via its Atarisoft label) (see Figure 10.3).

Namco and other video game developers wasted little time following up on the success of *Pole Position*. Namco released *Pole Position II* the following year, which offered two new racetracks and improved graphics. A flood of derivatives and clones followed for arcade, computer, and console markets. One of the most innovative was Epyx's *Pitstop*, a 1983 game for the Atari 8-bit, Coleco ColecoVision, and Commodore 64. The big innovation here was the titular pit stops, where players took control of a pit crew to refuel their racecar and change its tires. Another popular racing game of the era was Rick Koening's *Racing Destruction Set* (1985) for the Commodore 64 and Atari 8-bit line, which let players design their own tracks and then race on them (alone or with a friend) using a selection of modifiable vehicles.

1986 saw the release of Sega's *Out Run*, an influential game with much in common with *Pole Position*. However, here the player controls a Ferrari Testarossa convertible, and the game seems to take itself much less seriously than its rivals. Players could select among three different songs to listen to while driving and choose which route to take through the course. One version of the cabinet introduced a hydraulic system that became influential in later arcade racing games; it moved along with the car on the screen, greatly heightening the feeling of immersion.

Yet another great innovation came in 1988 with Atari's *Hard Drivin'*, which the company billed as "the world's first authentic driving simulation game." It offered a racing environment composed entirely of three-dimensional polygons, a highly realistic gear shift, and a steering wheel with "force feedback," which made it bump and vibrate in a manner that corresponded to the car's situation in the game. The game's most impressive feature was its accurate simulation of actual driving; it boasted a fun stunt track as well. It replaced the "above and behind" or chase-cam perspective of *Pole Position* and *Out Run* with a first-person or "windshield" view.

As we saw with flight simulation games in Chapter 7, fans of racing games soon diverged into two basic camps of casual and hardcore players. The former were less interested in accurate driving physics than they were in interesting themes or fun gameplay. We certainly see this in Bally/Midway's 1983 hit *Spy Hunter*, which combined a vertical-scrolling racing game with elements from shoot'em ups. We can also find an alternative to realism in Rare's *R.C. Pro-Am*, a 1987 game that put players behind remote controls instead of steering wheels. As with *Spy Hunter* before it, the gameplay was focused not only on racing but also on collecting power-ups for battling one's opponents. This trend would continue in later games like Nintendo's *Super Mario Kart* (1992), which inspired a whole genre of cutesy "kart racers," and in what we might call "crash simulators," such as Sega's *Crazy Taxi* (1999), Reflection's *Destruction Derby* (1995), and Angel Studios' *Midtown Madness* (1999).

Meanwhile, the trend toward increasingly realistic driving games continued in 1989 with Papyrus' *Indianapolis 500: The Simulation*, a game released for Apple Macintosh, Commodore Amiga, and PCs. Like *Hard Drivin'*, it offered a first-person view and focused on realistic physics and detailed graphics. What really set it apart was its "car setup" options, which allowed players to make all sorts of adjustments to their vehicle, such as gear ratios and tire pressure. It also offered a replay mode that let players study a race from six different perspectives. Sega's *Virtua Racing* (1992) took things a step further by offering fully rendered cars as well as environments and the ability to switch perspectives during the race. It was left behind a year later when Namco's *Ridge Racer* roared into arcades, once again raising the bar on realism.

As with flight simulation, the racing genre's best days seem to be ahead of it rather than behind. Modern fans have a number of superb games and franchises to choose from, such as *Forza Motorsport*, *Grid*, *Project Cars*, and *F1 2014* just to name a few. Some racing games such as *DiRT Rally* and *Live for Speed* are already offering support for Oculus Rift VR. Combined with one of the many steering wheel and pedal controller rigs, these setups could add a downright uncanny feeling of being on the track.

But despite their beautiful graphics, accurate physics, tight controls, or even virtual reality immersion, modern racers still owe a great debt to Toru Iwatani and his classic *Pole Position*.

10.1 Playing *Pole Position* Today

Considering how far racing games and sims have come since 1982, you might wonder why anyone would bother playing *Pole Position*. Even if you take nostalgia out of the picture, *Pole Position* is still quite fun today, and the vibrant graphics and distinctive sound effects hold up remarkably well.

If at all possible, hunt down an arcade machine, preferably the sit-down version, and prepare to qualify. At the time of this writing, there were several working arcade machines for sale on eBay ranging from $500 to $1500. If that's not an option, you can try emulating it with MAME, preferably with an optical steering wheel (with 360° movement), shifter, and pedal controllers. It is tricky getting all these set up, but the wiki at http://wiki.arcadecontrols.com/wiki/Driving_Controls should be enough to get you started.

Although the purist in you might prefer the original game, I prefer *Pole Position II* for its extra race tracks.

Chapter 11

Pitfall!: Activision's Fearless Fortune Hunter

David Crane, the creator of *Pitfall!*, is another towering figure of the video game industry, referred to by some as its Charles Schultz (see Figure 11.1). Like the famous and incredibly prolific cartoonist, Crane works tirelessly at his craft every day of his life, with an active career that reaches back over three decades. His influence extends well beyond the impact of the many best-selling video games he personally conceived, designed, and implemented. On October 1, 1979, Crane and a handful of former Atari employees jumped ship to form the first ever third-party developer of cartridge software. It was a move with awesome ramifications for the industry—today, almost all video games are developed and published outside the auspices of the console manufacturers themselves.

Crane was raised in Nappanee, a small town on the northern border of Indiana, where his father moved after serving as a skipper during World War II. To keep himself occupied, the young Crane took apart radios and televisions, and experimented with chemistry—even making his own gunpowder.[1] For a high school science fair, Crane built an elaborate Tic-Tac-Toe playing machine, but it burned up the night before.[2] His mother, perhaps to interest him in less dangerous hobbies, encouraged him to draw, paint, and play tennis.

The young Crane's dream was to invent an airplane that would be powered entirely by electricity. "I wanted to be the guy who solved the weight issue of an electric motor and its batteries that had enough power to lift its own weight plus a payload," said Crane. Shortly thereafter, he discovered someone had beaten him to it—a toy manufacturer from Japan. "That was something of an epiphany for me," said Crane. "I realized that time and time again the latest technology was finding a home in toys, games, and entertainment. And why not? If we can't make our time on earth more enjoyable, what good are we?"[2]

Nerdy well before nerdy was cool, Crane was a lifelong lover of math, science, and tragically bad haircuts. He proudly admits to wearing a suit "precisely three times in my adult life," preferring his plaid button-ups, and clings to his Red Wing shoes until they

---

[1] Amrich, Dan. "Interview: Pitfall! creator David Crane." *Activision Community*. September 13, 2012. https://blog.activision.com/community/10s/blog/2012/09/13/interview-pitfall-creator-david-crane (accessed May 29, 2015).

[2] Thomasson, Michael. "Interview David Crane." *Good Deal Games*. 2003. http://www.gooddealgames.com/interviews/int_David_Crane.html (accessed May 29, 2015).

Figure 11.1   David Crane, creator of *Pitfall!*, at Retro Gaming Expo 2011. (Photo courtesy of Joe Grand.)

fail to return the favor, crumbling around his massive size-14 feet.[3] His voice never raises above a nasally monotone, and his smiles look almost painful. Even today, after earning millions of dollars and international fame (at least among his fellow game developers), Crane wouldn't look a bit out of place in his hometown of the 1970s.

Crane decided to study electronic engineering technology at DeVry University in Phoenix. It wasn't MIT, but I doubt even the professors there could've taught him much he hadn't already learned on his

own. After graduating in 1975, he headed out to Silicon Valley to find an exciting job in his chosen field. He found one at National Semiconductor, where he designed integrated circuits.[1] At first, he found the work fascinating but gradually lost interest over the next 2 years as his life settled into a dull routine.

At least he still had tennis. One day, as he was enjoying a few sets on a warm Californian evening, he met a kindred spirit—Alan Miller.[3] Miller had been tasked with finding talented programmers to work on Atari's new console. A few days later, Miller asked for Crane's help proofreading the want ad he intended to put in the paper—perhaps a clever ploy to attract his first applicant. If so, it worked, because Crane interviewed the next morning and got the job.

When Crane first joined Atari in the fall of 1977, it was still being run by its founder, Nolan Bushnell. An engineer himself, Bushnell understood the eccentricities of those attracted to that profession, respecting the intelligence and recognizing the skills his employees brought to the table.

But after Bushnell departed, Ray Kassar took over, a buttoned-down business executive with little tolerance for "unprofessional" conduct. In Kassar's eyes, Atari's game developers were no more integral to the process than the minimum-wage factory workers assembling the cartridges, a fact he was quick to let them know when they asked for better compensation.

The final straw was a memo Kassar sent out intended to frighten the less talented developers into coding for their lives (or, at least their jobs). It showed that only four of Atari's designers were responsible for more than 60% of their sales—the others had better step up their game, or else. However, Crane and the other three top developers noted

---

[3] Covert, Colin. "Meet David Crane: Video Games Guru." *Hi-Res*, January 1984: 46.

something on the memo. They were only being paid $30,000 a year, but their games were making more than $100 million a year in profits for Atari. "That will get anyone thinking about a piece of the pie," said Crane.[4] A few days later, Crane cleaned out his cubicle, joining Miller, Jim Levy, Bob Whitehead, and Larry Kaplan on a bold, risky new venture: Activision.

Before Activision, it was assumed that the company that manufactured a console held exclusive rights to produce games for it. It was often compared to the razor business; sell the razor for cheap or even at a loss, and make up for it with expensive, patented replacement blades. Activision's entry into the industry as a third-party, independent game developer and publisher threatened to undermine this lucrative and efficient way of doing business.

Naturally, Kassar and Atari weren't going to sit idly by as their star talent set up their own shop across town. In 1980, Atari sued them for patent and copyright infringement, and even took out full-page ads intended to unite Atari fans against them.[5] Atari struggled mightily for years but never managed to shut them down. Activision, meanwhile, happily published its games for Atari's rival consoles, the Intellivision and ColecoVision, as well as the home computers of the era.

Activision's first four games hit the shelves in 1980 and made an immediate impression. They shipped in bright, colorful boxes that were quite distinctive, and for the first time, the names of the developers were there for all to see. Crane and his fellow designers at Activision had long resented the forced anonymity they'd had to endure at Atari. They didn't go as far as Trip Hawkins did at Electronic Arts, promoting designers as "rock stars," instead preferring to think of themselves as game "authors."

Crane wrote two of the games in Activision's initial offering—*Fishing Derby* and *Dragster* (see Figure 11.2). The latter title was a clone of an arcade game called *Drag Race* (1977), programmed and designed by Mike Albaugh for Kee Games, a secret Atari subsidiary. Despite all of Activision's rhetoric about designers getting proper credit for their work, they made no mention of Albaugh for this game or *Boxing*, which was based on Albaugh's design for an unreleased arcade machine.[6] In any case, adapting these coin-operated games for the Atari 2600 was no mean feat. Anyone could have ideas for a boxing or racing game, but precious few had the programming chops to implement it on such a humble device.

In the manual for *Dragster*, Crane is described as a designer who "specializes in games that other designers consider impossible." His reputation grew the next year, with two hits called *Freeway* and *Laser Blast*. However, the game that'd really establish his name came in 1982. It began as a simple animation of a running man he'd created

[4] Donovan, Tristan. "The Replay Interviews: David Crane." *Gamasutra.* January 3, 2015. http://www.gamasutra.com/view /feature/134618/the_replay_interviews_david_crane.php (accessed May 29, 2015).

[5] Fleming, Jeffrey. "The History of Activision." *Gamasutra.* 30 July, 2007. http://www.gamasutra.com/view/feature/129961 /the_history_of_activision.php (accessed June 1, 2015).

[6] Albaugh, Mike, interview by Dag Spicer. *Mike Albaugh Interview* (November 12, 2010).

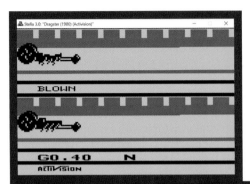

Figure 11.2 *Dragster* was one of Activision's first titles. It was a clone of Mike Albaugh's *Drag Race* arcade game.

2 years earlier. Crane thought it was the start of something great, but a suitable game design eluded him.

According to Crane, he decided one day he'd sit at his desk sketching out ideas until inspiration struck. "I literally sat there with a blank sheet of paper and drew a little running man," said Crane. "I gave him a path to run on ... obstacles. Scorpions and crocodiles ... I gave him

treasures to collect. And literally, in ten minutes I had the design document ... It took one thousand hours of programming."[7] The jungle theme was most obviously inspired by *Indiana Jones and the Raiders of the Lost Ark*, which had arrived in theaters a year previously. However, Crane also credits a classic cartoon called *Heckle and Jeckle*, whose intro shows the titular magpies hopping across a line of crocodiles just before their mouths snap shut. Nintendo's *Donkey Kong* had been out for nearly a year, but Crane had already designed a significant chunk of *Pitfall!* before he saw it: "Like *Freeway* and *Frogger*, [they] were developed simultaneously in Japan and California."[8]

Designing the game was the easy part; the real challenge was realizing the design in code. One of the greatest obstacles was dealing with the memory limitations of the 2600; Crane says he had to "get down to saving individual bytes to make it fit."[7] He also worked hard on the graphics, carefully selecting colors and bordering "on-screen color changes with black pixels to reduce color bleed. We were our most demanding critics, and we didn't stop until the game was better looking than anything we had seen."[5]

"The last hundred hours are spent on details you might never notice," said Crane:

> I made it easier for the guy to jump from a standing start. Originally you'd have to hit the joystick and the fire button right at the same time. Now, if you don't, the logic takes care of it. Just thinking about it, coming up with the idea and deciding to do it and getting it right took about a week. But it was a very important aspect of the game, making it play right.[3]

The end result of this genius and hard work was a game that was simply amazing (see Figure 11.3). It was the biggest selling game of 1982 and stayed at the number one position on the *Billboard* charts longer than any other game.[1] *Electronic Games Magazine*

---

[7] Crane, David. "Pitfall: Classic Game Postmortem." *GDC Vault*. 2011. http://www.gdcvault.com/play/1014632/Classic-Game -Postmortem-PITFALL (accessed June 1, 2015).

[8] This quotation is from my Twitter dialog with Crane on June 6, 2015. View the Tweet at http://tinyurl.com/p3tspvh.

praised its "superb graphics" and "varied play-action," which they felt were much better than those of Atari's licensed title *Raiders of the Lost Ark*.[9] Pitfall Harry even made it into CBS's *Saturday Supercade* cartoon—though even Crane admits that it was "really awful."[1] He did like the theme music, though, and used it in *Pitfall II: Lost Caverns*.

A major part of Activision's marketing was community engagement, which they encouraged with a wide variety of badges, contests, and newsletters. The manuals requested that fans write in to talk about

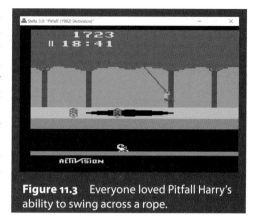

Figure 11.3 Everyone loved Pitfall Harry's ability to swing across a rope.

their experience with the game. According to Crane, *Pitfall!* received more than 14,000 of these letters in a single week![2] Crane even bought a personalized PITFALL license plate for his car. The sales set historical records for the Atari 2600, selling more than 4 million copies and becoming the second best-selling game of all time for the system (after *Pac-Man*).[10]

Like *Donkey Kong, Pitfall!* is a "platform" video game, a genre that is still quite popular today. These games are known for their precision jumping segments, anthropomorphic characters, and dangerous obstacles. As you'll recall, *Donkey Kong* was a series of four single-screen stages. *Pitfall!* gave the impression of a large, continuous level by snapping to a new screen whenever Harry makes it to the edge. Harry can also swing across vines, a fun maneuver enhanced with a *Tarzan*-inspired musical sequence.

Another major innovation of *Pitfall!* concerns playtimes. While still quite short compared to modern games, *Pitfall!* could be played for up to 20 min. Most other console games of the time were slavish imitations of arcade games, which needed a much shorter playtime to turn a profit.

Crane's *Pitfall II: Lost Caverns* followed a year later, and it once again raised the bar on what was thought possible on the Atari 2600. Crane took advantage of his background in hardware design to make a custom chip called the DPC (Display Processor Chip, or David Patrick Crane). It not only enhanced the graphics of the 2600 but also added memory and could generate three channels of music (plus a drum). *Pitfall II* was another stunning technological achievement. Now, Harry could not only move sideways but also climb up and down. Instead of a 20-min time limit, the sequel lets you play as long as you want, and "dying" merely brings you back to a save point rather than making you start all the way over. Harry can also swim and ride on balloons. Sadly for Crane, what is perhaps his greatest achievement was launched in the midst of what is now called The

[9] Katz, Arnie, ed. "Players' Guide to Heroic Fantasy." *Electronic Games Magazine*, June 1983: 47–58.

[10] Buchanan, Levi. "Top 10 Best-Selling Atari 2600 Games." *IGN*. August 26, 2008. http://www.ign.com/articles/2008/08/26/top-10-best-selling-atari-2600-games (accessed June 1, 2015).

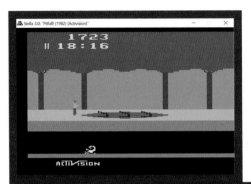

Great North American Video Game Crash of 1983.

It would be entirely possible to write a book on this industry-wide catastrophe, and it begs for a more in-depth analysis than what is possible here. The video game industry had seemed unstoppable going into 1982, but by October, it was clear that all was not well. Atari reported losses of $536 million, and thousands,

Figure 11.4   The famous crocodile sequence was inspired by a scene from the cartoon *Heckle and Jeckle.*

including Kassar, lost their jobs. Arcade operators were bemoaning drops in revenue of 40%.[11] Retailers were hit hard as well; sales had dropped by half (see Figure 11.4).

Hopes were high that Christmas sales would make everyone merry again. However, prices on cartridges and consoles had been reduced to "bargain bin" levels. Crane believed that, inadvertently, Activision was to blame for this dire situation. "We showed that you don't have to spend $100 million to produce a game console to make money in video games," said Crane.[4] Activision's amazing success had convinced 30 other companies to try their luck. Quaker Oats alone put out 14 games, but all of them were flops.[12] Even Purina put out a game: *Chase the Chuck Wagon*, based on their TV commercials. According to Crane, a liquidator bought up all these terrible games and sold them in barrels for $5 each during that holiday season. "When dad went in to buy junior the latest Activision game for $40," said Crane, "he saw that he could be a hero and get eight games for the same money. Sales of new games went to near zero."[4] Activision, which had every reason to expect a tremendous year, lost millions.

The most infamous disasters, though, were Atari's. While it's probably not fair to blame the crash on their wretched *Pac-Man* and *E.T.: The Extra Terrestrial* cartridges, they had definitely tarnished the company's reputation and eroded consumer confidence. Mattel's Intellivision was the first high-profile casualty, and Coleco found itself making far more off its Cabbage Patch dolls than ColecoVision. Atari racked up $536 million in losses and was unceremoniously sold off by Warner.[13] Christopher Kirby, an analyst for a New York investment firm, spoke for many when he declared that video games were just another fad, not much different than the C.B. radio craze of the early 1970s.[11]

---

[11] Kleinfield, N.R. "Video Games Industry Comes Down to Earth: COMPANY NEWS The Boom Is Over for Video Games." *New York Times*, October 17, 1983: A1.

[12] Alexander, Charles P., Lisa Towle, and Richard Woodbury. "Video Games Go Crunch!" *Time*, October 17, 1983: 72.

[13] Kent, Steve L. *The Ultimate History of Video Games: From Pong to Pokémon and Beyond: The Story Behind the Craze that Touched Our Lives and Changed the World.* Rocklin, CA: Prima Pub., 2001: 240.

Kirby, however, wasn't thinking of video games as a medium, but rather video games as dedicated devices—consoles and arcade machines. It's important to keep in mind that during this time personal computers were competing directly with the console manufacturers. For a little more than the price of a console, you could buy a cheap but powerful computer such as the Commodore 64 or Atari 800. Most popular games, including Activision's, were available for these systems, so you wouldn't be missing out on the gaming action. In passing, it's worth noting that Kitchen recreated *Pitfall!* to demonstrate his *GameMaker* tool, the first all-in-one video game construction kit. Activision published this award-winning product in 1985.

Crane and Kitchen left Activision in 1986 to found Absolute Entertainment. Absolute published *David Crane's Amazing Tennis* in 1992 for the Super Nintendo and Sega Genesis, which was generally well received. However, his next game, *A Boy and His Blob* (1989) was a bigger hit, and won "Best of Show" at the Consumer Electronics Show of 1989. After Absolute shut down in 1995, Crane and Kitchen founded Skyworks Interactive, which specialized in "advergames," or games made to promote a product or company. Though Crane mocked the Quaker Oats and Purina-branded games of yore, he was now doing it himself, shamelessly churning out browser-based games to promote Nabisco, Wrigley, and Kraft products.

In 1994, Activision made a game called *Pitfall: The Mayan Adventure* for a variety of platforms, but Crane was not involved. While some reviewers were kinder than others, it was clear to everyone that it was not the groundbreaking title that its predecessors had been—and, at worst, a shameless attempt to exploit whatever nostalgic value the "brand" still possessed. When Shane R. Monroe interviewed Crane in 2002, he asked if he felt the game was "an abomination of your original creation," expecting a spirited response.[14] Instead, Crane replied drily that it was "just a game," and seemed baffled by the idea that he might be protective or have any personal affection for Pitfall Harry.

Regardless of Crane's indifference about his "little running man," no one denies the technological and cultural achievement he represented. Here was not an abstract shape or spaceship, but a recognizable human figure. It was also a grand achievement for the Atari 2600—Crane had indeed achieved what others had thought impossible. Furthermore, the company he cofounded and wrote his best games for, Activision, marked a decisive turning point for the games industry, creating a space for independent game studios that persists to this day.

11.1 Playing *Pitfall!* Today

You can play *Pitfall!* for free at https://archive.org/details/Pitfall_Activision_1982. One version of the Atari Flashback retro-console (FB2) has *Pitfall!*, but most do not, so be wary. Another option is the Jakks Pacific Activision 10-in-1 TV Game, a plug-and-play device with a built-in arcade-style joystick.

---

[14] Monroe, Shane R. *RetroGaming Radio: The Interviews*. Amazon Digital Services, Inc., 2011.

Crane himself recommends playing it on a real Atari 2600. According to Crane, "The original game ran at a full 60 frames per second, and none of the emulated versions work at a fixed frame rate. The original Atari joystick was the best, and the game was tweaked for that controller."[1] You can usually find a working system on eBay for $100 or less, and loose *Pitfall!* cartridges run $5–$10.

Chapter 12

Flight Simulator:
The Sky's the Limit

Flight. There are few dreams as universal to humanity as taking wing, soaring through the air, free to explore our world in three glorious dimensions. Sadly, over a hundred years after the Wright brothers' first powered flights, most of us can still only experience flight as passengers. Even if you're willing to purchase or (more likely) rent an aircraft, there's still the considerable amount of training and courage you'll need to earn your license. In short, flying an airplane into the great blue yonder is still but a dream for the average person.

Thanks to Bruce Artwick, however, we can experience the thrills of flight with our feet firmly on the ground. In 1975, Artwick was an electrical engineering student at the University of Illinois at Urbana–Champaign, where he built logic circuits and designed graphic terminals for the Digital Computer Laboratory. He'd started off as a computer engineer, but decided that "electrical engineer" sounded more marketable (see Figure 12.1).

Artwick's roommate, Stu Moment, was majoring in organizational administration and organization psychology but also had a strong interest in math. However, his real love was airplanes, and he'd saved his earnings as a busboy for two full years to earn his pilot's license.[1] In 1973, he became an FAA (Federal Aviation Administration) Certified Flight Instructor and is now best known for his fabulous stunt shows (and impersonating Elvis Presley). Serendipitously, he was able to talk his roommate into taking a flight with him and later taught him to fly.

Part of Artwick's training included professional flight simulators. In his thesis, Artwick describes systems with "prefilmed movies and 'flying' television cameras," as well as "attempts" at computer-generated graphics.[2] The Aviation Research Lab had a Raytheon 704 computer and a Singer Link GAT-2 simulator (see Figure 12.2). The GAT-2 was a formidable beast, resembling a hacked-off cockpit section of a twin-engine aircraft, which moved and shifted to simulate the feeling of flight. While the instrument panel and controls were realistic enough, there wasn't a display. Artwick sought to remedy this problem,

---

[1] Moment, Stu. *Classic Airshows.* n.d. http://www.classicairshows.com/ (accessed May 16, 2015).

[2] Artwick, Bruce. *A Versatile Computer-Generated Dynamic Flight Display.* Urbana–Champaign: Aviation Research Laboratory, 1976: 1.

either by incorporating a CRT monitor into the panel or by simply putting a screen in front of the simulator's windshield and projecting an image onto it. The image, of course, would be created dynamically by the computer, but without expensive graphics hardware. The successful conclusion of Artwick's thesis shows the youth already thinking ahead to a space flight simulator, which he'd finally accomplish in 1994 with *Microsoft Space Simulator.*

Figure 12.1   Bruce Artwick, creator of *Flight Simulator,* in 2010, shown here at the PLATO@50 event hosted by the Computer History Museum.

Artwick stayed in school after his bachelor's degree, going on to earn a master's degree in May of 1976. He'd written a 75-page thesis on using Motorola's 6800 microprocessor to simulate flight. Written in FORTRAN, Artwick's program was designed to be "implemented economically with a bare minimum of graphics hardware and a sixteen-bit mini-computer."[2] A mini-computer, by the way, was much less expensive than a mainframe, costing less than $25,000, but still far more powerful

Figure 12.2   Commercial flight simulators like this one were much too expensive and impractical for consumers.

than home computers of the time. They were still, of course, far more expensive than the "home" or "personal" computers of 1977 (the Apple II, TRS-80, and Commodore PET).

After graduating, Artwick moved to Culver City, California, where he'd landed a job at Hughes Aircraft working on radar systems. After the "home computer" revolution of 1977, Artwick tinkered with the idea of adapting his mini-computer program for these machines. After all, the Apple II was powered by MOS Technology's 6502 microprocessor and designed by some of the same Motorola engineers who'd developed the 6800. It was only a sixth of the price of the 6800, though Artwick noted that "a 6800 program cannot run on a 6502 without major revision," owing to the completely different set of operation codes (or "opcodes").[3]

---

[3]   Artwick, Bruce. *Microcomputer Interfacing.* Englewood Cliffs, NJ: Prentice-Hall, 1980: 59.

An oft-repeated claim (that I've sadly been unable to confirm) is that around this time Artwick began writing some editorials for a magazine covering the nascent home computer industry. Some accounts say that these articles were only about a hypothetical three-dimensional (3D) graphics program; others suggest that he was already talking about flight simulation. An editor informed Artwick that readers were writing in asking where they could buy this program, inspiring him to get serious about his plans to found and incorporate his own software company.

A story from *Personal Computing* tells another story.[4] Artwick was at his home in Culver City when he heard a tremendous clamor outside. Rushing out to investigate, he found the smoldering debris of an airplane floating in his swimming pool! Understandably frightened by this event, Artwick decided to move back to Champaign, Illinois, and try his hand at running his own business.

In any case, Artwick teamed up with Moment to found subLOGIC, whose first products were 3D graphics programs, one written in BASIC and the other with 6800 assembly. Artwick outlined in the manual why such programs were so challenging to develop:

> 3D graphics programs are very complex, rely heavily on complicated mathematical theories and computations and are very hard to write, debug, and test ... Intricate software/hardware interactions are involved. Very few people simultaneously know enough about the mathematics of computer graphics, hardware, software design, and now microprocessors, to effectively write 3D graphics software.[5]

Fortunately for us, Artwick himself was one of this rare breed—and better yet, also had his own, as well as his partner Moment's, extensive knowledge of flying at his disposal. The pair was ready to put all these skills to use with a full-fledged flight simulator for the Apple II.

Artwick might have been inspired by a PLATO game called *Air Fight*, a flight simulator using the platform's vector graphics (see Figure 12.3). *Air Fight* was programmed by Brad Fortner in 1976, and it's a sophisticated 3D simulation. As the title implies, it's focused on combat, and could host up to 30 other pilots. Of course, this game ran on a far more powerful computer than the Apple II. When his colleagues suggested that he make a version for home computers, Fortner said, "It is flat out impossible to do a flight simulator on an Apple II. It can't be done. It doesn't have a floating point processor; it is impossible."[6]

Artwick, obviously, disagreed, and felt that the home computers' crude displays (compared to PLATO's) would lessen the need for such intense calculation. In 1979,

---

[4] Nelson, Robin. "Rough Air." *Personal Computing*, July 27, 1990: 43.

[5] Artwick, Bruce. *Three Dimensional Microcomputer Graphics*. Culver City, CA: SubLOGIC Company, 1977: 1.

[6] Computer History Museum. "PLATO—An Early Community of Multiplayer Games." *YouTube*. June 22, 2010. https://www.youtube.com/watch?v=dEyppAb_6ag#t=627 (accessed June 11, 2015).

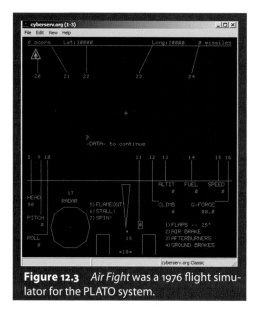

Figure 12.3   *Air Fight* was a 1976 flight simulator for the PLATO system.

subLOGIC published *Flight Simulator with British Ace 3D Aerial Battle Game* for the Apple II, followed a year later with a version for the Radio Shack TRS-80. Both versions of *FS1*, as it's come to be known, were completely coded in their respective machine code (6502 and Z80, respectively). SubLOGIC's plan was to advertise the product in magazines and sell copies by mail.

The Apple II version had a painfully low frame rate, rendered in only four colors, and shipped on a cassette for the 16K (RAM) Apple II (see Figure 12.4). Nevertheless, it contained all of the necessary elements to model flying an aircraft, in this case a slow, but maneuverable, Sopwith Camel, appropriate for the World War I theme. It sported a first-person view of the field (a 6 × 6 grid with mountains) above a rudimentary instrument panel. As crude as it might seem to modern gamers, it was soon considered a must-have title for the Apple II.

The TRS-80 version was lacking in some respects—there was no sound, and only black and white visuals at 128 × 48 resolution, which explains the lack of a graphical instrument panel. On the other hand, Artwick introduced an additional overhead, or "radar" view. As with the Apple II version, contemporary critics hailed it as a technological breakthrough. Roxton Baker, a writer for *The Alternate Source* (a magazine for the TRS-80 owners) is particularly effusive in his 1980 review of the game:

> This is a superb program. It is so innovative and advanced that it must be praised in parts; its whole effect is beyond comparison with any existing TRS-80 software. First, *FS1* is a highly realistic simulation of small aircraft flight. It combines with that a sophisticated, ingenious, and breathtaking 3-D graphics display. Finally it provides an exciting and challenging real-time dogfight game. In any one of these aspects *FS1* must be rated well ahead of its competition. Indeed for the graphics display it has no competition.[7]

At any time during a flight, the player could press the "w" key to declare war, which would immediately send five enemy planes into the air. It was then up to the player to engage the opposing planes and drop a bomb on their fuel depot before being shot down. It

---

[7]   Baker, Roxton. "subLOGIC FS 1 for the TRS-80 (1980)." *The Old Flight Simulator Vault.* 1980. http://fshistory.simflight.com/fsvault/fs1-trs80.htm (accessed May 16, 2015).

wasn't as fun as it sounds, but it seemed like a good way to broaden the game's appeal.

The subLOGIC team continued to refine and add new features, such as enhanced terrain, additional structures, altitude counter, and a crash screen for players who hit the ground too hard. However, these innovations paled in comparison to those ushered in with the first IBM PC version, *Microsoft Flight Simulator*, released in 1982 as an officially licensed product. IBM and Microsoft both wanted an exclusive license for an IBM PC port and were willing to pay top dollar. Artwick eventually signed a joint licensing agreement with Microsoft after being impressed by its "nice small company atmosphere" and the person of Vern Raburn, head of their consumer products division.[8] The deal allowed subLOGIC to continue making versions of *Flight Simulator* for other platforms, as well as spin-offs such as *Jet* (1985) and *UFO* (1989).

Figure 12.4 *Flight Simulator* running on an Apple II+ emulator.

Microsoft Flight Simulator was a huge leap forward for the program and demonstrated the audiovisual potential of the IBM PC. It took full advantage of its 64K RAM and CGA (four color) graphics card to show solid colors rather than wireframes. The aircraft this time around was a modern-day Cessna 182, complete with retractable landing gear, an instrument panel sporting eight gauges, a new coordinate system, four different flight areas (Chicago, Seattle, Los Angeles, and New York/Boston), 20 airports, weather conditions, and nine view directions. In other words, it was *Flight Simulator* taken to the next level. The game was a major success, and it's likely that many desk-turned-throttle jockeys upgraded their PCs just to see and play the game in its full glory (see Figure 12.5).

SubLOGIC took what it had learned during *Microsoft Flight Simulator* and brought it to *Flight Simulator II*, which it published for the Apple II (1983), Commodore 64 (1984), and Atari 800 (1984). In 1986, they released versions for the Apple Macintosh, Amiga, and Atari ST. All of these versions were well received, earning high praise from critics. Microsoft, meanwhile, continued publishing updated versions of *Microsoft Flight Simulator*, going through six before Artwick finally sold them his company, BAO, which he'd formed after quitting subLOGIC in 1988. He took the copyright to *Flight Simulator* with him, but sold it to Microsoft in 1996.

Meanwhile, Moment remained at subLOGIC, where he planned to continue releasing flight simulator programs, most notably a product called *Flight Assignment: Air Transport Pilot.* Microsoft insisted that it alone had the right to market *Flight Simulator*-related products for the PC, but Moment disagreed. Eventually, the two settled on the condition that subLOGIC remove the phrase "flight simulator" from its products and

---

[8] Grupping, Jos. "The Story of Flight Simulator." *Flight Simulator History.* March 4, 2005. http://fshistory.simflight.com/fsh /versions.htm (accessed May 16, 2015).

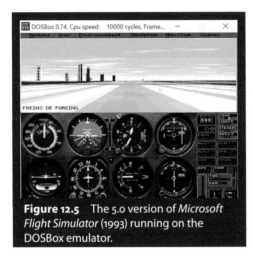

Figure 12.5 The 5.0 version of *Microsoft Flight Simulator* (1993) running on the DOSBox emulator.

marketing materials. Sierra acquired sub-LOGIC in 1995.

The flight simulator genre, of course, extends far beyond the offerings of either Microsoft or subLOGIC. Indeed, it's useful to split it up into two basic subgenres: Casual and Hardcore. The physics of flight are naturally quite complicated, requiring, as we've seen, significant training and experience to master. As computers and consoles evolved, they became more capable of including all of these factors into their simulation, resulting in products that were, on the one hand, more realistic, but, on the other hand, much more intimidating for nonpilots.

The industry responded by developing some games that simplified these physics, resulting in "casual" games that were easier to pick up and play—and arguably more fun. Examples of such casual flight sim games include Sega's *After Burner* and Konami's *Top Gun* arcade games (both 1987), which focused on the thrills of blasting enemy jets at supersonic speeds, not mastering the fine art of takeoffs and landings. Another example is Cinemaware's *Wings* (1990), a game set in World War I. This game has plenty of tense dogfighting and bombing missions, but, like most of Cinemaware's titles from this era, the emphasis is on story, context, and cinematic aesthetics, not hardcore physics.

There has remained, however, a viable if smaller market for "hardcore" flight simulators that do their best to recreate the actual physics and mechanics of a real-life aircraft. I had my first experience with one of these in 1989 with *Falcon* by Spectrum Holobyte, which shipped with a 100+-page manual complete with index and glossary. It took me the better part of a summer before I could successfully land my F-16 Fighting Falcon on the aircraft carrier! A more modern example of this type is *X-Plane 10* by Laminar Research (2012). Its marketing material makes it clear that it is "not a game, but an engineering tool," a fitting description given its heavy emphasis on accurate physics, weather simulation, and geography. Though tools such as this are probably more useful for pilots or pilots-in-training, some gamers just aren't satisfied with "dumbed down" physics and are more than willing to take on the challenge and learning curve associated with such a product.

Needless to say, flight simulation on modern PCs and consoles has come a very long way from Bruce Artwick's pioneering efforts on the Apple II and TRS-80. Most noticeably, 3D graphics have evolved tremendously, offering a level of complexity and detail that Artwick could only dream about. Meanwhile, flight sim developers have also continued refining the physics part of their simulations, resulting in products that are useful for actual flight training.

Microsoft's long-running *Flight Simulator* series nosedived in 2009, when the company discontinued it after poor sales. Its *Microsoft Flight* game in 2012 failed to take off, too. However, an English company called Dovetail Games has now acquired the rights to make new entries in the series and released an updated edition of *Microsoft Flight Simulator X* for Steam in 2014 to rave reviews from long-term fans as well as newcomers to the series.

The future of flight simulators looks bright at the moment, especially if we consider the impact that Oculus Rift Virtual Reality Headset might make in 2016. There are already four flight or space simulators out that take advantage of it, including *DCS World*, *Ambient Flight*, *War Thunder*, and *Elite Dangerous*. Third parties have begun developing hardware that complements the visual experience of Oculus Rift with "full body simulators" that move you around as you play, such as Somniacs' *Birdly* that lets you flap your arms like a bird. Artwick mentioned in a 2010 interview that he'd like to get back into the business by designing full-enclosure cabinets that would tilt and move along with the action—in short, a virtual successor of the mechanical simulators that inspired him back in the 1970s.

When I was a kid growing up in the 1980s, I was constantly assured that by the year 2000 (which sounded so far away at the time!), we'd all be flying our own jets, helicopters, or at least a hoverboard. Sadly, it's 2015, and obviously that's not happened. Still, thanks to Artwick and his vision for a PC-based flight simulator program, I can take to the skies whenever I feel like it—no pilot's license required.

12.1 Playing *Flight Simulator* Today

It's a snap to play the original *Flight Simulator* or its popular sequel, *Flight Simulator II*. Just go to http://www.virtualapple.org/flightsimulatordisk.html and install the Active GS add-on for your web browser. You can also download the disk images from this site to use in an Apple II emulator of your choice. I also recommend you try *Microsoft Flight Simulator*, though it can be a bit trickier to find and set up. At the time of this writing, it's available along with installation instructions at http://fshistory.simflight.com/fsvault /msfs1-pc.htm. After playing these classics, it's fun to switch immediately to a modern flight simulator such as the aforementioned *Microsoft Flight Simulator X* and marvel at how far the industry has come.

Chapter 13

Elite: The Stellar Sandbox

You need chutzpah to make a game like *Elite*, and anyone who's played it enough to achieve its highest rank must have it, too. *Elite* was more than a game—it was a line in the silicon for the countless nerds who spent hundreds if not thousands of hours in the cockpits of their Cobra MK IIIs, growing their reputation from Harmless to the glorious rank of—Mostly Harmless. The few stalwarts with the skill, fortitude, and, let's face it, the OCD (obsessive–compulsive disorder) to get all the way to Elite deserve whatever praise they got (assuming they had any friends or family left to bestow it!).

Yes, now we turn to a second breakthrough game from the United Kingdom, David Braben and Ian Bell's *Elite*, a "space trading sim" and one of the earliest and most influential "open world" designs (see Figure 13.1). It was a synthesis of several distinct gameplay styles that were well established by 1984—the open world concept of games like *MUD*, the three-dimensional (3D), first-person perspective of *Flight Simulator*, the procedural generation of *Rogue*, and a third category of games called space trading sims. *Elite* was greater than the sum of these parts, and certainly one of the greatest triumphs of the 8-bit era.

A game from 1984 might seem out of place in this section, but the UK computer game industry had followed a different trajectory than the American one. A substantial income gap meant that many UK computer gamers had to settle for less powerful "budget" machines than their American counterparts, with less memory and slower cassette tapes rather than floppy disks for storage. Some of the most popular machines, including the Sinclair ZX81, even lacked proper keyboards, relying instead on the less expensive (but also less usable!) membrane technology.

Nevertheless, UK developers more than made up for in ingenuity what they may have lacked in cutting-edge technology, as *Elite* clearly demonstrates.[1] The press created a virtual cult of the "bedroom coder," fixating on the vast sums these geeky teenagers were cranking out of their home computers. UK magazines regularly printed their code listings for other aspiring game makers to study and emulate. It was a fertile social environment for innovation; the severe limitations of these machines served only to goad these youths, who sought endlessly for any trick to save precious memory. The success or failure of an entire program could come down to a single byte.

Let's talk first about the "space trading sim" genre, which had been around a long time before *Elite*. Indeed, it can trace its roots back at least to the early 1970s, where two such

---

[1] I highly recommend Anthony and Nicola Caulfield's documentary film, *From Bedrooms to Billions*, for a fascinating and in-depth look at the UK side of the early games industry.

Figure 13.1   David Braben and Ian Bell, creators of *Elite*.

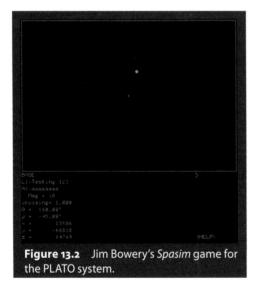

Figure 13.2   Jim Bowery's *Spasim* game for the PLATO system.

games appeared on the PLATO platform: John Daleske's *Empire* (1973) and Jim Bowery's *Spasim* (1974) (see Figure 13.2), both of which were inspired by the *Star Trek* television show. According to Daleske, *Empire* started off as a final project for his education class at Iowa State University.[2] The first version of this game was a turn-based "strategic simulation of economy, population, manufacturing, and trade," with support for up to eight players. Silas Warner (of *Castle Wolfenstein* fame) helped him develop it and later resurrected the project as *Conquest*. Daleske is humble about his possible status as the first developer of such a game, admitting that "some innovations are just plain intuitively obvious … I am not saying that I and only could I have seen it, nor implemented it." Later versions of *Empire* focused on space dogfighting.

Spasim was an incredibly ambitious game for its time, with up to 32 players. Like *Elite*, it let you fly around in 3D space, with ships depicted with wireframe graphics. The first version focused on combat, but a second version the following year introduced space stations and resource management. Docking in space stations bears an uncanny resemblance to *Elite*, though this similarity is coincidental. Neither Braben nor Bell had access to PLATO, and both games most likely borrowed the sequence from the film *2001: A Space Odyssey* (1968). Bowery is much less humble about his contributions than Daleske, offering a $500 reward to anyone who can document the existence of a "multi-player 3D virtual reality game prior to 'Spasim.'"[3]

---

[2] Daleske, John. "How Empire Came To Be." *Plato Empire.* 2008. http://www.daleske.com/plato/empire.php (accessed June 10, 2015).

[3] Bowery, Jim. "Spasim (1974) The First First-Person-Shooter 3D Multiplayer Networked Game." *Geocities (Wayback Machine).* 2001. http://www.geocities.com/jim_bowery/spasim.html (accessed April 10, 2001).

Among the earliest examples of space sims for home computers are Edu-Ware's *Space* (1978) and *Empire* (1981) for the Apple II, as well as Omniverse's *Universe* series (which launched in 1984 for a variety of home computers). All of these games offered many of the tropes seen in *Elite*. There are the same economic imperatives to sell cargo between and among countless planets, purchase upgrades for your ship, and the chance to battle as or against space-faring pirates. One recurring theme across this genre is the "sandbox" or "open world" style of gameplay. There is no right way to play these games, and plots (if they exist at all) have little bearing. Indeed, even in *Elite*, the missions were quite literally an afterthought. To create the illusion of a huge or even endless universe, planets are spawned and randomly assigned names or other attributes to planets or systems. Daunting manuals and interfaces are another hallmark of the genre; *Universe*'s 93-page manual came in a three-ring binder! *Elite*'s manual was a relatively modest 64 pages.

I've found no evidence that *Elite*'s creators were familiar with any of these games. They did, however, play *Traveller* and *Space Opera*, tabletop role-playing games with science fiction themes and several of the same tropes—indeed, the default character is named Jameson, the same as the sample character in *Traveller*. Regardless, the authors maintained that the game was "as original as any computer can be."[4] To be fair, these tabletop games owe much of their inspiration to "hard science fiction" novels, particularly those of Larry Niven, Poul Anderson, H. Beam Piper, and Jerry Pournelle. The authors working in this subgenre try their best to stay within the realm of plausible science, which for obvious reasons strongly appealed to computer nerds. In short, the ideas were out there, and it was really just a question of who could best implement them into a solid game design.

A more obvious inspiration for *Elite* was flight simulators, which, as we saw in the previous chapter, were quite advanced by 1984. Developers had been quick to adapt the traditional flight sim for space flight, including Activision's *Space Shuttle: A Journey into Space* (1982) and Edu-Ware's *Rendezvous: A Space Shuttle Simulation* (1982).

A more prescient predecessor is Doug Neubauer's *Star Raiders* game for the Atari home computer, published in 1979 (see Figure 13.3). Like *Elite*, this innovative game featured real-time 3D space battles, hyperspace jumps, and galactic charts for navigation. However, when asked if it inspired *Elite*, Braben replied, "It didn't. I know that's surprising, but the problem is I didn't have an Atari and none of my friends did. I didn't know anyone who had an Atari."[5]

The story of *Elite*'s development begins on Christmas morning, 1981, when 17-year-old Braben unwrapped a shiny new Acorn Atom and fell in love with programming.[6]

---

[4] Croft, Martin. "An Elite Crew." *Micro Adventurer*, January 1985: 15.

[5] Helion, Marcel. "The Elites: David Braben Talks Elite: Dangerous and Space Sims." *The Escapist.* February 13, 2015. http://www.escapistmagazine.com/articles/view/video-games/columns/gamedesign/12976-David-Braben-Discusses-Elite-Dangerous-and-Space-Sims (accessed June 11, 2015).

[6] Robinson, Martin. "The Resurrection of Elite: Braben Talks Dangerous." *Eurogamer.* July 3, 2014. http://www.eurogamer.net/articles/2014-03-07-if-elite-were-on-console-there-would-be-an-expectation-the-game-would-be-dumbed-down (accessed June 10, 2014).

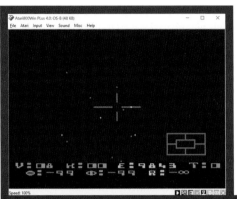

Figure 13.3 *Star Raiders* running on the Atari 800 Win emulator. Doug Neubauer's 1978 space combat game was far ahead of its time.

Braben was particularly interested in 3D graphics, and, thanks to the excellent technical documentation, BASIC, and assembly tools included with the system, had soon taught himself enough to make some impressive programs. Bell, meanwhile, had spent much of his spare time programming an Othello game on the computer in his dad's office.[7]

Braben and Bell met at Jesus College, Cambridge, and discovered their mutual love of programming computer games. While their personalities were quite different, they found that they worked well together, and set out to make a 3D space game. According to Bell, setting the game in space "was the easiest, because space didn't have anything in it. With a flight sim you've got the ground, but space is beautiful because it's a sparse environment."[7] It was enough to add pirates for space dogfighting, and they worked out the aforementioned docking sequence that is one of the game's most memorable moments. However, both felt the game was still lacking something.

According to Braben, the next idea came from playing games like *Space Invaders*, which typically awarded you an extra ship if you reached 10,000 points. He wondered—why an extra ship? What if I wanted more bullets instead? Why shouldn't I have a choice of how to spend my points? These thoughts eventually led him to the upgrade system of *Elite*, in which players start off with a barebones vessel and have to save up money to gradually upgrade its components.[8] One way to make money was by shooting the pirates and collecting bounties, but again they felt they needed more. The solution this time was a full-fledged interstellar economy and the ability to trade from planet to planet. Since it would likely take weeks, if not months, to work your way up to the best possible ship (and highest ranking—the vaunted "Elite")—they decided to let players save the game whenever they wanted.

Braben and Bell feared that their game was too complex for the arcade-loving crowd, who were used to short bursts of instant gratification and would never dream of reading a manual. They were right to be worried—the first publisher they approached with a demo of the combat and docking sequence, Thorn EMI, rejected it precisely on those grounds. They had more luck with Acornsoft, the software branch of Acorn Computers,

---

[7] Spufford, Francis. "Masters of Their Universe." *The Guardian*. October 18, 2003. http://www.theguardian.com/books/2003/oct/18/features.weekend (accessed June 10, 2015).

[8] *From Bedrooms to Billions*. Directed by Anthony Caulfield and Nicola Caulfield. 2014.

manufacturers of the Electron, Atom, and BBC Micro, who agreed to take on the project. Bell and Braben would write the game for their BBC Micro, model B first, and follow it up with a stripped-down version for the lesser-powered Electron.

All in all, it'd take the pair two full years and plenty of long nights to complete the game.[9] Their first major stumbling block was memory—even a humble 10 solar systems with hardcoded names and other variables would overwhelm the 22K of RAM they had to work with. "Then we had a Eureka! moment," said Braben in a 2011 GDC postmortem.[10] The solution was to use long number sequences that appeared to be random but were actually based on a generalized Fibonacci sequence.[11] This breakthrough allowed them to quickly generate names, locations, and other variables for each planet and system using only 6K of memory. Braben was fascinated by the fact that, even though they were fully aware of all the mathematics behind the procedure, it was still wondrous to explore the galaxies it generated. The system always managed to surprise them—such as when they stumbled upon a planet named "Arse" and realized they'd have to work out a scheme for eliminating naughty names! Some sources you'll find online claim that *Elite* was the first game to use procedural generation techniques; this is, of course, false (see Chapter 6, *Rogue:* Procedural Generation). Still, the massive degree to which *Elite* was able to leverage these techniques to create whole galaxies was unprecedented (see Figure 13.4).

To round out the *Elite* package, the publisher furnished a large box (most UK games at the time shipped in bags), stickers, a novella by Robert Holdstock, and the all-important manual (see Figure 13.5). According to Chris Jordan of Acornsoft, the game sold more than 100,000 copies between 1984 and 1989 for the BBC Micro, and 35,294 for the Acorn Electron.[12] Bell and Braben had reserved the rights to any ports of their game to other platforms and were now in a position to command top dollar for these rights, which they auctioned to the highest bidders. For their trouble, they received what Braben believed to be the first-ever six-figure advance for a game.[10] The wild success of the game ensured Braben and Bell a prominent role in the gaming press of the United Kingdom, who tended to be much more focused on the lives and personalities of game developers than their US counterparts. Ralph Bancroft of *Personal Computer News* called it the "most addictive game I have ever come across, and the first that truly could claim the title of 'mega game.'"[13] They even made the evening television news!

---

[9] Braben, David. "Elite Frequently Asked Questions." *Frontier Developments (Wayback Machine).* 1999. http://www.frontier.co.uk/elitefaq.html (accessed March 3, 2000).

[10] Braben, David. "Classic Game Postmortem—ELITE." *GDC Vault.* 2011. http://www.gdcvault.com/play/1014628/Classic-Game-Postmortem (accessed June 11, 2015).

[11] For a technical overview of how this works, go to http://wiki.alioth.net/index.php/Random_number_generator.

[12] Scholten, Wouter. "Elite: Claims about numbers sold etc." *Wouter's BBC Micro Software, Scans, Pictures, Etc.* February 12, 2014. http://wouter.bbcmicro.net/bbc/elite.html (accessed June 11, 2015).

[13] Bancroft, Ralph. "Gameplay." *Personal Computer News*, October 6, 1984: 47.

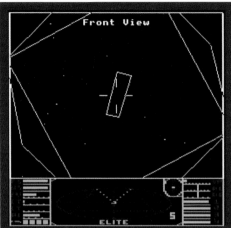

Figure 13.4   A shot of the BBC Micro's version of *Elite*. Shown here is the famous docking sequence. Expect to crash many times before getting it right.

Elite put players in control of a Cobra MK III, a high-quality and highly customizable intergalactic spaceship. The starter ship was armed only with the weakest of weapons, the slow-firing pulse laser. Likewise, the ship was lacking almost all of the exciting options and customizations, such as a larger cargo bay or an automatic docking computer. This last option was particularly valuable, given the complexity of the manual docking procedure—widely hailed as one of the game's most memorable, if frustrating, aspects. There were

many upgrades available, and not just for bigger lasers—indeed, players who disliked combat could outfit their ship with a mining laser, and spend their time in well-policed systems harvesting ore from asteroids.

Players who enjoyed dogfighting could buy military-grade lasers for the front and rear of the ship, homing missiles, energy bombs, and escape pods if the going got too rough. The fuel scoop let players refuel for free at stars, but it was also used to salvage cargo from beaten opponents. There were dozens upon dozens of possible configurations, and they made an immediate and noticeable difference to the gameplay.

Elite offered another means of measuring one's prowess: ranks. The rank was an indicator of one's overall combat skill. The

Figure 13.5   Firebird's dramatic box art. To thwart pirates, the game shipped with a plastic "Lenslock" device, an annoyance that was remedied in future versions. When my dad and I went to buy our copy, only one was left. Upon closer inspection, we discovered that someone had managed to get that box open in the store and swipe the Lenslock!

player began with the offensive "poor" rank, moving up through several stages from "competent" to "dangerous," and finally joining the vaunted "elite," the most fearsome pilots in space. There were also three reputation ranks: clean, offender, and fugitive. Players who consistently broke the law were hunted by the "galcops," who flew about in packs of vicious Viper-class ships. Pirates weren't the only threats lurking out in space—the insectoid Thargoid race was at war with humanity and its allies, and only the best pilots could hope to survive an encounter with their invasion ships.

The game consisted of two basic interfaces: a mostly text-driven menu interface for trading and upgrading, and a first-person, simulator-style view for spaceflight and combat. An intriguing sensor system at the bottom showed other ships and objects in three dimensions. Objects that were above or below the character were represented by dots connected to lines resembling narrow towers. Other aspects of the interface resembled a conventional flight simulator, but *Elite* adhered to realistic physics. For instance, the player could roll the ship clockwise or counterclockwise but could only turn by aiming in a direction and firing the engines. It took practice and patience to learn to maneuver the ship, and even more to maneuver it well enough to survive combat. Experts could even make special maneuvers on the basis of the gravitational force of planets or bodies. The game made high demands on players and had a low tolerance for incompetence. While this level of difficulty turned away some, others savored the challenge.

After *Elite*, Braben and Bell found that they had different priorities. Braben wanted to focus on making the physics and astronomy more realistic, but Bell thought this was a mistake. After Braben founded his own company, *Frontier Developments*, their friendship deteriorated into a bitter feud over royalties. Braben's company developed two official sequels to *Elite*—*Frontier: Elite II* (1993) and *Frontier: First Encounters* (1995).

Elite's intoxicating mix of trading and space dogfighting is seen in plenty of other games, most notably Origin's *Wing Commander: Privateer* (1993), Egosoft's *X* series (1999), Digital Anvil's *Freelancer* (2003), and *Eve Online* (2003). More recently, Chris Roberts' *Star Citizen* (expected 2016) raised more than $2 million in its much-publicized Kickstarter campaign. This massive, juggernaut of a project promises a full single-player campaign as well as a massive multiplayer component.

Braben himself went to Kickstarter in 2012, successfully raising 1.5 million pounds to fund a project called *Elite: Dangerous*. The game was launched on December 16, 2014, and has already sold half a million copies and generated more than 22 million in sales.[14] Reviewers of the game have been mostly positive, though some complained about "moments of emptiness, frustration, and boredom."[15] The bulk of the negative comments focused on the lack of narrative and long periods of inaction; some players need to feel that their actions have some meaning beyond the simple pursuit of wealth, status, and exploration.

---

[14] Cambridge News. "Frontier's Elite Dangerous Earnings Boost Cambridge Index." *Cambridge News.* April 28, 2015. http://www.cambridge-news.co.uk/Frontier-s-Elite-Dangerous-earnings-boost/story-26396543-detail/story.html (accessed June 11, 2015).

[15] Thursten, Chris. "Elite Dangerous." *PC Gamer.* December 22, 2014. http://www.pcgamer.com/elite-dangerous-review/ (accessed June 11, 2015).

I'm reminded of the unsettling conclusion of Holdstock's novella, *Elite: The Dark Wheel*, which seems to have as much relevance for *Elite: Dangerous* as it did for the original game:

"How does it feel to be rich?"
"Empty," Alex said, and Rafe Zetter laughed.
"You'll do for the Dark Wheel, Alex. You'll do..."

Elite was not an easy game, nor was it always an exciting one. Like most games worth playing, it was worthless to many. But it was a game that pushed you out of your nest, and if you fell, you fell.

But if you flew, you soared.

13.1 Playing *Elite* Today

There are many different versions of *Elite*, and each has its merits. You can check them out in the *Elite Forever* site (http://www.eliteforever.co.uk/downloads.html), which has graciously assembled them into self-extracting files complete with emulators. All you need to do is download and run the files. The site also hosts the sequels.

Of course, you might also try *Elite: Dangerous*, whose stunning audiovisuals make the original's look positively antiquated.

Chapter 14

Pinball Construction Set:
The Game of Games

Bill Budge's *Pinball Construction Set* arrived during a deliciously apropos historical moment. For much of its long history, the arcade was dominated by pinball, and early video games such as *Pong*, *Breakout*, and *Space Invaders* competed with these often elaborate and sophisticated machines for space, coins, and cultural status. As video game technology and manufacturing improved, however, the fickle public lost interest in the latest offerings from venerable names like Gottlieb, Sterns, and Williams. The newer video games took up less space, offered a much greater variety of gameplay, were easier to maintain, and, most importantly, made more money. While never dying out entirely, pinball machines moved from front and center to the dustier back corners of the arcade industry.

In the midst of this transition came a truly revolutionary product that not only let you play a realistic pinball simulation on your home computer—a remarkable achievement in and of itself—but also let you build your own tables! Even more impressive was that it let you do this in a natural, intuitive, and appealing way. It's hard to imagine a better tribute to the glory days of pinball.

Pinball Construction Set (hereafter *PCS*) was a stunning achievement for its 28-year-old creator, Budge, who admittedly wasn't much of a gamer (see Figure 14.1). In 1978, Budge was taking courses for a PhD in computer science from UC Berkeley. He scrimped and saved for an Apple II and became enamored with programming games for it. His first success was *Penny Arcade* (1979), a set of *Pong*-inspired games such as *Bumper Pool* and *Tennis*. Budge demonstrated the game at Apple, who happily traded the rights for a $700 printer.[1] It also landed Budge a job at Apple, where he was put to work creating software for the ill-fated Apple III computer.

At Apple, Budge became friends with Steve "Woz" Wozniak. Despite his status as one of the greatest visionaries of the computer industry, Woz was still a huge fan of pinball, and frequently discussed the finer points of the game with like-minded colleagues and friends. They were always "talking about catches, and how to pass the ball from flipper to flipper, and they really got into it. And I would go and watch them play and listen to them talk about it," said Budge.[1] Even though Budge himself described pinball as "sheer torture," he reckoned that a great pinball computer simulation might be just

---

[1] Kohler, Chris. "Trailblazing DIY Pinball Game Snags Pioneer Award for Bill Budge." *Wired.* January 21, 2011. http://www.wired.com/2011/01/bill-budge-pioneer/ (accessed May 26, 2015).

Figure 14.1   Bill Budge, legendary Apple II programmer and creator of *Pinball Construction Set*. (Photo courtesy of Jason Scott.)

the thing to impress his colleagues.[2] It also represented a substantial programming challenge, which he knew would put his graphics and physics skills to the test. He took Williams' *Firepower* table as his model and went to work.

Budge persevered, and his game *Raster Blaster* was hailed as "the best pinball-

Figure 14.2   Budge's *Raster Blaster* pinball game was the best in its class for many years.

game simulator for microcomputers"[3] and the "most popular program of 1981" according to *Softalk* magazine (see Figure 14.2).[4] Budge had managed to overcome some limitations of the Apple II's hardware, creating a game with much smoother animation and accuracy than many had dreamed possible. "The collision detection was kind of a nightmare," said Budge.

"No matter what I tried, the ball would sometimes stick to a wall and freeze or slide right through." His solution was both unorthodox and stunningly brilliant:

> I made a scan-line table; for each scan line on the screen I entered a list of wall locations, together with the slope of the wall at that point. To collision detect the ball with the game board, I used the ball y-coordinate to index into the table and the x-coordinate to check against all the walls at that y.[5]

To sell the game, Budge had teamed up with his more business-oriented sister, Ellen Beritzhoff, to form BudgeCo. Beritzhoff soon found herself submerged under a torrent of

---

[2] Darling, Sharon. "Birth of a Computer Game." *Compute!*, February 1985: 48.

[3] Mace, Scott. "Electronic Antics." *InfoWorld*, January 1984: 69.

[4] Tommervik, Margot Comstock. "The Most Popular Program of 1981: Raster Blaster." *Softalk*, August 1982: 163–167.

[5] Hague, James. "Bill Budge." *Halcyon Days*. March 1997. http://www.dadgum.com/halcyon/BOOK/BUDGE.HTM (accessed May 26, 2015).

tens of thousands of orders. When asked how she planned to follow up such an outstanding debut, she replied, "Well, I guess Bill will have to program another one."[4]

Budge, meanwhile, was "sick" of video games and was again working on software for the Apple Lisa, another ambitious Apple computer. The Lisa flopped in the marketplace despite its awesome innovation—it was the first home computer with a Graphical User Interface (GUI), complete with windows, icon, and a mouse-driven cursor. One of the programs Budge saw demonstrated was a simple painting program that let users draw pixels onto the screen.

Budge began to wonder if this concept could be expanded, allowing users to create and manipulate shapes. Then, he thought about how much easier—and more *fun* it would have been for him to create tables for *Raster Blaster* if he'd had access to such a tool. It dawned on him that others, particularly those with less programming skills, might enjoy this process even more. What began to take shape in his brain was a design for a program that, while technically not really a "game" at all, might turn out to just as much fun.

"You can't ask people what they want to see on a computer," said Budge in a 1984 episode of *Computer Chronicles*. "[Designers] have to write a program that *they* want to write, and that *they* want to use. When I started writing [*PCS*], it was something I really wanted to do—I really wanted to see it work."[6] This time, Budge had taken on an even greater challenge than he'd faced with *Raster Blaster*. Yet again, he'd struggle with collision detection, graphics, and physics, but would also have to work out a system for sharing files and editing artwork and sounds. He'd also be attempting to adapt some key functionality from the Lisa's GUI to the much humbler Apple II—which didn't yet support the mouse. It was a difficult, intimidating, and probably seriously misguided project that a publisher would have likely rejected out of hand. It's a good thing that Budge's sister was too busy stuffing *Raster Blaster* inserts into Ziploc bags to question him—and, besides, he had *that look* in his eyes again!

It took him several months, but at last *Pinball Construction Set* was ready for shipment. The pitch was simple, straightforward, and electrifying:

> *The Pinball Construction Set* contains the pieces and tools to make millions of hi-res video pinball games. No programming or typing is necessary. Just take parts from the set and put them on the game board. Press a button to play! Use the video tools to make borders and obstacles. Add game logic and scoring rules with the wiring kit. Create hi-res designs and logos using the BudgeCo magnifier. Color your designs with the paint brush.

The fact that Budge's own *Raster Blaster* could be recreated and even surpassed with *PCS* was enticing to anyone who'd ever dreamed of making a virtual pinball game. Exciting

---

[6] Budge, Bill, interview by Stewart Cheifet and Gary Kildall. "Computer Games." *Computer Chronicles*. PBS. September 28, 1984.

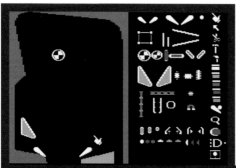

stuff even today, it was utterly fantastic in 1982—particularly considering that the Apple II had just 48K of RAM (see Figure 14.3).

PCS was a critical and commercial success for BudgeCo, but by 1983, Budge and his sister found themselves overwhelmed with the demands of running a software publishing business in an increasingly

Figure 14.3 *Pinball Construction Set's* drag'n drop interface seems uncannily modern. Just click and drag the components you want onto the highly configurable table. Genius!

sophisticated and competitive marketplace. Fortunately for them, Electronic Arts, an up-and-coming publisher, and its founder, Trip Hawkins, were more than eager to relieve their burden.

Hawkins' shtick was promoting developers as "electronic artists," just as worthy of veneration and fame as the stars of other entertainment media. He created cults of personalities around developers like Budge and was always quick with slick ad copy, intriguing packaging, and highbrow claims about the untapped artistic potential of games (see Figure 14.4). Compare the almost utilitarian text from the BudgeCo release of *PCS* (above) with that of Electronic Arts':

> Power. Pure, sheer and unadulterated. A nearly telepathic link between you and the machine. Here is the promise made good. Here is the reason you bought a computer in the first place. It's been called the best program ever written for an 8-bit machine. Boot the disk and find out why.

Budge, though, was a humble man, hardly one to brag or boast about his accomplishments. About to give a talk at an industry event, Budge was overcome with stage fright when he noticed Bill Atkins, creator of *MacPaint*, sitting in the front row. "I was so nervous," said Budge. "Atkinson is four or six times better a programmer than I am."[7]

Hawkins' goal, however, was not just to sell games, but to sell the medium, and Budge tried his best to play along. Hawkins put together a typically splashy, unreserved advertising campaign focused on the question "Can a computer make you cry?" and the claim that "We see farther." It's telling that even in the midst of such hyperbolic ad copy, Budge is quoted asking "Software artists? I'm not so sure there are any software artists yet. We've got to earn that title."

Budge later recounted a story of anxiously showing up to sign autographs at an electronics store in Boston. The manager promptly explained that his job would be to ring

---

7   Caruso, Denise. "People." *InfoWorld*, May 28, 1984: 18.

up sales, not to sign autographs, and he damned well wasn't going to do that until he'd found himself some *proper* attire. Budge quietly left to buy some clothes to replace his t-shirt and sneakers and spent the rest of a long, boring day behind the store counter. "That's when I realized maybe I wouldn't be a rock star," said Budge.[1]

Part of Budge's problem might well have been that he indeed saw farther—at least, farther than most gamers (and store managers!) of the era. "When everyone is still discovering *Pac-Man*," explained

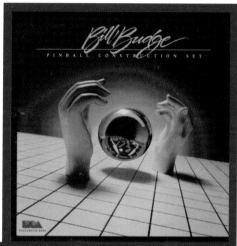

Figure 14.4   EA developed some stylish, if slightly creepy, cover art for the game's "rock album" style packaging.

Budge, "and a program comes along that tells them they can build video games—well, it doesn't register at first."[6] *PCS* wasn't really a "game" at all, but rather one of the very first software toys or "construction sets," programs that have more in common with Lego blocks or model train building than pinball or *Pac-Man*. A good construction set not only has to empower users to achieve their creative visions but also has to simplify that process, which of course entails heavily constraining one's options. The key is abstracting out just those parts of making a pinball simulation that would be fun for the average person.

To that end, *PCS*'s interface is consolidated to a single screen, split down the middle. Creating a board is a simple matter of dragging components from the right, such as bumpers, flippers, and alleys, onto the canvas or board on the left. At any time, you can play a quick game on your board, a critical feature for both experimentation and working out the kinks in a design. More advanced users can even tinker with the logic or physics of the game, such as adjusting scoring methods or even gravity. While some users liked to "keep it real," so to speak, you could just as easily create wild and crazy boards that could never function in reality.

PCS touched off a flurry of other construction sets, including Will Harvey's *Music Construction Set* (1984), Rich Koening's *Racing Destruction Set* (1985), and Stuart Smith's *Adventure Construction Set* (1985). *Music Construction Set* was intended more for education than entertainment, but was still popular. As a music composition notation program, it let users drag and drop notes right onto the staff, play back their creations, and print them out. *Racing Destruction Set* was a split-screen, isometric-perspective racing game that could be played in either racing or destruction modes, the latter allowing for offensive weapons like oil slicks and landmines. Vehicles included a variety of cars, including a jeep and

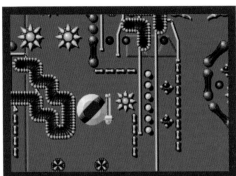

lunar rover, as well as motorcycles. Where *RDS* really dazzled, however, was letting you not only modify elements like gravity and vehicle components but also design your own courses. Finally, *Adventure Construction Set* (*ACS*), the most advanced of Electronic Arts' construction sets, let you make complete role-playing games. It came with toolkits for science fiction, spy, and fantasy-themed games.

Figure 14.5   Budge's next pinball construction set game, *Virtual Pinball*, didn't appeal to Genesis fans.

Meanwhile, Budge spent the next 5 years trying to outdo them all with what he called a "Construction Set Construction Set," whose goal was to let novices make any kind of game they liked. Unfortunately, this project proved too ambitious even for the likes of Budge, who finally had to give up in frustration. Arguably, Activision accomplished this goal with *Garry Kitchen's GameMaker* in 1985. This product was most popular on the Commodore 64, where it was used to create more than 100 games.[8]

After a long hiatus, Budge returned in 1993 with *Virtual Pinball* for the Sega Genesis (see Figure 14.5). The challenge of designing a pinball construction set for a device with no keyboard, disk, or mouse appealed to Budge, but the console crowd seemed resistant to the concept.

In any case, it's not hard to see the influence of Budge's "construction set" concept in later titles. Sensible Software's *Shoot'em-Up Construction Kit* (1987) was a hit among SHMUP fans, who created enough quality games with the software to warrant its own category: SEUCK games, which are still being made with it today. In 1991, fans of *The Bard's Tale* series could create similar adventures with *The Bard's Tale Construction Set*, and SSI's *Forgotten Realms: Unlimited Adventures* did the same for its "gold box" engine a few years later. Of course, in modern titles, "user-generated content," as it came to be known, is greatly aided by powerful tools such as Bethesda's *Skyrim Creation Kit* or Obsidian Entertainment's *Electron Toolset* for *Neverwinter Nights 2*. Often enough, these fan-made productions can rival or even surpass the popularity of the original game. Of course, creativity is at the heart of both *LittleBigPlanet* (2008) and *Minecraft* (2009), two of the most successful games in recent memory.

In 2011, Budge became the second recipient of the Pioneer Award from the Academy of Interactive Arts & Sciences, who recognized him for "revolutionizing game design and user interfaces." Will Wright was on hand to acknowledge his debt to the honoree: "*Pinball Construction Set* was the first game that introduced me to the idea of

---

8   See GameBase64's list of 125 *GKGM* games at http://tinyurl.com/ntyjx2k.

constructive games and systemic thinking. I doubt *SimCity* would have existed without it."[9] Budge accepted his award and signed autographs with his customary humility, and this time no one said anything about his t-shirt or sneakers.

14.1 Playing *PCS* Today

If you simply want to try out *PCS*, go to http://virtualapple.org and look for *Pinball Construction Set* for the Apple II. If you want to be able to save your boards, you'll probably need to download the disk ROMs from this site and load them into an appropriate Apple II emulator. I use *AppleWin*, a free emulator available at http://github.com/AppleWin.

There are ports of *PCS* available for a wide variety of platforms, including Atari 8-bit, Commodore 64, DOS, and Mac. Of course, there's also *Virtual Pinball* for the Sega Genesis, which is the most impressive from an audiovisual perspective. Modern pinball-making tools include BSP Design Software's *Future Pinball* and Randy Davis's *Visual Pinball*. Both options are free and boast some impressive features. Readers with Unity experience can purchase a template from the Unity Assets store called *Pinball PlayMaker Kit*.

---

[9] Chen, Debby. Academy of Interactive Arts & Sciences Names Bill Budge as its Second Pioneer Award Recipient. Calabasas, CA, January 21, 2011.

Chapter 15

King's Quest:
From Peanuts to Palaces

By 1984, the "home computer" industry had evolved far beyond the humble Apple II, TRS-80, and Commodore PET. Newer machines, such as the Apple IIe, Tandy Color Computer, and Commodore 64, offered substantially enhanced graphics capabilities and computing power for games over their predecessors. Therefore, it was a bit shocking when IBM, the world's largest and best-respected computer maker, finally entered the fray in 1981; its IBM PC had no sound beyond a puny built-in PC speaker or "buzzer," and graphics were limited to four-color CGA at 320 × 200 resolution (and many owners were quite satisfied with MDA, or monochrome graphics!). In any case, the IBM PC's high price (a barebones model ran $1565) sharply limited its appeal purely as a gaming platform. Though the IBM PC was a hit among business professionals, it posed little threat to the burgeoning commercial gaming market.

To address the situation, in November of 1983, IBM announced the PCjr, a lower-cost, more gamer-friendly home computer. Nicknamed "Peanut" by IBM's engineers, the PCjr could display 16 colors, output up to three channels of mono sound, and had two built-in joystick ports and two cartridge slots for instantly loading games. It was also roughly half the price of an IBM PC. Not everyone was impressed with the new kid on the block—in many ways the Commodore 64 was a much better value. However, IBM's name and deep pockets caught the eye of Sierra On-Line's president, Ken Williams. "What other machine would one develop software for?" he asked his audience at the 1983 Consumer Electronics Show.[1] Williams arranged a deal with IBM to publish their new game *King's Quest* exclusively for the new platform (see Figure 15.1).

Designed by Williams' wife, Roberta Williams, *King's Quest: Quest for the Crown* definitely had the potential to be the PCjr's killer app (see Figure 15.2). It single-handedly established many of the features we take for granted in modern adventure games, such as brightly colored animated graphics, a navigable three-dimensional (3D) environment, sight-based puzzles, and the quirky, irreverent humor so typical of the genre. It put the PCjr's enhanced audiovisual hardware to good use. IBM made it a central part of its marketing campaign for the platform, as we see in the following "review" (actually an

---

[1] Wierzbicki, Barbara. "Developers Embrace PCjr Despite Drawbacks." *InfoWorld*, December 19, 1983: 51–52.

Figure 15.1 *King's Quest* was the first of many best-selling graphical adventure games by Roberta Williams.

advertisement paid for by IBM) of the PCjr in *InfoWorld* magazine:

Sir Grahame's[2] movements ... are unusually smooth and realistic because multiple video buffers in main memory are used instead of a single chip to create the animation effects. PCjr's three voice sound creates an impressive variety of sound effects, such as a fanfare of horns when the castle door opens. And PCjr's ability to produce 16 colors lends a touch of realism to an imaginary kingdom.[3]

King's Quest made Sierra On-Line one of the biggest and most influential game publishers of all time and paved the way

Figure 15.2 Ken and Roberta Williams launched an empire with their hit series of graphical adventure games. It all started with *King's Quest*.

for a whole series of sequels and spin-offs. Sadly for IBM, however, *King's Quest* wasn't enough to woo gamers to its PCjr. The PCjr's high price and a combination of other factors (awful keyboard, limited memory, and compatibility issues) would take more than King Graham to save it. Fortunately for us, Sierra was able

to rerelease the game for other platforms the following year, including the Tandy 1000, a much more successful IBM PC-compatible computer inspired by the PCjr. Sales of the game soared as scores of gamers flooded into software shops, eager to see the game that all their friends were talking about.

---

[2] The character was renamed Graham in later versions.

[3] IBM. "Read Only: A Review of the IBM Personal Computer Family, Vol. 1, No. 2." *InfoWorld*, December 10, 1984: 37–40.

Ken and Roberta Williams founded "On-Line Systems" in 1980 (the name change to Sierra On-Line took place in 1982). Ken was a 26-year-old software engineer who, despite being a child prodigy who'd entered college at 16, dropped out two years later, married Roberta, and

Figure 15.3   *King's Quest's* iconic opening screen. Be careful not to fall in the moat!

began studying programming. After learning to code, he did contract work for a wide variety of companies.

After playing *Colossal Cave Adventure* (see Chapter 3) with Roberta one night in the late 1970s, the two concocted a plan to make a similar game but with graphics for the Apple II. As Roberta worked up some simple line illustrations and a story, Ken developed the engine. The result was the first-ever graphical adventure game, *Mystery House*, which turned out to be the right product at the right time. Though almost laughably crude-looking today, the game took the Apple II community by storm and provided the capital the Williams needed to fulfill their dream of moving out of the city and running their own business. By the time rumors began circulating about the IBM PCjr, the two had earned a solid reputation for innovative graphical adventures, including *The Wizard and the Princess*, the first such game with color graphics, and *Time Zone*, a huge game with more than 1400 rooms. The Williams saw in the IBM PCjr a chance to up the ante yet again.

Their goal was to make a game that would not only *look* better than the competition but offer a much freer range of movement. Although Roberta maintains in several interviews that she prioritizes plots and characters over audiovisuals, *King's Quest* was a technological marvel, requiring six programmers and artists $700,000 and 18 months to complete.[4] The result was stunning (see Figure 15.3). Not only were the 16-color animated graphics superior to her earlier works, but this time the player controlled a character that could move in three dimensions, all in real time! *King's Quest* isn't true 3D—the character does not shrink or expand as he moves up and down but can walk behind or in front of objects on the screen—but it was still spectacular for its time. Trivette of *Compute!* Magazine's response was typical: "The graphics and animation in the PCjr version of *King's Quest* are spectacularly better than in any other adventure game I've seen. The three-dimensional quality makes it seem like Sir Grahame is moving through an animated cartoon."[4]

Simplicity was an important goal while designing the interface, but no one was thinking of doing away with the text parser quite yet. While the character (Graham) is controlled by the arrow keys, players still had to type in commands and read plenty of textual descriptions. The parser wasn't nearly as sophisticated as Infocom's, and the

---

4   Trivette, Donald B. "Inside King's Quest." *Compute!*, February 1985: 136.

low resolution of the graphics made some objects hard to identify; what looked like a stone might actually be a walnut. Typing "TAKE STONE" would simply result in an error message; only "TAKE WALNUT" would work. While savvy players could find ways to deal with these problems (such as typing "LOOK AT GROUND" to learn the name of the object), others relied on hint books or advice from friends.

Even putting these interface issues aside, the game was still quite difficult. Graham was easily and frequently killed in the adventure, so frequent saves were necessary to prevent tedious repetition. Getting the game into an unwinnable state was a more insidious problem; you might play for days only to realize that something you did (or failed to do) early on has now made the game impossible to complete.

Roberta earned a reputation during these years for creating hard puzzles with obscure or even misleading clues. One such puzzle involves a condor. The idea is to stand in a certain spot on the screen (walkthroughs have gone so far as to offer close-up screenshots to help) and enter "JUMP" into the parser at just the right moment. The precise timing and placement, combined with the somewhat obscure command to jump (why not catch or grab?), stumped many gamers.

The most infamous puzzle is based on the old fairy tale about Rumpelstiltskin, but with a twist. When players were asked to name the gnome, they might not have realized that an earlier clue to "think backward" meant they had to transcribe the name Rumpelstiltskin using a backward alphabet, yielding "IFNKOVHGROGHPRM." Roberta acknowledged that she "received a LOT of letters about the old gnome's name. In retrospect, it was an awfully nasty puzzle," but points out that "it was a typical 'advanced' puzzle in those days."[5] A later sequence involves climbing a beanstalk, from which Graham will fall to his death at even the slightest deviation from the pre-established (and difficult to find) path. Even seasoned veterans were forced to save and restore countless times to get to the top of the beanstalk, a frustrating experience to say the least.

Later, Sierra adventure games (and those from LucasArts) were much more forgiving than *King's Quest*; players were encouraged to explore without fear of dying or making the game impossible to beat. Some fans of the older style disliked these changes, claiming that gamers simply weren't patient or intelligent enough to meet the challenge. Sharply disagreeing with this opinion is Ron Gilbert, designer of LucasArts' breakaway hit *The Secret of Monkey Island* (1990). His 1989 diatribe, "Why Adventure Games Suck," has been widely quoted and is worth partially quoting here:

> Some people say that following [my] rules makes the games too easy to play. I disagree. What makes most games tough to play is that the puzzles are arbitrary and unconnected. Most are solved by chance or repetitive sessions of typing 'light candle with match,' 'light paper with match,' 'light rug with match,' until something happens. This is not tough game play, this is masturbation. I played one game that required the player to drop a bubble gum wrapper in a room in order to get a trap door to open

---

[5] Williams, Roberta. *King's Quest Collection Series Manual*. Oakhurst, CA: Sierra On-Line, Inc., 1994.

(object names have been changed to protect the guilty). What is the reasoning? There is none. It's an advanced puzzle, I was told.[6]

Gilbert's essay is still relevant today, and it's easy to think that one reason the adventure game genre has declined in

Figure 15.4   Another scene from the first *King's Quest*. Note the fiddle in the lower right corner. Getting to it and figuring out its purpose are a few of the game's many puzzles.

recent years is that not enough developers have read and applied it. At any rate, at the time, gamers were sufficiently dazzled by the audiovisual spectacle of *King's Quest* to protest too loudly about the fairness of its puzzles.

The story of *King's Quest* was inspired by the classic fairy tales Roberta read

Figure 15.5   The second *King's Quest* game starred a new lead character. This early scene in the game is an effective teaser—look at all those intriguing locations in the background!

and reread growing up. The goal is to recover three stolen artifacts for the Kingdom of Daventry. These items are a shield that makes its bearer invulnerable, a chest that never empties of gold, and a mirror that shows the future. The mirror, which plays a strong role in later *King's Quest* games, was taken by a wizard who promises in exchange to "bring an heir" to the king and queen, who have been childless throughout their long and otherwise happy marriage. Rather than bear a child, however, the queen becomes deathly ill. Next, a dwarf shows up who offers to cure the queen in return for the shield. The dwarf takes the shield, but the queen dies shortly after. The miserable king, however, manages to rescue a beautiful princess, who he takes for his wife. When she learns about the chest, though, she takes off with it, leaving the king without a bride and the kingdom without its last magical artifact. The player's character, Sir Graham, shows up to help, and is promised the throne of Daventry if he can restore the three artifacts (see Figure 15.4).

The success of the game made a sequel all but inevitable (see Figure 15.5). To facilitate the process, Ken developed AGI, the Adventure Game Interpreter, similar in concept to Infocom's Z-Machine (see Chapter 3). As with the Z-Machine, AGI not only made it

---

[6] Gilbert, Ron. "Why Adventure Games Suck." *Grumpy Gamer.* 1989. http://grumpygamer.com/why_adventure_games _suck (accessed May 18, 2015).

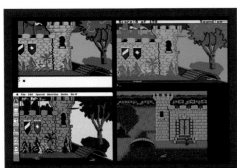

easier to port their games to other systems but also allowed them to hire specialized designers who needn't know much beyond the rudiments of coding (see Figure 15.6). While *King's Quest* remained their flagship adventure game series, Sierra also published Mark Crowe and Scott Murphy's *Space Quest* (1986), Al Lowe's bawdy *Leisure Suit Larry* (1987), Jim Walls' *Police Quest*

Figure 15.6   Shown here is the first *King's Quest* running on different platforms. Starting from the top left and going clockwise, they are Apple II, Atari ST, Mac, and the Sega Master System.

(1987), and Lori Ann Cole's *Quest for Glory* (1989). All of these series earned high acclaim for their designers and remain among the best-loved PC games of all time.

Sierra continued refining and pushing the boundaries of PC graphics technology with its *King's Quest* series well into the 1990s. *King's Quest V: Absence Makes the Heart Go Yonder* (1990), made another leap forward, this time to 256-color VGA. In her March 1991 review of the game in *Computer Gaming World*, Scorpia remarked that "this is the game to boot up when you want to show off your VGA system,"[7] a sentiment shared by plenty of other gamers and critics at the time. Another big change was a switch to icon-based interaction, with the cumbersome and oft-lamented text parser finally laid to rest. An updated CD-ROM version released a year later added digitized voices, but the shoddy voice acting made some question its value.

1990 also marks the release of the first remake of the original *King's Quest*, which featured enhanced graphics, sound, and a modernized interface (sans parser). It was the first project assigned to Josh Mandel, who candidly described the experience in a 2011 interview with me:

> It was tortuous. Every designer at Sierra, including me, had been brought up using the parser interface, which allowed us to create any type of puzzle we could imagine ... Now we were reduced from using an entire dictionary's worth of verbs, to four or five. It was difficult and painful for every designer to adjust their thinking to come up with ways to present, at least, an illusion of the old flexibility ... I felt like my arms and legs were cut off.

Though Sierra would never return to the old format, the negative reactions to the remake were enough to put them off future attempts to update their back catalog.

---

7 Scorpia. "Scorpion's View: When Is a Sequel More than a Sequel? Sierra's King's Quest V." *Computer Gaming World*, March 1991: 50–54.

King's Quest VI: Heir Today, Gone Tomorrow, released September 1992, is usually regarded as the highpoint of the series, and it shows up on several greatest game lists. It brought together two of Sierra's most celebrated designers: Roberta Williams and Jane Jensen, the designer responsible for the hugely popular *Gabriel Knight* series. The familiar blend of folk and fairy tales seems more thoughtfully and artistically explored here than before. What appears at first to be a very basic plot (Prince Alexander sets off to find Princess Cassima) expands rapidly. Alexander must contend with four different islands in the Land of the Green Isles, each with its own theme and personality. What makes the story worthwhile are the characters; neither Alexander nor Cassima act in the stereotypical ways we might expect from the previous games, and the inhabitants of each island have a unique theme and personality. Finally, and perhaps most importantly, the puzzles are much less frustrating than previous games, and the game is much more forgiving of mistakes. It's quite accessible to novices, especially when compared to previous entries.

The biggest change graphically was a lengthy introductory 3D cut scene; it was cutting edge for its day and provided gamers with yet another impressive sequence to show off the power of their systems. The intro is particularly impressive in the later CD-ROM release, which (mercifully) features professional quality voice acting. Both versions boast full 3D animation and dramatic music. Of course, the actual game is less impressive than its cinematic introduction.

The series declined after the sixth game, perhaps because Roberta was too engrossed in her *Phantasmagoria* project, an adult-oriented game with large amounts of full-motion video. *King's Quest VII: The Princeless Bride* appeared in November 1994, and seems to be an effort to create a game in the style of Disney's *Aladdin*. It featured cell animation and SVGA graphics, qualities that give the game a distinctly modern look despite its age. Its cutesy story, characters, and animation style seemed a rather sharp contrast to the previous game, and its simplified interface seems a response to Cyan's monster hit *Myst*, which had debuted the year before.

In 1996, Sierra On-Line was purchased by CUC International, an event that signaled the beginning of the end for their adventure game line. Since Sierra was a publicly traded company, the decision wasn't up to CEO Ken Williams. He said later that "I had no power to control things, and they got out of hand. I transferred out of the games division, primarily because I couldn't stomach watching my company ripped apart."[8] It's not hard to imagine how this drama behind the scenes affected the confidence, morale, and, ultimately, the quality of the final *King's Quest* games.

The final game, *Mask of Eternity* (1998), was controversial even before its release. The boldest change to the gameplay was the introduction of role-playing elements. Sierra had had great success with Lori Ann Cole's *Quest for Glory* series of adventure/RPG hybrids, but many fans were appalled to find them in a *King's Quest* game. Nevertheless, Roberta felt that a drastic change was necessary:

---

[8] Jong, Philip. "Ken Williams Interview." *Adventure Classic Gaming.* March 28, 2006. http://www.adventureclassicgaming .com/index.php/site/interviews/197 (accessed May 18, 2015).

I was trying to bring new blood into the genre ... thereby trying to keep it from dying. Times change, and tastes change ... they just do, and you've gotta do what you've gotta do to try and reach the biggest possible audience to keep a genre alive ... The old-style adventure game that we all know and love will just not cut it in today's world.[9]

Reactions to the game were mixed among fans and critics, with lots of grumbling about the combat and role-playing mechanics. It still managed to more than double the sales of its key competition that year, LucasArts' *Grim Fandango*.

The influence of *King's Quest* is immense, particularly during the "point-and-click" heyday of the 1990s. While there are literally hundreds of games we could mention, the most important are those developed by LucasArts (earlier, Lucasfilm Games). These include two classics by Ron Gilbert: *Maniac Mansion* (1987) and *The Secret of Monkey Island* (1990), which are indisputably among the greatest adventure games of all time.

Like Sierra, LucasArts created its own in-house development tool called SCUMM, or "Script Creation Utility for *Maniac Mansion*," and countless best-selling games were composed with it. *Maniac Mansion* offered a purely icon-based interface (no text parser) and was much more forgiving than Sierra's hits. *The Secret of Monkey Island* further refined the formula, making it impossible for the protagonist (Guybrush Threepwood) to die except in one place. Since players no longer had to be worried about sudden death or getting the game into an unwinnable state, they were much more comfortable exploring and experimenting, savoring the story and witty dialog. Gilbert's masterpiece has been translated into five languages and is certainly worth the attention of any *King's Quest* fan. LucasArts would go on to produce dozens of best-selling games but was never able to seriously threaten Sierra's dominance in the American adventure game market.

The influence of *King's Quest* still lives on today in modern point-and-click adventures such as Telltale Games' *The Walking Dead* (2012), Double Fine Productions' *Broken Age* (2014), and Ron Gilbert and Gary Winnick's *Thimbleweed Park* (expected 2016). Activision resurrected the series with a five-part episodic series of King's Quest games by The Odd Gentlemen. Their first episode debuted on July 28, 2015, and met with ecstatic reviews from fans and newcomers alike. Featuring prominent voice talent and modern graphics, these games tell the untold stories of Graham's life and times.

15.1 Playing *King's Quest* Today

The first question you should ask yourself about playing *King's Quest* today is whether you prefer a parser to a point-and-click style interface. The parser version is, of course, older and more venerated among purists. If you'd like to try it, the best way is to pick up a collection of the first three games from http://www.gog.com. These come with PDF manuals and a preconfigured installer.

---

[9] Sluganski, Randy. "Roberta Williams Speaks Out..." *Just Adventure.* March 1999. http://justadventure.com/Interviews/Roberta_Williams/Roberta_Williams_Interview_3.shtm (accessed June 11, 2004).

There's also an impressive enhanced edition of the first game developed by AGD Interactive, currently in its fourth version. It has great graphics, a full voice cast, and many other refinements, and, better yet, runs fine on a modern PC or Mac. You can download it (for free) at http://www.agdinteractive.com/games/kq1/.

Finally, it's surprisingly easy (and fun!) to make your own point-and-click adventure games. The best place to start is the Adventure Game Studio (AGS), a free download at http://www.adventuregamestudio.co.uk/. With this free, powerful, and intuitive tool, you can make your own games in the style of *King's Quest* or *The Secret of Monkey Island* in no time, regardless of your previous experience with coding.

Chapter 16

Wizardry: A New Perspective on Computer Role Playing

In all my years interviewing game designers and other game industry professionals, the one game that seems to come up most often is Sir-Tech's *Wizardry: Proving Grounds of the Mad Overlord* (1981). It was many gamers' first introduction to role playing on their home computer, and while the audiovisuals seem primitive today, they were more than sufficient to fire the imagination at the time. Furthermore, the game's infamously challenging difficulty level and the possibility of permanently losing your entire party (eradicating weeks, months, or possibly even years of work!) gave it an emotional resonance lacking in most other games. While it wasn't the only computer role-playing game (CRPG) on the market (we'll look at Richard "Lord British" Garriott's *Ultima* games in Chapter 17), *Wizardry* made an indelible impression on a generation of game designers and established many of the "dungeon crawling" paradigms still at work in modern CRPGs.

Wizardry was designed by two students at Cornell University, Andrew C. Greenberg and Robert Woodhead (see Figure 16.1). The two met at the campus computer lab, which offered access to PLATO. I could easily write an entire book about this fascinating computing platform, but it was essentially a nationwide network of high-tech terminals connected to a mainframe computer. The terminals featured plasma displays with 512 × 512 resolution with vector graphics and character sets. While the system was originally intended for educational uses (the name stands for Programmed Logic for Automatic Teaching Operations), users quickly found a myriad of social and entertainment applications for the technology, including chat rooms, e-mail, and multiplayer games. "PLATO was so hugely influential," said Woodhead. "It inspired a lot of what I did ... Everything that you like about computers—odds are, it was invented in the early 70s on PLATO."[1]

Greenberg worked as a lab technician, and one of his jobs was to keep people like Woodhead from playing games. Naturally, this led to some friction between the pair, even if Woodhead later acknowledged that it was precisely his addiction to PLATO that led to his flunking out of Cornell during his last semester. While Woodhead played all sorts of games on PLATO, his favorite was Jim Schwaiger's *Oubliette*, which was basically an early massively multiplayer online role-playing game (MMORPG) (see Figure 16.2).

---

[1] Woodhead, Robert, interview by Matt Barton. *Matt Chat 260: Robert Woodhead on Anime and Plato* (October 3, 2014).

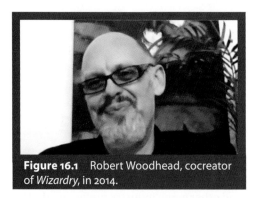

Figure 16.1   Robert Woodhead, cocreator of *Wizardry*, in 2014.

You have   1 hits left
    You are 1 st

You have been surprised
by   4 Footpad

Figure 16.2   Woodhead and Greenberg were inspired by *Oubliette*, an RPG for the PLATO system.

It let multiple simultaneous users explore a virtual world, forming into parties and battling their way through tough dungeons. The display showed a wireframe dungeon in a first-person perspective, and monsters and other enemies were rendered with simple line drawings. As we'll see, Woodhead and Greenberg were heavily inspired by this game, which, like many PLATO titles, seems uncannily ahead of its time.

Back home in Ogden, New York, Woodhead got a job at a Computerland store, and did whatever programming jobs he could find on the side.[2] Meanwhile, his mother, Janice Woodhead, who'd taken over the family's industrial resin business after her husband passed away, partnered up with a souvenir spoon manufacturing outfit run by Frederick Sirotek, Jr. Sirotek realized that the operation could be much more profitable if they could automatically coordinate their costs and

pricing using one of the new "home computers" he'd been hearing about. Janice saw an opportunity to bring her son into the business. Sirotek purchased a souped-up Apple II with extra RAM, and young Woodhead went to work, quickly developing a solution that greatly impressed Sirotek.

Woodhead sensed that his program might be valuable to other companies, and developed it into a product called *Info-Tree*. As it happened, there was a major computer festival going on at Trenton, and Woodhead felt it'd be a great opportunity to market his program. Unfortunately, Woodhead didn't drive, and Sirotek wouldn't let him mail or try to take the Apple II with him on a plane. Instead, he asked his son, Norman, to drive him there.

Norman wasn't interested in computers, but that changed after seeing the wonders at the Trenton Computer Festival. Woodhead finally talked him and his brother Robert Sirotek into going into business with him, an arrangement the elder Sirotek heartily

[2] Maher, Jimmy. "The Roots of Sir-Tech." *The Digital Antiquarian*. March 18, 2012. http://www.filfre.net/2012/03/the-roots-of -sir-tech/ (accessed May 27, 2015).

approved. Naturally, the question arose about what product the newly founded Siro-tech (later Sir-Tech) should develop next. That product was a *Star Trek*–inspired arcade game called *Galactic Attack*, which ended up garnering more media attention and sales than their database program had. Woodhead, who'd never really lost interest in *Oubliette* and PLATO, now wanted to do a game like it in PASCAL for the Apple II. He called the game *Paladin*.

Woodhead somehow ran into Greenberg, the lab technician at Cornell who'd tried vainly to keep him from playing so much *Oubliette*. Woodhead was stunned to learn that Greenberg had also been developing an *Oubliette*-style game, but in Apple BASIC. He called his project *Wizardry*. Woodhead and Greenberg were sufficiently impressed with each other's ideas to join forces. "I don't think the game would have been nearly as good if it'd just been me or just been him," said Woodhead. "I was better at banging out code, and he had a better understanding of the story and balancing out the monsters." Greenberg agreed that their game should be done in PASCAL, and the two were soon fleshing out a very promising design, with Greenberg's friends doing much of the play-testing (and many of whom were immortalized as monsters in the game).

The game's story concerned The Mad Overlord Trebor (Robert spelled backward), whose madness was caused by a magical artifact—an amulet. The evil wizard Werdna (Andrew spelled backward) manages to steal this artifact, but somehow sets off an earthquake in the process. Conveniently, the quake creates a 10-level dungeon beneath Trebor's castle, and in an effort to save face, Werdna claims that creating this *lair* was his intent all along. Trebor encourages adventurers to pursue Werdna and retrieve his arti-fact, promising them riches as well as a prestigious position in his honor guard should they succeed. It's not much of a story, to be honest, but something more elaborate might well have only detracted from its dungeon crawling appeal.

Rather than put the player in charge of a single character, the game allowed you to create a party of six, which could be made up of various combinations of four races, eight classes (four starter and four advanced), and three alignments. There was no system for automapping—serious players had to learn to map out the 20 × 20 dungeons onto graph paper, a process that some detested but others enjoyed. The magic system boasted 50 spells and nearly 100 types of enemies ranging from bubbly slimes and creeping coins to fire dragons and greater demons. Overall, the development took about 16 months to complete.

Right away, though, there was a problem. Woodhead's souped-up Apple II had more memory than the typical Apple II configuration, which he'd relied on with the expecta-tion that Apple was coming out with a 48K runtime version of PASCAL, which would allow his program to run on an unmodified system. Apple took longer than promised to deliver, but, on a positive note, the delay gave them more time to polish the program. Once 16K expansions became more widely available, Woodhead used it as a disk cache, substantially speeding up loading times.

When Woodhead got around to showing the game to Norman Sirotek, his partner wasn't impressed. "I remember late one evening telling Bob Woodhead to forget the new game and put his efforts into something worthwhile, like a business package. I said nobody wants or needs the game. Bob looked straight at me and said I was wrong and went back

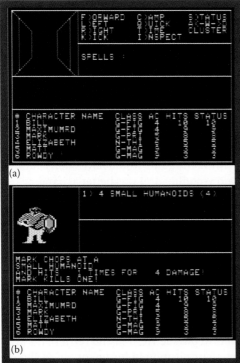

(a)

(b)

Figure 16.3   Shown here are two scenes from the Apple II version of *Wizardry*: (a) exploration mode and (b) one of the countless combat sequences.

to work."[3] Norman's younger brother, Robert, was much more excited. As the man responsible for marketing, he'd successfully made a case for shipping the game in a box rather than the plastic bags that were customary at the time—a first for the industry, according to Robert.[4]

The resulting product, *Wizardry: Proving Grounds of the Mad Overlord*, was an overnight sensation when it was finally released in September of 1981 (see Figure 16.3a and b). The back of the box quotes Neil Shapiro of *Popular Mechanics*, who called it "amazing," and Margot Tommervik of *Softalk Magazine*, who said, "It's not a game. It's a place." At first, they were selling their products by mail order, and the phone wouldn't stop ringing. Initially, they were shipping out a hundred disks per day; then five hundred—this game that no one wanted or needed was now rivaling

VisiCalc's sales! By 1984, they had sold more than 200,000 copies.[5] Sir-Tech eventually ported the game to the Macintosh, DOS, Commodore 64, and even the NES (see Figure 16.4). After their success with the first game, Woodhead and Greenberg developed three more scenarios using the same engine. The first two let you import your party from the previous games, but the third was an unforgiving reboot in which you played as Werdna.

Some have argued that *Wizardry* is, in significant ways, a clone of *Oubliette*. Chester Bolingbroke, aka the "CRPG Addict," though hesitant to make that claim himself, points out 11 of the more obvious commonalities between the two programs. The following are five of the more blatant ones:

- The overall structure of the game, with a castle and shops on top and a first-person wireframe dungeon below

---

[3] Salmons, Jim. "Exec Sir-Tech: Wizzing to the Top." *Softalk*, August 1982: 32–35.

[4] Sirotek, Robert, interview by Matt Barton. *Matt Chat 244: Robert Sirotek on the Origins of Sir-Tech* (June 8, 2014).

[5] Bateman, Selby. "Is a Picture Worth a Thousand Words?" *Compute!*, October 1984: 32.

- The specific types of shops and visitable locations on the castle level

- The system of rolling attributes first and then determining the character class

Figure 16.4   *Wizardry* running on the NES. The series became wildly popular in Japan, where it continues to this day.

- Some identical spell names and root syllables, identical spell effects, and the basic spell "slot" system

- The traps associated with chests found in the dungeon, which are exactly the same in both games[6]

However, Bolingbroke points out as well that there are substantial differences between the two games, most notably the switch from multiplayer to single player. "It seems clear to me that the *Wizardry* developers started with an *Oubliette* paradigm and worked from there," but calls it "slightly unforgivable" that the developers failed to acknowledge their inspiration in the game or manual.

Corey Cole, a co-designer of *Quest for Glory* and former PLATO user, responded to these criticisms in the comments on the post by pointing out that "copying an existing game or tool, then modifying it, was both common hacker practice and an excellent way to learn programming back in the 1970s." Furthermore, the source code couldn't have been directly copied, since the language and platform in question were totally different systems.

I contacted Jim Schwaiger and his fellow *Oubliette* authors to get their views on the matter. Incidentally, they released a commercial version of *Oubliette* for the Commodore 64 in 1983, and, more recently, an iOS and Android version in 2012 based on that version's source code. Schwaiger claims that he "only examined *Wizardry* on the Apple II once—spent just a short time, certainly less than 30 minutes, but could not find any meaningful difference with *Oubliette*." He even argues that the most distinguishing factor—single player rather than multiplayer—was a "necessary concession to reality rather than a deliberate failure to copy."

I agree with Cole. Many games in this book were commercial adaptations of free games running on mainframes. It makes no more sense to deride Sir-Tech than it would

---

[6] Bolingbroke, Chester. "Game 12: Oubliette (1977)." *The CRPG Addict.* October 17, 2013. http://crpgaddict.blogspot .com/2013/10/game-12-oubliette-1977.html (accessed May 27, 2015).

to blast Bushnell for ripping off *Spacewar!* or Infocom for plagiarizing *Colossal Cave Adventure*. Furthermore, focusing too much on what they borrowed distracts us from their real contributions. After all, adapting a game intended for a powerful mainframe computer for a humble home computer is no small feat, and as cool as PLATO and other mainframes were, only a privileged few had access. Atari, Infocom, and Sir-Tech helped bring these joys to the masses.

Wizardry in its turn inspired plenty of other games, including *The Bard's Tale* (1985), *Might and Magic* (1986), *Dungeon Master* (1987), *Pool of Radiance* (1988), and *Ultima Underworld* (1991) just to name a few. Though these games had much better audiovisuals and added their own innovations, you can still see the tropes of mapping out dungeons shown in first-person perspective, grinding out levels, grabbing loot, and dispatching wave after wave of randomly encountered enemies.

The original designers, Woodhead and Greenberg, left the series after *Wizardry V*, handing the reins over to David W. Bradley. Bradley oversaw a significant revamping of the engine for *Wizardry VI: Bane of the Cosmic Forge* (1990), which brought a much-needed overhaul to the aging interface. The last *Wizardry* game published by Sir-Tech was 2001's *Wizardry 8*, designed by Brenda Romero.

The series has remained commercially relevant in Japan, where it was localized in the early 1980s, and the series became nearly (if not more) influential there than it was in the United States. Chris Kohler notes that Yuji Horii and Koichi Nakamura were avid fans, and incorporated several of its core concepts into their hit *Dragon Quest* series.[7]

In short, *Wizardry* and Sir-Tech played a key role in bringing the CRPG to the masses. Even if the game owes more to *Oubliette* than its developers seem willing to admit, I still commend them for introducing so many of us to the dungeon crawler. I spent many happy weeks making my way through this game on my Commodore 64, even though I had better-looking games I could have played instead. *Wizardry* is dungeon crawling stripped down to its core essence, and for some of us, that's all we ever really needed.

16.1 Playing *Wizardry* Today

Playing *Wizardry* is as simple as going to http://www.virtualapple.org, where you can play it in a browser or download the ROMs for use in an emulator. I recommend the latter option, since you'll likely want to save your game (and possibly cheat by making backup copies of your disks!). You might also enjoy the NES version, which has better audiovisuals (including a nice musical score) and an interface designed for a controller.

---

[7] Kohler, Chris. *Power Up: How Japanese Video Games Gave the World an Extra Life*. Indianapolis: Brady Games, 2005: 86.

Chapter 17

Ultima: The Virtues of an Avatar

Around the same time that Woodhead and Greenberg were in New York devising plans for their *Wizardry* game, on the West Coast, a teenager named Richard Garriott was laying the groundwork for the greatest of all the computer role-playing game (CRPG) series: *Ultima*. The impact and legacy of his epic series would shape the computer game industry for nearly two decades, and make Richard "Lord British" Garriott one of the most influential developers and publishers of all time (see Figure 17.1).

But no one, particularly not Garriott himself, could have known any of this in 1979. Garriott was raised in Nassau Bay, Texas, a tiny city of 4000 near Galveston Bay. His father, Owen K. Garriott, was an astronaut who worked at the Lyndon B. Johnson Space Center there. Naturally, having an astronaut for a dad made a career in science and technology almost inevitable, but Garriott's dream wasn't to become an astronaut (though he'd later travel to space as a tourist). Instead, Garriott became fascinated with another kind of flight—the flight of fantasy, and the technology and potential of immersion.

"Really, what the root of it all is," said Garriott, "is Halloween. When I was a young trick-or-treater, going around the block, I went to one of my neighbor's houses. This woman had decorated the entry hall of her home like a witch's chamber, and she herself was in costume. She had all kinds of high-tech, electrostatic shock machines that you literally got shocked by as you came in ... It was the closest thing to being immersed in a virtual world of scariness that I'd ever seen. I began immediately after that to do my own—not just Halloween, but year round. Easter, Fourth of July—didn't matter. I was building these interactive things for my friends to come over and go through. This pre-dates *Dungeons & Dragons* and computers, but there was already live action role-playing at my house."[1]

Garriott next discovered the great classic fantasies of J.R.R. Tolkien and C.S. Lewis, which he read and reread endlessly. When *Dungeons & Dragons* debuted in 1974, Garriott was one of its first adopters. "What was interesting about the early game," said Garriott, "was that the rules were almost irrelevant. What it was, really, was a group of people sitting around the table having interactive narrative. When the game master would describe a scenario, as long as the participants described something clever, funny, or

---

[1] Garriott, Richard, interview by Matt Barton. *Matt Chat 196: Lord British on Ultima and Akalabeth* (June 2, 2013).

Figure 17.1   Richard "Lord British" Garriott in 2014.

interesting in some way—sure, it'd work … The only reason it would be fun is if you had a really great storyteller at the helm, and highly participating players on the other side." As the rules became more sophisticated and integral to the experience, Garriott began to lose interest.

Meanwhile, Garriott had discovered computers—specifically, the Teletype machine at Clear Creek High School. "I wrote 28 games on that Teletype that I called *D&D 1-28* before getting ahold of my first Apple." Indeed, Garriott's prowess was so obvious to his teachers that they let him create his own programming course. After he started work at a computer store, ComputerLand, he saved up to buy one of their shiny new Apple II computers in 1979. He rewrote the latest version of his *D&D* game, which became his first-ever commercial product, *Akalabeth: World of Doom* (see Figure 17.2). Like *Wizardry*, it featured an overhead world view, first-person dungeon perspective, wireframe graphics, and monsters rendered in the Apple II's "Hi-Res" graphics. The whole Garriott household had gotten involved, with his mother helping out with the artwork and his father with the math.[2]

Garriott had programmed his game in Applesoft BASIC, but software for personal computers was so scarce that a game like *Akalabeth* had solid commercial potential. Software was typically sold in local, privately owned computer hobby shops, copied by the developers themselves, and packaged in plastic baggies with amateurish inserts. Such was the case for *Akalabeth*. Garriott spent $200 on the plastic zipper storage bags and cover sheets, a serendipitous investment to say the least.

One of the eight copies he sold ended up on the desk of California Pacific Computer Company, the same company who'd published some of Bill Budge's early work. Garriott idolized Budge, and hoped to meet him. The publisher flew Garriott from Texas to California, where they worked out a deal for wider distribution. Although he didn't get to meet Budge, his deal with California Pacific was a success, providing him with $150,000 in royalties and the confidence to pursue a more ambitious goal.[3] He'd learned a great deal developing *Akalabeth* and felt he now had the experience and knowledge necessary to make a truly commercial-quality project: *Ultima*.

Garriott had struggled with the stiff memory limitations of the Apple II, particularly with the top-down overland view that showed when the player wasn't in a dungeon. The solution to this problem was "tile graphics." Tile graphics save memory by assembling scenes from a common set of tiles. Garriott had worked with a similar setup during his

---

[2] King, Brad, and John Borland. *Dungeons and Dreamers: The Rise of Computer Game Culture from Geek to Chic.* Emeryville, CA: McGraw-Hill/Osborne, 2003: 36.

[3] See footnote 2, p. 43.

Teletype days, when he'd built levels with asterisks and other characters. However, Garriott lacked the advanced programming techniques he'd need to implement something more ambitious on the Apple II. Fortunately for him, he'd made friends with a coworker at ComputerLand named Ken "Sir Kenneth" Arnold, a teenager like himself. Arnold knew enough assembly language to write a subroutine for tile

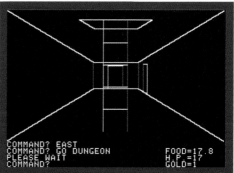

Figure 17.2 Garriott's first commercial product, *Akalabeth*, sold much better than he expected given his lack of training and experience. He determined that his future products would be much more professional.

graphics. Code in hand, Garriott went to work designing tiles and building levels on a much larger scale than before.

The tiled overhead view was used whenever the main character (known after the fourth game as "The Avatar") roams outside or in towns or villages (see Figure 17.3). The new graphics routine enabled a much vaster gameworld, and now players could see much more of it on-screen. However, when the character descends into a dungeon, the perspective shifted to the first-person, wireframe mode of *Akalabeth*; Garriott had recycled these routines from his earlier endeavor.

Garriott added plenty of new features, including quests and a scripted ending. There was also a clearly defined mission: destroy the evil wizard Mondain, hated ruler of Sosaria. Achieving this goal required traveling back in time to destroy a gem that granted the wizard immortality. Naturally, traveling back in time wasn't easy—in fact, the player had to travel to outer space! The fact that the game included both fantasy and sci-fi elements generated a great deal of buzz; it was one of the most ambitious games players had ever seen.

The underlying role-playing mechanics were fairly simple. Players were given 90 points to distribute among six stats (strength, agility, stamina, charisma, wisdom, and intelligence) and could play as a fighter, cleric, wizard, or thief. There were also four races to choose from, one of which was hobbits—an obvious allusion to J.R.R. Tolkien's famous fantasy works.

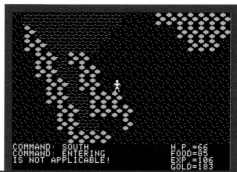

Figure 17.3 *Ultima* employed "tile-based graphics," which allowed him to make large, varied maps with very limited memory.

Ultima and its sequels not only set sales records but helped expand the market from a cottage industry into the multibillion dollar juggernaut it is today. Garriott's determination to up the ante with each new *Ultima* earned him a reputation as one of the world's best game developers, and his eagerness to take full advantage of the latest hardware and programming routines kept him (and fans) on the cutting edge of technology. In time, gamers and critics would look to the latest *Ultima* as a paradigm shift; not just a new installment in the series but the next stage of gaming itself.

However, Garriott's ambition and perfectionism occasionally brought him into conflict with publishers. After his publisher, California Pacific Computer, went bankrupt, Garriott recovered the rights to his series. By this point, *Ultima* was a well-respected brand, and Garriott was choosy—he wanted to find a publisher who'd agree to let him not only publish his games in nice boxes (rather than in cheap plastic bags) but also include a cloth map of the land. He'd gotten this strange idea from the movie *Time Bandits* (1981). Only Sierra On-Line was willing to agree to his demands, and published *Ultima II: The Revenge of the Enchantress* in 1982.

The new game offered several key improvements, most notably the option to talk to other characters. It was, like the earlier game, an immense undertaking that included both fantasy and sci-fi elements. It also marked a major leap for Garriott as a programmer, since he was now programming in assembly language rather than BASIC. The more advanced language allowed for more efficient routines and smoother gameplay. In any case, it says something about Garriott's personality that he risked creating a new game with a difficult language he hadn't yet mastered; indeed, he was learning as he went.

Ultima II was successful, but Garriott had become disillusioned with Sierra. One problem concerned the IBM PC port of *Ultima II*, which hadn't been discussed in his contract since that platform didn't exist (or at least wasn't viable) when it was drafted. Garriott thought Sierra was bilking him on royalties. Another problem was that Sierra felt its licensing agreement extended to making new *Ultima* games, even if Garriott wasn't involved in their production.

With yet another hit game under his belt, Garriott felt confident enough to found his own publishing company. Together with his father, brother, and a friend named Chuck "Chuckles" Bueche, he founded Origin Systems in 1983. In addition to their flagship *Ultima* series, Origin would also publish Chuckles' *Autoduel* (1985), Chris Roberts' *Wing Commander* (1990), and Paul Neurath's *Ultima Underworld* (1992). But that was all in the future. For now, the new company's fate rested solely on the success or failure of a single product. That product was *Ultima III: Exodus*, and Garriott was more determined than ever before to prove he had the right stuff.

By this time, Garriott had mastered assembly language and was ready to put his freshly honed skills to the ultimate test. *Ultima III*, which became the company's flagship product, introduced a number of bold changes, including the ability to create and control a party of adventurers rather than the lone Avatar. In an interview with Shay Addams, Garriott acknowledged that he was inspired by *Wizardry*.[4] Combat was also

---

[4] Addams, Shay. *The Office Book of Ultima.* Greensboro, NC: Compute! Books, 1990.

altered, now adopting a turn-based system with time limits; if players didn't move fast enough, the monsters got a free swing at the characters. This model may have served as the inspiration for the Active Time Battle system of the *Final Fantasy* series. There were also loads of new magical spells and weapons, including ranged weapons like bows. The dungeons, which were now central to the mission, had been upgraded from the monochromatic wireframe to solid color.

Finally, Garriott incorporated a dynamic musical score that took advantage of Sweet Micro System's new Mockingboard card for the Apple II. The Mockingboard compensated greatly for the Apple's limited sound capabilities and is a good example of how Garriott pushed the industry forward by catering to high-end, rather than just the far more numerous low-end gamers.

Exodus was a triumph for the series and a bestseller for Origin. It established the company as a world famous developer and Lord British as a master craftsman of CRPGs. The game was ported to most of the popular platforms of the era, including the Nintendo Entertainment System, and is easily the best of the early series. *GameSpot* selected it as one of its "15 Most Influential Games of All Time," citing it as the inspiration for later hits such as BioWare's *Baldur's Gate* (1998; Apple Macintosh, PC).

The immense popularity of *Exodus* had made Garriott a powerful and influential figure in the industry, but he didn't necessarily feel giddy. Indeed, he began to feel guilty about his previous work. A letter from a concerned parent convinced him that most games, including his own, did little to promote good, ethical conduct in players, instead rewarding them for pillaging and plundering. As one of the game industry's most powerful individuals, Garriott now believed he had a responsibility not just to entertain his fans but also to enlighten them.

The result of Garriott's soul-searching was *Ultima IV: Quest of the Avatar*, a 1985 release that debuted the "Age of Enlightenment," a trilogy of games exploring morality and society. The gameplay was reworked substantially from the previous game, and the difference was visible immediately. Rather than create a character or party based on stats, players were asked a series of questions pertaining to moral dilemmas. The system was based on eight virtues: humility, sacrifice, compassion, justice, valor, spirituality, honor, and honesty, each of which was linked to a particular character class. The goal was to let the player make a character that would truly conform to his or her own outlook and moral values, as well as take the game well away from its roots in "hack and slash" (see Figure 17.4).

The manual speaks of the game as a "search for a new standard, a new vision of life for which our people may strive,"

Figure 17.4 *Ultima IV* was a critical breakthrough for the series, introducing a highly influential "moral" component to the gameplay.

in short, a game that would make players into better people. This spiritual aspect of the game was reinforced with another feelie, this time a small metal ankh.

Quest of the Avatar was another massive hit for Origin, outselling its predecessor and reaping high praise from critics. It remains the favorite of many longtime fans of the series, and has shown up on plenty of "all time" lists; *Computer Gaming World* voted it the #2 game of all time in 1996, and 1Up.com named it as the 21st of its "Essential 50" list.

After *Quest of the Avatar*, Garriott set himself to converting the earlier games into full assembly language, updating the audiovisuals and releasing the set as Ultima Trilogy in 1987. The timing was perfect for such a compilation, since the countless thousands who had been introduced to the series with *Quest of the Avatar* now had a convenient way to familiarize themselves with its backstory. The trilogy sold exceptionally well.

The next game in the series, *Ultima V: Warriors of Destiny* (1988), was the last developed on the venerable old Apple II platform, and also the last time Garriott himself did a significant amount of coding. Whereas the first game had been about the Avatar's own quest for virtue, this game put players in a more ambiguous position: What happens when the state tries to force its own interpretations of moral virtues on its people? As players explored the world, they found that some bad people prospered and some good people were condemned; the lines between good and evil were often quite blurry.

The sixth game was *The False Prophet*. The moral theme this time is racism and xenophobia, and again players were faced with tough decisions with disturbing consequences. It was the best-looking game of the series so far, with 2048 different tiles in 256 colors. It also had support for the Roland and AdLib sound cards. As with his support of the Mockingboard earlier, here Garriott was a driving force behind the wider adoption of these graphic and audio standards. Countless gamers were more than willing to upgrade or purchase new systems to play the new *Ultima* game in its full glory.

Garriott's finest moment may well have been *Ultima VII: The Black Gate*, released in 1992 for the PC. The game's primary feature is a huge and robust interactive world, which was far more detailed than anything gamers had experienced before. Players could, for instance, plant seeds, grow wheat, bake it into bread, and sell it at the market; these diversions were compelling enough to make some players forget all about the main story and quest line! It also took advantage of the mouse, which had by that time begun to take root among PC users. Mouse control was perhaps a necessity given the alterations to the gameplay, which was now in real time; fast, precise control was essential. Garriott claims to have been inspired by *Times of Lore*, a game by Chris Roberts that Origin published in 1988, and FTL's *Dungeon Master* (1987; Apple IIgs, Atari ST, Commodore Amiga, etc.), a pioneering real-time game with first-person perspective and full-color three-dimensional (3D) graphics.[4] Though Origin spent a million dollars developing the game, they were back in black the first day it was released.

Ultima VII was a very tough act to follow, even for Garriott. *Ultima VIII: Pagan*, a 1994 game for PC, was really the first major misstep for the series. Garriott had signed on with Electronic Arts to publish the game, a deal he regretted after they harried him to rush the game through production. The gameplay is a sharply different affair than previous games, involving a great deal of running, jumping, and fast-paced combat, aspects that led some to mock the game as "Super Avatar Bros." While these sorts of games were becoming very popular on consoles, many found them out of place in *Ultima*. Peter Olafson of *Compute!* Magazine seemed upset that "your pals Iolo, Dupre,

Figure 17.5   *Ultima IX: Ascension* had fully rendered 3D graphics and looked awesome. However, it wasn't the game many longtime *Ultima* fans had longed for. (Photo courtesy of Good Old Games.)

and Shamino are nowhere to be found," though he applauded the enhanced graphics and wondered "how far are we from virtual-reality *Ultima*?"[5] Like most *Ultima* games, *Pagan* pushed the era's hardware to the limits; one reviewer called it "demonic when it comes to system resources."[6]

If *Pagan* disappointed some fans, the last *Ultima* game, *Ascension*, appalled nearly all of them (see Figure 17.5). Although Garriott had been touting the game for months, a long and drama-filled development cycle had done its damage. Perhaps still smarting from the sharp criticism he received for *Pagan*, Lord British seems to have become shaken and indecisive, forcing the code through four different versions. We should also keep in mind that *Ultima Online* was in production at this time, and Garriott may have struggled to stay on top of the two vastly different projects.

Ascension was fully 3D rendered in third-person perspective and involved quite a few action/reflex sequences. Greg Kasavin's review for *GameSpot* called it "both an epic and a farce," admiring its ambition but lamenting the poor implementation, which was fraught with bugs.[7] IGN's Trent C. Ward, a longtime fan of the series, faced the unpleasant task of reviewing a game he felt was "nearly unplayable," describing himself as "nearly paralyzed with disappointment over the way the last chapter turned out."[8] The criticisms were many, but the consensus was that Lord British had lost his way. It was a sad ending for this magnificent and influential series.

---

[5]   Olafson, Peter. "AD&D, R.I.P.?" *Compute!*, June 1994: 86.

[6]   Yee, Bernard. "Ultima VIII: Pagan." *PC Mag*, September 13, 1994: 471.

[7]   Kasavin, Greg. "Ultima IX: Ascension." *GameSpot*. December 10, 1999. http://www.gamespot.com/pc/rpg/ultima9ascension /review.html (accessed Nov 10, 2006).

[8]   Ward, Trent C. "Ultima IX: Ascension." *IGN*. December 10, 1999. http://www.ign.com/articles/1999/12/11/ultima-ix-ascension (accessed May 28, 2015).

Ultima's influence on the game industry is immense, as the size of this chapter attests. The games were discussed at great length in almost every gaming magazine of the day, and ports found their way onto virtually every viable platform. Compiling a list of commercial games that have been inspired by *Ultima* is a formidable task. Some, such as DieCom Production's *Gates of Delirium* (1980) for the Radio Shack Color Computer, are shameless and insipid clones. Others, such as SSI's *Questron* (1984) were authorized games based on Garriott's engine. *Questron* was admired for its smooth gameplay and accessibility to novices. This series led to SSI's later and more successful *Phantasie* (starting 1985), *Wizard's Crown* (starting 1985), and the "Gold Box" (1988) series of CRPGs.

Perhaps the influence of the *Ultima* series is most evident in Japan, where it inspired the countless games featuring top-down perspective, randomized combat, and roaming NPCs who must be found and interrogated. According to Koichi Nakamura, his friend Yuji Horii was a fan of *Ultima*, whereas he preferred *Wizardry*. "So both of us said, why don't we create a role-playing game? We were really into these role-playing games at the time. And that was how *Dragon Quest* started."[9] *Wizardry* and *Ultima*, blended together and simplified for the console audience, proved the right product at the right time. *Dragon Quest* (also known as *Dragon Warrior*) was a huge hit, eventually selling more than 2 million copies in Japan and becoming a "cult hit" when it was exported to America.[10]

The fan base remains active and committed to keeping the *Ultima* games playable and relevant for modern gamers. The site *Ultima Codex* tracks a myriad of these projects. One of these is *Ultima IX: Redemption*, an effort by a group called Titans of Ether that hopes to "live up to the *Ultima* greatness that the original game ... failed to achieve. It will feature total freedom in moral decision-making (which the original didn't grant), as well as multiple endings." It's being built with the *Morrowind: The Elder Scrolls* engine. An older project called *Exult* is a "cross-platform reworking of *Ultima 7*" for modern systems, including Android and Linux.

In 2015, Garriott and his new company Portalarium launched a Kickstarter project for a game called *Shroud of the Avatar: Forsaken Virtues*, which managed to raise nearly 2 million dollars. I'll have more to say about this project when we discuss *Ultima Online* in Chapter 36.

17.1 **Playing *Ultima* Today**

Once again, our friends at Virtual Apple II have made it quite easy to play *Ultima* in your browser. Just visit http://www.virtualapple.org and look for their *Ultima I* page. Of course, you'll probably want to download the disk images and run them in an emulator if you're serious about completing the game.

---

[9] Parish, Jeremy. "Koichi Nakamura Interview: On the Birth of the Console RPG." *1up.com*. August 7, 2012. http://www.1up .com/features/koichi-nakamura-interview-console-rpg (accessed May 29, 2015).

[10] Kohler, Chris. *Power Up: How Japanese Video Games Gave the World an Extra Life*. Indianapolis: Brady Games, 2005: 87, 223.

A better option still is to purchase the *Ultima* trilogy from GOG, which comes with PDF scans of the manuals, clue books, and maps. Pick it up for Windows or Mac at http://www.gog.com/game/ultima_1_2_3. You can find the other *Ultima* games there as well, all set up and ready to run on a modern system. I'd also suggest checking out the *Ultima Codex* site at http://ultimacodex.com/. Besides information about the games themselves, there are interviews, fan projects, news, wikis, forums, and more.

Part III
The Early Majority

And now we come to the third of Rogers' category of adopters: the "early majority." These were the folks who'd shown little interest in *Pong*, found all that *Pac-Man* nonsense childish, and would never have dreamed of buying one of those so-called home computers or an Atari 2600. These were the folks smugly saying "told you so" after the Great Video Game Crash of 1983.

This cynical attitude was keenest among American retailers, who had zero interest in enduring another gruesome loss on the video game "fad" or flooding their warehouses with unwanted game cartridges.

To put it simply, the rusting pipes of the American game industry were clogged so tight with crap that nothing was going in or coming out. Thankfully, a plumber was on the way.

By far, the most important event of this generation was the launch of the Nintendo Entertainment System (NES), a Japanese import that not only put an end to the Great Video Game Crash of 1983 but also expanded the industry far beyond Atari and Activision's wildest dreams. Nintendo wouldn't make the same mistakes that doomed their predecessors, and their vicious stranglehold over the industry wouldn't be seriously threatened until the arrival of Sony's PlayStation a decade later. In fact, if I had to divide the whole history of video games into just two big periods, I'd call one B.M. and the other A.M.—before and after Mario!

Figure PIII.1   *Defender of the Crown* was the first of many Hollywood-inspired productions by Cinemaware. The Amiga version was one of the earliest games to demonstrate the possibilities afforded by its advanced hardware.

The NES's hardware and games may seem primitive today, but they were a giant leap from the precrash consoles of the early 1980s. The increase in memory and the meticulous programming of games such as *Super Mario Bros.* and *The Legend of Zelda* began to shift the role of video games in mainstream culture.

Gone were the days when a console's claim to fame was how well it could approximate an arcade hit. Now, console gaming was growing into its own, with much longer games featuring memorable characters and increasingly detailed stories. Pretty soon, every family with a disposal income just had to have a "Nintendo" in the house. Poorer families needn't despair, either—they could always rent one from their local Blockbuster!

A few years later, Nintendo revolutionized the industry yet again with its Game Boy handheld, which many people bought just to play the greatest game ever to emerge from Russia, if not the greatest game, period—Alexey Pajitnov's *Tetris*. Once again, these units appealed to a diverse audience, not just nerdy young men or boys.

This period also sees the last gasp—or perhaps I should say the last great punch—of the arcade industry. As computers and consoles evolved to rival and then surpass arcade machines, the coin-operated business dried up. However, in 1991, a game called *Street Fighter II* provided the arcade with an extra life, turning it into a virtual arena for teenagers hoping to prove themselves in vicious one-on-one combat. An explosion of sequels, spin-offs, clones, and rip-offs followed, and the "competitive fighting game" genre was born.

These were also great times for computer gamers. New machines such as the Commodore Amiga, Atari ST, and Apple Macintosh offered substantially more power than their predecessors. During this period, we find such vital games as Cinemaware's *Defender of the Crown* (1986) (see Figure PIII.1), FTL's *Dungeon Master* (1987), Interplay's *Wasteland* (1987), SSI's *Pool of Radiance* (1988), Jordan Mechner's *Prince of Persia* (1989), and Will Wright's *SimCity* (1989). By the end of this period, MS-DOS would be the undisputed champion of home computing platforms, with the Macintosh a distant second.

Chapter 18

Super Mario Bros.: Mario and the Mushroom Kingdom

Whenever I try to think of someone outside the video games industry to compare to Mario's creator Shigeru Miyamoto, I inevitably come to Walt Disney. Both were artists by training, and relatively shy men, shunning the spotlight despite their staggering successes. Both possessed genuine affection for "children of all ages" and committed themselves to creating virtual worlds for them to savor, albeit by very different means. But more to the point of this chapter, if Mario is the Mickey Mouse of video games, then *Super Mario Bros.* is it's "Steamboat Willie."

Bear with me a moment.

Steamboat Willie was the classic short that not only debuted two of the most famous cartoon characters of all time (Mickey and Minnie) but also was a remarkable technological achievement—the first cartoon with synchronized sound. This amazing feat was but a small step for Disney; he'd barely embarked on the glorious career that would make him the greatest animator of all time. By the end of it, Steamboat Willie was positively archaic, with its grainy black and white footage, simplistic (even incoherent) narrative, and an all-too-brief 7-min running time.

Yet, when Disney first showed Steamboat Willie to an audience in 1928, the "effect was nothing less than electric. They responded almost instinctively to this union of sound and motion ... It was terrible, but it was wonderful! And it was something new!"[1] Nearly 60 years later in 1985, when American children played *Super Mario Bros.* for the first time, their reactions were identical. But I would add one more exclamation point: "It was fun!" For *Super Mario Bros.* was more than just an animation. It was animation you could control. And that has made all the difference.

Walt Disney and Shigeru Miyamoto were artists of a special breed, men who, with pencils or pixels, showed the rest of us what'd they'd seen on blank paper and an empty screen. But Disney put aside his brush to build a Magic Kingdom of bricks and mortar, concrete, and steel. Miyamoto's dreams led to equally imaginative worlds enjoyed by

---

[1] Maltin, Leonard. *Of Mice and Magic: A History of American Animated Cartoons.* New York: New American Library, 1987.

countless children of all ages—but not a single one of them ever had to stand in line (see Figure 18.1).

Mario has sold more games and consoles than any of his rivals, and pretty much single-handedly resurrected the video game industry, or at the very least the console, from the ashes of the Great Video Game Crash. But I think you get the point: Miyamoto was a big deal, maybe bigger than Disney. But unlike the animator, who happily took credit for his works, Miyamoto preferred to think of himself as an employee of Nintendo. Much of this is cultural, as Nick Paumgarten explained in an expose of Miyamoto for *The New Yorker*:

Figure 18.1   *Super Mario Bros.* made Miyamoto an international superstar among game developers.

The corporate ethos in Japan, and especially at Nintendo, is self-effacing; the humility that has kept Miyamoto at the company for three decades, rather than in, say, Silicon Valley seeking his billions, also governs the apportionment of credit. Miyamoto has been a superstar in the gaming world for more than two decades, but neither he nor the company seems inclined to exploit his stardom. They contend that the development of a game or a game console is a collaborative effort—that it is indecorous to single out any one contributor to the exclusion of the others. Miyamoto is also guarded about his private life. The fact that anyone would be curious about it baffles him.[2]

Well before he began work on *Super Mario Bros.*, Miyamoto had already established his reputation with *Donkey Kong*, the megahit arcade game that put Nintendo's name on the radar (see Chapter 9). But the games Miyamoto designed after it, *Popeye* (1982), *Donkey Kong Junior* (1982), *Donkey Kong 3* (1983), and even Mario's debut title, *Mario Bros.* (1983), weren't as successful. Perhaps he'd peaked. Or, maybe Miyamoto was only perfecting his craft, testing out new innovations and refining his techniques in preparation for something truly extraordinary.

The original *Mario Bros.* is a case in point. "Jumpman" from *Donkey Kong* was given a new occupation as a plumber and officially named Mario. At Yokoi's suggestion, Mario was given a brother, Luigi, who was controlled by a second player. Luigi

---

2   Paumgarten, Nick. "Master of Play." *The New Yorker*. December 20, 2010. http://www.newyorker.com/magazine/2010/12/20/master-of-play (accessed June 17, 2015).

could either collaborate with his brother or compete with him, sabotaging his efforts by bumping or shoving him into enemies.

The level design consisted of a number of platforms with pipes at the top and bottom on each side, from which the game's turtle-like "shellcreeper" adversaries entered and exited. Mario and/or Luigi had to defeat each wave of these creatures by first bopping them from below the platform they're walking across, causing them to temporarily flip over on their backs, helpless. Then, Mario or Luigi could stomp on them from above. It was a fun, even if illogical, gameplay mechanic. Later stages introduced tougher enemies and other perils. Make no mistake, *Mario Bros.* is not nearly the game its successor would be, but you can clearly see the painstaking attention to even the minutest details. The distinctive green color of the pipes, for example, was the result of careful experiments; no design or aesthetic decision was taken lightly.

Japan had not suffered the same retail catastrophe that had all but destroyed the American industry, and in 1983, Nintendo successfully introduced an advanced console there called the Family Computer Disk System, or Famicom for short. After selling half a million of these systems in Japan, they decided to try their luck in America.[3]

After a deal with Atari fell through, greatly angering Yamauchi, Nintendo's formidable president, they decided to go it alone and devised a cunning two-pronged strategy. The first prong was a toy robot named R.O.B., and a light gun called the Zapper. These accoutrements allowed Nintendo to market the device as a gee-whiz electronic toy like the highly successful *Simon* or *Electronic Battleship* games and distance itself from the dread category of "video game console."

The second prong was equally unprecedented: a money-back guarantee. Nintendo of America's president, Arakawa, had proposed this risky, and frankly desperate, scheme to further allay the fears of retailers. Yamauchi—Arakawa's son-in-law—could see no reason for it, but Arakawa was convinced it was the only way. The department stores who signed on to sell the NES now were committing only to floor space. Even this degree of risk was too much for some, but others signed on. The die was cast.

Arakawa's plan worked, but not as well as he'd hoped. The NES only sold a modest 50,000 units.[4] The problem was likely the games—neither *Duck Hunt* nor *Gyromite*, which were bundled with the system, nor the other 15 games available at launch, were sufficient reason to get excited about the system. When Arakawa picked up the phone to call his father-in-law boss, the imperialistic Yamauchi, he must surely have experienced déjà vu.

Once again, Yamauchi tapped his star designer, Miyamoto, to save his American branch.

The design of *Super Mario Bros.* was a rather organic process. Miyamoto was joined by Takashi Tezuka, a fellow designer, who'd often sit beside him drawing on the same maps.[5]

---

[3] Kent, Steve L. *The Ultimate History of Video Games: From Pong to Pokémon and Beyond: the Story Behind the Craze that Touched Our Lives and Changed the World.* Rocklin, CA: Prima Pub., 2001: 280.

[4] See footnote 3, p. 298.

[5] deWinter, Jennifer. *Shigeru Miyamoto: Super Mario Bros., Donkey Kong, The Legend of Zelda.* New York: Bloomsbury Academic, 2015.

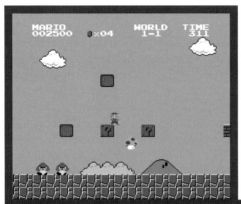

Figure 18.2   *Super Mario Bros.* was an effective demonstration of the NES's technology as well as Miyamoto's skill as a designer.

The pieces gradually fell together after a great deal of brainstorming and trial-and-error. Miyamoto had been trying to find something innovative to do with platform games, which had exploded in popularity since *Donkey Kong* and the original *Mario Bros.* One of these tests involved a double-sized Mario, which was fun to control, but they found out it was more fun if he started off small. Miyamoto claims that *Alice in Wonderland* had nothing to do with his

decision to use a mushroom as the power-up to trigger this transformation—"There has always been a relationship between mushrooms and magical realms," he claimed.[6] In any case, mushrooms were a major theme of the setting, which had moved from the sewers of New York City to a fantasy land called "The Mushroom Kingdom."

Though 4 years had passed since *Donkey Kong*, the graphics technology of the NES still necessitated significant compromises; therefore, Mario kept his hat, overalls, and mustache from the earlier game (see Figure 18.2).

A larger innovation was a scrolling screen, rather than a fixed screen. Miyamoto was familiar with the technique from one of his earlier projects, *Excitebike*, a racing game. Allowing the screen to scroll as Mario or Luigi advanced through the levels allowed for much more detailed and elaborate level designs. Instead of the black background customary at the time, Miyamoto chose bright colors to suggest different environments (bright blue for outdoors; black for underground, and so on) (see Figure 18.3).

Several elements from the original *Mario Bros.* were repurposed or adapted to great effect in *Super Mario Bros.* For example, jumping up to hit a block could now not only destroy or harm an enemy walking on top of it, but the block itself might be destroyed—occasionally revealing a hidden treasure (gold coins) or power-up. The shellcreepers of the game were replaced with the "Koopa Troopas." When Mario or Luigi stomped on them, they retreated into their shells, which could then be kicked or carried to use as a weapon.

The controls were straightforward and simple to master, thanks mostly to the NES controller. It had a directional pad (D-pad) on the left and two buttons, A and B. Each button had a main function and a secondary function, depending on the environment or status of the character. For instance, the A button was used for jumping on most levels, but for bobbing up while swimming. Holding down B while Mario was running sped

---

[6] Iwata, Satoru. "New Super Mario Bros: Volume 1." *Iwata Asks.* n.d. http://iwataasks.nintendo.com/interviews/#/wii/nsmb/0/0 (accessed June 3, 2015).

him up, but it also shot fireballs if he had a fire flower power-up. It was a wonderfully intuitive scheme that was eminently suited to the NES controller.

For a story, Miyamoto returned to the "rescue the damsel in distress" theme of *Donkey Kong*, sending the brothers on a quest to save Princess Toadstool[7] from Bowser, an evil turtle-like being.[8] Bowser and his Koopas turned the denizens of the

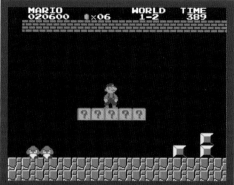

Figure 18.3   With a quick switch of color palettes and music style, the game took on a vastly different look and feel for underground levels.

Mushroom Kingdom into stone, bricks, and plants, and only the Princess has the power to turn them back. This whimsical tale worked well with the bright, cartoony graphics and Koji Kondo's charming score, which is certainly among the most memorable of any ever composed for a video game.

Super Mario Bros. was indeed the killer app Arakawa needed to overcome the American resistance. He lost little time in replacing it as one of the "pack-in" or games bundled with the system, and reportedly sold more than 40 million copies, though as a bundled game, it's unclear how many of those people would have bought it if it were only available separately.[9] By 1988, Douglas McGill of the *New York Times* could write "for boys in this country between the ages of 8 and 15, not having a Nintendo is like not having a baseball bat."[10] McGill credited Nintendo's "colorful names and eccentric cast of characters," of whom none loomed larger than Mario.

Nintendo of America released *Super Mario Bros. 2* in 1986 and *Super Mario Bros. 3* in 1988. The first of these was actually a conversion of a different game called *Yume Kōjō: Doki Doki Panic*, which had been rebranded to serve as the American sequel. The original Japanese sequel was thought too difficult for Americans.[11] Though some consider it the black sheep of the series, it sold well. However, the third game fared much better, becoming the system's greatest bestseller (see Figure 18.4). Today, it's ranked

[7]   She was called Princess Peach in Japan; this name eventually became standard everywhere.

[8]   Some sources claim that Miyamoto had intended Bowser to be an ox, but his animator misinterpreted his drawing. See http://www.theguardian.com/technology/gamesblog/2010/sep/13/games-gameculture.

[9]   Cifaldo, Frank. "Sad But True: We Can't Prove When Super Mario Bros. Came Out." *Gamasutra*. March 28, 2012. http://www.gamasutra.com/view/feature/167392/sad_but_true_we_cant_prove_when_.php (accessed June 16, 2015).

[10]   McGill, Douglas. "Nintendo Scores Big." *New York Times*, December 4, 1988: F1.

[11]   McLaughlin, Rus. "IGN Presents: The History of Super Mario Bros." *IGN*. September 13, 2010. http://www.ign.com/articles/2010/09/14/ign-presents-the-history-of-super-mario-bros (accessed June 16, 2015).

high (if not #1) on most of the net's "greatest video games" lists. It offered several new features and refinements, and even played a prominent role in Todd Holland's film *The Wizard* (1989).

Speaking of movies, one of the more infamous moments in the history of Mario came in 1993, when the film *Super Mario Bros.* debuted in theaters. Starring Bob Hoskins as Mario and John Leguizama as Luigi, the movie was a miserable flop. Siskel and Ebert gave it two thumbs down,

Figure 18.4   The highly anticipated *Super Mario Bros. 3* was everything you thought it'd be, and so much more.

with the latter calling it a "complete waste of time and money." Making a successful movie based on a video game has always been a challenge, but the high profile this one enjoyed explains some of the rancor one still finds for it online.

Nintendo's flagship franchise has played a key role in defining each of its consoles, maintaining a brand consistency despite radical changes in the underlying technology: *Super Mario World* (1990) was more than enough incentive to buy a Super Nintendo Entertainment System (SNES), and *Super Mario 64* (see Chapter 37) not only sold Nintendo 64 consoles but also was many gamers' first experience with immersive three-dimensional graphics and controls. But these games are just the tip of Mario's iceberg. Wikipedia lists more than 200 games featuring Mario, several of which are successful franchises in their own right. Some of the best known are *Dr. Mario* (1990), *Super Mario Kart* (1992), *Mario Party* (1998), *Super Smash Bros.* (1999), and *Mario & Luigi* (2003). Needless to say, there's a lot more I could write about Mario's legacy.

At the start of this chapter, I compared *Super Mario Bros.* to Steamboat Willie, but there's a key difference. I don't imagine that many people today are still interested in watching the Disney classic, at least outside of historians. By contrast, *Super Mario Bros.* is still very much in active circulation today, and just as much fun as it was in 1985. Furthermore, hundreds of avid fans have taken to YouTube to showcase their efforts to become the world record holder for the shortest completion time (a "speed run"). At the time of this writing, the record is 4.57.693, claimed by a German player going by "i_o_l." *Super Mario Bros.* might look primitive compared to modern games, but any rumors of its obsolescence are greatly exaggerated.

In 2015, Nintendo announced *Super Mario Maker* for its Wii U, a highly anticipated construction kit for making Mario-style platform games. It featured four themes, including the original *Super Mario Bros.* The tool promised to make creating levels feel as simple as sketching them out on paper, which was in fact how Miyamoto and Tezuka designed the original. It's certainly a fitting way to celebrate Mario's 30th anniversary, and the promised ability for users to easily share their levels with others bodes well for the future of the genre.

Super Mario Bros. was the last game for which Miyamoto would (and could) oversee every last detail. After it, the size and scale of the projects, as well as his increased responsibility for multiple simultaneous projects, meant delegation. Like Disney, the franchise Miyamoto had fathered would grow from its "primitive" roots into a genuine cultural phenomenon.

The influence of *Super Mario Bros.* on the rest of the gaming industry was deep, profound, and lasting. Gone forever were the days of console games slavishly mimicking the arcades, and dour predictions about the future of the industry—taken quite seriously in 1983—seemed outright preposterous after *Super Mario Bros.* Indeed, the continued relevance of the side-scrolling platform game was evinced quite clearly in 2006, when Nintendo rolled out *New Super Mario Bros.* While this successful and critically acclaimed game offered a substantial audiovisual overhaul and lots of other fun features, the influence of the original game is evident.

One of many professional game designers inspired by *Super Mario Bros.* was Will Wright, designer of *SimCity* and *The Sims.* "The breadth and the scope of the game really blew me away," said Wright. "It was made out of these simple elements, and it worked according to simple rules, but it added up to this very complex design."[12] Wright would develop these ideas into his "possibility space" concept, the founding principle of his best-selling games.

The platform mechanics the game popularized would show up in countless other games, but few of these even came close to rivaling it. To compensate, lesser designers turned to licensing whatever television or Hollywood title they could force fit onto a platform engine, such as Capcom's *Disney's Adventures in the Magic Kingdom* (1990), Hi-Tech Expressions' *Barbie* (1991), Ocean's *The Addams Family* (1992), or T*HQ's *Wayne's World* (1993), just to name a few. My personal favorite clone of the game is Time Warp Productions' *The Great Giana Sisters*, which swaps out Mario for a female punk rocker. Unfortunately, the game was close enough to *Super Mario Bros.* for Nintendo to take notice and stop sales of the game.

18.1 Playing *Super Mario Bros.* Today

There are several legal and convenient options for anyone hoping to play the original *Super Mario Bros.* Assuming you're not up for buying an original NES console on eBay, you can buy *Super Mario Bros.* on Nintendo's Virtual Console.

In 2005, many of Nintendo's patents expired, making it legal for other manufacturers to make hardware clones (though they're still not allowed to use any of Nintendo's trademarks or violate their copyrights). Two of the more popular of these units is Retro-Bit's NES Retro Entertainment System and Hyperkin's Retron 1 NES System. Of course, you'll still need to find a copy of the game, and a purist will naturally prefer the original hardware.

---

[12] Seabrook, John. "Game Master." *The New Yorker.* November 6, 2006. http://www.newyorker.com/magazine/2006/11/06/game-master?currentPage=all (accessed July 7, 2015).

Chapter 19

The Legend of Zelda:
A Link to the Future

In 1987, American gamers took their first trip to Hyrule, the fantasy world of *The Legend of Zelda*. Designed by the celebrated creators of *Super Mario Bros.*, Shigeru Miyamoto and Takashi Tezuka, *Zelda* was a challenging "action adventure" without a platform, mushroom, or Goomba to be found. Instead, players took on the role of Link, a boy tasked with an epic quest: retrieve the eight pieces of the legendary Triforce of Wisdom and save Princess Zelda from the vile clutches of Ganon, the Prince of Darkness.

Instead of running and jumping their way across side-scrolling levels, *Zelda* had players exploring a large tile-based world, shown from an overhead perspective comparable to early *Ultima* games. Unlike Mario, Link could travel freely in all four cardinal directions, exploring the world in the order you saw fit. Traveling across the sprawling "overworld," or surface level, you'd eventually find entrances to the game's nine dungeons.

Naturally, there were plenty of monsters to slay, but Link would first need to acquire a sword from a mysterious old man, who tells him, "It's dangerous to go alone! Take this" (see Figure 19.1). If Link's "life hearts" were at full capacity, he could throw his sword and have it magically reappear in his hand; otherwise, he'd have to kill them at close range. In any case, the monsters eventually reappear after clearing a level, but players soon discovered the trick of leaving one monster intact—thus preventing them all from respawning. Link could also find an upgrade for his shield and a magical bow and arrows. In addition to weapons and upgrades, there were also keys, maps, rings, candles, and other useful items.

These elements were not enough to warrant its designation as a role-playing game (RPG), which was never Miyamoto's goal: "I personally have a fundamental dislike of the RPG system," said Miyamoto.[1] He specifically didn't like the mechanic of starting off weak, barely able to move, and only gradually becoming powerful. Nevertheless, *Zelda* still possessed a sophistication missing in most other console games of the time. Although the Nintendo Entertainment System (NES) was significantly more advanced than the previous generation of American consoles, the bulk of its library was still simple action games. This situation was in stark contrast to the computer game market, where complex adventure, RPG, and strategy games were far more prevalent. Furthermore,

---

[1] Kohler, Chris. *Power Up: How Japanese Video Games Gave the World an Extra Life*. Indianapolis: Brady Games, 2005: 88.

many believed the NES's user base was made up mostly of young children, an idea that Nintendo seemed to reinforce with its strict censorship policies, cartoony mascots, and family-friendly advertisements. Although adult gamers could easily enjoy *Super Mario Bros.* or *Duck Hunt*, they were mere diversions compared to the expansive worlds and tactical gameplay offered by computer games like *Ultima* or *Wizardry*. If nothing else, *The Legend of Zelda* proved that this perceived gap

Figure 19.1   Every self-respecting Nintendo fan will recognize this famous scene from early in the game. According to Glitterberri's "Retranslation Redux," the line should have read "It's dangerous to go alone. I shall grant you this."

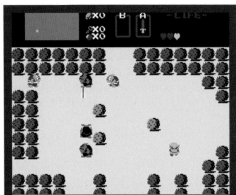

between console and computer gamers wasn't so wide after all; both audiences could appreciate a well-designed and imaginative game that demanded more than quick thumbs. If Miyamoto's *Super Mario Bros.* was a good reason to buy an NES, *The Legend of Zelda* was a good reason to keep it (see Figure 19.2).

According to Miyamoto, "The *Mario* games ... aren't particularly suited to having a very heavy story, whereas the

Figure 19.2   *The Legend of Zelda* had a huge map to explore, but you needed to be careful. There were all kinds of monsters wandering about!

Zelda series is something that lends itself more naturally to that idea."[2] Both games certainly had their challenges, but *Zelda* required players to explore and navigate a large game world, find all sorts of hidden items, and ensure that Link was properly geared before taking on certain enemies. Significantly, it was the first game cartridge with a battery, which allowed players to conveniently save and resume their progress. Before this innovation, games with save options required players to write down and input long codes, an arduous process that also made it easier to cheat. To highlight its special

2 Kohler, Chris. "Q&A: Nintendo's Shigeru Miyamoto on Mario, Zelda, Project Natal and More." *Wired.* June 6, 2009. http://www.wired.com/2009/06/shigeru-miyamoto-interview/ (accessed June 17, 2015).

nature, Nintendo placed it in a distinctive gold cartridge, which stood out from the standard gray (see Figure 19.3).

Miyamoto said later that he wanted to create a "miniature garden that [players] can put inside their drawer."[3] Miyamoto wished to share with players some of the thrills he had as a young boy, exploring

Figure 19.3   Just to make sure you'd know that *The Legend of Zelda* was special, Nintendo placed it in a stunning gold cartridge. (Photo courtesy of Dave or Atox.)

the fields, forests, and caves near his family's home in Kyoto. Koji Kondo's magnificent soundtrack for the game contributed to the sense of wonder and potential danger.

Minoru Arakawa was anxious that American gamers wouldn't be able to figure out *Zelda* and would probably demand refunds if they got lost. To that end, he set up a toll-free hotline for stumped players to call for help.[4] Soon, players were calling the number not just for help with *Zelda* but with other games as well, and the operators were swamped. The problem became an opportunity, however, when Arakawa switched the number to a 1-900, pay-by-the-minute service. Players could also turn to *Nintendo Power* magazine for help with the game, which published maps and provided players with strategies and tips. This magazine was another of Arakawa's brilliant ideas, and it remained in publication from July 1988 to December 2012.

Zelda wasn't quite as phenomenally successful as *Super Mario Bros.*, but it was a terrific bestseller for Nintendo, eventually selling more than 7 million units.[5] Indeed, it's estimated that 1 in 10 console owners had the cartridge. It's hard to imagine a game achieving this level of worldwide penetration today. Link's image was plastered on cereal boxes, bed sheets, and Saturday morning cartoons.

The next *Zelda* game was *Zelda II: The Adventure of Link*, released in the United States in 1988. Although the success of the first ensured its high sales, it's generally considered the black sheep of the series. It had a number of features that are found in no other *Zelda* game. The most noticeable change was a two-dimensional, side-view mode for combat and in-town scenes (the overhead perspective was maintained for overland travel). This is also the only *Zelda* game that qualifies as a true RPG, since Link now gained experience points and attack, magic, and life levels.

---

[3] Vestal, Andrew, Cliff O'Neill, and Brad Shoemaker. "The History of Zelda." *GameSpot*. November 14, 2000. http://www.gamespot.com/gamespot/features/video/hist_zelda/ (accessed July 1, 2006).

[4] Kent, Steve L. *The Ultimate History of Video Games: From Pong to Pokémon and Beyond: the Story Behind the Craze that Touched Our Lives and Changed the World*. Rocklin, CA: Prima Pub., 2001.

[5] Nichols, Max. "Zelda: Sales Numbers in Context." *Zelda Data*. June 14, 2014. http://www.zeldadata.com/zeldadata_SalesInContext2014.html (accessed May 18, 2015).

©1991.1992 Nintendo

The third *Zelda* game and the first for the Super Nintendo Entertainment System (SNES) is *The Legend of Zelda: A Link to the Past*, published in the United States in 1992 (see Figure 19.4). It returned to the overhead perspective of the first game, but took advantage of the SNES's superior technology to offer substantially

Figure 19.4   The arrival of the *Zelda* series to the SNES was more than enough reason to own the system.

improved audiovisuals. The game's enormous sales helped Nintendo's new platform establish itself in the market and eventually outperform its rival, the Sega Genesis—which had beaten Nintendo to the 16-bit era.

Sega, always struggling to "do what Nintendon't," introduced a CD-ROM add-on for the Genesis in 1992, and new titles with full-motion video (FMV) were all the rage. There were other, short-lived standalone CD-ROM consoles available. One of these was Philips' CD-i, released in 1991, which plays a small role in the *Zelda* story.

Nintendo was reluctant to follow Sega's lead. On the one hand, CD-ROMs had enormous storage capacity and were much cheaper than cartridges. On the other hand, Nintendo feared they would be copied and distributed illegally. Still, they seemed willing to at least explore the option, first partnering with Sony, and then Philips, to create a CD-ROM add-on for its SNES. However, by the time the unit was ready, much of the hype over FMV had died down, and Nintendo decided to cancel their agreement. In an unusual, even bizarre move, they granted Philips a license to create some games based on *Zelda* for its CD-i console.

Philips moved quickly to exploit the arrangement and, in addition to developing Mario-themed titles, released three infamously bad *Zelda* games for its console: *Link: The Faces of Evil* (1993), *Zelda: The Wand of Gamelon* (1993), and *Zelda's Adventure* (1994). Like most early CD-ROM games, these were loaded with unplayable FMV sequences (the first two are animated; the last has live actors). All three of these games were poorly contrived and had none of the polish and attention to detail that characterized Nintendo's games. Few fans of the series consider these wretched games worth playing today, but their notoriety makes them valuable to collectors.

Zelda made its first appearance on a handheld in 1993, with *The Legend of Zelda: Link's Awakening*, for Nintendo's Game Boy. A year and a half in the making, it sold millions of copies and received praise from nearly all major critics.

However, 1998's *The Legend of Zelda: Ocarina of Time* is the game most fans of the series consider its finest moment. We'll return to this game in Chapter 41.

The Legend of Zelda is a foundational game, one of a small handful of titles that can truly be said to have defined the industry. Its popularity and name recognition are second only to *Super Mario Bros.* and *Pac-Man*, and the franchise it spawned is still going strong today.

19.1 Playing *The Legend of Zelda* Today

Probably the easiest way to play this game today (outside of acquiring a cartridge and an NES console or compatible device) is to buy it from Nintendo's Virtual Console store. Versions are available for Wii, Wii U, and 3DS. Any competent NES emulator will support the game just fine, but this option isn't exactly legal.

Chapter 20

Final Fantasy: Console Games Get a Level Up

As we saw in Chapter 19, *The Legend of Zelda* showed that there was a promising market in North America for complex and sophisticated games for consoles. Naturally, this led several Japanese developers to consider exporting more of these kinds of games to the West.

One of the earliest was Chunsoft's *Dragon Quest*, which was renamed *Dragon Warrior* when it was brought to the United States in 1989. Inspired by *Ultima* and *Wizardry*, its designer, Yuji Horii, thought these computer role-playing games were simply too difficult for average gamers. He set about simplifying their admittedly cumbersome interfaces and mechanics for a mainstream audience. The resulting game was published in Japan in 1986 and, after some timely promotion in a manga publication, became a best-selling and influential title. It sold more than 2 million copies and won many awards.[1] The sequels made it even more popular, and by 1990, the franchise was a roaring cultural phenomenon. When the highly anticipated third game was released in 1988, it sold 1 million copies in a single day, and police arrested nearly 300 school-aged kids who'd played hooky from school to snag a copy early[2] (see Figure 20.1).

Strangely, when it was translated and localized for the American Nintendo Entertainment System (NES), *Dragon Warrior* was only moderately successful. Ron Duwell, author of a detailed history of the series' localization, argues that the issue was timing; the Japanese version had looked cutting edge in 1986 but was seriously outdated 4 years later.[3] By that time, NES programmers had devised effective techniques for optimizing and enhancing the platform's graphics, but these discoveries weren't leveraged for *Dragon Warrior*. Duwell also points out the swap in the box art; the Japanese covers were done by Akira Toriyama, a famous manga artist. Believing that Americans wouldn't appreciate Toriyama's "super deformed" style, they swapped it out with a dull, generic fantasy image. Finally, Duwell notes that the menu-driven interface may have baffled gamers who weren't accustomed to it.

However, the problem might well have been that *Dragon Quest* was "too Japanese, too soon," if you will. While anime and manga are commonplace in America today, this was

---

[1] Kohler, Chris. *Power Up: How Japanese Video Games Gave the World an Extra Life*. Indianapolis: Brady Games, 2005.

[2] Keizer, Gregg. "One Million Sold in One Day." *Compute!*, June 1988: 7.

[3] Duwell, Ron. "History of Dragon Quest Localizations." *TechnoBuffalo*. October 11, 2014. http://www.technobuffalo.com/2014/10/11/history-of-dragon-quest-localizations-1989-to-2001/ (accessed June 18, 2015).

not the case in 1989. Therefore, American gamers were largely unaccustomed to *kawaii*, or the "aww"-evoking cuteness, that tends to crop up in Japanese popular culture in ways that can be quite jarring to the uninitiated.

A perfect example is slime. One of the monsters encountered in *Dragon Quest* is a cheerful, smiling dollop of slime, which resembles a Hershey's Kiss candy. American gamers accustomed to "serious" fantasy games like *Wizardry* might

Figure 20.1   *Dragon Warrior* was a sensational hit in Japan, but only a minor title in the United States.

well have balked at this adorable little slime ball. The slime in *Wizardry*, by contrast, looks far more menacing, with bits of bone in some versions and a menacing scowl in others. To put it bluntly, *Dragon Warrior* looked childish to many Americans who'd come to role playing by way of *Wizardry*, *Ultima*, or *Dungeons & Dragons*. However, even in Japan, there were those who desired a grittier take on the genre.

Final Fantasy was designed by Hironobu Sakaguchi, a senior game designer at Square who'd joined the young new company, along with his roommate, Hiromichi Tanaka, as a part-time gig in 1984 while they were off for spring break from Yokohama National University.[4] The pair ended up staying on, however, when the early games they designed turned out to be big hits. However, Sakaguchi longed to return to school to finish his degree, so he agreed to do one final game and then call it quits. Fate had other plans.

Sakaguchi was a huge fan of *Wizardry*, which he loved playing until the wee hours of the night on his roommate's (Hiromichi Tanaka) Apple II. Still, as fun and addictive as the game was for Sakaguchi, he felt it lacked something—it needed graphics, sound, and music to match its gameplay—features that Nintendo's Famicom system had at its disposal.

As it happened, an ace programmer at Square, Nasir Gebelli, was also a fan of the Apple II—and was something of a hero among Apple II programmers for both his skill and speed at coding for the machine. His claims to fame were *Space Eggs* and *Gorgon*, bestsellers that really brought out the best of the Apple II's hardware. The Great Video Game Crash of 1983 had destroyed his company, Gebelli Software, so he was happy to take the job offer at Square. "I was a huge fan of his," said Sakaguchi. "When the president brought him into the company, I was all, 'Wow, it's Nasir; let me have your autograph!' "[5]

---

4   See footnote 1, p. 91.

5   Gifford, Kevin. "Hironobu Sakaguchi on Final Fantasy I's Roller-Coaster Development." *1up.* December 21, 2011. http://www.1up.com/news/hironobu-sakaguchi-final-fantasy-roller-coaster (accessed June 19, 2015).

Unfortunately, the hotshot coder Gebelli knew zilch about role-playing games. "I had to explain everything," said Sakaguchi. "I'd say the character's hit points go down at this point, and he'd reply, 'What're hit points?'"[5] Fortunately, Gebelli caught on quickly.

Sakaguchi wanted *Final Fantasy* to stand out from *Dragon Quest* in several important ways. For one, he wanted a "sabishii" (lonely) style look instead of the "kawaii" or cutesy style. When he was looking for a suitable artist to design characters, Koichi Ishii, a co-designer, recommended Yoshitaka Amano, who'd worked on the darkly ominous *Vampire Hunter D* graphic novels. "Never heard of him," said Sakaguchi. He then showed Ishii some clippings he'd cut out of magazines. "I want this guy, instead."

"Uh, that's Amano," replied Ishii.

Final Fantasy would also boast a more sophisticated storyline than *Dragon Quest*. At first, it would appear to be another "rescue the damsel in distress" cliché, but that was only the prologue. Afterward, players discovered a much more involved quest involving four light warriors, crystals, and the mythical elements (fire, water, earth, and air). The characters the player met along the way were better developed, too, and there was always the possibility of deception. "We weren't making a product but a creation," said Sakaguchi. "It was putting our soul into the production ... not saving anything for the sequel."[6]

Final Fantasy was a hit in Japan, where it sold more than 400,000 games, a figure that convinced Sakaguchi to stay on at Square rather than resume college (see Figure 20.2a and b).[5] According to a report on Square Enix's website, 780,000 copies of the game were sold outside of Japan, for a total of 1.9 million. Anecdotal evidence also suggests the game was widespread. However, apparently the sales were insufficient to warrant localizing the next two games, which were only released in Japan (see Figure 20.2a and b).

Americans had to wait for the fourth installment, which was confusingly published as *Final Fantasy II* in 1991 for the Super Nintendo Entertainment System (SNES). This critically acclaimed title sold more than 4 million copies and established a new standard for console role-playing games. The big leap came with *Final Fantasy VII*, which leveraged the CD-ROM to spectacular effect—but we'll cover that game in Chapter 39.

Both *Dragon Quest/Warrior* and *Final Fantasy* were hugely successful in their home country but were elsewhere only modest contenders. Of the two, *Final Fantasy* was more popular in America, perhaps because its grittier aesthetic appealed more to Western audiences than the cutesier *Dragon Quest*. In any case, a few years and a generation of consoles later, American gamers took to the series in droves, finally establishing the franchise as a true global phenomenon. I speculate that we might explain this lag simply by age. The 8-year-old who'd bought an NES back in 1985 was now 13, the perfect age to fully appreciate a game like *Final Fantasy* (see Figure 20.2a and b).

---

[6] Fear, Ed. "Sakaguchi Discusses the Development of Final Fantasy." *Develop-Online*. December 13, 2007. http://www .develop-online.net/news/sakaguchi-discusses-the-development-of-final-fantasy/0102088 (accessed June 19, 2015).

(a)

(b)

IMP

FIGHT   RUN
MAGIC
DRINK
ITEM

MATT
HP 35

AAAA
HP 30

AAAA
HP 33

AAAA
HP 30

Figure 20.2   Shown here is the (a) exploration and (b) combat modes of *Final Fantasy*.

20.1 Playing *Final Fantasy* Today

The easiest way to play *Final Fantasy* today is simply to buy it on Nintendo's Virtual Console for Wii U or 3DS. If you prefer a remastered version with enhanced graphics and other features, you could try *Final Fantasy* (2007) for Sony's PSP handheld. This version is also available for Android, iOS, and Windows Phone. Sadly, there's no legal way to play it on a modern PC.

Fans of the series are divided over whether it's desirable to start your *Final Fantasy* experience with the first game, which hasn't held up as well as *Final Fantasy II/IV*. If you want to start there instead, I recommend the DS or 3DS versions.

Chapter 21

Tetris: The Perfect Video Game?

Tetris is the greatest video game ever to come out of Russia, or arguably anywhere else in the world for that matter. It has been endlessly cloned and ported for almost every viable platform, and is still widely played on all manner of devices by all manner of people. It is a game for all ages, for the ages.

Many have pondered what makes *Tetris* so universally appealing. Its design is simple, clean, and elegant, but its audiovisuals—the bread and butter of most games—are notably Spartan. A novice programmer could code it in an afternoon, but we play it all our lives and still find it compelling. It is, in short, sublime; a game greater than the sum of its blocks.

Though it's based on a puzzle game with wooden blocks, *Tetris* is only feasible as a video game.[1] Yet, it runs well on even the cheapest hardware. It's one of those basic designs that we think we could or should have thought of ourselves, but not even the 28-year-old Russian computer engineer who invented it, Alexey Pajitnov, has been able to surpass or even match its brilliance (see Figure 21.1).

Today *Tetris* is usually categorized as a "casual game." This term is broadly applied but is usually confined to low-tech games that run in a browser or on low-budget hardware. They are also "casual" in the sense that they can be picked up, played for a few minutes, and put down without concern. This is in stark contrast to most popular games for computers and consoles, which take far more time to learn and play.

However, there was nothing "casual" about *Tetris* in the Soviet Union of the 1980s, which was behind Japan and the United States in computer technology. Indeed, the Academy of Science of the USSR's Elektronika 60 minicomputer, on which Pajitnov programmed *Tetris*, was a clone of DEC's LSI-11, an ancient model less powerful than an Apple II or Commodore 64, and it lacked support for any kind of sound or graphics. Furthermore, there was no market for personal or "home computers" in the USSR; all that existed were "do-it-yourself" models based on designs printed in electronics magazines. According to Pajitnov, the Soviet Union's scarce computing resources were "used mainly for science and research. They weren't even seriously used in any commercial purposes."[2]

---

[1] Though you can see a YouTube video of an electromechanical version called *Mekaniskt Tetris* at https://www.youtube.com/watch?v=EHgLK8-snaM. Judging by the video, it does not keep score or erase finished lines.

[2] Nutt, Christian. "Alexey Pajitnov—Tetris: Past, Present, Future." *Gamasutra*. June 28, 2010. http://www.gamasutra.com/view/feature/134248/alexey_pajitnov__tetris_past_.php (accessed June 23, 2015).

Figure 21.1   Alexey Pajitnov, designer of *Tetris*. (Photo courtesy of Eunice Szpillman.)

Part of Pajitnov's job was to determine the capabilities of whatever computers the Academy was able to scrounge together, and games were an ideal way to do so. Pajitnov, always a fan of puzzles, decided in June of 1984 to design a video game based on pentominoes—a popular "brain teaser" type game with 12 polygon-shaped blocks. Players try to arrange these blocks into various designs or patterns described in an enclosed booklet. Anyone looking at these games today couldn't help but think about *Tetris*, but it was actually a stroke of genius on Pajitnov's part to reimagine these meditative logic puzzles as a fast-paced action game.

Since the Elektronika 60 had no graphics, Pajitnov was forced to work with punctuation symbols to form the pieces. Since it was too difficult to form all 12 pieces, he simplified it to 7. After he'd created the pieces, Pajitnov tried to figure out what to do with them:

> Next I put together the procedures for manipulating the pieces: pick a tile, flip it, rotate it. But the playfield filled up in 20 seconds flat. Also, once you'd filled a line, it was kind of dead, so why keep it on the screen? So I made each full line disappear, which was key. I was a pretty good programmer and it took me about three weeks to get something controllable on screen.[3]

Pajitnov himself became the first victim of *Tetris* addiction; he told his supervisors that the program needed more debugging, but in reality he was enamored with his own creation. A few of his closest colleagues got hold of it, and soon everyone else at the USSR's Academy of Science was hooked. These early fans included a 16-year-old high school student, Vadim Gerasimov, who helped Pajitnov add new features and made a version of it for the PC (see Figure 21.2).

While Pajitnov and his colleagues were playing *Tetris*, the General Secretary of the Communist Party, Mikhail Gorbachev, was introducing his policies of "glasnost" and "perestroika," which ultimately led to the lifting of the Iron Curtain, the toppling of

---

[3] Hoad, Phil. "Tetris: How We Made the Addictive Computer Game." *The Guardian*. June 2, 2014. http://www.theguardian.com/culture/2014/jun/02/how-we-made-tetris (accessed June 23, 2015).

the Berlin Wall, and finally the collapse of the Soviet Union itself. Unfortunately for Pajitnov, it was still a difficult (and potentially dangerous) time for a Russian citizen to publish his own software. Therefore, he signed over the rights to the USSR for 10 years, after which they'd revert back to him.

What happened next is worthy of a James Bond movie. The full story would take too long to recount here and has been covered in detail in other books

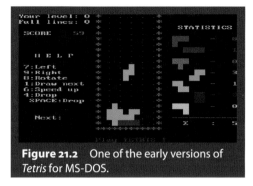

Figure 21.2   One of the early versions of *Tetris* for MS-DOS.

(including our own *Vintage Game Consoles*) and documentaries. In short, Gerasimov's PC version was smuggled to Hungary, and from there distributed to the rest of the world by several different companies, each claiming to have the legal authorization to do so.

For our purposes, the most important of these companies was Spectrum Holobyte, an American developer and publisher best known for its flying and racing simulations. Spectrum Holobyte kept the gameplay intact but improved the graphics and played up its origins with Russian-themed background scenes and music. It hit the shelves in 1987 for over a dozen computers, including the Amiga, Atari ST, DOS, and Macintosh. Reviewers praised its simple yet compelling gameplay and emphasized its addictiveness. A reviewer of the Atari ST version humorously described it as a Soviet secret weapon:

> Once it hit the shelves, we'd be helpless addicts, mindlessly tapping the keys until we fell to the floor, victims of the deadly game as the Red Army marched in to effortlessly conquer us.[4]

One of many who played Spectrum Holobyte's *Tetris* was Henk Rogers, whose job was finding suitable games and licensing them for Japan's video game market. He first became aware of *Tetris* at Spectrum Holobyte's booth at the Consumer Electronics Show of 1988. "I was hooked instantly," said Rogers. "I licensed every version on every system I could through Spectrum Holobyte. But it turned out their parent company, Mirrorsoft, had already given some of the Japanese rights I thought I owned to Atari"[3] (see Figure 21.3).

Rogers was primarily interested in *Tetris* because he judged correctly that it was the perfect game for Nintendo's new Game Boy handheld system. Rogers approached our old friend Arakawa, president of Nintendo of America, and told him, "If you want little boys to buy your machine include Mario, but if you want everyone to buy your machine,

---

[4]   Chadwick, Ian. "Tetris." *ST-Log*, October 1989: 91.

Figure 21.3   Spectrum-Holobyte added colorful backgrounds and Russian music. They also enhanced the look of the pieces.

Figure 21.4   The GameBoy version of *Tetris* was a killer app, not just for the system, but for handheld gaming in general.

include *Tetris*."[5] Arakawa agreed, and *Tetris* was soon revealed as the killer app of mobile gaming, selling more than 35 million copies.[6]

Since so many other companies were claiming to have rights to the game, Rogers traveled to Moscow to straighten out the mess with Elorg, the government bureau that handled software exports. There, surrounded by the KGB, lawyers, and Pajitnov himself, he learned something very disturbing:

The director of Elorg, a Mr. Belikov, told me they had never given rights to anybody. I was in deep kimchi, because I had 200,000 game cartridges at $10 apiece being manufactured in Japan, and I'd put up all of my in-laws' property as collateral.[3]

Fortunately, Rogers was able to make a hasty deal with the Russians, securing exclusive rights (this time officially) for the Nintendo Entertainment System (NES) and the GameBoy versions (see Figure 21.4).

Atari jumped the gun, however, and released an NES version under its Tengen label. This version was superior to Nintendo's because it allowed two players to simultaneously play the game on juxtaposed boards—a cool feature that ramped up the competitive factor. Those who bought it in time were lucky; Nintendo took them to court and had it taken off the shelves.

---

[5] Peckham, Matt. "Tetris at 30: An Interview with the Historic Puzzle Game's Creator." *Time*. June 6, 2014. http://time.com/2837390/tetris-at-30-pajitnov-interview/ (accessed June 23, 2015).

[6] Wynne-Jones, Jonathan. "Computer Game Tetris Celebrates 25 Years." *The Telegraph*. June 6, 2009. http://www.telegraph.co.uk/technology/news/5460283/Computer-game-Tetris-celebrates-25-years.html (accessed June 23, 2015).

Even though *Tetris* is one of the most abstract video games, it still made an indelible mark on popular culture. The annual *Tetris* World Championship is now in its fifth year and was the subject of a 2011 documentary film called *Ecstasy of Order: The Tetris Masters*. It also appears in an exhibit at New York City's Museum of Modern Art and played on the side of skyscrapers! *Tetris* has been referenced in several films and television shows. *Tetris* merchandise ranges from stackable LED desk lamps to nifty animated alarm clocks. There's even *Tetris*-themed board games and a fun "Bop It" electronic toy from Hasbro.

The unexpected and unprecedented success of *Tetris* predictably led to a sea of imitators and derivatives called "tile-matching" games. One of the best known is *Dr. Mario*, a 1990 game for the NES with branding from its popular Mario franchise. Here, the *Tetris*-style gameplay is given a medical theme. Instead of blocks, players guide pills (consisting of two pieces) that fall from the top of the screen to a set of viruses toward the bottom. Players win the game by matching up pills and viruses of the corresponding color (red, blue, or yellow). There was also a popular two-player mode available, which employed side-by-side simultaneous gameplay.

Other early tile-matching games are Sega's *Columns* (1990), Taito's *Puzznic* (1989), Compile's *Puyo Puyo* (aka, Puyo Pop, 1991), Taito's *Puzzle Bobble* (aka, Bust-a-Move, 1994), and PopCap Games' *Bejeweled* (2001). While always popular, these games really took off after the smartphone and tablet revolution, where their bright colors, casual gameplay, and low demands on hardware made them ideal. It's easy to see the influence of *Tetris* on modern hits such as King.com's *Candy Crush Saga* (2011), PopCap's *Bejeweled Blitz* (2013), and, of course, Electronic Arts' *Tetris Blitz* (2013).

Pajitnov made several games after *Tetris*, and the reputation he'd earned for *Tetris* was more than sufficient to interest publishers. The first was *Welltris*, a 1989 title published by Spectrum Holobyte. The gimmick was a third dimension, which made it look as though you were playing *Tetris* down the sides of a well (thus the name). Later efforts included *Hatris* (1990), which replaced the blocks with colorful hats; *Wordtris* (1991), which had players arranging letters to make words; *Hexic* (2003), a game with hexagonal tiles; and *Marbly* (2013), the first game Pajitnov designed exclusively for mobiles. Sadly, none of these games have come anywhere close to the success of *Tetris*.

Sadder still is that Pajitnov himself profited little from the runaway success of his greatest achievement. "I don't really like to talk about that because when I think about those things I lose my sense of humor," Pajitnov told an interviewer.[7]

Things did improve after 1996, when Pajitnov reclaimed the rights. He'd emigrated to the United States and teamed up with Rogers to form *The Tetris Company*. Their goal was to extract royalties from the many companies making *Tetris* games. However, although the company claims the exclusive right to the *Tetris* name, their control does not extend to the "look and feel" and basic concept of the game. This loophole allows people to make

---

7   Almaci, Hasan Ali. "Interview: Tetris—The Making of an Icon." *Kikizo*. December 5, 2007. http://archive.videogamesdaily .com/features/tetris_iv_dec07_p1.asp (accessed June 24, 2015).

unauthorized *Tetris* clones as long as they call them by other names, such as Wolfgang Strobl's *Klotz* (1989), Tingly Games' *Atlantris*, or Absolutist's *Pentix*.

At least Pajitnov was able to get a personalized TETRIS license plate on his Tesla. Now nearing 60, the famed designer spends his days driving around Bellevue, reading Russian fantasy novels, working out, and playing tennis or mobile games. When he does get the urge to design, he works with paper and pen, not a computer. Will he ever manage to top *Tetris*, one of the best-selling games of all time? "I have a project in the back of my mind," said Pajitnov, "but I'm not literally doing it."[8] No matter what he comes up with, though, I doubt it'll distract the hordes of *Tetris* addicts for long.

21.1 **Playing *Tetris* Today**

There are countless ways to play *Tetris* today, but I recommend going to the official page at http://tetris.com to play it for free (legally!) online. Otherwise, Vadim Gerisamov hosts downloads of the original MS-DOS version on his site at http://vadim.oversigma.com /Tetris.htm. You can also play *Tetris* on consoles or mobile devices by visiting the relevant app store, or, for maximum chic, kick back on a *Tetris* 3D cushion while playing it on a watch, bracelet, or even a business card![9]

[8]   Gravning, Jagger. "The Man Who Made 'Tetris'." *Motherboard*. November 20, 2014. http://motherboard.vice.com/read /the-man-who-made-tetris (accessed June 24, 2015).

[9]   See http://www.arduboy.com/.

Chapter 22

Street Fighter II: The Arcade Comes Back Swinging

By the time *Street Fighter II: The World Warrior* debuted in North America in 1991, the arcade side of the industry was all but irrelevant. The throngs of teens who'd once crowded around *Pac-Man* and *Donkey Kong* were gone, their only vestiges the gum wads stuck on the back of the well-worn machines. Computer and console games had moved far beyond the days of slavishly imitating these games and now offered much longer and more sophisticated experiences.

But now there was a new game firing up at the arcade, one that wouldn't just put this sorry situation on its head—it'd give it a spinning pile driver. It was a fateful day when a friend said to you, "Hey, I bet I can kick your ass in *Street Fighter II*!" (see Figure 22.1).

Ryu, Ken, E. Honda, Guile, Chun-Li, Zangief, Dhalsim, Sagat, and M. Bison—do they really need an introduction? If so, you're overdue for a serious Shoryu-Ken. Capcom's *Street Fighter II* is the most important arcade game of the 1990s. A decade earlier, the pride of posting one's initials on the high score list was all it took to bring the masses—but now that all seemed petty. *Street Fighter II* offered something better, something meaner; something much more visceral and satisfying. This game let you beat your opponents to a pulp, showing off your own prowess at the controls while simultaneously shaming your rivals. There was posturing, trash talk, even the occasional real-life fight as emotions and egos raged.

This new game touched off a tsunami of imitators rivaled only by *Space Invaders*, single-handedly carving out a new genre of competitive or "versus" fighting games that's still going strong. *Street Fighter V* was one of the most highly anticipated games of 2016 and sold over a million and a half copies despite some problems caused by a rushed launch.[1] Wikipedia lists more than 350 other titles in the "versus fighting games" category. These games are as diverse as Nintendo's *Super Smash Bros.* (1999), which had Mario, Donkey Kong, and Pikachu battling it out, and NetherRealm Studios' *Injustice: Gods Among Us* (2013), which featured popular characters from DC Comics. However, despite the enhanced audiovisuals and distinctive themes, stories, and characters, the core mechanics of these games has changed little in the 25 years since *Street Fighter II*.

---

[1] Williams, Mike. "Street Fighter V's Sales Below Expectations, Capcom Plans 'Full-Scale Offensive.'" *US Gamer.* May 9, 2016. http://www.usgamer.net/articles/street-fighter-vs-sales-below-expectations-capcom-plans-full-scale-offensive (accessed July 7, 2016).

Figure 22.1 Victory or defeat came quickly in *Street Fighter II*. Would you go home in shame, or beg mom for another quarter?

While there were several great fighting games before it, *Street Fighter II* trumped them all with spectacular graphics, sound effects, numerous characters, and technically sophisticated, even artistic combat. A seemingly endless line of teenagers lined up in front of these machines, eager to demonstrate their virtual street fighting skills—or at least their mastery of its esoteric combat system. For countless gamers growing up in the 1990s, *Street Fighter II* wasn't just a game, but a rite of passage (see Figure 22.2).

An important point to consider is that *Street Fighter II*'s emphasis on competition made it uniquely suited to the arcade; playing it at home alone against the computer was for training purposes only—the real challenge came from other players. The game's producer, Yoshiki Okamoto, explained that this emphasis on player-versus-player was inspired by his team's efforts to make arcade machines profitable again. The problem with games like *Space Invaders*, Okamoto felt, was that players felt cheated when they hit the "game over" screen too soon. Of course, the brief play times were necessary to keep the quarters rolling in. On the other hand, while you could get away with charging 50 cents for visually stunning games like Cinemaware's *Dragon's Lair* (1983) or *Space Ace* (1984), which streamed cartoons off a laserdisc, the cost of the necessary hardware jacked up the cost of the machine. According to Okamoto,

Figure 22.2 *Street Fighter II* offered a wide variety of protagonists to choose from. Shown here in mid-arc is Chun Li, the only female contender in *The World Warrior* version.

> We thought about it more and came to the conclusion that if two people played at once, operators would get twice the money. Players would essentially split the cost so they could both play for longer ... If we dictated the difficulty, players could always get frustrated. But if players were competing against each other, whether they won or lost would be up to them.[2]

This brilliant tactic not only doubled the quarters the machine could bring in, but did so in a way that felt justified—you only had to pony up another quarter if you lost to another player, and that was your fault, not the game's (see Figure 22.3).

To better understand *Street Fighter II*'s appeal, it's helpful to look at its predecessors. As usual, there's debate about what game really deserves credit for being the first "true" fighting game, whatever that means, but two of the best were Technos Japan's *Karate Champ* (1984) and System 3's *International Karate* (1986). Both games rode the wave formed by John G. Avildsen's blockbuster film *The Karate Kid* (1984), which raked in more

---

than $90 million and helped popularize the sport of karate for a generation of American youth.[3] Everyone was saying "wax on, wax off" in their best Mr. Miyagi accent and bowing in at their local dojo. The time was right for a good karate game.

Karate Champ fit the bill nicely, with an arcade cabinet featuring two pairs of joysticks, one for moving and the other for fighting.[4] As with *Street Fighter II*, players squared off *mano a mano*, trading punches and kicks, but there was no health bar. Instead, the round was over as soon as someone landed a hit. There was significant skill involved; you only earned half a point for a normal hit, but a successful counter or high-risk maneuver awarded a full point. The winner

Figure 22.3   A *Street Fighter II* machine at the Bradford Media Museum. Note the six-button layout. (Photo courtesy of John Turner.)

was treated to a bonus round. Data East published ports for home computers and the Nintendo Entertainment System (NES), but none of these were as good as the arcade version.

International Karate (also known as *World Karate Championship*) was a similar game published by Epyx for home computers. Its gameplay was considered superior to the *Karate Champ* home versions and was successful enough to invite a lawsuit from Data East USA, who sued them for copyright infringement. The courts eventually ruled in favor of Epyx, resolving that no one game company could monopolize an entire sport, and the creative elements (backdrops, graphics, sounds, etc.) weren't close enough to constitute infringement. Thus, anyone could make a karate game as long as they didn't copy the artwork, music, and other "creative" elements[5] (see Figure 22.4).

This decision led to a cavalcade of computer, arcade, and console games based more or less on *Karate Champ* released in the mid to late 1980s. One of many such games was Capcom's first *Street Fighter* in 1987. While it offered better audiovisuals than *Karate Champ* and had health bars instead of one-hit rounds, the controls were inaccurate

---

[3] IMDb. "The Karate Kid." *Box Office Mojo.* June 29, 2015. http://www.boxofficemojo.com/franchises/chart/?id=karatekid .htm (accessed June 30, 2015).

[4] The original version was single player only; the more popular Player versus Player edition followed a few months later.

[5] Kent's *The Ultimate History of Video Games* offers a detailed account of these legal proceedings.

and frustrating. Furthermore, there were only two, almost identical characters to choose from (Ryu and Ken). The audio-visuals were impressive, but it was still a humble beginning for one of the world's best-known game series.

The original controls were a joystick and two pneumatic pads. The not-so-brilliant idea behind this setup was that players needed to smack these pads as hard as possible to maximize the damage done by their character. It sounded good on paper, but overzealous players inevitably wrecked the machines. Later versions replaced these pads with the now familiar six-button setup.

Street Fighter also featured three secret techniques that players had to discover

Figure 22.4   *Karate Champ* was an instant hit with fans of *The Karate Kid* movies.

on their own. It was a great design decision, but executing these techniques required split-second timing and were difficult to pull off.

Despite its shortcomings, the original *Street Fighter* was successful enough to impress a rival company, SNK, who managed to woo its design team away from Capcom—its designer, Hiroshi Matsumoto, would later create the *Art of Fighting* for the Neo Geo platform.

To fill the void, Capcom tapped Yoshiki Okamoto, a tempestuous 30-year-old who'd been fired by Konami despite his success with *Time Pilot* (1982) and *Gyruss* (1983), two of my favorite arcade games. He soon proved his value to his new employer with *1942* (1984), a hit scrolling shoot'em up game that is still widely admired and played today. However, before Okamoto finished his game, Tecnos Japan's *Double Dragon* landed in arcades.

Double Dragon was a "beat'em up," a genre with side-scrolling levels occupied by large numbers of enemies, who players must dispatch with martial arts and, in the case of *Double Dragon*, a variety of fun weapons (whips, baseball bats, dynamite, and more). From an operator's perspective, the game's brilliance lay in its cooperative multiplayer, which doubled the number of quarters it could earn at one time.

In response to *Double Dragon*'s enviable success, Okamoto seized the moment and abandoned his plans for a *Street Fighter* sequel. Instead, he produced *Final Fight*, a beat'em up designed by Akira Nishitani and Akira Yasuda. "Capcom was in trouble at the time," said Okamoto. "If *Final Fight* didn't sell well, Capcom [was] in danger of going under."[2]

Fortunately, the game was a hit, and Okamoto was asked to make a sequel for it, but there was a problem—"I don't generally do what people ask," said Okamoto. The nonconformist decided that now was the right time to go back to his earlier plans for a *Street Fighter* sequel.

Capcom threw money at Okamoto, who swelled his team to include more than 20 artists to create characters, backgrounds, and other assets. The original *Street Fighter* had only had two characters, but now the sequel would have many more, each with a distinctive look, fighting style, theme song, and national origin: Japan, the United States, Brazil, China, the Soviet Union, and India were all represented by player characters, lending the game an international appeal, even if some objected to the rather blatant stereotyping. The artists and designers enjoyed a friendly competition to see who could create the best characters.

The most celebrated feature of the game—the combos—was a fortuitous accident. The team had decided that the special moves in *Street Fighter* were too hard to pull off, so they cut players some slack with the timing. Much to their chagrin, however, they soon discovered that players could manipulate the process, stringing together special moves into powerful combinations, or "combos" as they became known. Considered a bug at first, combos turned out to be one of the game's most popular and endearing features. Each character had his or her own appropriately themed moves. Chun-Li, a Chinese martial artist, had the "Spinning Bird Kick," whereas Dhalsim, an Indian fighter, could do the "Yoga Smash." Later games in the series would add tons more characters and moves, but the original had plenty enough to keep you busy.

Okamoto had taken a big risk making *Street Fighter II; Final Fight II* would have been a much safer bet. The tension escalated after the game launched in Japan to a lukewarm reception. "Nobody fought against other people," said Okamoto. Earnings were less than a third of what they'd predicted. "People around me were saying, 'Your game tanked.'"[2] However, it was just a slow start—once these solo players had finished their "training" by defeating the computer-controlled opponents, they challenged their friends. Word quickly spread.

The game got off to a stronger start in the United States. Jeff Walker, Capcom USA's VP of Sales and Marketing, grew anxious when one of his operators in Fort Lauderdale, Florida, asked for a second machine. "I'm afraid if I put a second one in there I'm gonna cannibalize it. I'm gonna have two doing $600 [instead of one doing $1200]. Not the case at all. They both did $1400 ... Now we know we've got a juggernaut on our hands."[2] Capcom eventually sold more than 200,000 *Street Fighter II* cabinets, a figure that no one had seen since *Pac-Man* and *Space Invaders*, the only games that top its estimated 3.5 billion dollars in earnings.[6,7]

Street Fighter II: The World Warrior was a staggering success for Capcom and the arcade industry as a whole. Capcom released dozens of variations over the years, adding or revising content or tweaking the gameplay. *Street Fighter II* aficionados endlessly debated the merits and limitations of each port, sequel, and remake.

---

[6] Rignall, Jaz. "Top 10 Highest-Grossing Arcade Games of All Time." *US Gamer.* May 22, 2015. http://www.usgamer.net/articles/top-10-biggest-grossing-arcade-games-of-all-time (accessed July 1, 2015).

[7] This figure adjusted for inflation. It's $2.3 billion in 1995 dollars.

Naturally, *Street Fighter II* spurred a huge number of clones and spin-offs. SNK added several key games to the genre, including *Fatal Fury: King of Fighters* (1991), *Art of Fighting* (1992), and *Samurai Shodown* (1993), just to name a few of the best known examples. However, the most (in)famous of all was *Mortal Kombat*, a 1992 game developed by Midway Games' Chicago studio, where Americans Ed Boon and John Tobias—both fans of *Street Fighter II*—decided to take the genre in a much darker direction (see Figure 22.5).

Mortal Kombat looked more realistic than *Street Fighter II* because it was made with live actors who had been filmed over a bluescreen and digitized—a technique pioneered in Atari Games' otherwise insignificant *Pit-Fighter*, released a year earlier. Word quickly spread of the game's "fatalities," which allowed victorious players to perform gruesome finishing moves on the fallen competitor. Perhaps the worst offender was a "spine rip" fatality performed by the character Sub-Zero. The over-the-top violence, coupled with the realistic graphics, ignited a firestorm in the media that led to US Senate hearings. Unfortunately for those concerned about the effects of such violence on youth, the political furor amounted to little more than free publicity for

Figure 22.5 *Mortal Kombat* offered a bloodier take on the genre. Fans loved the realistic look, but some worried that they might encourage real-life violence.

Midway, who ended up selling more than 24,000 cabinets and grossing over a half-billion in profits.

While most of the excitement around *Street Fighter II* and *Mortal Kombat* happened at arcades (or wherever an arcade machine could be found!), they were ported to most computer and console platforms in various editions. *Street Fighter II Turbo/Champion* was adapted for the Super Nintendo Entertainment System (SNES), Turbo-Grafx 16, and Sega Genesis, and even if none of these could hope to achieve 100% fidelity with their arcade equivalents, they were critically acclaimed and drove system sales. It was especially vital for Nintendo, who managed to get first dibs. It sold more than 6.3 million copies and was a major coup for Nintendo.[8]

Mortal Kombat's excessive violence led to plenty of controversy when it came to adapting it for consoles. Nintendo had a family-friendly policy, and naturally *Mortal Kombat* needed a serious scrubbing. The fatalities were toned down or taken out completely, and the blood was recolored gray and referred to officially as sweat. Even though Sega had tried to distinguish itself from Nintendo by projecting an edgier image, they also censored it—but by entering a special code, gamers could bring back the violence. Once this information leaked out, Sega's version was the preferred choice.

Both *Street Fighter II* and *Mortal Kombat* received live action silver screen treatments. The first was Steven E. de Souza's dreadful *Street Fighter*, a 1994 starring Jean-Claude Van Damme, whose earlier movies had been the inspiration for *Mortal Kombat*. Paul W. S. Anderson's film *Mortal Kombat*, which debuted in 1995, fared much better both critically and commercially, with a solid story, awesome soundtrack, and excellent martial arts action.

As the 1990s drew to a close, developers kept searching for ways to keep the genre fresh. Sega had a surprise hit in 1993 with its arcade game, *Virtua Fighter*, a pioneering attempt at a three-dimensional (3D) fighting game (see Figure 22.6). Critics raved about its realistic fighting system and impressive 3D graphics. The *Virtua Fighter* series inspired several other 3D fighting games, including Namco's *Tekken* (1995) and Team Ninja's *Dead or Alive* (1996). Both games led to best-selling and long-running series. The *Dead or Alive* series gained some measure of fame for its scantily clad female characters, a trend that culminated in *Dead or Alive Xtreme Beach Volleyball* (2003) for the Microsoft Xbox—a volleyball game that starred the series' female cast in next to nothing.

There are, of course, plenty of other interesting and innovative one-on-one fighting games worth mentioning, such as Squaresoft's *Bushido Blade* (1997; Sony PlayStation), a realistic weapons-based game featuring one-hit kills; Arc System Works' *Guilty Gear* (1998), featuring beautiful anime-style graphics; and Namco's *Soulcalibur* (1999), a weapons-based fighter with greater freedom of movement.

---

[8] Patterson, Eric L. "EGM Feature: The 5 Most Influential Japanese Games Day Four: Street Fighter II." *EGM Now.* November 3, 2011. http://www.egmnow.com/articles/news/egm-featurethe-5-most-influential-japanese-gamesday-four-street-fighter-ii/ (accessed July 1, 2015).

An interesting trend in fighting games is the "crossover fighting game," which mixes together characters from other franchises or even different media entirely. The most popular of these are *Marvel vs. Capcom, Capcom vs. SNK, Mortal Kombat vs. DC Universe*, and the aforementioned *Super Smash Bros.* games, but there are plenty of others. Personally, I'd love to see *Marvel vs. DC Universe*; stranger things have happened!

Figure 22.6   Sega's hit *Virtua Fighter* brought the genre into three dimensions.

The widespread adoption of broadband reduced the demand for the arcade slugfests. On the plus side, it's easier than ever to find worthy contenders to play with, as it's always butt-kicking o'clock somewhere in the world. On the downside, though, there's something to be said about putting the smack down on someone standing within kicking distance, especially with an appreciative audience to admire your technique.

Space Invaders and *Pac-Man* were certainly influential but seemed more suited to individuals than communities of gamers. Competition was indirect and based on an abstract high score table. It was like runners competing by comparing lap times rather than racing down the track together. *Street Fighter II* was, if nothing else, very clear about winning and losing. As players competed, they talked, either to taunt their opponent or compare notes. Serious players analyzed the game's ins and outs with the same dedication a sports fanatic lavishes on her favorite team.

Okamoto and Capcom left themselves wide open by introducing such a complex and sophisticated game. Arguably its greatest feature was a bug, and it broke with that age-old advice to "be easy to learn, but hard to master." *Street Fighter II* was hard to learn, and as far as mastery is concerned, I'll quote Daigo Umehara, one of the world's most famous *Street Fighter* players and world record holder:

> Though I've been called "God's Hand" and "The Beast," I've never thought of myself as someone with talent. Actually, if we're only talking about talent, I think there are a lot of people who have more of it than I do.[9]

Humble words. Mr. Miyagi would be proud.

[9] Taylor, Nicholas. "Daigo Umehara." *Event Hubs*. May 30, 2013. http://www.eventhubs.com/news/2013/may/30/daigo -umehara-ive-never-thought-myself-talented-talks-about-his-gaming-career-and-views-what-winning-means/ (accessed July 1, 2015).

Figure 22.7   A promotional screenshot of *Street Fighter V*, due in 2016. (Photo courtesy of Capcom U.S.A.)

22.1 Playing *Street Fighter II* Today

While historical purists might prefer the original *Street Fighter II: The World Warrior*, many prefer the revised versions: *Street Fighter II: Champion Edition* or *Street Fighter II Turbo: Hyper Fighting*. These offer additional moves, balance refinements, and characters. The next installment, *Super Street Fighter II: The New Challengers*, switched to CP System II hardware, which enabled enhanced audiovisuals. There are dozens of other authorized editions, and many more bootleg editions. Which of these countless variations is best comes down to individual preference, but if you're just starting out, you may wish to stick to *The World Warrior* for the sake of simplicity and nostalgia.

Capcom published *Super Street Fighter II Turbo HD Remix* in 2008, and it's available on Xbox Live and the PlayStation Network. Many consider it to be the definitive version, and definitely worth checking out if you're into the series. Sadly, it's not yet available for PCs, though there are petitions circulating online to bring it to Steam. You can play *Street Fighter IV* or *Ultra Street Fighter IV* there, though, and *Street Fighter V* may be out by the time you read this (see Figure 22.7).

In any case, don't even attempt to play this game without an appropriate controller. Ideally, you'll use an arcade fighting stick. There are many to choose from, but I recommend X-Arcade's Dual Joystick. This sturdy unit will bring you pretty close to the look and feel of the arcade version on whatever platform you choose.

Chapter 23

SimCity: A City of Silicon

Would you know a great game if you played it? Maybe you would, but we've already seen several instances where even the savviest publishers said "no, thanks" to a smash hit.

One cringe-worthy example occurred at a trade show in 1980, where marketing executives were offered their choice of four Namco arcade games: *King and Balloon*, *Tank Battalion*, *Rally-X*, and *Pac-Man*. You'd think that anyone would've known *Pac-Man* was something special, but that's the benefit of hindsight. Midway's president, David Marofske, shared Namco's opinion that *Rally-X* was by far the best in show.[1] In Marofske's defense, "strategic multiplayer racing game" sounded much better on paper than "wedge-shaped creature gobbles pellets as monsters pursue him through a maze."

If *Pac-Man*'s premise seemed ludicrous, imagine a game about adjusting tax rates, assigning zones for development, and laying water pipes, streets, and power lines. How could any of that possibly be any fun? There wasn't even a clear way to win or lose; you just played until you got bored and started over again. "I told people I was going to do a game about city planning," said the game's designer, Will Wright, who was then 25 years old. "They'd just look at me, roll their eyes, and say, somewhat dubiously, 'Oh good, Will, you go do that.'"[2] The "unmarketable" concept only made sense to Wright, who'd gotten into the business after giving up (temporarily, at least) on his dream of building robots and colonies in space. But there was one dream he couldn't let go of; one idea his colleagues could not quite convince him was stupid; one tiny sim who would not do as he was told.

Then and now, most games are based on activities that are intrinsically fun, such as pinball or *Tetris*, or those that immerse us in exciting scenarios, like fighting, racing, or exploring. We play these games to escape from reality; we dream of being lion tamers, not chartered accountants.

"Will has a reality-distortion field around him," said his friend and business partner Jeff Braun. "He comes up with the craziest idea you've ever heard, and when he's finished explaining it to you the world looks crazy—he's the only sane person in it."[3] Wright's idea was brilliant, but it was one of the toughest sells in the history of the industry (see Figure 23.1).

---

[1] Kent, Steve L. *The Ultimate History of Video Games: From Pong to Pokémon and Beyond: The Story Behind the Craze that Touched Our Lives and Changed the World.* Rocklin, CA: Prima Pub., 2001: 142.

[2] Keighley, Geoff. "Simply Divine: The Story of Maxis Software." *GameSpot.* 1999. http://www.gamespot.com/features /maxis/index.html (accessed May 8, 1999).

[3] Seabrook, John. "Game Master." *The New Yorker.* November 6, 2006. http://www.newyorker.com/magazine/2006/11/06 /game-master?currentPage=all (accessed July 7, 2015).

Wright's interest in the video game industry began in the early 1980s, after he bought an Apple II and played Bill Budge's *Pinball Construction Set* and Nasir Gebelli's games. He was inspired by Bruce Artwick's *Flight Simulator*, but it wasn't so much the plane as the world around it: "For the first time, there was this consistent, microscopic little world ... It just amazed me," he said.[4]

Wright also singles out Dan Gorlin's *Choplifter* (1982) game as an influence; this was a great 2D helicopter game that had you shooting tanks, planes, and rescuing

Figure 23.1   Will Wright at GDC 2010. (Photo courtesy of Official GDC.)

hostages (see Figure 23.2). As we'll see, helicopters were never far from Wright's mind. He cherished the memories of flying in them with his father, who died when Wright was only 9 years old. His dad had never told his son his ideas were crazy or misguided. Instead, he'd sat with him on many a night, pointing up at stars and wondering what sort of creatures might live there. Wright's father was gone from the earth, but the stars were still there.

The program that had the strongest impact on Wright's life and his career was not really a game at all, but rather a simulation. It was John Horton Conway's *Game of Life*, a simulation of cellular automation that dated back to 1970 (see Figure 23.3). It was based on four simple rules—algorithms—that determined the growth or decay of the cellular system—life at its most abstract. The *Game of Life* was fascinating then, and it's fascinating now—with so little input, the computer spawns wondrously complex, elegant, beautiful patterns; spaces of the possible. Wright became obsessed with the *Game of Life* and spent a year programming versions of it in PASCAL and later machine language.

As Wright's confidence grew in his programming, he decided the time was right to try making his own game. He knew his Apple II inside and out, but the Commodore 64, the most popular computer the world had ever seen, was the surest route to success. He bought one and set to work learning to code it, and, like many Apple II programmers, found it painfully deficient, like typing with one hand. Wright found the situation intolerable, so he built an interface that allowed him to program on his Apple II and then run his code on the Commodore. It wasn't an elegant solution, but it worked, and "good enough" is the mantra of every wealthy programmer.

Of course he'd choose to make his first game about helicopters. However, this would be much more than a *Choplifter* clone. Instead, he'd use Conway's *Game of Life* algorithms to simulate a dynamic, virtual world; a "world large enough to get lost in," as he

4   Wright, Will. "Classic Game Postmortem: Raid on Bungeling Bay." *GDC Vault.* 2011. http://www.gdcvault.com/play/1014635 /Classic-Game-Postmortem-RAID-ON (accessed July 8, 2015).

described it.[4] At a time when most designers would have been satisfied just to have
a smoothly scrolling tiled background,
Wright wanted a working ecosystem, or a
"clockwork universe," as he put it.

The world he created for his game was
a group of islands. Boats traveled between
them, delivering resources to tanks on the
islands, which would transport them to

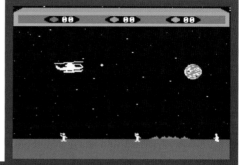

Figure 23.2   *Choplifter* was a hit Apple II helicopter rescue game. It was developed by Dan Gorlin and published by Brøderbund in 1982.

the six factories the player was tasked with
destroying. The factories were defended by
turrets, tanks, and fighters, and the factories would expend resources to rebuild any
that were destroyed. Meanwhile, the scien-
tists in the factories were furiously developing more advanced technologies, such as
heat-seeking missiles.

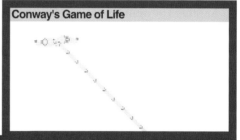

Conway's Game of Life

Figure 23.3   Conway's *Game of Life* is a simple simulation of cellular automation, but its tendency to produce mesmerizing patterns showed Wright how complexity could emerge from very humble origins.

Brøderbund, who'd brought out *Choplifter* in 1982, published *Raid on Bungeling Bay* in 1984 as a sequel of sorts—the "Bungeling Empire" introduced in that game was carried over to maintain some continuity (it also appeared in Douglas E. Smith's *Lode Runner*). They ported it to the Nintendo Entertainment System (NES) and MSX (a Japanese platform) a year later. Critics were impressed with both the graphics and movement, but few even mentioned its greatest innovation, the one for which Wright was so proud: the clockwork universe. "It was totally opaque to people," said Wright.[4] He blamed himself; he didn't even depict the resources the boats collected, thus masking the entire process. It was a failure of design, not concept, but he still earned "enough money to live on for several years"[3] (see Figure 23.4).

Like Bill Budge, Will Wright had more fun making his game than he did playing it. This was especially true of his game world: "I was more interested in creating the build-ings on the islands than in blowing them up."[3] However, just putting up buildings on a map wasn't much of a game. There was something missing.

He talked it over with his next-door neighbor, who happened to be the city planner for Oakland, California. He gave him a copy of *Urban Dynamics*, a controversial book by Jay Wright Forrester, the father of system dynamics. The book's argument was that city

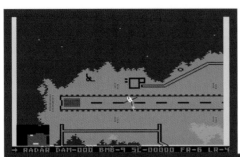

managers tend to treat symptoms rather than the actual causes of a problem. To get at the real causes, we have to dig much deeper into a system's structures and policies; often a group of three of more "interacting feedback loops."[5] These complex relationships were much too difficult for a human to fathom, but a computer

Figure 23.4   Will Wright's *Raid on Bungeling Bay* was a fun action game, but it was easy to overlook what really made it special—its living game world.

could simulate its behavior, revealing its true characteristics. It was heady stuff, but perfect thought fodder for Wright, who'd always been an electric and fervent reader.

Another key influence was a short story by Polish author Stanislaw Lem called "The Seventh Sally," in which a robot builds a miniature kingdom whose description could serve for *SimCity*: "It was only a model, after all. A process with a large number of parameters, a simulation, a mock-up for a monarch to practice on, with the necessary feedback, variables, multistats..." The robot in the story made his simulation a little too perfect; the tiny citizens eventually became self-aware and turned on their master, who'd became a despot—much like the countless fans of his game, few of whom could long resist the temptation to unleash disaster on their city just for the fun of it.

Wright spent the next year adapting Forrester and Lem's ideas into a playable game for the Commodore 64, a formidable task given that machine's limitations. In the meantime, the Macintosh, Amiga, and Atari ST had popularized the graphical user interface, and Wright tried his best to apply these concepts (as well as multitasking) into a program he called *Micropolis*, which he completed in 1985. Though it lacked many of the features of the later versions, it was already an impressive achievement (see Figure 23.5).

Wright himself was proud of the unpredictable citizens that populated his virtual city, the "sims." "They don't obey," said Wright. "That's what makes it fun ... You keep trying to keep this city together, but it keeps falling apart ... You have a certain amount of control, but there's a certain amount of entropy of the system, and it's balanced just right ... It's life at the edge of chaos. Shit happens."[6] Much like the despot in Lem's story, players could spend hours manipulating the variables, then sit back to witness the long-term effects of their playing at God.

Unfortunately, Brøderbund was baffled by its open-ended design. "They kept saying, 'Where's the ending? When do you win or lose?' And they wanted to have an election where you got kicked out of office or not. And I was like, 'No, it's even more fun if you're doing it

---

[5] Forrester, Jay Wright. *Urban Dynamics*. Cambridge, MA: MIT, 1969: 108.

[6] Kelly, Kevin. "Will Wright: The Mayor of SimCity." *Wired*. January 1994. http://archive.wired.com/wired/archive/2.01/wright.html (accessed July 8, 2015).

badly.' And they just parked it. They decided they weren't going to release it."[7] He fared no better with other publishers, who simply couldn't imagine anyone actually wanting to play a game about city building.

In 1986, Wright attended a pizza party thrown by investor Jeff Braun. Braun had made his fortune with a business that made

POWER LINES

Figure 23.5   The first version of *SimCity* was done on the Commodore 64. It wasn't much to look at, but the gameplay was deep and addictive.

factory-floor automation systems, but after learning about the Commodore Amiga, "decided it was going to change the world," and invited a bunch of game developers in hopes of snagging a few into a new venture.[8] When Braun asked Wright what kind of games he made, the despondent developer sighed, "You won't like the games I make. They're really bad."[9]

Braun was eventually able to coax Wright into showing him his game anyway, and unlike the executives at Brøderbund, he immediately recognized the game's potential. "It was a breakout, something I had never seen before," said Braun, who partnered with Wright to develop it for the Amiga and other computers under their own label, Maxis.[8] Brøderbund reluctantly agreed to distribute the product, but only after they'd added scenarios based on historical cities (Hamburg of 1944, Detroit in 1972, etc.) (see Figure 23.6).

Braun, like Trip Hawkins of Electronic Arts, was wrong about the Amiga; a few years later, it was all but irrelevant. As the weeks crept into months after *SimCity* hit the streets, it looked as though he was wrong about it, too. "It was such a strange thing; nobody knew what to make of it," said Braun.[9] If the sluggish sales weren't worrisome enough, he was soon the target of a lawsuit by Toho, the Japanese film company, who claimed the unnamed monster in *SimCity* impinged on their Godzilla trademarks.

And this might have been the end of Maxis and *SimCity* were it not for a full-page review that appeared in *Newsweek.* The reviewer, Bill Barol, sums up the game's appeal quite aptly: "Control. The exhilarating ability to manipulate an environment. Maybe even their own environment, by proxy of imagination. In a world where cities seem to have ungovernable lives of their own, that's a gift."[10] It was the first time *Newsweek* had ever published a game review, and it sent the game's sales through the roof. By 1992, it had sold more than

[7]   Sinclair, Brendan. "Spot On: 'Here's the Pitch…'." *GameSpot.* December 7, 2007. http://www.gamespot.com/articles/spot-on-heres-the-pitch/1100-6183997/ (accessed July 8, 2015).

[8]   Bryant, Adam. "Computer Games with Principles." *New York Times*, November 7, 1993: ED36.

[9]   Buckleitner, Warren. "Dust or Magic 2009: Jeff Braun on the Early Days of Maxis, Will Wright, and SimCity." *YouTube.* July 30, 2010. https://www.youtube.com/watch?v=3g1OZljodSQ (accessed July 8, 2015).

[10]   Barol, Bill. "Big Fun in a Small Town." *Newsweek*, May 29, 1989: 64.

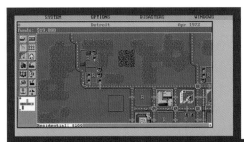

Figure 23.6 *SimCity Classic* running on the DOSBox emulator. If you didn't want to start a city from scratch, you could load one of several included scenarios to test your mettle as a city planner.

a million copies, and Russell Sipe, the publisher of *Computer Gaming World*, proclaimed it had "changed the face of computer entertainment software."[11]

Further critical acclaim followed. "In 1989, there was no award we didn't get," said Braun.[9] The appeal went well beyond traditional gamer circles. It soon found its way into classrooms, government offices, labs, executive boardrooms, and, of course, architect and designer studios. *The Journal*, the biggest newspaper in Rhode Island, had the five candidates for mayor play the game as a test of their fitness for the office. Most failed spectacularly, but Vincent Cianci, who "solved a housing crunch, avoided new taxes, and left office with a small budget surplus," did end up winning the election.[11]

Wright didn't rest on his laurels, and immediately went to work with *SimEarth: The Living Planet* (1990). It put players in control of a planetary ecosystem, which they could affect by altering its temperature, atmosphere, and landmasses, and then observing how these conditions influenced the evolution of living organisms. It was based on another of Wright's informal scholarly pursuits, James Lovelock's Gaia hypothesis. The hypothesis describes the earth itself as a living organism; its organs are living and nonliving entities that interact in powerful and dynamic ways. Lovelock himself contributed to the game's manual, a 212-page document loaded with facts, theories, and cheesy one-liners: "Is this a random world or did you planet?" Corny jokes aside, the game's steep learning curve and complex interface (described in the manual as a "planetary spreadsheet") turned away those looking for a *SimCity* successor, and it wasn't nearly as successful.

Next up was *SimAnt*, released in 1991. This ant colony simulation attracted more attention than *SimEarth*, probably because of its more intuitive interface and appealing subject matter. A lifelong "ant lover," Wright was inspired this time by ant expert E.O. Wilson, whose massive book *The Ants* is considered the definitive work on the subject and was richly influential in ecology and sociobiology. Wright read this and all of Wilson's other works. Wright took the chance to interview him for NPR's *Open Mic* program in 2009 and discovered a mutual admiration. When asked if he thought there was a place for games in education, Wilson responded that "Games are the future in education ... I envision visits to different ecosystems that the student could actually enter, taking this path, going to that hill, with an instructor ... I hope I'll meet you sometime, maybe walking together through a Jurassic forest."

"I'll start working on it," replied Wright.[12]

Wright followed *SimAnt* with an even more abstract title called *SimLife* (1992), which focused again on ecosystems, but this time players could modify the genetic code of plants and animals. Wright would return to this theme in 2008 with *Spore*. In 1993, Maxis released *SimFarm*, a game that, as the title suggests, had players managing a farm. *SimLife: Missions in the Rainforest* followed in 1995, an unsuccessful game by Matthew Stibbe (see Figure 23.7).

None of these spin-offs achieved anywhere near the popularity of the original, which finally received a true sequel, *SimCity 2000*, in 1993 (see Figure 23.8). This game marked a great leap forward in audiovisuals, with the city now shown

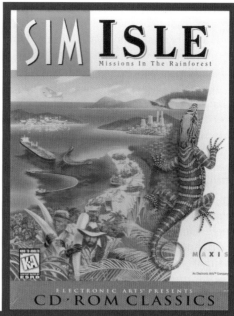

Figure 23.7   *SimIsle: Missions in the Rainforest* was a 1995 game designed by Matthew Stibbe outside of Maxis. Despite its intriguing premise, it was one of many SimFails.

in isometric perspective instead of the top-down view of the original. This angled perspective made the structures look more three-dimensional (3D); taller buildings visibly looked taller. The sequel also added many new structures, such as subways, airports, and seaports. While the new features pleased fans and critics, others were more impressed with the *SimCity*

Figure 23.8   *SimCity 2000*'s sharper visuals and new structures made it a must-have for fans of the series.

Urban Renewal Kit, which allowed players to alter the in-game images to represent particular buildings or settings. The award-winning game was another crowd-pleaser for Maxis and is considered the best of the series by many aficionados.

---

[12] Montagne, Renee. "E.O. Wilson and Will Wright: Ant Lovers Unite!" *NPR.org*. September 1, 2009. http://www.npr.org /templates/transcript/transcript.php?storyId=112203095 (accessed August 26, 2015).

Despite the financial success of *SimCity 2000*, Wright himself was tired of doing sim games. Instead, he spent several fruitless months designing a "freeform adventure game with a flight simulator," based on the Hindenburg airship disaster.[2] Wright eventually scrapped the ill-conceived project, fearing that some might think he was a Nazi sympathizer (the German LZ 129 *Hindenburg* had giant swastikas on its tail fins).

It took a sim game based on his old flame, helicopters, to bring Wright back to the table. *SimCopter* (1996) was a 3D game that put you in the cockpit of a helicopter soaring over a simulated city. Gameplay consisted of redirecting traffic, apprehending criminals, fighting fires, performing daring rescues, and transporting people to and fro. You could even import maps from *SimCity 2000*. It was also the first appearance of Simlish, the fictional language of the Sims.

The last *SimCity* game that Wright himself designed was *SimCity 3000*, whose development began in 1996. By this point, first-person shooters with 3D graphics were all the rage, and it seemed to make sense to bring *SimCity* into the third dimension as well. Sam Poole, a former sales executive with no game development experience, was now running Maxis and promising "photo-realistic 3D graphics and an enhanced simulation model" in time for Christmas.[13]

Unfortunately, this challenge proved far more formidable than Maxis anticipated, and all they had to show for their efforts at E3 a month later was a brief trailer with blocky, outmoded graphics. Soon after this dismal showing, Maxis was acquired by Electronic Arts, and Luc Barthelet became the general manager. He moved decisively, gutting the staff and reducing *SimCity 3000* back down to two dimensions.

The resulting product may not have been 3D, but it looked great in 2D and did offer more sophisticated choices. Naturally, there were more structures to build, which now included farms and wastewater management services. Players could also interact with neighboring cities to work out business deals or purchase services. There was also a greater emphasis on land values. A jazzy score by Jerry Martin rounded out the package. Electronic Arts published *SimCity 4* in 2003, which was also warmly received. Unlike the previous games, which focused on a single city, this time the planning was at a regional level, with interactions between neighboring cities.

The latest entry in the series was confusingly titled *SimCity* (unofficially, it's known as *SimCity 5*) (see Figure 23.9). This 2013 release was a high-profile disaster for Maxis and Electronic Arts, caused mostly by the decision to require an online connection to a persistent universe. It wasn't necessarily a bad idea, but there were many issues in practice. Like many other players, I had troubles logging in and staying connected when I did. To soothe bitter tempers, EA gave owners a free game and made the online connection optional, but the damage was done. In March of 2015, EA shut down Maxis' studio in Emeryville, where the *SimCity* games were made.

SimCity inspired plenty of games from rival companies eager to cash in on the "city management" craze. One of the earliest and most successful was David Lester's *Caesar* game, which was popular enough to warrant three sequels. As the title implies, the series

---

[13] PR Newswire. "Next Generation in Best Selling SimCity Line Set for Holiday Release." *PR Newswire*, May 16, 1997.

had players managing cities in Ancient Rome rather than modern times. Other rivals focused on the business side of things, such as Trevor Chan's *Capitalism* (1995), which put players in charge of a major corporation. Phil Steinmeyer's *Tropico* series (2001) has also proven quite successful, combining the familiar

Figure 23.9   The new *SimCity* had a lot of promise, but connectivity issues plagued its launch and incensed many devoted fans. Shown here is a promotional screenshot courtesy of Electronic Arts.

city-building aspects with political and cultural satire. The latest of these, *Tropico 5*, was published in 2014. Other *SimCity*-inspired games are the *Tycoon* and *Empire* series, such as Sid Meier's *Railroad Tycoon* (1990–2006) or Chan's *Restaurant Empire* (2003). There are dozens of these themes to choose from, including hospitals, theme parks, and zoos.

Sometimes, Peter Molyneux's *Populous* (1989) game is mistakenly lumped in with such games. However, this game had players in the role of a god, not a mayor or park manager—a substantial difference, I'd argue. Furthermore, the player doesn't decide what to build where, but rather raises and lowers land tiles to facilitate settlement by your minions or followers. Gradually, their devotion grants you divine powers to create, well, acts of God, and also to promote followers to higher ranks. Honestly, it deserves its own chapter in a book like this, but suffice it to say, it was in many ways an equally brilliant and influential game.

We'll come back to Wright when we talk about his greatest game, *The Sims*, in Chapter 32.

23.1 Playing *SimCity* Today

Purists should try *SimCity* for the Commodore 64, which was the first version and also the simplest. Unless you have a C64 lying around, though, you'll need an emulator—I recommend Cloanto's *C64 Forever*. However, the later versions for MS-DOS, Amiga, and other platforms have superior audiovisuals and more features.

A great option for modern PCs (and free!) is *Micropolis*, an open source version of the original *SimCity* by Don Hopkins. You can download a copy or play it online at http://micropolis.mostka.com/.

Chapter 24

Civilization: Just One More Turn

A few years after Will Wright's *SimCity* tore into the industry like a rampaging Godzilla, another designer, Sid Meier, was developing another touchstone of strategy gaming: *Civilization*. Like *SimCity*, its production was an uphill battle and could easily have been canceled. The many of us who enjoy playing "*Civ*" today owe much to Meier, who knew the game was worth the struggle (see Figure 24.1).

Sid Meier, a Canadian-American, got his start in the industry by majoring in computer science at the University of Michigan in the early 1970s. While there, he worked on an IBM 360 mainframe and learned FORTRAN.[1] After college, he landed a job programming microcomputers at General Instrument.

One of John's colleagues there was John "Wild Bill" Stealey, a manager with a sideline as a US Air Force fighter pilot. Meier was a quiet, modest type who only raised his voice to sing in his church choir. Stealey was the opposite, a man who was only comfortable streaking through the sky at supersonic speed. What brought the unlikely pair together was their shared interest in the Atari 800. Meier had bought his to learn how to program games; Stealey bought his for a single game: *Star Raiders*, Doug Neubauer's amazing space combat simulator.

One day at a Las Vegas trade show, the two worked their way down to a basement to see an arcade game exhibit. Stealey, cocky as ever, challenged Meier to each one, but was quickly humbled. He thought he'd turn the tables, though, when he spied a flight simulator—Atari's *Red Baron* arcade game. Surely, Stealey reasoned, his thousands of hours in the cockpit would give him an edge. He fought his way up to the third rank on the high score table—75,000 points—and sat back, smug, no doubt, as Meier put in his quarter.

Imagine the look on Stealey's face when his companion managed to match his high score and then *double* it. Feeling that he'd made his point, Meier finally let his plane crash, more bored than challenged. "I was really torqued," said Stealey. "This guy outflew an Air Force pilot?"[2] Meier only shrugged, admitting that while he lacked Stealey's experience in an actual jet, he knew programming and had simply figured out *Red Baron*'s algorithms.

"I could design a better one," Meier said off-handedly.

[1] Edwards, Benj. "The History of Civilization." *Gamasutra*. July 18, 2007. http://www.gamasutra.com/view/feature/1523/the_history_of_civilization.php (accessed July 29, 2015).

[2] Schreier, Jason. "Sid Meier: The Father of Civilization." *Kotaku*. June 26, 2013. http://kotaku.com/the-father-of-civilization-584568276 (accessed July 30, 2015).

Figure 24.1   Sid Meier in 2015. (Photo courtesy of Guerric.)

Figure 24.2   *Hellcat Ace* was one of many flight simulator games Meier developed before *Civilization.*

"If you could, I'd sell it," offered Stealey, and a partnership was born. Meier, of course, would do the computer work while the brash fighter pilot took care of the business and sales side of things—aspects that Meier detested. The two founded Microprose in 1982, and Meier delivered on his promise with *Hellcat Ace* a couple of months later.[3] A reviewer for *ROM Magazine* wrote that "it's the type of game you'll have many 'all nighters'"[4] (see Figure 24.2).

Stealey lived up to his end of the bargain, too, taking the game to software shops and haranguing managers to put *Hellcat Ace* on the shelf. If that failed, he wasn't above guile:

I would call computer stores and ask to buy *Hellcat Ace.* And when they didn't have it, I would yell and scream at them … I would do that three times in three weeks, each time pretending to be a different person. And the fourth week I'd call and say, "Hello, this is John Stealey. I'm a representative with Microprose, with this game called *Hellcat Ace*." They'd say, "Hey, hey, hey, everyone's been calling about that; can you help us get that game?"[2]

Stealey's approach worked, and soon he and Meier were making healthy profits and earning a name for themselves in the flight simulator genre with *Spitfire Ace* (1982), *Solo Flight* (1983), and several more by other designers. Meier appears to have shared Wright's interest in helicopters and the game *Choplifter* as well; though his *Chopper Rescue* (1982) was a more straightforward derivative than Wright's *Raid on Bungeling Bay.*

---

[3] There's some debate about which is Meier's first commercial game. Other contenders are *Formula 1, Chopper Rescue,* and *Floyd of the Jungle,* all circa 1982. *Formula 1* was published by Acorn Software Products. Read more at http://web.stanford.edu/group/htgg/cgi-bin/drupal/?q=node/237.

[4] Cockroft, Jason. "Jake the Software Dude." *ROM Magazine,* October/November 1983: 11.

Microprose's flight simulators were very profitable, and Stealey's background in aviation made it a great fit for him. Meier, however, felt a constant itch to experiment with radical new designs rather than imitate other successful games. The first of these to really take off was *Sid Meier's Pirates!* in 1987, which let players experience the life of a swashbuckling pirate in the Caribbean

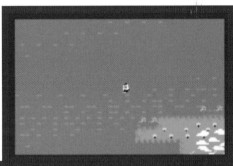

Figure 24.3 *Pirates!* was one of Meier's most influential games. Shown here is the Commodore 64 version.

(see Figure 24.3). Since it was such a radical departure from the games Microprose normally published, Stealey decided to make its designer's name part of the title—a suggestion offered by the comedian Robin Williams at an industry event.[5] Microprose fans were familiar with the name from title screens, but this move significantly enhanced Meier's reputation as a master game designer.

Pirates! was based more on Hollywood and popular myth than actual history, but that didn't seem to bother anyone. Most players and critics appreciated its open-ended, player-directed gameplay; there was no prescribed way to play; you could be a vicious pirate or an honest trader. The variety of activities was especially impressive, with fun swordfights, sea battles, and political intrigue. Meier designed it on a Commodore 64, but it was ported to most platforms of the day, including the Nintendo Entertainment System (NES).

Meier's next project was a game based on trains, a preoccupation of the earliest nerds (remember that *Spacewar!* was developed by members of MIT's Tech Model Railroad Club). *Sid Meier's Railroad Tycoon* hit the rails in 1990 and became the first in a series of such games. Much like *Pirates!*, *Railroad Tycoon* gave players leeway in how they approached the game, and many elements were inspired by Wright's *SimCity*, which had debuted a year before.[1] The game was another big hit for Microprose, sweeping up awards (see Figure 24.4).

Meier's collaborators on *Railroad Tycoon* were Bruce Shelley and Max Remington. Shelley had been hired away from Avalon Hill, an influential maker of strategy board games. "Board games were at a tough point at Avalon Hill. I didn't think I had any future there. When I found out the company had created the Commodore 64 game *Pirates!*, I looked into trying to get a job there."[1]

Shelley and Meier worked so well together their colleagues started calling the pair "The A*Team." Meier's design methodology was to simply start immediately on a prototype, making huge changes to the design as he went along. Occasionally, he'd show his project

---

5 Birnbaum, Ian. "How Sid Meier Became One of the Most Recognizable Names in Gaming." *PC Gamer*. June 27, 2013. http://www.pcgamer.com/how-sid-meier-became-one-of-the-most-recognizable-names-in-pc-gaming/ (accessed August 1, 2015).

IDENTIFY THIS LOCOMOTIVE

Grasshopper	Planet
Norris	Patentee
American	Iron Duke
Mogul	DX Goods
Ten-Wheeler	Stirling
Consolidation	Spinner
Pacific	Webb Compound
Mikado	Hamilton
Challenger	A1 Class
F3A-Series	A4 Class

Figure 24.4   To derail pirates, *Railroad Tycoon* required players to correctly identify a locomotive. Unless you happened to know a member of the Tech Model Railroad Club, you'd probably need to consult the documentation.

to Shelley, who'd playtest it and give Meier feedback. "He must have relied on me to be his sounding board," said Shelley, "to represent average gamers around the world."[1] He became Meier's go-to source for second opinions on his designs.

If Meier had stopped after *Railroad Tycoon*, he'd probably still be recognized

as a preeminent designer. However, he'd yet to make his magnum opus, a game that would take place over the entire course of human history, starting with the first city and progressing through all the centuries up to the present and beyond. While there was a board game called *Civilization*, Meier claims not to have played it before making his game. Instead, his inspiration was the classic board game *Risk*, which he wanted to "bring to life on the computer," and along the way added the technology tree that became the core of the game.[1]

Meier's original plan was to do something more akin to *SimCity* and his own *Railroad Tycoon*, which were both real-time games. However, Meier was also a fan of the classic computer strategy game *Empire*, a turn-based war game created by computer programmer Walter Bright in 1971. *Empire* was a brilliant game that had players conquering cities, which produced a range of military units (planes, tanks, and ships) that could be controlled individually. Like *Civilization*, game maps could either be procedurally generated or based on actual continents, and an important early step was exploration (a fog of war covered unexplored areas). The similarities to *Civilization* are hard to miss, but there's no tech tree, and it's entirely focused on military production (see Figure 24.5).

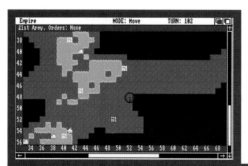

According to Shelley, one day Meier asked him to come up with 10 ways that *Empire* could've been better. It's not clear if the tech tree was on Shelley's list, but, at any rate, the idea occurred to them that it might be more fun if instead of being allowed to build all the various types of units from the beginning, you'd have to research and develop them first—and

Figure 24.5   *Civilization* was heavily influenced by this classic turn-based strategy game, *Empire*. My dad and I spent many pleasant weekends playing the Amiga version, shown here.

thus have to make decisions about which ones to prioritize. This led naturally to a richer historical aspect; why not start off with primitive weapons like clubs and spears and proceed throughout the ages, ending up with nuclear weapons and beyond? Finally, more for flavor than anything else, Meier delved into some actual history but was careful to avoid the dreaded "educational" label. To that end, their research was limited to the "children's section of the library," said Shelley.[1]

Working with a team of 10 people, Meier was able to get the game done in a year. "It started to go viral within the company," said Brian Reynolds, one of Meier's collaborators and designer of *Civilization II*.[2] Frequently, those who played it came up with their own ideas for the game, and Meier was always happy to take them into consideration—"feedback is fact," he was fond of saying. Just because he liked an idea was irrelevant if others didn't. However, he was more concerned with taking things out than putting more stuff in; the complexity and scale of the game made even small additions tricky to implement—rather like adding extra gears to a pocket watch.

Meanwhile, Meier had distanced himself from Stealey and the management of Microprose. He believed that their focus on arcade and console versions of their computer games was a mistake, and stepped down. His fears were well grounded; the company was soon nearing bankruptcy and had to go public. Meier stayed on as a contractor, and a new VP, Kip Welch, took over his production responsibilities.

Unfortunately, Meier's new status as an outside contractor meant that there was less incentive within the company (namely, personal bonuses) to support his projects. According to Shelley, "The VP of production got no bonus for what Sid published. So he wanted to put resources on stuff he was being paid for. It was a struggle to get the people we needed to finish *Civ*."[1] The only employees of Microprose who weren't already promising to stop playing the game "after just one more turn" were the upper management, who Shelley believes would have canned the project if Meier had still been his employee. "I don't think management had much of a clue about what it was until it started selling," said Shelley.[1]

When they finally cobbled the final pieces together, Meier was further disappointed to learn that Microprose would not be actively promoting it. If the game was to succeed, it'd have to be by word of mouth.

A few months later, Stealey called Meier to inform him that his game had just won an award. The gaming public still respected the name Sid Meier, even if his own company had all but forgotten he existed. Indeed, the game sold better than Meier's other hit games—more than 850,000 copies by 1996. *Computer Gaming World* gave it five stars and called it "more addictive than crack. It should come with its own warning label."[6] Keith Ferrell penned as nearly an effusive review for *Compute!*, and took a worthy stab at articulating its broad appeal:

---

[6] Brooks, M. Evan. "The Modern Games: 1950-2000." *Computer Gaming World*, June 1992: 121.

Meier's accomplishment here is, ultimately, the creation of a game whose peaceful developmental aspects can be as fulfilling as its warlike aspects, perhaps even more fulfilling. How many war games can you think of in which you have the choice between producing weapons of mass destruction or build-

Figure 24.6   *Civilization* has come a long way since the first game, shown here, but much of the core gameplay remains the same.

ing Shakespeare's theater? The presence of that option indicates Meier's growth as a designer; that plowshares can in some ways be as fundamental to success as swords indicates the sophistication of the game.[7]

The game's unprecedented success set a high bar for Meier, who was happy to let Reynolds take responsibility for the sequel while he worked on *C.P.U. Bach*, a program that used algorithms to create original musical compositions. It was a niche product at best, and it didn't help that it was published exclusively for Trip Hawkins' short-lived 3DO platform. "I realized if I tried to top *Civilization* right away I'd probably go crazy," said Meier. "I didn't want to … try to top what we had done."[8] Meier designed several noteworthy games after *Civilization*, such as *Sid Meier's Colonization* (1994), *Sid Meier's Alpha Centauri* (1999), *Sid Meier's SimGolf* (2002), and more recently, *Sid Meier's Civilization: Revolution* (2008), a simplified version of *Civilization* for consoles. However, none of these or Meier's other games has come close to matching the appeal of his undisputed masterpiece (see Figure 24.6).

For his part, Meier seems content to rest on his laurels. "If that's what's on my epitaph—'Did *Civilization*'—that would be fine," said Meier.[1] The continued success of the franchise bodes well for his legacy. While the later games in the series offer plenty of welcome refinements, the core design hasn't changed as radically as some might assume—and Meier was not involved with their design and his name on the games is only a matter of branding. In any case, most modern fans prefer *Civilization V* (2010) or *Civilization IV* (2005), but even *Civilization III* (2001) is still actively played. A *Civilization VI* seems all but inevitable, though no official announcements have been made to date—and I have no reason to believe Meier would be more involved with it than he was with previous sequels.

---

[7] Ferrell, Keith. "Sid Meier's Civilization." *Compute!*, January 1992: 86.

[8] Jenkins, David. "Sid Meier Interview—A Lifelong Strategy." *Metro*. March 12, 2015. http://metro.co.uk/2015/03/12/sid-meier-interview-a-lifelong-strategy-from-pirates-to-starships-5099845/ (accessed August 1, 2015).

On a personal note, I have spent more than 600 h playing *Civilization V*, mostly with my friends on Steam. It always surprises me how well the game can keep us all engaged to the end, no matter how many times we've played from start to finish. It truly seems timeless, more like a great board game, whose appeal comes almost solely from a brilliant design, not fancy graphics or a gripping narrative. I wouldn't be surprised if fans are still playing some form of *Civilization* a hundred years from now, and it'd only be fitting if the game itself was memorialized in some future edition as a Great Work of Art.

24.1 Playing *Civilization* Today

Sadly, the original *Civilization* is no longer available commercially, so you'll need to use an appropriate emulator such as DOSBox. Alternatively, you can play FreeCiv, a free and open source clone of the game for modern systems. It's available at http://play.freeciv .org and can be played right in your browser. *Civilization III* and later sequels are still being sold—look for them on Steam.

Chapter 25

Pool of Radiance: The Gold Box Games

By 1988, there were plenty of great computer role-playing games (CRPGs) on the market—you had your pick of Origin's *Ultima*, Sir-Tech's *Wizardry*, Epyx's *Apshai*, or New World Computing's *Might and Magic,* just to name a few. All of these were based more or less on older pen-and-paper or "tabletop" role-playing games.

By far the most influential of these was *Dungeons & Dragons (D&D)*, designed by Gary Gygax and Dave Arneson in the 1970s. It introduced millions of people to the concept of role-playing, where players assume the role of a character and participate in a campaign managed by a GM (game master). *D&D* combined an effective rule system for combat with rich fantasy settings like *Dragonlance* and *Greyhawk*; the adventures were only as limited as the players' own imaginations.

Developers were quick to see the potential of *D&D* as a computer game but devised their own rules and settings rather than deal with TSR, who owned the rights. The upside was they didn't have to pay royalties or licensing fees, but their systems were seldom as sophisticated or as battletested, so to speak, as TSR's. The first officially licensed *D&D* videogames were for Mattel's Intellivision console, but none of those approached the sophisticated mechanics of the tabletop games.

The first serious effort at integrating the official ruleset came in 1988, with the arrival of SSI's *Pool of Radiance* for home computers (see Figure 25.1). SSI's design team leveraged the extensive Forgotten Realms campaign setting, with all its lore, history, bestiary, and geography, as well as its well-honed rules for combat, magic, and leveling. However, TSR gave SSI their own region of the Forgotten Realms to develop just for the game, so they wouldn't have to worry about breaking continuity with modules for the tabletop. It was a win–win situation for both companies.

Pool of Radiance built on the foundation established by Sir-Tech's *Wizardry*, with its first-person, three-dimensional exploration mode, but switched to a tactical isometric view for combat. Like TSR, SSI had started off making war games and, by 1988, had a well-earned reputation in that genre. They'd also developed the RPGs *Wizard's Crown* (1986) and *The Eternal Dagger* (1987), which borrowed freely from the tactical and strategic dimensions of their strategy titles. Their game *Questron* (1984) was a hit as well, though its similarity to *Ultima* was close enough to warrant a reaction from its creator, Garriott, but they managed to come to a licensing arrangement. They were best known,

Figure 25.1   Behold, *Pool of Radiance*, a CRPG worth its weight in gold.

however, as the publishers of Winston Douglas Wood's *Phantasie* series, which debuted in 1985.

When TSR began soliciting pitches for a licensing deal, SSI moved quickly to put together an effective pitch. However, its president, the 29-year-old Joel Billings, had "only played *D&D* once in high school and hated it."[1] However, Brors ran a campaign the night before their presentation to TSR and managed to turn his president onto the game: "Keith is a great Dungeon Master and I really enjoyed it—he showed me what it was like if you had a good DM."

Naturally, SSI wasn't the only company at the table—Electronic Arts and Origin were also vying for the license. SSI's strategy was to put together a more comprehensive package than the rest, with a full series of RPGs and a line of action games through their partner, US Gold. The clincher was their plan to make a program to assist Dungeon Masters with the tabletop version. "We showed them how Paul and Keith were hardcore role-playing game fans—they were hardcore gamers that knew what TSR was all about ... We were real gamers and not just another computer company."[1]

Billings later described the immediate impact of acquiring the lucrative 5-year exclusive license to publish *Advanced Dungeons & Dragons* (*AD&D*) software (see Figure 25.2):

> As soon as we got the license, we were able to start hiring more developers; we hired our first artists ... Before that, the programmers did all their own art. Now there was a whole art team, a team of scripters for encounters, the story behind the game. In a couple years, we went from a development team of ten people to forty.[2]

The newly expanded team was led by 35-year old Chuck Kroegel, who had a year to develop TSR's assets into the gold standard of CRPGs. Paul Murray and Keith Brors set to work designing and programming the new engine, paying special attention to the enemy's behavior in combat. They'd already developed sophisticated AI routines for

---

[1] Ritchie, Craig. "Developer Lookback: Strategic Simulations, Inc." *Retro Gamer*, October 11, 2007: 82–87.

[2] Billings, Joel, interview by Matt Barton. *Matt Chat 184: Joel Billings on the Gold Box Series* (February 10, 2013).

Wizard's Crown; it was now just a matter of integrating TSR's ruleset.

To stave off any potential conflicts with TSR, SSI kept them in the loop as the project progressed, especially TSR's head of product development, Jim Ward. This was a smart move; TSR was well known for its "iron fist" approach with its licensees and were ready to veto anything they didn't feel was in the spirit of their game.

The result of this surge of talent, care, and resources was *Pool of Radiance*, the first in a long line of games that finally did justice to the revered *AD&D* license. Their distinctive boxes with gold trim earned

Figure 25.2   Joel Billings, president of SSI.

them the nickname "Gold Box games," which sported covers by TSR's renowned artists.

The game was set in Phlan, a formerly great city that now lay in ruins. The player's job was to create up to six characters, who'd form a party to help reclaim and ultimately rebuild the city for resettlement. Naturally, there were those opposed to this plan—namely, the monsters, bandits, and greater adversaries who'd set up in shop in the long-abandoned parts of the city (see Figure 25.3).

The game took weeks, if not months, to complete—and that's assuming you didn't get skewered by the hordes of skeletons at Sokal Keep or crushed by trolls and ogres in the city's slums. It was a difficult and challenging game even for veterans of *AD&D*, but SSI published helpful guides with combat tips and detailed maps.

Ken St. Andre, who designed a popular rival to *D&D* called *Tunnels & Trolls*, wrote a review of the game for *Computer Gaming World*. He was impressed with how well the team had integrated the "Byzantine perplexity" of the *AD&D* system: "[It] keeps track of all the rules and the player interface is beautifully transparent. That gives one the real feel of playing *AD&D* without needing to have all of the rulebooks close at hand. Frankly, this has proven irresistible to me."[3] He also praised the detailed graphics and the morale checks during combat—enemies who felt overwhelmed would surrender, saving the player the trouble of killing them.

To get around the problem of memory limitations—and to serve as a form of copy protection—the game shipped with an "Adventurer's Journal" and a code wheel. The Journal contained a numbered set of text passages, to which the player would be referred during appropriate moments of the game. Without this booklet, the player would miss out on flavor text, but also a few crucial pieces of information. The code wheel was for translating runes during the game as well as during the loading sequence. These methods may have curtailed some piracy, but they more likely just irritated those of us who inadvertently lost or wore them out by playing the game too much!

---

[3] St. Andre, Ken. "It's Only D&D, But I Like It!" *Computer Gaming World*, December 1988: 28, 60–62.

Figure 25.3 *Pool of Radiance* offered exceptional tactical turn-based combat. The larger battles could take hours.

SSI used the engine it created for *Pool of Radiance* for that game's sequels (*Curse of the Azure Bonds*, *Secret of the Silver Blades*, and *Pools of Darkness*). While you could start each of these with a new set of characters, you could also import your party from game to game—albeit with some concessions for the sake of game balance.

SSI also developed and published several spin-off series. There were three games based on TSR's *Dragonlance* campaign, two games by Stormfront Studios set elsewhere in *The Forgotten Realms* and a series of Buck Rogers games. In 1991, Stormfront Studios adapted the Gold Box engine for online play. Their *Neverwinter Nights* game ran on America Online for 6 years and boasted more than a hundred thousand players at its peak.

In 1993, SSI published MicroMagic's *Forgotten Realms: Unlimited Adventures*, which let you create your own Gold Box–style games for DOS or Mac. This popular product is still in use today; the *UA Archive* site hosts more than 500 modules made with the original and hacked versions of the program.

In addition to the Gold Box series, SSI published a "Black Box" series of TSR-licensed games developed by Westwood Associates. We'll come back to these when we talk about *Dungeon Master* in Chapter 27.

After its success with its Gold Box series, SSI struggled to maintain its momentum, and eventually TSR revoked their license. The next company to properly assume the *AD&D* mantle was BioWare, whose epic *Baldur's Gate* revived the moribund genre in 1998.

25.1 Playing *Pool of Radiance* Today

Pool of Radiance was originally designed on and for the Commodore 64. Again, I'll recommend Cloanto's commercial emulator C64 Forever, which provides a handy GUI (graphical user interface) for getting ROM files up and running. However, you may prefer to play the MS-DOS version, since the final game in the series, *Pools of Darkness*, is only available for that platform. MS-DOS emulation is a breeze with the free program DOSBox. Otherwise, the Amiga or Atari ST versions have better graphics than the C64.

Chapter 26

Wasteland: Hot, Mean, and Radioactive

Another seminal role-playing game (RPG) of 1988 was Interplay's *Wasteland*, which diverts from the well-trodden path of swords and sorcery to explore an equally compelling scenario: the aftermath of a global nuclear holocaust. It was designed at Interplay by Brian Fargo and a group of tabletop RPG designers: Ken St. Andre, Michael Stackpole, Dan Carver, and Liz Danforth. This trio had worked for Flying Buffalo, designing and creating materials for *Tunnels & Trolls*. *Wasteland* inspired Interplay and later Bethesda's hit *Fallout* series, but had to wait 26 years to get its own official sequel. That project raised nearly $3 million on Kickstarter and put this classic RPG back on the map.

Interplay scored its first hit in 1986 with *Tales of the Unknown: Volume I—The Bard's Tale* (see Figure 26.1). Designed by Fargo's high school chum Michael Cranford, this classic dungeon crawler expanded on the concepts pioneered by Sir-Tech's *Wizardry* series, but with better graphics and an updated interface. It was a terrific success for both Interplay and its publisher, Electronic Arts, and two equally impressive sequels followed in 1986 (*The Destiny Knight* and *Thief of Fate*). Interplay also did a do-it-yourself dungeon maker called *The Bard's Tale Construction Set* in 1991, which allowed gamers to make their own standalone games.[1] Fargo produced a parodic RPG called *The Bard's Tale* in 2004, which, despite its name, diverged sharply from the original games and was widely panned by critics. Nevertheless, Fargo managed to raise $1.5 million on Kickstarter for *The Bard's Tale IV* in 2015.

Despite the success of *The Bard's Tale* series, Fargo had an itch to try something different. He loved postapocalyptic fiction, especially the *Planet of the Apes* films and *Kamandi: The Last Boy on Earth*, a comic book series he read as a boy.[2] He was also enamored with the films *Mad Max* and *The Road Warrior* and knew their director, George Miller. The dystopic vision of the future presented in these films and stories was often dark and gritty, but not without opportunities for adventure and heroism.

---

[1] The site http://bardstale.poverellomedia.com/constructionset.html hosts two of these fan-made productions: Alex Ghadaksaz's *The Bard's Quest* (1996) and John H. Wigforss' *The Bard's Lore* (1998).

[2] Kosman, Marcin. "Brian Fargo: 'The Golden Era of Computer RPGs is Yet to Come'." *Polygamia*. June 24, 2013. http://polygamia.pl/Polygamia/1,112250,14171391,Brian_Fargo___The_golden_era_of_computer_RPGs_is_yet.html (accessed July 22, 2015).

Furthermore, as Fargo argued, "Post-apocalyptic universes seem more plausible for the most part over straight up sci-fi."[2] "I don't think I'm going to be flying around in a spaceship anytime soon, but this stuff feels … its gritty realism. Women in wheelchairs with machine guns—it's gritty stuff."[3] The postapocalyptic setting was simultaneously familiar and exotic.

There'd been RPGs set in postapocalyptic worlds before. A prominent example is Chuck Bueche's *Autoduel* (1985), based on Steve Jackson's *Car Wars* tabletop game.

Figure 26.1   *The Bard's Tale* was a massive hit for Interplay.

But the setting wasn't the only aspect that set *Wasteland* apart from the mainstream. "One thing that made *Wasteland* such a big deal at the time, and why so many people still have a positive memory of it," said Fargo, "is that it was the first sandbox game. It was open world: Do anything you want, any order you want, and see ripple effects that could happen one minute or thirty minutes later."[4] There had been "go anywhere and do anything" games before, but *Wasteland* emphasized the short- and long-term consequences of your actions. For instance, choosing to kill rather than ignore a group of mocking children will ultimately lead to a lake drying up, which in turn makes a town uninhabitable.

Furthermore, the world was persistent, meaning that areas didn't reset until you started completely over. If you lost your original group, you could create new ones and start off again in the same world.

Fargo's original plan called for a story similar to the film *Red Dawn*, but St. Andre talked him out of it. "I developed another idea that I thought would be more fun. It was Arizona Rangers versus Terminators in the deserts of New Nevada … I chose Arizona because I live here and know the geography very well, and the desert seems like a post-nuclear wasteland already."[5]

The player was put in charge of four Desert Rangers, former US Army soldiers who now struggled to maintain some semblance of order in the chaotic wastes: Hell Razor, Angela Deth, Thrasher, and Snake Vargas.[6] In addition to *Mad Max*–inspired punks and

---

[3] Barton, Matt. *Honoring the Code: Conversations with Great Game Designers*. Boca Raton, FL: CRC Press, 2013: 67.

[4] See footnote 3.

[5] Paik, Eric. "Wasteland Interview." *GameBanshee*. August 23, 2006. http://www.gamebanshee.com/interviews/28345 -wasteland-interview.html (accessed July 24, 2015).

[6] You could create your own party if you didn't like the premade group.

scavenger types, these Desert Rangers have a greater enemy—a powerful computer programmed to eradicate humanity.

Instead of the first-person perspective of *The Bard's Tale*, *Wasteland* opted for a top-down, tile-based system similar to *Ultima* (see Figure 26.2). The combat mode, however, was similar to *The Bard's Tale*'s, with an animated picture of the enemy on the left and the rest of the screen

Figure 26.2   Don't let its bright tiled graphics fool you—*Wasteland* is a dark and gritty game.

occupied by a textual description of the action and the party's stats below (see Figure 26.3). The bright color palette of the exploration mode lends the game a more lighthearted tone than the packaging or theme suggests.

Wasteland's character creation system was more complex than most, consisting of a series of stats as well as 27 skills, which ranged from fighting techniques

Figure 26.3   The designers ran wild with the postapocalyptic setting. Here, my party faces off against a killer bunny.

to metallurgy. Later, the player could recruit computer-controlled characters (NPCs), and it was also possible to split up the party into separate groups to deal with special situations. The sprawling story was told mostly in the form of a printed journal that accompanied the game; as with *Pool of Radiance*, players were periodically referred to a numbered passage.

Wasteland was a hit with most critics, winning *Computer Gaming World*'s "Adventure Game of the Year" award in 1988. James V. Trunzo's review in *Compute!* summed up the game's appeal: "Maybe the end of the world will be like this. If it is, I don't think I want to be part of it. That's why playing *Wasteland* is such a vicarious thrill—I get to experience something that I *really* don't want to ever have happen."[7]

Playing the game back in 2012, what struck me was the over-the-top violence and incredibly dark humor. It's hard to imagine a game nowadays that lets you wantonly

---

[7] Trunzo, James V. "Wasteland." *Compute! Magazine*, November 1988: 78, 82.

murder children and even babies. Emil Pagliarulo, lead designer on *Fallout 3*, remarked that this level of violence "seems gratuitous, unnecessary, and cruel," and refused to "cross that line," which he felt the ESRB would never allow anyway.[8] To a large extent, the cartoony tile graphics and hilarious encounters with enemies like "Harry, the Bunny Master" provide some counterbalance to the darker aspects of the game. That said, no one would ever mistake *Wasteland* for Disneyland.

26.1 Playing *Wasteland* Today

There's good news for anyone wanting to play the original *Wasteland*—you can pick it up on Steam or GOG, all set up and ready for play on modern machines.

---

[8] Pagliarulo, Emil. "Emil Pagliarulo Writes for Edge." *Edge-Online*. October 26, 2008. http://www.edge-online.com/blogs /emil-pagliarulo-writes-edge (accessed November 14, 2008).

Part IV
The Late Majority

Rogers' fourth stage of the diffusion of innovations is called the "late majority," which the sociologist describes as skeptical or apathetic about a new technology. By the early 1990s, the bulk of Americans had at least played a video game before, and many already owned systems and already considered themselves "gamers." However, there were still a fair number who weren't quite sure what to make of this "whole video game thing," or assumed it was only for children or nerds. Some simply didn't have the money to indulge in a gaming hobby, or felt they lacked the supposed education or technical skills to enjoy them. I suspect most simply felt it wasn't respectable for someone like them to enjoy a video game.

This situation began to change dramatically in the mid-1990s as both consoles and computers made huge leaps forward. The younger markets were never in question; they accepted the new breed of video game consoles (the SNES Sega Genesis) with enthusiasm. What was more remarkable was the upsurge of adults who dove into Trilobyte's *The 7th Guest* and Cyan's *Myst*, whose incredible popularity led to rapid adoption and development of CD-ROM technology. As these games were attracting people who'd never played games before, a community of "hardcore" gamers was forming around a shareware title from an obscure company called id. Their obsession with *Doom* and the "first-person shooter" genre it spawned led to massive gatherings called "LAN parties" and drove research and development in three-dimensional graphics technology.

Meanwhile, *John Madden Football* became a hugely successful franchise after launching on the Sega Genesis in 1991, bringing in hundreds of thousands of adult sports enthusiasts who couldn't have cared less about *Sonic the Hedgehog.* Another major console title of this era was Square's *Final Fantasy VII* (1997) for the new Sony PlayStation, which effectively demonstrated the cinematic possibilities of console gaming, whose audience was growing up and demanding more sophisticated fare.

By the end of this era, most Americans had either a console or a computer in their home, or both. The technology was cheaper, more powerful, and easier to access than ever before. There were still holdouts, of course—the laggards who still had no interest in entertainment technology beyond a television or stereo. They wouldn't join the fun until the Internet and the smartphone made video games available to anyone who cared to participate in modern life.

Chapter 27

Dungeon Master: Real Time Hits the Big Time

We'll begin this section with FTL Games' *Dungeon Master*, first published for the Atari ST back in 1987. Even though it's older than other games in this section, it was very much ahead of its time and influenced much of what was to follow. Most importantly for fans of modern computer role-playing games (CRPGs), it was *Dungeon Master* that shrugged off the slavish imitation of tabletop RPGs that characterized the bulk of its predecessors. Instead of trying to recreate the tabletop experience on a computer, Doug Bell and Andy Jaros used the power of the new Atari ST and Commodore Amiga computers to provide a more immersive experience, with real-time action, three-dimensional (3D) perspective and sound.[1] It was an ambitious plan, but Jaros and Bell were up for the challenge. Their game *Dungeon Master* was a smash hit on both platforms, won dozens of major industry awards, and established a new paradigm for RPGs that is still in use today (see Figure 27.1).

Bell and Jaros met as students at the University of California. Jaros had brought his parents' Apple II+ computer with him to college, and the two spent many a pleasant evening playing their way through *Ultima* and *Wizardry* games. Bell was "The Wild Man," a nickname he earned by blowing things up with dynamite and indulging in extreme sports: "I love the feeling of risking my life," said Bell.[2] Jaros, who majored in chemistry, was a much quieter man. He turned to the video game industry after a 2-year stint as a Quality Control Chemist for 3M. "The prospect of a lifetime titrating carcinogenic chemicals for a salary that crept upward only once a year was not my idea of a real career," said Jaros.[3]

One day, Bell decided that he should try his own hand at making a game and partnered with Jaros to found a company they called "PVC Dragon." They managed to sell enough shares to family and friends to fund development of their first game, *Crystal Dragon.*[4] The pair worked on this project for 2 years but ran out of money before it was

---

[1] *Dungeon Master* was not the first game to achieve this feat. Dyna-Micro's *Dungeons of Daggorath* (1982) for the Tandy CoCo and Philip Price's *Alternate Reality: The City* (1985) were even further ahead of their time, but not as successful.

[2] Schneider, Boris. "Licchtschnell zur Spitze." *Power Play*, April 1988: 82–83.

[3] Mitchell, Andy. "Behind the Mask—Chaos Revealed." *ST Action*, June 1990: 34–36.

[4] McFerran, Damien. "The Making of Dungeon Master." *Retro Gamer*, January 1, 2011: 30–31.

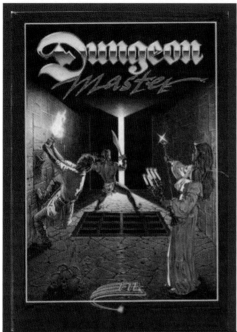

finished. Now living in San Diego, the two sought out a publisher willing to take on their project. They found Wayne Holder, owner of FTL Games, a three-person outfit who'd developed a popular space trading game called *SunDog: Frozen Legacy.*

According to Bell, "Wayne decided to take us on for a few months to get the game to work state," but news of the upcoming launch of the Atari ST changed everything. "The Atari was a much more capable computer than the Apple, and better suited to *Crystal Dragon*, where we were spending a great deal of our time trying to fit it in the Apple's 64K."[4] It soon became apparent, however, that they'd never be able to finish it in time for the ST's launch. Not willing to waste this golden opportunity, Bell and Jaros put their game on

Figure 27.1   The cover art for *Dungeon Master*. The man pulling on the torch is Andy Jaros, co-designer of the game.

hold and worked with Holder to port and enhance *SunDog* for the new computer. It was a wise decision; the game was the best-selling ST game that year and gave the team much-needed experience on the new platform.

With *SunDog* filling FTL's coffers, Bell and Jaros went back to work on their game, which they were now calling *Dungeon Master*. They thought of it as "the dungeon equivalent of a flight simulator."[5] However, their game wouldn't allow smooth movement like a flight simulator but a grid-based system of discrete moves through the dungeon. Even with this limitation, Bell's coding skills were put to the test. "We started with a proof of concept to use a painter's algorithm (drawing from back to front) to create the dungeon," said Bell. This made substantial demands on the hardware, so Bell spent the next 3 weeks teaching himself C and rewriting his code, which he'd done in Pascal.[4]

Jaros, meanwhile, was working on the graphics for the game. A consummate perfectionist, he spent several days creating and refining his designs for each monster.[2] About half were familiar monsters such as mummies, but he created many on his own, drawing inspiration from animals. He had never taken any art classes in school but

---

5   Atari Roundtables. "Interview of FTL Team." *DMWeb*. January 1990. http://dmweb.free.fr/?q=node/94 (accessed July 27, 2015).

had a passion for the subject and studied the works of many famous artists.
"My favorites include Escher, Frazetta,
Boris, Dean, Mead, Corben, Woodroffe,
the Hildebrants, Rowena, Segrelees,
and Rodney Mathews to name a few,"
said Jaros.[3] To make the art for *Dungeon*

Figure 27.2   Combat in *Dungeon Master* was fast, furious, and surprisingly fun.

Master, Jaros used a program called N-Vision, which "had a very handy tool that could
change one color to another (or swap them) in a user-defined area. This was useful for
finding the most aesthetic color combinations in the dungeon, menus, and inventory
screen"[3] (see Figure 27.2).

Holder's job was the sound effects, which he programmed to grow or lessen in volume according to the characters' proximity to their source. This feature would become
one of the more memorable aspects of the game, and the manual declared that it was
best experienced with stereo headphones. Indeed, anyone who's played the game has at
least one story of being jolted by a sudden noise.

Holder's wife, Nancy, was tasked with writing the game's storyline. This decision
wasn't made for the sake of convenience or nepotism; she was a *New York Times* best-
selling author and won the Bram Stoker Award for horror writing on four separate occa-
sions. For *Dungeon Master,* Holder penned a 20-page prologue, printed in the manual. It
amounted to a quest to retrieve a magical "Firestaff," but a nice twist was that the player's party was composed of resurrected heroes who had already fallen victim to one of
the dungeon's many perils.

Two additional programmers, Mike Newton and Dennis Walker, filled the gaps, but it
was still a very small team for such an enormous project. The real challenge was getting
all the code and assets to fit onto a single 360K floppy disk, which the Atari ST used as
its storage media. It would've been much easier to simply span the game across multiple
disks, but this would've necessitated frequent disk swapping—which the developers felt
would shatter the immersion. The raw data was well more than 1.6 megabytes, but the
team crammed it onto a single disk with sophisticated compression and memory management techniques. "No game ever got as much onto a 360K floppy disk or into the Atari
520ST's memory as *DM*," said Bell.[4]

With a few exceptions, most CRPGs before *Dungeon Master* that offered a 3D perspective restricted the player's view of the world to a small window. The rest of the screen was
used to display statistics and textual descriptions of the action. *Dungeon Master*'s view-
ing window was much larger, dominating the screen. Health and mana bars were used
instead of numbers, and the game was designed to be completely controlled by a mouse
(a row of buttons with directional arrows were clicked for movement). The mouse was
also used to click on switches, items, buttons, and many other items (see Figure 27.3).

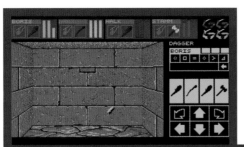

Combat tended to be a furious affair. Each character's attack had a timeout period, and spells were cast by stringing together arcane runes—a process requiring some considerable coolness under pressure as well as dexterity. You could also reorient your characters to protect

Figure 27.3   Do you see the hidden lever on the wall? *Dungeon Master* was filled with secrets like this one, rewarding patient, careful exploration of each area.

the party's flank. There were four basic character classes (fighter, ninja, priest, and wizard), but many characters were hybrids of two or more of these types. Characters gained more expertise in these areas by practicing the corresponding skills; casting lots of wizard spells, for instance, built up that skill, whereas throwing lots of shurikens would spike the ninja skill. Furthermore, rather than relying on a numbered series of levels, the characters progressed through stages like "novice," "journeyman," and "artisan." It was an intuitive and logical system.

To add further realism, the characters required food and water. Thankfully, they used up these resources very slowly, and there were lots of these items lying about. If your stomach churned at the idea of noshing on a turkey leg that's been sitting in a dusty corner of a dungeon for days, if not weeks, you could try eating some of your vanquished foes. Players also had to manage torches; run out and you'd be lost in the dark. Health and mana were replenished by napping but also left you vulnerable to wandering enemies.

When the game was finally published in 1987, ST owners were delighted. Heidi Brumbaugh's review for *START* magazine summed up the general enthusiasm:

> First, turn off your ST. Turn on a lamp. Open the package and take out the instruction booklet. Read the short history of the adventure on which you're about to embark. Now take a deep breath. Go around the house gathering supplies you'll need: scratch paper, grid paper, pencils, rulers, blank disks, blankets—and food and water for eight hours. Ready? Then put the disk in your drive, turn on your ST and be prepared to shed every preconception you ever had about computer games. This is *Dungeon Master*.[6]

Brumbaugh also mentioned that CompuServe was a good place to look for help with the game, since the *Dungeon Master* forum was the "single longest discussion on the entire service." The game sold at unprecedented numbers, eventually outselling all other games for the Atari ST. The team scored another triumph a year later, when they released

---

[6] Brumbaugh, Heidi. "Into the Dungeon with You!: The Dungeon Master Experience." *STart The ST Quarterly*, September 1988: 23.

a version for the Commodore Amiga. Versions for Apple IIgs, MS-DOS, Super Nintendo Entertainment System (SNES), and Japanese computers followed these successful ports.

Indeed, FTL had become so focused on making ports of *Dungeon Master* for other systems that they neglected their plans for expansions and sequels. The plan all along had been to use the engine for expansions and other scenarios, including some intriguing horror, science fiction, and spy games. Fans had to wait until 1989 to get *Chaos Strikes Back*, the first of a planned series of "expansions." Despite this designation, however, it did not require the first *Dungeon Master* to run. In any case, critics were dismayed by the game's severe difficulty and lack of any substantial improvements to the original. After this game, FTL focused on the Japanese market, quietly fading from the scene.

If FTL itself wasn't willing or able to follow up on the success of *Dungeon Master* in North America and Europe, other studios were happy to take their place. Perhaps the best known of the *DM*-likes, if you will, were the *Eye of the Beholder* series (1991–1995), developed by Westwood Associates and published by SSI. These games wedded the *DM*-interface style to TSR's *AD&D* ruleset. Westwood's popular *Lands of Lore: The Throne of Chaos* (1993) was also a *DM*-style game. There were plenty of lesser known (though not necessarily less innovative) *DM*-inspired games, such as *Bloodwych* (1989), *Captive* (1990), *Crystals of Arborea* (1990), *Black Crypt* (1992), *Ambermoon* (1993), and *Hired Guns* (1993).

Perhaps the most influential successor was *Ultima Underworld: The Stygian Abyss*, a 1992 game by Blue Sky Productions (later Looking Glass Studios). Paul Neurath, who designed it, said that he played *Dungeon Master* on his Amiga. "While the game play was fairly standard fare," said Neurath, "its first person 3D perspective, with detailed bitmapped walls and animated sprite monsters, had more impact and immediacy than prior CRPGs. This game provided a glimpse into the future."[7] Neurath's game updated the *DM* formula with continuous rather than grid-based movement, an important step forward in terms of immersion.

However, not all gamers were ready to abandon *DM*'s "obsolete" grid-based movement style. In 2012, Almost Human, a Finnish indie studio, released *Legend of Grimrock*, a *DM*-style game with updated graphics. It was enough of a hit to warrant a sequel in 2014. These critically acclaimed games do more than pay homage to their predecessors and provide a nice alternative to the now-mainstream first-person shooter-style movement of *The Elder Scrolls* and similar games.

Now that we're so accustomed to continuous movement, it might be hard to imagine how incredibly immersive *Dungeon Master* felt in 1987. Not everything about it has aged well, but gamers willing to see past its outmoded graphics will still find much to enjoy. Just turn off the lights, put on your headphones, and see if you don't feel your hair stand up the first time you hear a monster shuffling somewhere down one of those dark, dank corridors.

---

[7] Neurath, Paul. "The Story of Ultima Underworld." *TTLG Forums*. June 23, 2000. http://web.archive.org/web/20010309140053; http://www.ttlg.com/articles/uw1.asp (accessed July 28, 2015).

27.1 **Playing *Dungeon Master* Today**

Purists will want to play the original Atari ST version. There are many emulators to choose from, but Hatari seems the best supported—go to http://hatari.tuxfamily.org. Otherwise, the Amiga version is also superb, and you can use Cloanto's Amiga Forever emulator to get it up and running in no time.

There are also many unofficial open source clones and remakes of *DM* and its sequels for modern systems. A full list of these is maintained at http://dmweb.free.fr.

Chapter 28

Myst: Creating Worlds, One Tent at a Time

Cyan's *Myst*, published in 1993 for the Apple Macintosh and later for PC and other platforms, is a game loved by most everyone but gamers. It was made by two Christian brothers whose inexperience was their most valuable asset. No one was around to tell them that their concept was flawed, their design unsound, their understanding of the market hopelessly naïve. And yet the Miller brothers made *Myst*, a computer game that outsold all that came before it (see Figure 28.1).

Myst played no small part in popularizing the CD-ROM—a vital innovation that dramatically increased the amount of data developers had at their disposal. Game developers struggled to find a suitable use for this unprecedented increase in storage, and some chose simply to ignore it. The old guard had come to power when space was scarce; they didn't know how to deal with the sudden abundance. Floppy disks, the storage media of the time, typically held only 1.44 megabytes, and many games shipped on four or more. Revolution Software's *Beneath a Steel Sky*, an excellent sci-fi adventure game from 1994, shipped on 15! All those disks added to production and shipping costs, and no one liked having to constantly swap them out as they played. A single CD-ROM could hold the equivalent of 486 of these disks and costs less to boot. A multitude of skills, practices, and habits had suddenly become, if not obsolete, certainly much less relevant. Someone needed to rewrite the rule book.

Rand and Robyn Miller, cofounders of Cyan, had never read that book. They were newcomers to the video game industry and had no preconceived notions about "proper" game design. The only game either of them had actively played was *Zork* in the early 1980s, and there was certainly not much of a "games industry" in Spokane, Washington. Thus, when their first game, *The Manhole*, won the Software Publishers Association's award in 1988 for "Best New Use of a Computer," Robyn was genuinely surprised. The game, if you can properly call it that, had players (ostensibly children) following "Mr. Rabbit" through a manhole and into a wonderland-like world (see Figure 28.2). There was no real "point" to it or puzzles to solve; you just explored the place, reveling in the general weirdness and wisdom of its cutesy denizens. "No one else has shown near the creativity that they have," said James Bradbury, the editor of *MacUser*.[1] What Bradbury assumed was

---

[1] Jones, Grayden. "Software Developers Strike Gold." *Spokane Chronicle*, March 8, 1991: A12.

Figure 28.1   Robyn and Rand Miller, the creators of *Myst*.

I love to sleep while standing on one leg!

Figure 28.2   Before *Myst*, there was *The Manhole*.

creative brilliance might easily have been dumb luck—or, as the brothers might argue, divine inspiration.

Rand and Robyn were 32 and 25, respectively, when they began work on *Myst*. They were sons of Ron Miller, an evangelical "Tentmaker" preacher who traveled from church to church as his faith moved him. Tentmakers are committed to equipping young Christians with more than just scripture and moral teaching. They emphasize the need for a strong imagination, practical skills, work ethics, and a commitment to free enterprise.

Despite the frequent relocations prompted by their dad's career in the ministry, the boys had a happy childhood. The family played board and card games after dinner, and the boys spent much of their free time exploring the many locales in which they found themselves. "No matter where we lived," said Rand, "we were out on jeep trails or exploring old Indian ruins or going to canoe on rivers. We were exploring the world, and that felt a lot like play."[2] The brothers held onto their faith, and credited God for inspiring them to do *Myst*.[3] Divine source or not, the game did originate as a paper-based prototype that Rand played with his church group.[4] While the series wasn't explicitly Christian oriented, it lacked violence, sex, and other elements that some Christians find objectionable.

After their success with *The Manhole*, the Miller brothers made two more children's games in a similar fashion: *Cosmic Osmo and the World Beyond the Mackerel* (1989) and

[2] Swain, Lisa. *Myst and Halo: A Conversation with Rand Miller and Marty O'Donnell*. Louisville: Westminster: John Knox Press, 2010.

[3] Ostermiller, Tim. "Riven!" *Christianity Today*. 1998. http://www.christianitytoday.com/iyf/hottopics/faithvalues/8c6034.html (accessed August 3, 2015).

[4] Hanlon, Patrick. *Primbranding: Create Zealots for Your Brand, Your Company, and Your Future*. New York: Simon and Schuster, 2006.

Spelunx and the Caves of Mr. Seudo (1991). You can easily see the influence of their father's emphasis on imagination and "learning by doing" in all three, such as a lightning simulator in *Spelunx* that taught kids about the speed of sound. The games were doing remarkably well, and

Figure 28.3   *Myst* opens quite mysteriously with an unnamed character falling through a fissure. What the heck is going on here?

the brothers suspected that there were plenty of adults buying their games despite the children's label. The next logical step, it seemed, was to make a more sophisticated game for an older audience. That would mean going head-to-head with Sierra and Lucasfilm Games, venerable developers who dominated the adventure game market.

Myst deviated sharply from the paradigms established by *King's Quest* or *Maniac Mansion*. Unlike those games, which emphasized plots, characters, and humor, *Myst*, like Cyan's earlier works, was all about immersion in fantastic, highly imaginative worlds (see Figure 28.3). "We're not game designers," said Rand. "We were place designers ... We just started drawing maps, and the maps fueled the story."[5] The team used their drawings to design terrain, structures, and other objects on their Macintosh, drawing them first in grayscale to indicate height (lighter colors meant taller features). They then used a program called StrataVision 3D to render them into three dimensions— 2500 images in all. They also created more than an hour's worth of video clips, filming themselves over a blue screen and using QuickTime, a multimedia tool that had just shipped from Apple.

Perhaps the most unorthodox aspect of the Millers' development process was their reliance on HyperCard. As its name suggests, it was a hypermedia programming tool based on the concept of a Rolodex card stack. The cards would hold various kinds of data and GUI (graphical user interface) elements (check boxes, buttons, etc.) and the user could then write a script to direct a user through the stack. It was an early form of hypertext or hypermedia and was intended to give nonprogrammers an easier way to build dynamic content. It was a hit among academics, but most game developers would have found it hopelessly limiting and clunky. It'd be like trying to build a game using a wiki or blog engine today; possible, certainly, but hardly ideal for most purposes.

Using HyperCard wasn't the only "mistake" the young duo made as they developed *Myst*. "We didn't see a reason for buttons," said Robyn, an artist and anthropologist by training. The brothers believed that the bulky on-screen menus seen in games like *The Secret of Monkey Island* and *Gabriel Knight: Sins of the Fathers* were too distracting: "We intuitively didn't like the artifice of game stuff ... If you're playing a game, you should

---

5 Yoshida, Emily. "Lost to the Ages." *Grantland*. September 24, 2013. http://www.webcitation.org/6JvoME936 (accessed August 3, 2015).

be in that world as much possible ... When you go to movies, you don't have to deal with that kind of thing."[5] They also "failed" to add an inventory system, so that players could pick up and use objects. This had been a convention of almost every adventure game since Will Crowther's

Figure 28.4   The iconic opening scene of *Myst*. What is that strange structure off in the distance? Gamers at the time were mesmerized by the incredibly realistic graphics.

breakthrough *Colossal Cave Adventure*. Omitting it was, if not heresy, at least a line in the sand between Cyan and the rest of the industry. Rather than cater to gamers, the brothers were more interested in their parents or even their grandparents. "We didn't want [anything] to stand in the way of anyone playing the game," said Rand[5] (see Figure 28.4).

Finally, whereas most games made the player's mission obvious from the get-go (collect treasures, get off the island, save the princess, etc.), *Myst*'s now-iconic opening only served to bewilder players. It begins when The Stranger (the player's avatar) is literally sucked into a mysterious book about an island. As The Stranger learns more about the world of Myst, he or she learns about the authors of the books, powerful beings who link to parallel dimensions with a magic script. The central dilemma of this game concerned two brothers and their father. All are trapped in the books; it was up to the player to collect their missing pages and decide their fates. These "linking books" opened to reveal distorted full-motion video segments; each restored page sharpened the videos and eventually let the player hear and see the brothers (see Figure 28.5).

The brothers accuse each other of murdering their father, but a savvy player soon discovered that neither is trustworthy. However, *Myst* spelled out nothing; instead, players pieced the story together themselves, considering what they saw and heard as they explored the large gameworld. Although there was no way for The Stranger to die, only one of the game's possible endings was a happy one.

The game was presented through The Stanger's eyes in a first-person perspective but was not free-roaming like modern three-dimensional (3D) games. Instead, the player clicked "hot spots" on the screen, special locations that enabled possible actions. For instance, clicking on an exit moved the perspective to a new location, whereas clicking on a lever

Figure 28.5   *Myst* made judicious use of full-motion video, using it more as a plot device than a cheesy gimmick.

raised or lowered it. The interface was easily controlled entirely by the mouse. This setup was radically different from most adventure games of the era, which were usually represented in third-person perspective, with on-screen avatars the player directed with the mouse or keyboard. *Myst*'s interface and eerie ambience lent the game a timeless, Zen-like quality that starkly contrasted with other adventure games, which usually featured cartoony aesthetics and geeky, self-referential humor.

Unlike Cyan's previous works, *Myst* did have a number of challenging logic puzzles to solve. Most of these required finding clues or working out the strange mechanics of mysterious contraptions. Working out these conundrums allowed The Stranger access to new areas and eventually enough of the linking book pages to complete the game. It's not hard to see the influence of Robyn's anthropological training at work; The Stranger is given very little information upfront about the purpose of anything or anyone on the island. It's up to him or her to figure things out by studying their devices, artwork, architecture, and fragments of writing.

The game was launched quietly in 1993, mostly to negative reviews from the gaming press. To them, *Myst* was little more than eye candy; a series of prerendered, static images and a handful of digitized video clips. The severest critics lumped *Myst* along with *The 7th Guest* and other early CD-ROM games as mere technological curiosities; evolutionary dead ends. *Edge*, *Electronic Gaming Monthly*, *Power Play*, and *GameSpot* all gave it miserably low scores, describing it as boring, dull, and repetitive—almost offensive to a real gamer's sensibilities. Even today, there seems to be a consensus among traditional gamers that *Myst* was terrible. "It's hard to believe we let this game slide," wrote *IGN*'s Jack DeVries in a review of the 2008 DS version. "These gameplay mechanics were boring and outdated 14 years ago ... At its best it's a poorly aged, arbitrary puzzle-filled slideshow adventure."[6] But the Miller brothers were never interested in the traditional gamer demographic anyway. They pinned their hopes on a broader, much larger audience: everybody else.

Cyan pitched *Myst* to Brøderbund, who'd published *Spelunx* (Cyan had published their own games before that). Their CEO, Doug Carlston, was looking for something different. "I see a lot of hotshot groups right out of college who just need ten million dollars," said Carlston. "A lot of their work has a kind of sameness to it, the stuff they played when they were teenagers."[4] Carlston had never seen anything like *Myst*, and that was precisely what he was looking for.

The brothers caught a major break when Jon Katz of *Rolling Stone* magazine got hold of it. "*Myst*'s strange, mystical world rewards not the quick reflexes of *Super Mario Bros.*, but creative reasoning," wrote Katz:

> Users need to keep a detailed journal of their observations, of the graphics and symbols they encounter in their travels. The process makes the consumption of even

---

6 DeVries, Jack. "Myst Review." *IGN*. May 16, 2008. http://www.ign.com/articles/2008/05/16/myst-review-2 (accessed August 3, 2015).

most forms of computer entertainment seem lazy by comparison … It is *War and Peace* compared with most video games.[7]

Katz' article reinforced a reputation forming around the game as a sort of high-tech IQ test; a game for the literati. Jon Carroll of *Wired* also waxed eloquently about this aspect and the supposed genius of its designers: "*Myst* is designed to be played in 40 hours by the 'average' first-time player. Rand Miller once did it in two hours."[8] The fact that Rand, as a designer, would've known all the solutions to the puzzles must have been lost on Carroll along with his objectivity. Indeed, his review reads like ad copy: "*Myst* was good. *Myst* was better than anything anyone had ever seen. *Myst* was beautiful, complicated, emotional, dark, intelligent, absorbing. It was the only thing like itself; it had invented its own category." If mainstream gaming magazines weren't impressed with *Myst*, Carroll and other members of the popular press were absolutely enraptured. *Myst* fans "talk about the game in the transported tones of a convert," wrote Steve Daly of *Entertainment Weekly*.[9]

The Millers themselves were more humble. "People ask me all the time if *Myst* was art," said Rand. "I don't even know what art is."[5] Perhaps to avoid any hint of blasphemy, they preferred calling themselves "subcreators" rather than "creators" of worlds. "We know how much work it took to create *Myst*, and how puny and unreal it is compared to the real world … It just makes us realize how great God is."[8] They fervently denied having any specific "agenda" for the game and were unsettled by the reactions overzealous fans had for the game. "As long as there's nobody claiming to be the leader, there's no cult. We're going to keep reminding ourselves of that," said Robyn.[9]

Cyan followed *Myst* with five sequels, which, with one exception, were well received by critics and gamers. The first of these, 1997's *Riven*, was the most highly anticipated game of the year. By that time, *Myst* had sold more than 3.5 million copies, and game sites and magazines had been buzzing for months about the upcoming sequel.[10] When it was finally released, critics praised it and obsessed *Myst* fans lined up to purchase it. For *Riven*, Cyan had a much larger budget and team to work with, which now included a former Disney designer. The game also offered much more full-motion video than *Myst*, though the enthusiasm for this technique was waning by 1997. The story picked up after the first game and had the player chasing down Gehn, a villain who had captured Atrus' (the father in the first game) wife Catherine.

After *Riven*, the Miller brothers went their separate ways. Rand stayed on at Cyan while Robyn left to pursue writing, music, and film. Rand's next project was

---

[7]   Katz, Jon. "Rom & Roll." *Rolling Stone*, April 7, 1994: 43.

[8]   Carroll, Jon. "Guerillas in the Myst." *Wired*. 1993. http://archive.wired.com/wired/archive/2.08/myst_pr.html (accessed August 4, 2015).

[9]   Daly, Steve. "The Land of Myst Opportunity." *Entertainment Weekly*. October 7, 1994. http://www.ew.com/article/1994/10/07/land-myst-opportunity (accessed August 4, 2015).

[10]   Sengstack, Jeff. "Riven: The Sequel to Myst Review." *GameSpot*. November 3, 1997. http://www.gamespot.com/reviews/riven-the-sequel-to-myst-review/1900-2532838/ (accessed August 4, 2015).

realMyst: Interactive 3D Edition (2000), which updated the engine to allow free-roaming movement and used real-time 3D graphics instead of static images. Unfortunately, it ran too slowly on the PCs of the era to live up to its potential.

The next *Myst* game was *Myst III: Exile* in 2001, a project Rand had outsourced to Presto Studios. Cyan was busy developing

Figure 28.6   *Myst Uru* was a radical departure from the previous games. It was originally intended as an MMO.

a project called *Uru* and didn't have the time or resources to allocate to the sequel. Presto Studios had earned a solid reputation with *The Journeyman Project* (starting 1992) series of adventure games for the Macintosh and other platforms, and seemed a good choice for the project. *Exile* proved to be another successful game in the series, with good production values, well-designed puzzles, and good acting. The game sold well, but wasn't a media darling like its predecessors.

The *Uru* project mentioned above—*Uru: Ages Beyond Myst*—was nearly the end for Cyan (see Figure 28.6). The idea was to bring the *Myst* concept to a massively multiplayer format, which by 2003 had become a vital sector of the game market. It had potential: Individual players would be able to create their own realms and puzzles, adding value to the game far beyond Cyan's initial investment. It was also the only *Myst* game to offer a third-person perspective and the ability to create a unique avatar. Unfortunately, the developer ran out of time and money, and the resulting product was a dismal effort to salvage the material for use as a single-player game. Critics were appalled by the high number of bugs and the cumbersome control scheme, made worse by an inexplicable addition of precision action sequences: "It was an odd addition to a series that in the past had never required much hand–eye coordination," wrote Charles Herold for the *New York Times*. "It alienated many *Myst* fans but failed to make the game any more interesting for action gamers."[11] "Cyan and Ubisoft have completely ruined the *Myst* experience for me," wrote Murray Peterson in his scathing review for *Brass Lantern*.[12]

---

[11] Herold, Charles. "Tackling the Mystery of the Missing Game: URU, Ages Beyond Myst." *New York Times*, March 4, 2004: G5.

[12] Peterson, Murray. "Uru Review." *Brass Lantern*. 2003. http://www.brasslantern.org/reviews/graphic/urupeterson.html (accessed August 4, 2015).

Rand blamed the publisher, Ubisoft, for the game's demise:

I think it was simply lack of commitment and cold feet ... Because *Uru* was a very different type of online entertainment we were convinced we needed a year of uptime to really test the waters and grow the idea ... Meanwhile Ubisoft was watching *The Sims Online*'s lack of overwhelming success and instead of a year commitment they pulled the plug before we even launched ... It would have been nice to pick up the pieces and do it ourselves at that point, but we were completely spent.[13]

Myst IV: Revelation was developed by Ubisoft Montreal and released in 2004. Critics were much more impressed with *Revelation* than they'd been with *Uru*, and for good reason. It boasted the best audiovisuals and some of the best puzzles yet seen in the venerable series.

For the fifth and final entry in the series, 2005's *Myst V: End of Ages*, Rand Miller resumed the helm. The series at last abandoned prerendered graphics for real-time 3D. The end result may not have been as pretty as *Revelation*, but it was still well received by many critics, who admired its detailed models and quality voice acting. It received many accolades, but not all reviewers were impressed. The *New York Times* commentator quipped that it "does less with its real-time 3D engine than 1997's *Riven* did with pre-rendered backgrounds and some clever animations," and claimed it lacked imagination.[14] Twelve years had passed since two outsiders from Cyan had stunned the world with *Myst*; now, they were established developers, relying more on reputation than innovation to drive sales.

Rand and Robyn returned to the industry in 2013, launching a Kickstarter funding campaign for *Obduction*, a spiritual successor to *Myst* and *Riven* that raised $1.3 million. Although it will be an "entirely new property," it will have "the same framework that made Cyan's earlier games such a wonderful experience: stunning landscapes, deep storyline, engaging characters, dramatic soundscapes, and challenging yet intuitive puzzles."[15] Like the original *Myst*, the game will "plop" you into the middle of a mysterious, unknown location, with little initial information to go on. It will be built with the Unreal Engine 4, a far cry indeed from the days of HyperCard!

Despite the unprecedented success of *Myst* and *Riven*, few other developers successfully imitated Cyan's approach. There were, of course, many derivatives such as Dreamcatcher's *The Crystal Key* (2000), Knut Muller's *Rhem* (2003), and Detalion's *Sentinel: Descendants in Time* (2004), to more creative offerings like Her Interactive's *Nancy Drew* series (starting 1998), XXv's *Dark Fall* (2003), Kheops Studio's *Return to*

---

[13] Pearce, Celia. "The Ending Is Not Yet Written: A Conversation with Rand Miller." *Game Studies*. April 2010. http://gamestudies.org/1001/articles/pearce_celia (accessed August 4, 2015).

[14] Herold, Charles. "The Final Chapter in a Most Influential Series." *New York Times*, October 1, 2005: D7.

[15] Cyan, Inc. "Obduction." *Kickstarter*. October 17, 2013. https://www.kickstarter.com/projects/cyaninc/obduction/description (accessed August 4, 2015).

Mysterious Island (2004), Nucleosys' *Scratches* (2006), and Omni Adventure's *The Omega Stone* (2006).

More recently, *Myst*'s influence is evident in *The Talos Principle* by Croteam, a 2014 game that was met with rave reviews. There's also HyperSloth's *Dream* (2015), White Paper Games' *Ether One* (2014), and Krillbite Studios' *Among the Sleep* (2014), just to name a few of many indie developers churning out quality first-person adventure games and selling them on Steam. These modern takes on the genre offer fluid 3D movement rather than the perspective switching of the originals. The earlier method is still found in certain casual games, though, such as Artiflex Mundi's *Grim Legends: The Forsaken Bride* (2014) and *Enigmatis: The Ghost of Maple Creek* (2011), and Kheops Studio's excellent *Safecracker: The Ultimate Puzzle Adventure* (2006).

As all these titles suggest, the spirit of *Myst* lives on but is not as pervasive as fans or the developer would like. According to Rand, "It wasn't that [*Myst*] didn't take over. It was that it didn't create its own big fork in interactive entertainment ... Gaming just settled back to what it was ... They're all used to shoot aliens or zombies, for the most part."[5] And so what if the tourists have left? *Myst* was always a quiet, solitary place, once bustling, but now disturbed by none but the occasional wandering stranger, poking here and there among the ruins.

28.1 Playing *Myst* Today

Unless you're a historian or *Myst* purist, I'd recommend starting your adventure with *real-Myst: Masterpiece Edition*, available on Steam and Good Old Games. This 2014 remake updated the original's graphics with gorgeous new textures, models, and dynamic lighting and shadows. If you do want to try the older format, you can play *Myst: Masterpiece Edition*, which is also available on Steam. There are also versions for most mobile devices and consoles. On a side note, Cyan is hosting *Uru* (*Myst Online*) and allowing totally free play on their server. You can learn more at http://www.mystonline.com.

Chapter 29

Doom: Profound Carnage

In 1994, Matt Firme of *PC Gamer* wrote a feature for the magazine's premier issue about a shareware game called *Doom*. Like so many others, Firme found himself describing it in terms of addiction:

> *Doom* has taken control of my life. I can't stop playing the game, can't just turn off the computer and walk away. No matter what I should be doing, I play *Doom* instead. My wife can come home from work, eat dinner, and go to bed without my ever looking away from the computer. Ed McMahon could pound at my front door, shouting, "You are our latest millionaire" through a megaphone, and I'd never hear him. I'd just keep playing *Doom*.[1]

Even if Firme was being a bit tongue-in-cheek, there truly was something alarmingly addictive about *Doom*. Wandering through the exhibits at the Winter Consumer Electronics Show that year, Firme saw the game everywhere. Everyone he talked to asked if he'd played it yet.

"We knew we had made the best game ever, and we knew that because we were gamers," said John Romero, who helped design it. Romero, with his long dark hair and Californian accent, spoke in almost reverent tones: "The development of *Doom* was so smooth that it really felt like it was just our destiny."[2] Destiny or not, one thing's for sure—*Doom* didn't just turn the industry on its head.

Doom blew its head clean off.

Amazingly, the game that brought the industry to the next level did not come from a large, well-funded studio in Silicon Valley. Rather, Romero was one of four young, hotshot developers from id Software, a company they founded themselves in 1991 (see Figure 29.1). It was composed of former Softdisk developers, a "disk magazine" based in Shreveport, Louisiana. Disk magazines, or diskmags, thrived in the days before the Internet and were especially popular with people who lacked access to electronic bulletin board systems. Available at newsstands or by subscription, they were a convenient way to get regular infusions of new software.

Some of the programs on diskmags were public domain or fully functional programs that could be copied and distributed freely by anyone. However, others were

---

[1] Firme, Matt. "Doom: Why It Took Over My Life." *PC Gamer*, May 1994: 50–52.

[2] Barton, Matt. *Honoring the Code: Conversations with Great Game Designers*. Boca Raton, FL: CRC Press, 2013.

"shareware," which came in different forms. In most cases, you were free to copy and distribute a shareware program, but you were expected to pay the author if you liked it or found it useful. This try-before-you-buy approach became quite popular.

Of course, many users lacked the scruples to pay even for products they

Figure 29.1   The boys of id, circa 1990. As the saying goes, a picture is worth a thousand words. The man in blue is John Carmack; to his right is John Romero. The screaming man to his right is Tom Hall.

used frequently, so shareware publishers developed techniques to encourage them. The approach that Romero and many others employed was to offer the core game with a few levels for free, but charged for the fully expanded version. Thus, diskmags were a great way for shareware developers—what we'd probably call "indie developers" today—to get their wares in front of a larger audience, some of whom would happily pay for the full version of a program they enjoyed.[3]

The story of *Doom* begins, oddly enough, with a quirky two-dimensional platformer game called *Commander Keen*.[4] It was designed by John Romero, John Carmack, and Tom Hall, and first published in 1990 with the shareware arrangement discussed above. Anyone playing it today probably wouldn't think much of it, but it was a breakthrough for PC gaming. Until that time, it was commonly assumed that smooth, side-scrolling games like *Super Mario Bros.* weren't possible on DOS-based machines.

Romero had managed to get Carmack hired on at Softdisk after seeing a *Tennis* game he'd done for the Apple II (see Figure 29.2). A talented programmer himself, Romero could tell from that game's smooth animation that Carmack was a true master of the discipline. He was finally able to talk the reluctant Carmack into joining him at Softdisk. The two hit it off immediately—the spirited, charismatic Romero and the quiet, contemplative Carmack were equally obsessed with making games, and, working together, had the means to achieve their wildest ambitions.

---

[3] On a side note, while it was always possible to illegally copy and distribute the full versions of these programs without the author's consent, in my experience there was a certain shame in "screwing over" a shareware developer, who was likely a small team (or even a lone individual) and not associated with a big company. Even hardened pirates I knew strongly discouraged it.

[4] The full story of Romero and Carmack's rise to prominence has been told elsewhere; I recommend David Kushner's *Masters of Doom,* as well as Brad King and John Borland's *Dungeons and Dreamers* books for starters. This chapter is just a sketch of a long and fascinating story.

Romero had been doing a series of fixed-screen platformer games called *Dangerous Dave* (1988) for the Apple II. After the IBM PC became the industry standard, he worked on porting these games for CGA (4-color) and the hot-new EGA card (16-color). Carmack, meanwhile, had been studying and experimenting with scrolling techniques. One day, Romero came into his office and found a

Figure 29.2   After playing Carmack's *Tennis* game, Romero would stop at nothing to recruit him to his team. It may not look like much to us, but Romero was savvy enough to know that the Apple II animation that ran this smoothly took genius.

disk labeled *Dangerous Dave and Copyright Infringement* on his desk. Carmack had managed to replicate the smooth scrolling of *Super Mario Bros.* on the PC, mimicking its initial level perfectly (thus the joke in the title) (see Figure 29.3).

Figure 29.3   When Romero saw what Carmack had achieved with *Dangerous Dave and Copyright Infringement*, he realized they'd outgrown Softdisk. It was time to strike out on their own.

"I knew when I saw the horizontal scrolling that we had a Nintendo on the PC," said an awestruck Romero. "Boom! Here it is. We're out of here." Romero, convinced that Softdisk wouldn't recognize the game's potential, talked Carmack and two other Softdisk employees—artist Adrian Carmack and designer Tom Hall—into founding id Software in 1991. At 27, Hall was the oldest of the bunch—John Carmack, the youngest, was only 21.

Romero's instincts were good; id's *Commander Keen* series, which implemented Carmack's scrolling techniques, was a stunning achievement. Sandy Petersen, who'd later work for id, wrote a review of the game for *Dragon* magazine. "When Nintendo first made its appearance," wrote Petersen, "arcade games for home computers took a blow from which they have never really recovered ... [but] *Commander Keen* is one of the best games of its type that I've played ... In a number of ways, it stands above its rivals."[5] Petersen was most impressed with the small touches, such as Keen's ability to hang on to a ledge by his fingertips and look up and down to scope out a level. Barry Simon of *PC Magazine*

---

[5] Petersen, Sandy. "Eye of the Monitor." *Dragon*, September 1993: 60.

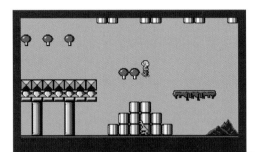

wrote about the game's "Nintendo feel" and marveled at its "smoothly scrolling scenery"[6] (see Figure 29.4).

Id might well have stopped there, simply churning out more *Commander Keen* games until the series ran out of juice. But as impressive as it was from a technological perspective, the fact was you

Figure 29.4   Id's *Commander Keen* games brought NES (Nintendo Entertainment System)-style platforming to DOS.

could already play plenty of games as good if not better on consoles. What Romero and Carmack really wanted was something that would not just set them apart from other DOS developers, but from all other developers, period. Id launched that game in 1992: *Wolfenstein 3D*, the first first-person shooter.[7]

Wolfenstein 3D was loosely based on the much older *Castle Wolfenstein*, a pioneering stealth game Silas Warner had written for the Apple II. Id's original design had included many elements from the Apple II classic that didn't make it into their finished game, like dragging and searching bodies or picking locks. "But that stopped you from killing, from slowing shit down," said Romero. "So we got rid of it." The team also wisely figured that just using a mouse and keyboard to control a character in three dimensions would be enough challenge for many people. The first episode did loosely follow the plot of Warner's game; your task was to recover secret Nazi war plans and escape a heavily guarded castle.

The game also drew heavily from two of id's previous games, *Hovertank One* and *Catacombs 3-D*, completed in May and November of 1991, respectively (see Figures 29.5 and 29.6). Each was an important step toward *Wolfenstein 3D*. For *Hovertank One*, Carmack developed a "raycasting" technique for efficiently drawing graphics onto the screen, as well as digital sound effects. Carmack devised a texture mapping routine for *Catacombs 3-D*, which allowed for more detailed surfaces on its models.[8] It was also notable because players controlled a person, not a tank or other vehicle. The character's hand was shown on screen instead of crosshairs. Carmack expanded on these concepts for the new game, most notably switching to the 256-color palette of the new VGA standard and adding digitally sampled sound effects.

---

[6] Simon, Barry. "Arcade Game Offers Nintendo-Style Action with Scrolling Graphics." *PC Magazine*, June 25, 1991: 480–481.

[7] Some have contested this claim, as we saw in Chapter 7. In any case, later first-person shooter developers looked to *Wolfenstein 3D* for their model, not *Spasim* or *Maze War*.

[8] There's some debate about the extent that Carmack's texture mapping routines may have been inspired by an early demo of the game *Ultima Underworld* by Looking Glass Studios, which employed a similar technique.

Peterson's review of the game for *Dragon* magazine summed up the game's unique appeal quite nicely:

> There is nothing else quite like *Wolfenstein*. While a few other games boast 3-D and scaled sprites (such as *Ultima Underworld*), *Wolfenstein's* greatest asset is its speed—you can

Figure 29.5   *Hovertank* was an early stab at a 3D game. It's generally not considered an "FPS" because the player is in a vehicle, not on foot.

> careen down the fortress halls at an astonishing rate for 3-D, racing past highly detailed posters of der Führer while Nazi guards shout at you.[5]

Petersen also commented on the gore factor, calling it "bloodily violent." "If wholesale slaughter disturbs you, this game

Figure 29.6   You're supposed to rescue the people in the building, not shoot them. Oops!

is *not* for you" concluded Petersen (see Figure 29.7).

Chris Lombardi of *Computer Gaming World* was similarly enthusiastic: "In *Wolfenstein 3-D*, the player is 'there' like no game I've ever played." Like Petersen, Lombardi expressed concerns about the violence: "Though I killed hundreds

Figure 29.7   Id's *Wolfenstein 3D* was fast and bloody, and had amazing 3D graphics.

of stick-figure guards in the original *Castle Wolfenstein* and never thought twice, the first-person perspective with the graphic detail and digitized sound really brings the act of killing home."[9] The fact that both reviewers seemed anxious about this aspect of the game says something about the unprecedented realism of its engine. As crude as it might look today, *Wolfenstein 3D* was sufficiently immersive to unnerve sensitive players, who seemed both anxious and excited about the potential of the first-person shooter.

---

[9] Lombardi, Chris. "The Third Reich in the Third Dimension." *Computer Gaming World*, September 1992: 50, 52.

Former US Army Colonel Dave Grossman called them "murder simulators" and feared that they might be conditioning children to kill.[10] Scientific evidence linking them to school shootings has yet to be produced, however.

In any case, *Wolfenstein 3D* did exceptionally well for id, which sold more than 100,000 copies of the game by 1993. Id's shareware model also meant that it was able to retain a much larger share of the profit than the traditional publisher model. A copy cost id less than $5 to produce, but they sold it for $50—a "profit margin any software company would envy."[11] Romero and Carmack now had the financial resources to do whatever they wanted—and what they wanted was to make an even better game than *Wolfenstein 3D*.

Their first move was to cut ties with Apogee, Scott Miller's shareware company. Even though Miller had given them an unheard of 50% royalty deal, Jay Wilbur, whom id had appointed its CEO, urged them to go it alone; to "grab opportunity by the scruff of the neck and pull it through."[12] Another casualty was Tom Hall, who'd become disillusioned with the company. He wanted id to return to their roots, with cutesy, zany *Commander Keen*-style games. He was also insistent that their games have well-developed stories; Carmack thought stories in games were as irrelevant as "a story in a porn movie; it's expected to be there, but it's not that important."[12] These creative differences led unsurprisingly to Hall's departure.

According to Romero, the hype around id's new project began early: "In January of 1993, we put out a press release that had everything we wanted to put in the game. We told everybody: This is *Doom*, and it'll be out at the end of the year. Everything was groundbreaking, and we hadn't done any of it. But we *knew* we could. It was like it was predetermined."[2] The press release promised "light diminishing and light sourcing," a "seamless world—inside and outside," "incredible movie-like cinematic sequences," and, most exciting of all, "four players at once on LANs, two by modem."[13]

Carmack's new engine was also far more advanced in terms of level design. Unlike *Wolfenstein 3D*, whose levels were limited to flat, rectangular grids, *Doom* let level designers put floors, walls, and ceilings wherever they wanted. Carmack had also set up a texturing system that allowed for some parts to be transparent—a useful feature for creating windows. Romero took full advantage of these new features:

---

[10] Grossman, David. "National Commission to Stop the New Violence." *The Schiller Institute*. May 20, 2000. http://www .schillerinstitute.org/new_viol/ctte_grossman.html (accessed August 7, 2015).

[11] Antoniades, Alexander. "The Game Developer Archives: 'Monsters from the Id: The Making of Doom'." *Gamastura*. January 15, 2009. http://www.gamasutra.com/php-bin/news_index.php?story=21405 (accessed August 5, 2015).

[12] Kushner, David. *Masters of Doom: How Two Guys Created an Empire and Transformed Pop Culture*. New York: Random House, 2004.

[13] id Software. "15. Doom Press Release." *5 Years of Doom*. 1993. http://5years.doomworld.com/doombible/section15.shtml (accessed August 6, 2015).

I started playing around with height, making ceilings really high up, and putting bal-
conies in the walls ... I played around with stairs leading up to [the room], changing
light values, making recessed stuff. I wanted to demonstrate the feeling of going from
a closed-in area, down a hallway, and now you're upstairs—now that was different.
Whoa, stairs! Then you go up, and the room opens up into this huge thing.[2]

Romero felt he'd achieved the right look for *Doom* (see Figure 29.8).

The team had also made breakthroughs in AI. "*Doom* was the only game I'd played
where the emergent behavior of the monsters felt unpredictable," said Romero. "Even
if you made the level, the game would always have some mystery to it." Different monsters would attack each other; hear gunshots through windows; even lure them into
ambushes. Monsters weren't the only perils awaiting the player. Ceilings caved in, slime
could be radioactive, and barrels could explode—blowing up a reckless player, but also
a way for savvier players to destroy monsters.

Finally, *Doom* added an impressive array of weaponry, including pistols, shotguns,
chainguns, a rocket launcher, and the ultimate weapon—the BFG9000, the "Big Fucking
Gun" that could kill almost anything with a single shot. There were also health and armor
pickups, as well as radiation suits and "stimpacks," a "booster enzyme that make[s] you
feel like a new man," according to the game's manual.

Doom went live on December 19, 1993, and rapidly made its way across electronic bulletin board systems and FTP servers. Tens of thousands of gamers raced to their modems

Figure 29.8 *Doom* was an instant success for id, turning the them into the new superstars
of the industry.

to download the game, far too impatient to wait for mail. "It was a mob scene the night *Doom* came out," said Rogers of AOL's game forum. "If we weren't on the other side of a phone line, there would have been bodily harm."[12] Downloads of the game and the networked multiplayer crashed the networks on college campuses and beyond—even Intel had to ban the game after its systems were overloaded.

Id was quick to follow up the original *Doom* with many upgrades, sequels, and spin-offs. *Doom II: Hell on Earth* appeared in 1995, which was basically the same game, though with a larger area to explore. The critical difference was that *Doom II* was never released as shareware; it was a commercial product that sold upward of 2 million copies and earned id, who'd self-published it, more than $80 million in revenue.[12] This game received several official expansion packs, many of which were based on levels designed by users: *The Ultimate Doom* (1995), *Master Levels for Doom II* (1995), and *Final Doom* (1996).

Id has also published spin-off games with *Doom*'s engine. These include Raven Software's *Heretic* (1994) and *Hexen* (1996), well-received games set in a fantasy setting. These games were noted for a more sophisticated inventory system and the ability to look up and down.

In 1996, id released *Quake*, another definitive first-person shooter. This tremendously successful game and its sequels again put players in the boots of a soldier. Government officials experimenting with teleportation technology ("slipgates") unwittingly granted access to a race of vicious "death squad" marauders, and, of course, it's up to the player to enter the slipgate and kill "Quake," a mysterious and powerful enemy responsible for the death squads (see Figure 29.9).

Despite *Quake*'s success in the market, Romero himself was disappointed. He'd wanted to achieve another giant leap forward like the one between *Wolfenstein 3D* and *Doom*. Instead, they'd settled for more of the same. "It wasn't the same place anymore," said Romero, who afterward quit id to work on his own project, an ill-fated game called *Daikatana* that tarnished his reputation.

Meanwhile, other developers were making their own first-person shooter games. Two of the most influential were Valve's *Half-Life* (1988) and Bungee's *Halo: Combat Evolved* (2001). *Half-Life* introduced several ambitious innovations but was perhaps most notable for weaving in a more sophisticated narrative—a successful challenge to Carmack's belief that stories are unimportant in games. Its sequel, *Half-Life 2* (2004) was even more story focused, with characters and a plot as good as any science fiction film. The ever-popular *Counter-Strike* game started off as a modification of *Half-Life*.

Halo: Combat Evolved was also acclaimed for its excellent story and writing but was more noteworthy for successfully

Figure 29.9   *Quake* was an awesome game, but Romero felt it lacked ambition.

adapting the genre for the console market. There had been earlier attempts (including ports of *Doom*), but with the key exceptions of Rare's *GoldenEye 007* (1997) and *Perfect Dark* (2000) for the Nintendo 64, these had largely failed. The complex control scheme demanded by the genre seemed to necessitate a keyboard and a mouse. Bungee and Microsoft solved the problem with a specialized controller. Indeed, now even many PC gamers prefer game controllers to a keyboard and mouse set.

There are, of course, a multitude of other vital first-person shooter games, such as Looking Glass Studios' *System Shock* (1994), Red Storm Entertainment's *Tom Clancy's Rainbow Six* (1998), Dynamix's *Starseige: Tribes* (1998), Digital Illusion CE's *Battlefield 1942*, Infinity Ward's *Call of Duty* (2003), Crytek's *Far Cry* (2004), and Monolith's *F.E.A.R.* (2005). All these games contributed new ideas and are worth playing. The first-person shooter genre proved quite versatile for rebooting older game franchises, such as Bethesda's *Fallout 3* (2008), Starbreeze Studio's *Syndicate* (2012), and, of course, 3D Realm's *Duke Nukem 3D* (1996) and Retro Studio's *Metroid Prime* (2002).

As for *Doom*, id released the third official sequel in 2004, which rebooted the franchise and ignored the story arcs of the previous games. While many praised its graphics and purely technical achievements, other aspects felt antiquated. The style of gameplay that was so fresh and exhilarating back in 1993 was now stale. Bethesda published an enhanced remake of the game called *Doom 3 BFG Edition* in 2012. Another reboot of the series is planned for 2016.

Andrzej Bartkowiak's *Doom* film hit theaters in 2005. Roger Ebert gave it one star and quipped, "*Doom* is like some kid came over and is using your computer and won't let you play."[14] It did fairly well on its opening weekend, but quickly dropped into obscurity.

It's been more than two decades since gamers got their first taste of *Doom*, but the paradigms it introduced are alive and kicking today, and I suspect they'll stay with us regardless of the progress of the underlying technology. In 1997, to preserve its legacy and support future generations of game programmers, id facilitated this process by releasing the *Doom* source code under a not-for-profit license.

29.1 Playing *Doom* Today

Even if modern first-person shooters make *Doom*'s once-stunning graphics look crude by comparison, its brilliant level design more than makes up for it. You can buy various editions of *Doom* on Steam, all set up and ready to run. It's also helpful (and quite entertaining) to watch John Romero's own in-game commentary on his level design—look for DoubleFineProd's "Devs Play" *Doom* series on YouTube.

---

[14] Ebert, Roger. "Doom." *RogerEbert.com.* October 20, 2005. http://www.rogerebert.com/reviews/doom-2005 (accessed August 6, 2015).

Chapter 30

John Madden Football: The Greatest Play

Electronic Arts' (EA's) *Madden* series is one of the most consistently profitable video game franchises, having earned its publisher well over $4 billion in the course of its long, storied history.[1] The *Madden* franchise looms large not just in sports but over the entire industry, selling millions of each of its near-annual releases. It moves technological innovation forward even without the goad of serious competition. If you want to play a football game, there's *Madden* and then there's … soccer.

"I really knew what *Madden* accomplished when I was at Fox," said John Madden, the legendary coach who has always eagerly lent EA his expertise as well as his name on their product (see Figure 30.1). "The president of Fox Sports had a meeting with a bunch of us, and he said, 'What we want to do is make our game in television look like the video game.'"[2] It was a textbook example of life imitating art, or, to be more precise, a sport imitating a game. I'm reminded of a prescient observation by Jean Baudrillard, a French sociologist and philosopher:

> Simulation is no longer that of a territory, a referential being, or a substance. It is the generation by models of a real without origin or reality: a hyperreal. The territory no longer precedes the map, nor does it survive it … The desert of the real itself.[3]

The real football field that the video games once struggled to imitate now imitates the simulated one—but the similarities between *Madden* and actual football don't stop with graphics and physics. The stuntmen who don futuristic-looking motion-capture suits to perform tackles, tosses, and other moves for the game often end up as bruised and battered as the athletes themselves.

The game's impact on the NFL runs deep. Many pros play it actively, and more than a few coaches use it as a training tool. Everyone pays attention to the in-game ratings it assigns

---

[1] Gaudiosi, John. "Madden: The $4 Billion Video Game Franchise." *CNN Money*. September 5, 2013. http://money.cnn.com/2013/09/05/technology/innovation/madden-25/ (accessed August 10, 2015).

[2] Bissell, Tom. "Kickoff: Madden NFL and the Future of Video Game Sports." *Grantland*. January 26, 2012. http://grantland.com/features/tom-bissell-making-madden-nfl/ (accessed August 10, 2015).

[3] Baudrillard, Jean. *Simulacra and Simulation*. Ann Arbor: University of Michigan Press, 1981.

to each athlete, which can have surprising consequences for their public perceptions and careers. That process is Byzantine in its complexity as well as its politics. It's "the secret process that turns NFL players into digital gods," according to Neil Paine, senior sportswriter for FiveThirtyEight.[4] Arnie Stapleton wrote that Donny Moore, the former "ratings czar," was often "the most reviled man in NFL locker rooms.

Figure 30.1   The title screen of the first *John Madden Football* game. Apple II version.

Sometimes older stars first recognize their careers are on the downslopes when the new *Madden* games arrive in August and their ratings have slipped."[5] Not everyone takes it lying down. Kerry Rhodes of the New York Jets took to YouTube to rant about his and his teammate Nick Mangold's ratings in a video called "WTF Madden!"

For many years, John Madden himself graced the cover of the games that bore his name, but now they feature exemplary NFL athletes like Odell Beckham, Jr. of the New York Giants. The honor brings a great deal of celebrity. "Teams go on the Wheaties box," said Josh Cribbs, a kick returner for the Cleveland Browns, "but, individually, when you make the cover of *Madden*, you've arrived" (see Figure 30.2). Cribbs is obviously unconcerned about the "*Madden* curse," a popular superstition that arose after a series of honorees met with disaster.

Most date the origins of the *Madden* series back to the late 1980s, where it played a large part in making EA the third-largest game publisher in the world. However, we should probably go back two decades earlier. As a boy, EA's charismatic founder, Trip Hawkins, dreamed of creating an alternative to his favorite board game, *Strat-O-Matic*. *Strat-O-Matic* came out in the early 1960s and was developed by Hal Richman, a math major. Richman used his background in math to simulate sports (football, baseball, and others) with a combination of dice and cards full of performance statistics. The player managed a team of these athletes and then used the dice and information on the cards to simulate a game. It might sound a bit like fantasy football, and, indeed, the company refers to it as "the ancestor of fantasy sports."

As a teenager, Hawkins made and tried to sell his own take on *Strat-O-Matic*, which failed miserably. Nevertheless, Hawkins clung to his dream, and created a computerized version on a PDP-11 while he was a student at Harvard. Finally, after a highly lucrative stint as an employee at Apple (where he was nicknamed "Junior Steve Jobs"), Hawkins cashed in his

---

[4] Paine, Neil. "How Madden Ratings Are Made." *Fivethirtyeight.com.* February 25, 2015. http://fivethirtyeight.com/features/madden/# (accessed August 12, 2015).

[5] Stapleton, Arnie. "Madden Ratings Guru Has the Players' Attention." *Denver Post.* August 25, 2014. http://www.denverpost.com/business/ci_26389107/madden-ratings-guru-has-players-attention (accessed August 12, 2015).

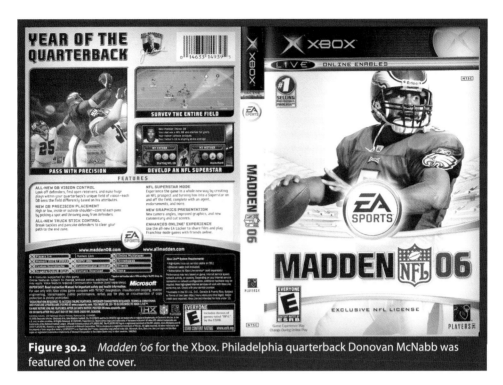

Figure 30.2 *Madden '06* for the Xbox. Philadelphia quarterback Donovan McNabb was featured on the cover.

Apple stock and used the millions to found EA.[6] As you'll recall from Chapter 14, Hawkins fostered an ideology of game designers as rock stars and published several innovative and influential games for early home computers. Among these was a hit basketball game, Eric Hammond's *Dr. J and Larry Bird Go One on One*, which EA published in 1983. The game was celebrated for its realistic animation, which, given the technology of the era, did a great job imitating the style of the titular athletes, who Hawkins had licensed for a mere $25,000 each.[7] Licensing actual athletes costs far more than just using generic or made-up names, but it was a brilliant marketing ploy. EA would use it again for *Earl Weaver Baseball* in 1987.

Of course, Hawkins had always been interested in doing a football game, and knew exactly who he wanted to grace the cover: Joe "Cool" Montana, the famous quarterback for the 49ers. Unfortunately for Hawkins, Atari had beaten him to the punch. Crestfallen, Hawkins tried for his second choice: former Vikings quarterback Joe Kapp. Kapp was available and interested, but only if EA paid him royalties, a deal-breaker for Hawkins. Finally, however, Hawkins found a suitable candidate willing to agree to his terms: John Madden, the Super Bowl–winning coach and color commentator.

---

[6] Hruby, Patrick. "The Franchise: The Inside Story of How Madden NFL Became a Video Game Dynasty." *ESPN Outside the Lines.* August 5, 2010. http://sports.espn.go.com/espn/eticket/story?page=100805/madden (accessed August 10, 2015).

[7] Nelson, Murray R. *American Sports: A History of Icons, Idols, and Ideas.* Santa Barbara, CA: Greenwood, 2013: 371.

Madden and Hawkins made an interesting pair. With the exception of his well-known love of the telestrator, a device he used to draw diagrams on sports plays, the former coach was no fan of technology. Indeed, Hawkins and Joe Ybarra, Hawkins' second-in-command, were asked to meet with Madden on a train—he refused to fly, and knew precious little about computers. What he did know, of course, was football. He was impressed with Hawkins, who he considered a "computer genius," but he had a problem with the proposal. Hawkins

Figure 30.3   This photo of John Madden and designer/programmer Robin Antonick appeared on the inside front cover of the game box.

and Ybarra, knowing full well the constraints of the home computers of the era, had in mind a simplified version of the sport with six-man teams. "If it isn't 11 on 11, it isn't real football," insisted Madden, who wouldn't budge on the issue.[8]

Reluctantly, Hawkins agreed, but these and other technological demands turned out to be more formidable than anticipated. "We were trying to model NFL football on a computer with less horsepower than your watch," said Ybarra. The task of turning Madden's vision into working code fell to Robin Antonick (see Figure 30.3).[9] Madden once said that the fewer rules a coach has, the fewer rules there are for players to break. Ybarra and Antonick found a corollary: the more players there are, the more ways there are for a program to fail. "All my memories are of pain," said Ybarra.[6] The project consumed so much time and resources that some around the office took to calling it "Trip's Folly."

Sadly, the struggle was mostly for naught. By the time *John Madden Football* finally hit store shelves in 1988 (see Figure 30.4), the time of *Madden's* development and release, the computer gaming market was in an awkward transition from 8-bit computers like the Apple II and Commodore 64 to 16-bit machines, but neither the Atari ST nor the Commodore Amiga could get much traction against the IBM PC despite its higher price and lackluster graphics. Finally, EA's product faced stiff competition from the likes of Brøderbund's

---

[8] Michaels, Al. "IGN Presents the History of Madden." *IGN.* August 8, 2008. http://www.ign.com/articles/2008/08/08/ign-presents-the-history-of-madden (accessed August 11, 2015).

[9] There's significant dispute about Antonick's actual involvement. Antonick sued EA in 2011, asserting that it owed him billions in unpaid royalties. Hawkins claimed that he was just one of many people who worked on the game, and not "the person driving the game" (Pham 2011). However, as mentioned above, Antonick is credited as a designer on the box, where he's featured in a photo. It also includes this signed statement from him: "Thanks to Trip for believing in me and the project, to EA for the opportunity … to pursue a dream come true—John Madden Football." In any case, Antonick left the company in 1992 and wasn't involved in the Genesis version. EA eventually won the case.

Playmaker Football, Data East's *ABC Monday Night Football*, Micro Sports' *MSFL Pro League Football*, and, most detrimentally, Cinemaware's *TV Sports Football*, whose stunning audiovisuals made it a hit even among nonfootball fans.

Meanwhile, the American console market had crashed a few years earlier, and though the Nintendo Entertainment

Figure 30.4 The Apple II version was an impressive technical feat but wasn't nearly as successful as the later Genesis version.

System (NES) had taken over, Hawkins was wary of Nintendo's policies and attitudes toward third-party developers. In addition, the NES already had a hit football game called *Tecmo Bowl* (1987), an arcade port with the names of actual NFL athletes (but not the names of their teams). Another Japanese console maker, Sega, had tried to level the playing field with its Master System, but couldn't tear Americans away from Mario and Zelda. Hawkins believed, however, that their next system, the Genesis, had a much better shot—especially if he threw the full weight of EA behind it.

John Madden Football for the Genesis was going to make their earlier effort look primitive by comparison. It boasted an extensive playbook, variable field conditions, passwords for saving games, digitized voice clips, tons of statistics, and an amazing pseudo-3D perspective with multilevel parallax scrolling. The distinguished C-64 composer Rob Hubbard did the soundtrack.

Hawkins played a smoke-and-mirrors game with Sega, demanding an insultingly low fee per cartridge ($2 rather than the typical $10) and an unprecedented $2 million cap even on that.[6] Meanwhile, Hawkins put a team on reverse engineering the console to bypass the fee altogether—a feat they accomplished in short order. Sega finally consented to Hawkins' demands. It wasn't worth it to get bogged down in a court battle with EA, and if they lost, they'd lose everything. According to Hawkins, "That $2 million cap saved us $35 million."

If Hawkins screwed Sega over with this deal, his next move was outright dastardly. Sega had planned to do its own football game starring—you guessed it—Joe Montana. Sadly, the team Sega had working on it was unable to deliver, at least not in time for the all-important Christmas season. Out of desperation, Hayao Nakayama, Sega's president, called Hawkins personally and asked if he'd consider trading Montana for Madden. Instead, Hawkins agreed to make both games, though in the case of *Joe Montana Football*, "We made sure it was totally inferior."[6] EA essentially gutted the best features of their flagship game, including the impressive pseudo-3D perspective. Surprisingly, both games did exceptionally well regardless, and helped make the Sega Genesis the console of choice for sports fans (see Figure 30.5a and b).

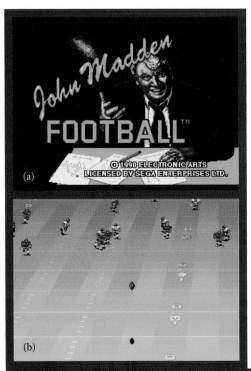

(a)

(b)

As impressive as *John Madden Football* for the Genesis was, however, it was totally eclipsed by its sequel, *John Madden Football '92* (see Figure 30.6a and b). It had 28 pro teams and the "All-Madden" team, improved AI, more plays, instant replays, two-player co-op, playoffs, more weather conditions, and more "audibles," or digitized voice clips. Most (in)famously, if a player got injured, a badly driven ambulance rushed onto the field, running over anyone in its path—a hilarious bit of comic relief that some fans sorely missed in later versions. For *John Madden Football '93*, EA turned development over to Paul Neurath's Blue Sky Productions studio, who needed the money to finish their *Ultima Underworld* game. They made a few minor improvements, but nothing spectacular. It was the first *Madden* game published for the Super Nintendo Entertainment System (SNES).

Figure 30.5   *John Madden Football* on the Genesis was a critical breakthrough for EA, Sega, and the industry in general. Shown here is the game's title screen (a) and gameplay (b).

EA finally acquired an NFL team license for *Madden NFL '94*. Twenty-eight teams were now officially represented along with classic Super Bowl teams. John Madden was a much more audible presence, greeting players when they booted the game and delivering his trademark exclamations like "Amazing!" and "Boom!" *Madden NFL '95*, released in 1994, was the first version with the full names of most NFL players, not just their numbers, and had full-season stat tracking. It was available for lots of platforms, including the Game Boy and Sega Game Gear handhelds. *Madden NFL '96* added classic teams and a create-a-player feature. A planned Sony PlayStation version was canned after Sony showed an early version of its *NFL GameDay*, a wonderfully advanced game that some deemed a *Madden* killer. "If you want to play next year's *Madden* early, buy this year's *GameDay*," quipped Kelly Flock, head of Sony Interactive Studios. He also poked fun at *Madden*'s "Liquid AI," which EA's press releases claimed would allow the computer to "react exactly as a human would." Flock called it "the crap that ran down EA's leg when they saw *GameDay*."[6]

GameDay did temporarily bring *Madden* down the charts. But, ultimately, Flock's routine was just a lot of tough acting—and *Madden NFL '97* brought the Tinactin. It had full 3D, a much-loved franchise mode, and solid AI (see Figure 30.7).

Madden hit another bump in 1999, when *NFL 2K* hit the Dreamcast—a platform that EA had rejected. Developed by Visual Concepts Entertainment, who'd formerly worked on *Madden* ports and the PlayStation *Madden NFL '96*. *NFL 2K* was a critically acclaimed masterpiece, with incredible 3D graphics, smooth controls, and realistic physics. EA's *Madden NFL 2000* wasn't nearly as impressive (see Figure 30.8). EA pulled out all the stops for *Madden NFL 2001*, which Ryan MacDonald of *GameSpot* called "the most realistic and complete video game interpretation of the sport of football ever."[10] "Grass fields look just like real grass, which can actually get lodged in the corner of a player's facemask after he sinks his head into the soil after a missed dive tackle," wrote the awestruck critic. *Madden* was back on top.

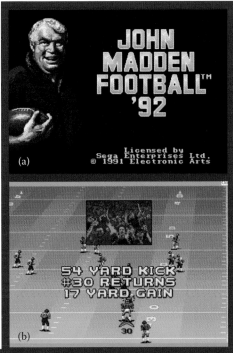

Figure 30.6 *John Madden Football '92* was an even greater success. Shown here is the game's title screen (a) and a crowd-cheering sequence (b).

Year after year, EA would add and loudly tout new features for each new *Madden*, even if cynics dismissed them as mere graphical tweaks and roster updates. After the cancellation of Sony's *NFL GameDay* and Sega's *NFL 2K* series in 2004, *Madden* unveiled its "hit stick" feature in *Madden NFL 2005*. This feature let you use the analog stick to ram into or tackle a ball carrier—provided your timing was good. Alex Navarro of *GameSpot* called it "the best defensive innovation made in any football game, ever ... absolutely phenomenal."[11] If the success of this game wasn't enough to solidify *Madden*'s position as the undisputed king of football games, the NFL's decision to give them an exclusive license certainly did. Through it all, Madden himself has stayed almost parentally involved in each game's production, lending the designers his expertise and insisting they meet his high standards.

As of this writing, *Madden* fans are pining for *Madden NFL 16*, with an impressive array of features. The most interesting (especially given the discussion of hyperreality at the start

---

[10] MacDonald, Ryan. "Madden NFL 2001 Review." *GameSpot*. October 13, 2000. http://www.gamespot.com/reviews /madden-nfl-2001-review/1900-2640511/ (accessed August 12, 2015).

[11] Navarro, Alex. "Madden NFL 2005 Review." *GameSpot*. August 6, 2004. http://www.gamespot.com/reviews/madden-nfl -2005-review/1900-6104310/ (accessed August 12, 2015).

Figure 30.7   *Madden '97* for the short-lived Sega Saturn.

of this chapter) is the "playmaker broadcast." The game's "presentation director," Brian Murray, explained it as follows:

This year, the team wanted to continue to push the envelope and go beyond what normal broadcasts are able to do. While we respect broadcast and the way they produce NFL games, our team does not have to worry about restrictions like player and cameraman safety in the game.[12]

Murray claims the system is "grounded in reality," that is, based on systems and technologies that are used in actual NFL broadcasts. However, Murray's field cameras can be wherever and whenever they're needed to maximize the spectacle. Unlike the wirecam you might see zipping around on television, Murray's can "track action and be right next to the QB right before the ball is snapped. With sweeping shots during a pass play or circling the QB before he gets

Figure 30.8   *Madden 2000* Nintendo 64 cartridge.

sacked, the Wirecam has truly changed the way we view our game." In short, it's quite possible that these and future innovations of this sort might not only make *Madden* indistinguishable from a televised broadcast, but more immersive and entertaining—even for spectators.

As for Hawkins himself, the boy who once dreamed of a computerized *Strat-O-*

Matic game left EA in 1991 to found 3DO, a pioneering but short-lived console and publishing company. The 3DO was the first 32-bit console and used CD-ROMs rather than

---

[12] Murray, Brian. "Go Beyond the Broadcast with Madden NFL 16 Presentation." *EA Sports.* July 9, 2015. https://www .easports.com/madden-nfl/news/2015/madden-16-presentation (accessed August 12, 2015).

cartridges for storage. Sadly, its high price put it out of reach of most gamers. It was viable long enough for Hawkins' former company to publish a *Madden* game for it. It was significantly ahead of its time, with tons of digitized animations, 3D stadiums, and color commentary by John Madden. It was an impressive game, but not enough to save 3DO, especially after Sony launched its PlayStation the following year.

"Sony committed more than $2 billion, and not only beat 3DO but pushed aside larger and stronger competitors like Sega and Nintendo," said Hawkins. "I was trying too hard to push the envelope ... I think many of us young entrepreneurs are trying to find out exactly who we are and where our edges are, and you don't know where the edges really are until you fall off a few times."[13]

Hawkins may be long gone from EA, but John Madden, who's even more involved with the series now that he's retired from broadcasting, hasn't forsaken him. "John and I have a special shared feeling from what got created there, a mutual appreciation," said a teary-eyed Hawkins. "It wouldn't have been created as well without the both of us. He could have thrown me under the rug. But he knows what we did."[6] What they did was score the most points—and, as Madden once put it, "Usually, the team that scores the most points wins the game."

Perhaps the greatest legacy of *Madden* was demographic in nature—it made it "okay" for adult men to play console games. These men—and no doubt some women, too—couldn't have cared less about Sonic or Mario, but they were passionate enough about football to overcome whatever social stigma they felt about gaming. Love it or hate it, *Madden* helped make video games a respectable hobby that adults could enjoy without shame.

Hawkins once said that EA could "see farther." Madden would've probably added, yeah, especially if they had their contacts in.

30.1 Playing *John Madden Football* Today

Playing the original Apple II version of the game is easy enough; just go to http://virtual apple.org and look for "John Madden Football." Keep in mind, though, that this game bears little resemblance to the Genesis version that made it famous. Although it's possible to emulate the Genesis version in a browser as well, trying to control it with a keyboard isn't much fun. Besides, it's cheap and easy to find a working Sega Genesis, and a *John Madden Football* cartridge is to be had for little more than the cost of postage. Most Genesis fans perceive *Madden NFL '95* as the best, though others argue for '92 (that ambulance!) and '93. In any case, playing one of these versions from a simpler time will be much easier for football novices than a modern *Madden*.

---

13 Ramsay, Morgan. *Gamers at Work*. New York: Apress, 2012.

Chapter 31

Sonic the Hedgehog: Faster than a Portly Plumber

Since the Nintendo Entertainment System (NES) and *Super Mario Bros.* game burst onto the scene in 1985, the name "Nintendo" was virtually synonymous with the term *video game*. Nintendo had a stranglehold on the console market and was more than willing to use its vast power to crush whatever competition dared raise its head. Determined not to repeat the mistakes of its predecessor, Atari, Nintendo ruled with an iron fist, and third-party developers had no choice but to obey a strict set of guidelines that highly favored the manufacturer. Got a problem with that? Deal with it. If you were a console developer who wanted to keep the lights on, you appeased Nintendo.

Nintendo's monopoly wasn't healthy for any industry, and unsurprisingly, stymied innovation, which suited them just fine. Committed to Yokoi's policy of "lateral thinking with withered technology," Nintendo saw no reason to replace its aging NES hardware. After all, upstarts like NEC and Sega had been trying that tactic for years with little to show for it. Even as NEC's PC Engine replaced their Famicom as the system of choice in Japan, Nintendo dragged their heels. They still dominated the far more lucrative American market. Everyone there knew that Nintendo was big, slow, and untouchable.

Perhaps, however, if President Yamauchi at Nintendo's headquarters in Kyoto had looked out his window, he might have seen the little blue dot in the distance, a dot that grew larger even as he watched it. What the hell was *that*?

That was *Sonic the Hedgehog* (see Figure 31.1). He was fast—hypersonic, in fact, with a temper to match. He was a nice guy if you really got to know him, and once you did, you'd know there was only one thing that *really* set him off: oppression.[1] And, whether he liked it or not, Yamauchi and Sonic were about to get very well acquainted.

Sonic's story begins in the late 1980s. Sega's efforts to penetrate the American market with its Sega Master System (SMS) console had failed miserably, despite its technical superiority to the NES. Sega responded with an even better console, the Sega Genesis in 1989.[2] The Genesis—called the "Megadrive" internationally—was a huge leap forward

---

[1] From the *Sonic Adventure* manual: "With a strong love of freedom, the only thing Sonic hates is oppression. Despite his short temper, deep down he's a really nice guy who is 100% committed to helping those in trouble whenever and wherever he can" (20).

[2] NEC unveiled its lesser known TurboGrafx-16 2 weeks later. It was a hit in Japan (where it was called the PC Engine), but lagged far behind Nintendo and Sega in the United States.

Figure 31.1   *Sonic the Hedgehog* was Sega's answer to Mario.

technologically, but American gamers were far more excited about *Super Mario Bros. 3* than "blast processing," whatever that was.

The problem was that the Genesis lacked a brilliant game. As we saw in Chapter 30, Electronic Arts (EA) was throwing the weight of its sports franchises behind them, but they still lacked a "killer app" that could go toe-to-toe with Mario. Contrary to some popular histories, Sega did have a mascot, albeit an unofficial one—*Alex Kidd*, who made his debut in 1986's *Alex Kidd in Miracle World* on the SMS. He was an adorable little boy with big pointed ears and a red and yellow jumpsuit. The game and character were popular, but Sega of Japan's president, the volatile Hayao Nakayama, didn't think Kidd was the best choice for the new console. So he literally sent his "AM8" team to the drawing board to come up with ideas for a new character. The best design would become the new face of Sega. The only imperative was that whatever they came up with, it'd better not look *anything* like a certain rotund plumber whose name must not be mentioned.

There were lots of intriguing ideas, but one stood out to Nakayama, and not just because he looked cool. The pair who pitched it hadn't merely created a character, but a game design to go with it—a design that was not only appropriate for the new character, but was suitably ambitious, and would take full advantage of the Genesis hardware. He was blue, spiky, and fast as hell. His name was Mr. Needlemouse.

The winning team was composed of Naoto Oshima and Yuji Naka (see Figure 31.2). Naka was a stellar programmer, obsessed with games, who'd jumped right into the indus-

Figure 31.2   Oshima and Naka in 2010.

try after high school—he didn't have time for college. He applied to Namco, but the famed creators of *Pac-Man* weren't interested in an "uneducated" man like Naka. Their loss. He got a job at Sega instead, whose president was a college dropout himself. At Sega, Naka worked on the best-selling *Phantasy Star* games and eventually climbed his way up to a lead programmer position.

In his spare time, Naka knocked out a tech demo that showed a sprite moving smoothly along a curve. This breakthrough led to a concept for a game involving rolling balls and long, winding tubes. It'd be like a cross between a pinball and a platform game. Naka was describing all this to his colleague Oshima, an artist and designer. Pinball and platforming had been done before, but one thing Naka said caught the artist's attention: "He can curl up into a ball to attack its enemies."

"You're talking about a hedgehog," said Oshima.[3] Thinking about what could further set the character apart from Mario, Oshima added, "a very *fast* hedgehog." Oshima grabbed his pencils and went to work, sketching out an anime-style hedgehog character, complete with fangs, sharp quills, and big, manga-style eyes. Oshima said later that Sonic's boots were inspired by Michael Jackson's from the album *Bad*, but thought their black color was boring—so he recolored them red because of Santa Claus, who has … black boots. This makes only slightly more sense than Oshima's claim that Sonic's personality was inspired by President Bill Clinton.[4]

I suspect he might have been inspired more by Oshima's boss, Nakayama, whose prickly persona and short temper were legendary. It's easy to see why Oshima would want to keep this information to himself. "Few people, especially in the United States, have heard of Mr. Nakayama," wrote Andrew Pollack for the *New York Times*. "He is a sometimes whimsical but often demanding executive who is held in fear by his subordinates."[5] "He speaks extremely rapidly and impatiently orders [them] around in a whiny voice."

Mr. Needlemouse wasn't the Sonic that we know and love today, but the character coupled with the game idea was enough for Nakayama. Now, it was time to refine Naka's concept. For one thing, they discovered there was such a thing as *too* fast: the game made them nauseated. Once they'd found the sweet spot for speed, Hirokazu Yasuhara started mapping out levels. He had a tough job. On the one hand, it was important that players who'd mastered a level should be able to zip through it with style, finesse, and above all, speed. On the other hand, it shouldn't be so difficult that a casual gamer would give up in frustration. He was also very conscious of the need to differentiate it from *Mario*, in terms of both aesthetics and gameplay. He succeeded admirably; no one would mistake the spectacular Green Hill or Star Light zones for *Mario* levels (see Figure 31.3).

Sonic was not a purely Japanese creation; Sega of America took pains to "Americanize" the concept. Indeed, their project manager, Madeline Schroeder, became known as the "Mother of Sonic." Schroeder felt that Oshima's Sonic was "too Japanese" and redesigned him with softer lines and removed his fangs. She also rejected the proposed backstory; Sonic was originally a singer in a rock band and had a sexy (human) girlfriend named

---

3 Horowitz, Ken. "Sega Stars: Yuji Naka." *Sega-16*. June 22, 2005. http://www.sega-16.com/feature_page.php?id=42&title=Sega%20Stars:%20Yuji%20Naka (accessed May 21, 2011).

4 Gametap. "Sonic the Hedgehog GameTap Retrospective." *YouTube*. February 9, 2009. https://www.youtube.com/watch?v=6D9h-4vQUHM (accessed August 13, 2015).

5 Pollack, Andrew. "Sega Takes Aim at Disney's World." *New York Times*. November 3, 1993. http://www.nytimes.com/1993/07/04/business/sega-takes-aim-at-disney-s-world.html (accessed August 14, 2015).

Madonna. The Japanese team was furious, but relented—after all, Sega's success hinged on pleasing Americans.

Sega of America's president was Michael Katz, who'd formerly worked for Atari. He'd been waging war since the launch of the Genesis, with irreverent ads that directly challenged Nintendo. "We had to create awareness, to make a noise and grab attention," said Katz.[6]

Figure 31.3   Sonic was so fast he could even defy gravity. Shown here is one of the iconic loops from the first level of the game.

When one of his copyrighters suggested the slogan "Genesis does what Nintendon't," Katz latched onto it, hammering the gaming public with the notion that Sega's console was technologically superior. According to Shinobu Toyoda, who was executive vice president of Sega of America, Katz waited to tell Nakayama about the ads until it was too late to stop the broadcasts.[7] "I learned that it was considered inappropriate in Japan to do competitive advertising," said Katz.[6]

Despite the "guerilla" marketing campaigns and efforts to differentiate Sega from Nintendo by emphasizing their licensed sports titles and a Michael Jackson game, there was clearly something missing. What that something was, Katz wasn't sure, but it certainly wasn't *Sonic the Hedgehog*. "Nobody even knew what a hedgehog was," said Katz. "We went into the game room, stuck it in, and it really wasn't very fun."[6] Nakayama had had enough. He fired Katz and replaced him with Tom Kalinske, the former president of Mattel.

If anyone knew what American boys wanted, it was Kalinske—he'd launched the Master of the Universe line and revived Hot Wheels. However, it was doubtful even the great Kalinske could replace Mario in the hearts and minds of 6- to 11-year-olds, but he thought there might be a chance with older kids. *Sonic the Hedgehog* looked like the perfect game to help him do that; the hedgehog wasn't nearly as cutesy as Mario, and older boys and girls would love his bad boy persona.

In fact, Kalinske liked the game so much he planned to bundle it with the Genesis, a suggestion that infuriated Nakayama, who demanded a face-to-face board meeting in Japan. As soon as the Americans walked in, the president tore into them. He insisted that they were in the business of selling software, not hardware. Then as now, consoles were usually sold at cost or even at a loss; the real profits were made when the owners

---

[6]   Stuart, Keith. "How Sonic Helped Sega Win the Early 90s Console Wars." *Kotaku*. October 31, 2014. http://kotaku.com/how-sonic-helped-sega-win-the-early-90s-console-wars-1653185046 (accessed August 14, 2015).

[7]   *Sonic: The Birth of an Icon*. Directed by Anthony Caulfield and Nicola Caulfield. Produced by Gracoius Films. 2011.

bought games for them. In Nakayama's mind, Kalinske's plan was like a rancher giving away milk in order to sell more cows. Abruptly, Nakayama leapt to his feet and kicked his chair, sending it soaring across the room. The room erupted in chaos, shouting in Japanese, and Kalinske must have feared for his job, if not his life.

But before he stepped out the door, Nakayama abruptly turned and calmly asked Kalinske, "Will this will really help us beat Nintendo?"

"Yes, it will," said Kalinske, undaunted.

"Then do it," said Nakayama, and slammed the door. As much as he detested the idea of giving away Sega's best game, he was prepared to do whatever it took to knock Nintendo off their perch.

If the first two parts of this plan were risky, the last bit was sheer hubris. At the Consumer Electronics Show where *Sonic the Hedgehog* would be unveiled, they'd actually have the game running side by side with *Super Mario World* on the Super Nintendo Entertainment System (SNES), Nintendo's new 16-bit console that was certain to be the talk of the show. Keep in mind that the SNES supported 128 simultaneous sprites compared to 80 on the Genesis, and twice as large to boot. It could also show 256 colors compared to 64 on the Genesis, from palettes of 32,768 to 512, respectively. This wasn't risky; this was suicide.

Al Nilsen, the director of marketing, sat in the Sega booth, biding his time until the exhibitor's hall opened. The first event of the day—the main event—was Nintendo's unveiling of its shiny new SNES. Nintendo's marketing team had gone all out, outspending Sega 10-to-1. A large and imposing-looking man, Nilsen must have cringed each time he heard that massive audience erupt with applause. Imagine Schroeder standing next to him, the "mother of Sonic," already sweaty in her *Sonic the Hedgehog* mascot costume. Nilsen checked his watch. An only slightly muffled chant of "Nintendo, Nintendo, Nintendo!" echoed through the cavernous hall.

And then, after one last thunderous cheer, the doors burst open, and out came the flood of journalists, critics, developers, merchandisers, and pretty much anybody who was anybody in the games industry. One smug journalist headed over to Nilsen, flipped open his notepad, and demanded, "The Super Nintendo has 32,768 colors. Your Genesis only has 512. What are you going to do about that?"

Nilsen motioned toward a screen behind him. On the left was *Super Mario World*, running on a spanking new SNES. On the right was *Sonic the Hedgehog*, running on a 3-year-old Sega Genesis. "Which has more colors?" asked Nilsen. The reporter leaned in to take a closer look, comparing one, then the other. He couldn't tell. "It's not how many colors you have," said Nilsen at last. "It's how you use them."[7]

If it looked good, it played even better. Lines began to form—everyone wanted to play this new hedgehog game they kept hearing about. Was it really as fast as they said?

It was obvious to anyone who played it that day that *Sonic the Hedgehog* was a killer app—one of those rare titles that's worth buying a system just to play. Well, almost anyone. Stewart Cheifet of *Computer Chronicles* observed that Sega had announced "two new games, one featuring a well-known mouse [*Mickey Mouse and the Castle of Illusion*], the other a lesser-known ... hedgehog." Unbeknown to Cheifet, within 5 years, Sonic

would not only be better known than Mickey, but far more popular.[8]

Just to sweeten the deal even further, Sega dropped the price of the Genesis to $149, making it $50 cheaper than the SNES. Sega sold 15 million consoles, and by the time Nintendo's SNES hit the American market, Sega had seized 55% of the market (see Figure 31.4).[9] Nintendo

Figure 31.4   The *Sonic the Hedgehog* cartridge. Collectors tend to shun these "Not for Resale" versions, which makes them cheap and easy to find.

had tried to crush Sega. But as many a predator has discovered to its dismay, stomping on a hedgehog hurts like hell.

Of course, all these sales and market penetration wouldn't mean zilch if Sega couldn't sell all those new Genesis owners a game they'd actually have to pay for. Obviously, *Sonic the Hedgehog* needed a proper sequel, and if it bombed, Sega's newfound market share would come and go faster than a Sega Scream.

Then, Yuji Naka, the "father" of Sonic, quit. Unlike Nintendo's Miyamoto, Naka was not content to sit by as he was passed over for promotions despite his obvious value to the company. Fortunately, Mark Cerny of Sega Technical Institute (STI) heard about Naka's resignation and begged him to come work for him in California. Yasuhara, whose fabulous levels were a key part of the first game's appeal, accepted his offer.

Cerny was no stranger to game design. He designed the amazing *Marble Madness* arcade game in 1984 and the SegaScope 3D Glasses for the Master System. His love of teaching made him a natural choice to head STI, a skunkworks operation that paired talented novices with seasoned developers from both countries. It sounded good on paper, but the cultural differences were larger than Cerny expected and eventually proved insurmountable. But they did manage to do a spectacular follow-up to Sega's killer app: *Sonic the Hedgehog 2* (1992) (see Figure 31.5).

The biggest innovation by far was Tails, Sonic's friend. Having two playable characters on screen at the same time was a programming challenge, but the newly configured team pulled it off. It was even more ambitious than its predecessor had been, with more levels, secrets, enemies, and a new "spin dash" maneuver. They were less successful with a split-screen competitive mode, which scrunched the graphics, but it was still fun to play.

[8] Arenot, Susan. "Dice: Creating Characters that Last." *Wired.* February 7, 2008. http://www.wired.com/2008/02/post-1-12/ (accessed August 14, 2015).

[9] Parish, Jeremy. "Sega Genesis 25th Anniversary: The Rise and Fall of an All-Time Great." *US Gamer.* August 14, 2014. http://www.usgamer.net/articles/the-true-16-bit-experience-segas-genesis-turns-25 (accessed August 14, 2015).

The game debuted on "Sonic 2s Day," November 24, 1992, an unprecedented worldwide launch. It was Nilsen's idea, who figured it would be great for publicity. "We're going to start in Japan, move to Europe, and then end in the U.S.," Nilsen told Schroeder. "No trucks, no boats: everything will be delivered by plane exactly one day before ... We're

Figure 31.5 *Sonic the Hedgehog 2*, a game no Sonic fan could live without.

going to have the world's first global launch."[10] These and other high-profile marketing efforts paid off; *Sonic the Hedgehog 2* eventually sold more than 6 million copies and became the second best-selling game for the Genesis (after the first *Sonic*).[11]

Sonic the Hedgehog 3 launched on February 2, 1994, and was even more ambitious than its predecessors. Knuckles the Echidna joined the cast in what many Sonic fans consider to be the best game in the series. A "surprise" sequel followed a few months later—*Sonic & Knuckles*, which snapped into a special slot on the *Sonic the Hedgehog 3* cartridge. In addition to new content, it let you play through the earlier game as Knuckles. Both were well received.

Sega would fall on hard times after the launch of Sony's PlayStation. Neither their Saturn nor Dreamcast consoles came anywhere close to matching the success of the Genesis. Unlike Mario, who made a seamless transition into 3D with *Super Mario 64*, Sonic just couldn't seem to catch up. After a "conspicuously long absence," Sonic made his (pseudo) 3D debut in *Sonic 3D Blast* (1996) (see Figure 31.6), which received mixed reviews. "Had this game been more action oriented, with more enemies and much faster gameplay, it would have truly lived up to the Sonic name," wrote Jeff Gerstmann for *GameSpot*.[12] *Sonic Adventure* (1998) for the Dreamcast fared better, but not enough to save Sega's flagging console line.

Fortunately, Sonic survived Sega's transition out of the hardware business intact. To date, he's been in more than 60 titles for other consoles and computers, including some with his former archrival Mario (*Mario & Sonic*). There's *Sonic Heroes* (2003), *Sonic Rush* (2005), *Sonic Unleashed* (2008), and *Sonic the Hedgehog 4: Episode 1* (2010), just to name a few. The last title was an homage to the hedgehog's origins on the Genesis and was published for just about every viable system.

---

[10] Harris, Blake. *Console Wars: Sega, Nintendo, and the Battle that Defined a Generation.* New York: HarperCollins, 2014.

[11] Boutros, Daniel. "A Detailed Cross-Examination of Yesterday and Today's Best-Selling Platform Games." *Gamasutra.* August 6, 2006. http://www.gamasutra.com/view/feature/130268/a_detailed_crossexamination_of_.php (accessed August 15, 2015).

[12] Gerstmann, Jeff. "Sonic 3D Blast Review." *GameSpot.* December 12, 1996. http://www.gamespot.com/reviews/sonic-3d -blast-review/1900-2534101/ (accessed August 15, 2015).

Even if Sonic and Mario have buried the hatchet, there's no denying the impact their rivalry had on the modern game industry. Thanks largely to Sega, Nintendo was forced to step up its game, and American publishers like EA were able to break successfully into the console market. If EA's *John Madden Football* series made it "okay" for adults to own a console, Sonic did the same for older children. Console gamers—and the games they played—were growing up.

31.1 Playing *Sonic the Hedgehog* Today

If you don't own a Genesis, consider picking one up. I come across them quite often in thrift stores and pawnshops, and they are usually much cheaper than

Figure 31.6   *Sonic 3D Blast* had potential, but it was no *Super Mario 64*.

a NES or SNES. *Sonic* cartridges are also plentiful and cheap. If you'd rather have a new machine, there are several retro consoles and handhelds available with built-in *Sonic* games. If you prefer playing on a modern system, try *SEGA Classics: Sonic the Hedgehog* on Steam, or check your console's virtual store. The game is also available for smartphones and tablets.

Chapter 32

The Sims: The World's Most Profitable Ant Farm

Will Wright's *The Sims* is one of the best-selling game franchises of all time, with sales in the hundreds of millions (see Figure 32.1). Its appeal extends far beyond the stereo-typical gamer—at least 40% of its fans are girls and women.[1] Like Pac-Man and Mario before them, the Sims made their mark on the broader pop culture. They've appeared on *The Drew Carey Show*, *Malcolm in the Middle*, and *30 Rock*, and Depeche Mode, The Black Eyed Peas, and Katy Perry have recorded their hit songs in Simlish, the fictional language Wright and Marc Gimbel created for the games.[2] It's even been used for coun-seling and psychotherapy.[3]

IGN's contemporary review of the first *Sims* game adroitly sums up its broad appeal:

> EA shipped us a few copies of the game nearly two weeks ago, and we've kept playing and playing them until someone had to physically pull the disks out of our hands. The game isn't just addictive; it's downright dangerous. Whether you loved playing with a dollhouse as a kid, or blowing up that dollhouse with M-80s, I feel safe in saying that you may have just found yourself a new religion.[4]

In his review for the *New York Times*, J.C. Herz waxed philosophically about how the game's simulation of modern life was at once "crude" and "disturbing in its accuracy":

> Where does the metaphor break down? *The Sims* asks that question in an elegant and provocative way. And to that degree, it succeeds as art ... By building a window into *Sims'* souls, it prompts us to consider our own.[5]

---

[1] Seabrook, John. "Game Master." *The New Yorker*. November 6, 2006. http://www.newyorker.com/magazine/2006/11/06/game-master (accessed August 16, 2015).

[2] Frum, Larry. "New Game Celebrates 10 Years of *The Sims*." *CNN*. October 28, 2010. http://www.cnn.com/2010/TECH/gaming.gadgets/10/26/sims.anniversary/ (accessed August 25, 2015).

[3] Skigen, Deidre. "Taking the Sand Tray High Tech." In *Popular Culture in Counseling, Psychotherapy, and Play-Based Interventions*, by Lawrence C. Rubin, 165–180. New York: Springer Publishing Company, 2008.

[4] IGN Staff. "The Sims." *IGM*. February 4, 2000. http://www.ign.com/articles/2000/02/05/the-sims-6 (accessed August 26, 2015).

[5] Herz, J.C. "The Sims Who Die With the Most Toys Win." *New York Times*, February 10, 2000: G10.

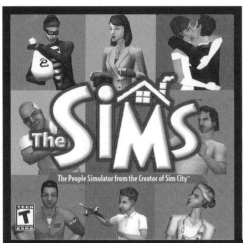

For its more intellectual fans, *The Sims* was a sort of antigame; a Dadaist work that called into question the supposed distinction between art and life. And like a certain other infamous Dadaist work, it all began with a toilet.

"We couldn't get the marketing or product development people behind it," said Jeff Braun, cofounder of Maxis. "They thought we were completely out of our minds."[6] Wright was forced to work with a shoestring budget, quietly assembling his "Experimental Domestic Simulator" with a tiny team. The earliest

Figure 32.1   *The Sims* was the best-selling PC game of all time.

prototype had only one functioning piece of equipment: a commode. Wright's colleagues at Maxis thought it was some kind of joke. "It was referred to as 'The Toilet Game.' It was the game where you clean the toilet," said Wright.[7] Even he had his doubts. "I thought the game would either do a million units ... or fifty," said Wright. "It would be a hit or a total dog."[8]

Fortunately for fans of *The Sims*, three of Electronic Arts' (EA's) executives, Bing Gordon, Don Mattrick, and John Riccitiello rallied behind the product. "We thought *The Sims* might be a killer app," said Gordon, over the loud objections of Sam Nelson, who'd produced a similar-sounding product for Activision called *Little Computer People* in 1985. Designed by David Crane of *Pitfall!* fame, *Little Computer People* never managed to rise above niche status despite glowing reviews from critics. To Nelson, Wright's "toilet game" sounded suspiciously like Crane's "house-on-a-disk" and feared it would fare no better.[9]

[6] Buckleitner, Warren. "Dust or Magic 2009: Jeff Braun on the Early Days of Maxis, Will Wright, and SimCity." *YouTube.* July 30, 2010. https://www.youtube.com/watch?v=3g1OZljodSQ (accessed July 8, 2015).

[7] Whitehead, Dan. "The History of The Sims." *Eurogamer.* March 19, 2008. http://www.eurogamer.net/articles/the-history -of-the-sims-article (accessed August 25, 2015).

[8] Gillen, Kieron. "Making of The Sims." *Rock Paper Shotgun.* January 18, 2008. http://www.rockpapershotgun .com/2008/01/18/making-of-the-sims/ (accessed August 26, 2015).

[9] Sheffield, Brandon. "Bing There, Done That." *Gamasutra.* May 23, 2007. http://www.gamasutra.com/view/feature/129855 /bing_there_done_that_eas_cco_.php (accessed August 26, 2015).

An avid reader, Wright has cited many academic inspirations for his game.[1] A quick glance at the titles of four of these works is quite revealing:

- *A Pattern Language: Towns, Buildings, Construction* by Christopher Alexander et al.

- *Time for Life: The Surprising Ways Americans Use Their Time* by John Robinson and Geoffrey Godbey

- *Maps of the Mind: Charts and Concepts of the Mind and Its Labyrinths* by Charles Hampden-Turner

- *A Theory of Human Motivation* by Abraham Maslow

To my mind, each item on this list is a "must-read" for serious game designers, but *The Sims* was not just a synthesis of Wright's reading material. In 1991, he lost his house in Oakland Hills to a massive fire. Fortunately, no one was injured in the blaze, but Wright and his family now faced the necessity of replacing all of their lost belongings. Luckily, Wright had just finished coding his game *Sim Ant*, and had moved the source code from his house to his office just a few weeks before. When he returned to view the ashes of his former home, he was pleased to find survivors—a colony of ants who had burrowed deeply enough into the soil to avoid the searing heat. "I watched as they came up and carried off the dead ants on the surface," said Wright. "They were feeding off their comrades."[10]

Wright might well have envied the ants their breakfast, especially since he now faced an even less palatable task. "I hate to shop," said Wright, "and I was forced to buy all these things, from toothpaste, utensils, and socks up to furniture."[1] "All these objects end up sucking up your time, when they had been promising to save you time." Wright also points to his earlier work on the *SimAnt* we discussed in Chapter 23. "I began wondering whether there was a way we could simulate human behavior in a more distributed sense in the way the ants do."[8]

The final design incorporated two distinctive types of gameplay: caring for your Sims and decorating their house. The first is comparable to a "virtual pet" game like Aki Maita's Tamagotchi toy. Each Sim had five adjustable personality attributes: neat, outgoing, active, playful, and nice (see Figure 32.2). The aggregate of these attributes was calculated as a sign of the zodiac. You could also choose their skin tone, sex, and age, and customize their appearance with different heads and outfits. Caring for your Sims meant satisfying their many needs or "motives." These were hunger, comfort, hygiene, bladder, energy, fun, social, and room. While some of these needs were straightforward (characters who don't get to a bathroom will soil their clothes), others were more complex and affected by the personality traits. For instance, a very playful character had more fun playing a game than reading a book.

---

[10] Taylor, Tracey. "Inspired to Make the Sims After Losing a Home." *Berkeleyside*. October 17, 2011. http://www.berkeleyside.com/2011/10/17/will-wright-inspired-to-make-the-sims-after-iosing-a-home/ (accessed August 26, 2015).

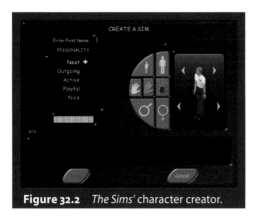

Figure 32.2   *The Sims'* character creator.

The Sims were conspicuous consumers, deriving much more satisfaction from high-end products than cheap stuff. While many players simply entered a cheat code to get instant cash, the Sims could earn their own money by getting a job. The type of job depended on a Sims' skills: cooking, mechanical, charisma, body, logic, and creativity. While cooking and mechanical skills were improved by reading, charisma required a mirror and body required physical exercise. Logic and creativity were increased by playing chess or the piano, respectively. The original game included 10 career tracks, including crime (pickpocket) and "x-treme" (daredevil). Sims could get married (same sex was allowed) and even have children.

The Sims didn't talk to each other using English or any other language, but rather a form of gibberish called "Simlish." Simlish was spoken, but also depicted with small icons in comic dialog bubbles. Simlish, which had originally debuted in the earlier *SimCopter* game (1996), became one of the series' defining characteristics. Since Simlish was a made-up, nonsense language, there was no need to worry about translating it for other locales.

Why was anyone willing to spend so much time catering to a virtual human being? One explanation is offered by Maita, designer of the cute little egg-shaped Tamagotchi toy mentioned above. Tens of millions of children loved these virtual pets, feeding, playing, and cleaning up after them with surprising dedication. "It is dependent on you—that's one reason," said Maita. "I think it's very important for humans to find joy caring for something."[11] Like *The Sims*, Tamagotchi was a hit with girls as well as boys.

Although many players enjoyed caring for their Sims, others focused on building or shopping for items to decorate their "dollhouse." The game offered countless ways to customize and renovate homes, turning players into Bob Villas or Martha Stewarts. Players could add pools, fences, columns, plants, stairs, wallpaper, and windows, and each object had dozens of variations. Ambitious builders could even add extra stories (see Figure 32.3).

Obviously, a project as ambitious as *The Sims* presented a formidable technical challenge. The final product offered a combination of two-dimensional (2D) and three-dimensional (3D) graphics that smoothed performance on the era's hardware. Only the Sims were rendered in 3D; the buildings and objects were rendered in 2D. One area that didn't compromise was sound, especially the upbeat, catchy music.

On December 17, 2002, EA published Maxis' *The Sims Online*. The idea seemed logical; if players were having so much fun playing with *virtual* people, wouldn't they have

---

11 Mutsuko, Murakami. "Just Another Day's Work." *Mimitchi*. February 25, 1998. http://www.mimitchi.com/html/aki.htm (accessed August 26, 2015).

even more fun with *actual* people? There were several key changes to the gameplay to accommodate online play, including replacing Simlish with English dialog. Players were also limited to a single sim, rather than a whole family. In practice, it amounted to little more than an expensive chatroom, and it flopped miserably.

The following year, however, a company named Linden Research enjoyed

Figure 32.3   The Sims were needy little people.

remarkable success with its *Second Life* MMO. It quickly became the most successful of all social-based MMOs, winning many awards and substantial investment from businesses and universities. *Second Life*'s developers emphasized "user-generated content," which ranged from custom objects to new gestures and animations for characters. Players could buy and sell all manner of things from other players (users retained copyright of the objects they created). The media was full of reports of people earning their living simply by playing *Second Life*, exchanging their in-game money for real-life dollars.

Meanwhile, the demise of *The Sims Online* didn't diminish enthusiasm for the stand-alone versions or their many expansions and spin-offs. EA Games released *The Sims 2* in September of 2004 (see Figure 32.4). The key additions were a 3D engine, lifetime aspirations, and genetic inheritance. Now, the Sims had memories as well as genes to pass on to subsequent generations. The aspiration system was for players who disliked the open-ended nature of the first game. Now, players could spend their time fulfilling specific goals. *The Sims 2* was a rousing success. *The Sims 3* followed in 2009, selling more than 10 million copies, and a fourth iteration debuted on September 2, 2014. It met with mostly lukewarm reviews, especially when critics compared it to a fully expanded version of the third installment. Of particular note was the omission of a toddler stage for Sims and swimming pools. Many longtime supporters of the series were disappointed or even outraged, and, at least for the moment, the future of the franchise is uncertain.

As for Wright, his next big idea—*Spore*—was one of the most anticipated

Figure 32.4   *The Sims 2* was another smash hit for the franchise.

games of the decade by the time it finally arrived in 2008. Critics praised it and sales were brisk at first, but it soon became obvious that it was not the next *Sims* franchise.

Wright parted ways with Maxis a year later to form Stupid Fun Club, a self-described "innovative think-tank" that merges the video, toy, and game industries. One of their first products, appropriately enough, is the Ant Farm Revolution, a futuristic ant farm with transparent "tunneling gel" instead of soil, LEDs, and a projecting lens. I'm not sure if Wright wrote the accompanying "Ant Watcher's Manual," but the following passage seems a fitting way to end this chapter:

> As you study your ants, you'll find that they plan their world very much as we plan ours. They engineer their homes and highways carefully. They seem to consider artistic form as well as function in their building. The highways and tunnels in the ants' world are always arranged in smooth curves, and their hills are well balanced ... If you treat your ants properly, they'll let you in their secret world and keep you fascinated.

32.1 **Playing *The Sims* Today**

Sadly, I was unable to find the original *Sims* game available for sale online. It's not hard to find used copies on online auction sites, however. Keep an eye out for *The Sims: Complete Collection*, which includes all seven expansion packs. *The Sims: Deluxe Edition* might be easier to find, which includes the *Livin' Large* expansion pack and Creator tool for customizing your Sims' appearance. I was able to get my copy of the original game working on Windows 7 without any issues. Most fans of the series prefer *Sims 3*, which is much more widely available. Be sure to check Origin, EA's equivalent of Steam, for deals on compilations. I routinely come across the games and expansions in thrift stores, in pawnshops, and on Craigslist, so check locally before placing a hefty bid on an auction site.

Chapter 33

Diablo: Click Click Boom

By the mid-1990s, the once-mighty computer role-playing game (RPG) genre was in a dark, dank place. After striking gold with *Pool of Radiance* and *Eye of the Beholder*, SSI was much less successful with *Dark Sun: Shattered Lands* (1993) and *Menzoberranzan* (1994). Richard Garriott's mighty *Ultima* series had stumbled greatly with *Ultima VIII: Pagan* (1994), and even the mighty Interplay failed to impress with *Stonekeep* (1995) and *Descent to Undermountain* (1997). These and similarly lackluster titles were enough to make the very term *RPG* an anathema to PC gamers.

One bright moment in this period was *Ultima Underworld: The Stygian Abyss* (1992), a brilliant take on the genre that shared *Doom*'s first-person perspective and real-time action (see Figure 33.1). Despite glowing reviews and awards, its steep hardware requirements and overall complexity limited its impact. Bethesda and New World Computing had better luck in 1996 with *The Elder Scrolls: Daggerfall* and *Might and Magic VI*, respectively, but most PC gamers were having too much fun rocket jumping in *Quake* to care about esoteric RPG mechanics.

Meanwhile, American console gamers were falling in love with Japanese RPGs (JRPGs). Square's *Final Fantasy II* (*Final Fantasy IV* in Japan) struck the Super Nintendo Entertainment System (SNES) in 1991, and *Secret of Mana* (1993) and *Chrono Trigger* (1995) weren't far behind. While these games did have much in common with the computer RPGs (CRPGs) of yore, they were much more focused on colorful characters and stories than stats and dungeon crawling. Above them all loomed Miyamoto's *Legend of Zelda* series, an "action adventure" with only a superficial resemblance to the likes of *Ultima* or *Wizardry*. In any case, Nintendo's stern censorship policies and their cutesy, manga-derived aesthetics stood in stark contrast to the blood-soaked death matches gamers were reveling in on PCs.

What was needed was an RPG for the PC that was just as visceral, gritty, and addictive as *Doom*. While developers like Bethesda and New World Computing tried to graft CRPG mechanics onto first-person shooter engines, a tiny developer named Condor looked to another inspiration: Mythos Games' *X-COM: UFO Defense* (1994). Designed by Julian and Nick Gollop, this seminal sci-fi game was an intoxicating mix of management simulation and turn-based tactical combat. David Brevick, a programmer at Condor, was most impressed by the latter element, particularly with its mouse-driven interface (see

Figure 33.1 *Ultima Underworld* was a groundbreaking three-dimensional CRPG from 1992.

Figure 33.2). It was also a dark and gritty game, with enough blood and gore to please the PC crowd (see Figure 33.3).

Brevick was a big fan of tabletop RPGs as well as *Wizardry*, *Bard's Tale*, and *Ultima*. But his real passion was roguelikes such as *Angband* and *Moria*.[1] As we saw in Chapter 6, these mainframe games lacked sprite-based graphics,

Figure 33.2 David Brevick, designer of *Diablo*. (From http://www.3news.co.nz /entertainment/diablo-creator-calls-nz-a-gaming-hub-2014091916#axzz3rs8hKEWr.)

relying instead on ASCII or ANSI characters. Brevick loved their procedurally generated dungeons and was convinced they were "crying out for an update." He reverse-engineered *X-Com*'s user-friendly interface and graphic engine, which showed the action from an isometric rather than the top-down perspective of *Rogue*.

Brevick's company was eventually bought out by Blizzard Entertainment and renamed Blizzard North. The new bosses liked Brevick's idea except for one thing—the turn-based combat. "We actually took a vote," said Duane Stinnett, an artist at Blizzard. "Raise your hand if you would buy this game if it were turn-based. I think two people raised their hands ... Allen [Adham] went in and called Dave Brevick and said, 'Look, you've got to make this real-time.'"[1] Initially skeptical of this executive decision, Brevick changed his mind after he implemented the change. "The light from heaven shone through the office down onto the keyboard," said Brevick. "I remember very vividly: I clicked on the monster, the guy walked over, and he smashed this skeleton, and it fell apart onto the ground ... I said, 'Oh my God, this is so amazing.' It was the defining moment of my career."

Much like Romero and Carmack had done with *Wolfenstein 3D*—avoiding any gameplay elements that distracted from the action—Brevick and his team avoided complex RPG mechanics. The difference was obvious from the start. Instead of having characters create a whole party of adventurers, or allocate attribute points, *Diablo* simply offered a choice between warrior, rogue, and sorcerer (see Figure 33.4). Once in the game, players

---

[1] Craddock, David. *Stay Awhile and Listen: How Two Blizzards Unleashed Diablo and Forged a Video-Game Empire.* Canton, OH: Digital Monument Press, 2013.

were treated to a remarkably intuitive interface; they simply clicked the mouse to move or attack an enemy. Leveling up was as easy as selecting a choice on a branching skill tree, the result of which was obvious immediately afterward. Then, there was the loot—tons and tons of loot. Previous CRPGs had tended to be stingy with valuable items or powerful weapons, but *Diablo* showered you with them. However, it soon became obvious

Figure 33.3   The terrifying demon from *Diablo*'s opening cinematic.

that some items were better than others, and the rarest and best items required either incredible luck or, more likely, persistent grinding (see Figure 33.5).

Finally, the frightening, gory nature of *Diablo* was apparent from the opening cut scene, an *Evil Dead*-like sequence littered with corpses and terrifying demons. This was no *Legend of Zelda*. This was a true "action RPG," and it was straight out of hell.

Figure 33.4   Unlike many CRPGs, which started with a lengthy character creation process, *Diablo* got you into the action quickly.

Diablo finally hit store shelves on December 31, 1996, narrowly missing the critical holiday buying season. Fortunately, word of mouth quickly spread. Reviewers loved the sinister art, addictive gameplay, and Matt Uelmen's mesmerizing score (see Figure 33.6). Trent Ward of *GameSpot* wrote, "*Diablo* is the best game to come out in the past year, and you should own a copy.

Figure 33.5   One more pile of bodies, one more pile of loot.

Period,"[2] a sentiment shared by millions of gamers.

Like *Doom, Diablo* was terrific fun for a single player, but it was even more fun to play with friends. Online play was enabled by Blizzard's *Battle.net* servers, which were provided as a value-add for purchasers of the game. Soon, these servers were swarming with die-hard *Diablo* fans, and some weren't above cheating.

Figure 33.6   The town of Tristram offered some welcome respite from the dungeons. Matt Uelmen's haunting guitar melody played in the background.

After publishing a lackluster expansion called *Diablo: Hellfire* in 1997, Blizzard North released the long-awaited *Diablo II* in 2000. It was a smash hit, selling more than a million copies in just 2 weeks. It improved on the gameplay of its predecessor and is still widely played by fans today. Blizzard Entertainment released a third sequel in 2012, but without Brevick's involvement.

More significantly, *Diablo* inspired a host of imitators whose productions culminated in a new genre: the "action role-playing game." Some of the better known of these are Larian Studios' *Divine Divinity* (2002), Gas Powered Games' *Dungeon Siege* (2002), Ascaron's *Sacred* (2004), *Marvel: Ultimate Alliance* (2006), and Iron Lore Entertainment's *Titan Quest* (2006), but there are many more. More recently, Runic Games' *Torchlight II* (2012), Grinding Gear Games' *Path of Exile* (2013), Crate Entertainment's *Grim Dawn* (2013), and Larian Studios' *Divinity: Original Sin* (2014) proved there's still a healthy market for these games.

Not all fans of CRPGs traded their D20s for *Diablo*'s "secret sauce," and BioWare restored much of the older games' complexity with *Baldur's Gate* just a few years later. Still, *Diablo* showed how the mechanics of these games could be distilled into something far more accessible.

33.1 Playing *Diablo* Today

Until recently, Blizzard included the original *Diablo* with its *Diablo Battlechest*, but the new version sadly omits it. It's easy enough to find a used copy, but I wasn't able to find a way to legally purchase it as a download. Be advised—you might have issues running it on a modern system; be sure to search for a patch if you're having trouble. The second game is still available from Blizzard's website.

---

[2] Ward, Trent. "Diablo Review." *GameSpot.* January 23, 1997. http://www.gamespot.com/reviews/diablo-review/1900 -2538662/ (accessed August 28, 2015).

Chapter 34

Starcraft: The ESport Zerg Rush

There was a time when the term *esports* would've sounded like, at best, a futurist's dream; at worst, a punchline. Who would pay money just to watch somebody else play a video game? Wasn't "interactivity" the whole *point* of video games? How could watching someone quietly moving a mouse or tapping on a gamepad possibly compare to the spectacle of real sports?

Hall of Fame baseball player and manager Tommy Lasorda once said that "in baseball and in business, there are three types of people. Those who make it happen, those who watch it happen, and those who wonder what happened."

What happened was 50 million Koreans were watching *StarCraft* on their televisions (Figure 34.1). The *New York Times* sent Seth Schiesel to find out what happened.

"It's all part of a of a dynamic that has taken technologies first developed in the West—personal computers, the Internet, online games like *StarCraft*—and melded them into a culture as different from the United States as Korean *pajeon* are from American pancakes," wrote Schiesel.[1] He watched incredulously as throngs of fans swarmed around the 27-year-old *StarCraft* professional Lim Yo-Hwan. "Without covering myself up in disguise it's really difficult to go out in public," Lim confided. Kim Byung Kyu, a manager at one of the nation's largest banks and host of a *StarCraft* league, told Schiesel that "When I'm in the U.S., I don't see games in public. They don't [even] have game television channels." He added, "Perhaps the United States will follow and Korea will be the model."

Actually, organized video game competitions were nothing new in America, even if they paled in comparison. Atari, Sega, and Nintendo regularly hosted competitions as part of their marketing strategy, and WTBS aired a syndicated video game TV show called *Starcade* during the 1980s. Walter Day's tireless efforts to maintain an official scoreboard for classics like *Pac-Man* and *Donkey Kong* were brought to public attention in the documentary *King of Kong* (2007). But even American arcade champs like Billy Mitchell still had to work for a living; their "pro" gaming work was for personal glory, not riches.

Thanks largely to *Starcraft*, there are now thriving, well-funded organizations like Major League Gaming and highly publicized events like The International DOTA 2 Championships and Intel Extreme Masters. According to the site *E-Sports Earnings*, the top three players (Saahill Arora and Peter Dager of the United States and Kurtis Ling of Canada) are the highest paid professionals, earning nearly $2 million each in prizes—and likely far more in

---

[1] Schiesel, Seth. "The Land of the Video Geek: Are Online Gaming Champions the Rock Stars of the 21st Century?" *New York Times*, October 8, 2006: A1.

Figure 34.1   In South Korea, esports are a national pastime.

licensing deals. Two million dollars, by the way, was the average NFL salary in 2013 according to Forbes.[2] *DOTA 2* and *League of Legends* are the dominant esports as of this writing, but *StarCraft II* (2010) and the comparatively ancient *StarCraft: Brood War* (1998) aren't far behind.

This level of professional competition seemed inevitable given the massive size and profits enjoyed by the video game industry. What was less obvious was that a game once derisively dismissed as "orcs in space" would be the catalyst that sparked that phenomenon.

Two years before *Diablo*, Blizzard published a real-time strategy (RTS) game called *Warcraft: Orcs & Humans* (see Figure 34.2), the first title released under its new Blizzard Entertainment label. It was hardly the first such game; Westwood Studios' *Dune II: The Building of a Dynasty* had been out for 2 years (see Figure 34.3). With a few notable exceptions, most strategy games before *Dune II* were "turn-based."

Turn-based computer games were like chess or checkers, in which a player must wait as her opponent contemplates his next move. If we wanted to play chess as a real-time game, the players would not sit idle as the other player strategized but would move their pieces as frequently as they could. However, the difference between RTS and turn-based strategy (TBS) games are a bit more profound than this analogy suggests. A set of real-time rules for chess would probably include penalties for moving across certain squares, or a "cooling off" period for certain pieces or abilities. For instance, whereas in

2 Patra, Kevin. "Odell Beckham: NFL Players Should Get Paid More." *NFL.com*. May 18, 2015. http://www.nfl.com/news/story/oap3000000493131/article/odell-beckham-nfl-players-should-get-paid-more (accessed August 28, 2015).

traditional chess the queen can move an unlimited number of spaces per turn, in a real-time version, she might only move one square every 10 s, whereas a pawn could only move one square per minute. Castling or becoming king might require longer cool-down periods. Obviously, such factors would be difficult, if not impossible, to account for in the board game, but computers can effortlessly track such variables, enabling possibilities not feasible in a board game. Fans of real-time games claim that they are more exciting, whereas turn-based fans argue that having more time allows for more sophisticated gameplay.

Figure 34.2   *Warcraft: Orcs & Humans* was Blizzard's take on the genre established by Westwood's *Dune II.*

Dune II and later RTS games put the computer's ability to time so many different events to good use. Structures and units took time to build; resources took time to harvest; and units took time to travel across the map. Keeping track of all these different simultaneous events required great concentration and no

Figure 34.3   *Dune II* was the first of what became known as RTS games.

small amount of dexterity with the mouse, but fans certainly didn't mind. Indeed, it took "one more turn" to the next level; the pace was so frenetic that hours felt like minutes!

Westwood was slow to follow up their groundbreaking title, so Blizzard stepped in to fill the gap with *Warcraft: Orcs and Humans*. Chris Lombardi summed it up as a "pretty good game set in the Tolkienesque mythos," but then outright accused Blizzard of "creative larceny": "Replace the overhead graphics of orcs and humans with Atreides and Harkonnen, substitute timber and gold with Spice, and rename the various buildings ... and you have Westwood Studio's *Dune 2*."[3] Lombardi praised the multiplayer, but bashed the AI and "carpal calisthenics" required to play the game

---

[3] Lombardi, Chris. "War Crime in Real Time." *Computer Gaming World*, January 1995: 228–232.

effectively. Despite these and other perceived flaws with the game, it nevertheless filled Blizzard's coffers, and everyone agreed that the head-to-head multiplayer option was an essential feature.

Westwood, meanwhile, had been working on its next RTS, *Command & Conquer*, which was finally released on the final day of August in 1995. This epic title sold millions of copies and wowed critics. Chris Hudak of *GameSpot* called it "one of the finest, most brilliantly-designed computer games I have ever seen," praising the keen attention to detail and riveting cut scenes.[4] With such stiff competition on the market, Blizzard's designers knew they'd need something special.

They achieved it with *Warcraft II*, which sold more than 2 million copies and was the best-selling PC game of 1996.[5] They not only managed to address the issues that plagued the first game—including the bad AI, and added a great fog-of-war system and improved online multiplayer options. Blizzard's success with this game and *Diablo* established its reputation as a premier developer.

Warcraft II was unquestionably a great game, but rather than start work on a third iteration, the team decided to try something different—a sci-fi RTS. Early screenshots were less than impressive, and skeptics began referring to it as "orcs in space." The aesthetics were eventually worked out to everyone's satisfaction, but what really set it apart was an extra playable race. Furthermore, each of the three races (Terrans, Zerg, and Protoss) were quite distinctive, with different types of units and strategic considerations. *StarCraft* at last debuted on March 31, 1998 (see Figure 34.4). Once again, critics and RTS fans were enamored, but 7 months later, Blizzard released the *Brood War* expansion. It added new missions, multiplayer maps, and units, but, more importantly, rebalanced the gameplay. It was a must for any serious fan of *StarCraft*.

Meanwhile, something very interesting was happening in South Korea. Fifty percent of Korean households had high-speed broadband Internet access, compared with a dismal 10% in the United States.[6] More importantly, though, a phenomenon called the "PC Bang" was raging across the country; hordes of people would crowd into dedicated game rooms to play *StarCraft*. The reasons were mainly cultural. Unlike most American gamers, who don't mind playing alone at home, their Korean counterparts preferred being with their friends, and the game rooms were a comparatively cheap form of entertainment. Kim Gi Beum, who owned one of those game rooms, stressed another factor: Korean parents were obsessive about their kids' grades; gaming at home was often forbidden. Naturally, Korean gamers traveling to the game rooms would want to play whatever their friends were playing, and that, more often than not, was *StarCraft*.

---

[4] Hudak, Chris. "Command & Conquer Review." *GameSpot*. May 1, 1996. http://www.gamespot.com/reviews/command-and-conquer-review/1900-2538453/ (accessed August 29, 2015).

[5] Blizzard Entertainment. "Blizzard Timeline." *Blizzard.com*. 2015. http://us.blizzard.com/en-us/company/about/b20/timeline.html (accessed August 28, 2015).

[6] French, Howard W. "Korea's Real Rage for Virtual Games." *New York Times*, October 9, 2002: A8.

But why *StarCraft*? After all, there were many other games with fun online multiplayer. "The question of why *StarCraft* is so popular in Korea is not an easy one to answer," a Blizzard spokesperson told Kotaku. Nick Ramus, a writer and filmmaker based in the country, argued that Koreans love competitive activities that require rapid thinking and decision making, and *StarCraft* fit the bill perfectly.[7]

Figure 34.4 *StarCraft* traded the fantasy setting of the earlier *Warcraft* series for sci-fi.

The term *actions per minute*, or APM, was invented to measure a player's performance. Proficient players can easily make a hundred or more, and it's a dazzling, perhaps even terrifying spectacle to behold.

Blizzard acknowledged the South Korean's love of their game by announcing the development of the first sequel at a special event hosted in Seoul in 2007. The game wasn't released, however, until the summer of 2010. There was much speculation about whether it would catch on like the first, especially after *Warcraft 3* failed to gain much traction there. After investing so many hard hours into practicing and training for a game, skilled *StarCraft* players were naturally reluctant to jump into a new game.

As of this writing, *StarCraft II* has still not eclipsed the original in Korea. Beyond the factors mentioned above, some experts claim it has more to do with Blizzard's crackdown on pirated copies. This came at a time when enormously popular alternatives like Riot Games' *League of Legends* were free to play (see Figure 34.5). Finally, Blizzard cut ties with the Korean e-Sports Player's Association (KeSPA) after failing to agree on fees for broadcasts. Meanwhile, a high-profile match fixing scandal certainly didn't help matters.

StarCraft II's failure to replace *StarCraft: Brood War* in the hearts and minds of so many Koreans does raise some questions about esports versus other kinds of video games. In 2011, Dustin Browder, director of *StarCraft II*, spoke for an hour at GDC on the difficulties of designing a sequel for an esport, comparing it to making "Basketball 2." The metaphor was apt, though probably not how Browder intended. Basketball, like any well-established sport, wouldn't last long if officials kept monkeying with the rules. Indeed, even relatively "common sense" changes, like the NCAA's decision to allow referees to use instant replay to review fouls, are not made lightly.

Another problem with esports is that sequels may not only fail to replace their predecessor, but destroy whatever support it had left. Patrick Howell O'Neill summed the situation up quite aptly: "In esports, sequels can kill." "It takes a dynamic competitive

7 Ashcraft, Brian. "Why Is Starcraft So Popular in Korea?" *Kotaku*. July 24, 2010. http://kotaku.com/5595262/why-is-starcraft-so-popular-in-korea (accessed August 29, 2015).

community to maintain an esport," wrote O'Neill. "When high-profile sequels come along and suck the life out of the original game's fan base, once-populous servers can become ghost towns."[8] Other esports, such as the aforementioned *League of Legends*, generate profits not from unit sales but with in-game micro-transactions

Figure 34.5   *League of Legends* is currently the most popular esport.

for access to certain characters or "skins" to modify their appearance. *League of Legends* is frequently updated, and not always without controversy, but Riot Games' Brent Critchfield insists "there will never be a *League of Legends 2* ... I want my great grand-children playing this game."[9]

Blizzard may not have done everything right with *StarCraft II*, and their success with the first might well be more a product of good timing than anything else. Still, regardless of its continued popularity as a Korean esport, there's no denying *StarCraft*'s status as a masterpiece of real-time strategy.

34.1 Playing *Starcraft* Today

Fortunately, Blizzard still sells the original *StarCraft* and its expansion on its website at us.blizzard.com. You can also pick up the *StarCraft Battle Chest* online or at a well-stocked video game retailer.

---

[8] O'Neill, Patrick Howell. "StarCraft: Brood War Proves the Best Esports are Timeless." *The Daily Dot*. January 30, 2014. http://www.dailydot.com/esports/starcraft-brood-war-starleague-esports-survive/ (accessed August 29, 2015).

[9] Gera, Emily. "There Will Never Be a League of Legends 2, says Riot Games." *Polygon*. June 11, 2014. http://www.polygon.com/e3-2014/2014/6/11/5799166/league-of-legends-2-riot-games-pc (accessed August 29, 2015).

Chapter 35

Pokémon: Gotta Catch'em All

Pokémon is the second in what I like to call Mobile's Killer App trilogy, the other two being *Tetris* and *Angry Birds*. While there are certainly plenty of other influential mobile games, these three did the most to popularize handheld gaming, each appealing to a much broader audience than the typical hit game. Even people who've never played any of the *Pokémon* games will likely recognize its most popular character, the adorable Pikachu. Today, *Pokémon* is a multibillion dollar franchise known the world over. There are *Pokémon* toys, films, soundtracks, card games, manga, bed sheets, clothing, and all manner of other merchandise. The franchise's catchphrase, "Gotta catch'em all," is as engrained in American culture as Nike's "Just do it."

Many children who grew up with the game have not "grown out" of their *Pokémon* habit. "I've been playing *Pokémon* games since I was 13," wrote Andrew Cunningham of Ars Technica, "and I've felt just a little too old for the game pretty much the entire time."[1] A quick search for "Am I too old for *Pokémon*?" revealed dozens of anxiety-ridden posts from 20- to 30-year-olds asking that question. If you're wondering—no, you're never too old for *Pokémon*.

Pokémon is all the more remarkable for making its American debut in 1998 on the nearly decade-old Game Boy system (see Figure 35.1). Many had considered the Game Boy obsolete-on-arrival; the Atari Lynx and Sega's Game Gear were much more impressive. However, these machines lacked *Tetris*. By the late 1990s, though, the *Tetris* craze had diminished, and many of the millions of Game Boy units bought for the sake of *Tetris* were now in the hands of the children or younger siblings of the older generation. These kids and their crusty old Game Boys turned out to be the perfect audience for Nintendo's new, ultra-cutesy export.

The story of *Pokémon*'s development begins in 1990, when Satoshi Tajiri, a designer and programmer at Nintendo—and friend of Shigeru Miyamoto—observed some children playing with their Game Boys, which they'd connected using a Game Link Cable. This device was an accessory that allowed two players to play with or against each other, assuming the game in question supported it and both players had copies. Tajiri had a vision of small bugs traveling along the cable and back again, and from that vision began conceiving a game (see Figure 35.2).

---

[1] Cunningham, Andrew. "Aren't You a Little Too Old for That?" *Ars Technica*. October 19, 2013. http://arstechnica.com/gaming/2013/10/arent-you-a-little-too-old-for-that-14-years-of-playing-pokemon/1/ (accessed September 11, 2015).

Figure 35.1 *Pokémon* became a global phenomenon.

Figure 35.2 Satoshi Tajiri, creator of *Pokémon*.

Tajiri's childhood nickname was "Dr. Bug," which he earned because of his fascination with the insects that he and his friends collected around the rice paddies and forests in their Tokyo suburb.[2] Later, urban sprawl eliminated most of these bug habitats, which greatly saddened Tajiri. Bug collecting had been a vital part of his youth and a great way for kids to learn about and experience nature. Now, many kids were stuck in their homes alone playing video games, but Tajiri thought that perhaps a bug collecting game might encourage them to go outside and meet the other kids in the neighborhood.

Like many others, Tajiri spent the better part of his teenage years playing *Space Invaders* and other arcade games. His interest in them went far beyond most, though—he studied their design to the point where he was publishing his own strategy guides, and he taught himself programming. He even took apart his Famicom system and studied its components. All this learning culminated in founding his own studio, Game Freak, and Namco publishing his first game, *Mendel Palace* (*Quinty* in Japan) in 1989.

Tajiri's first collaboration with Nintendo was *Yoshi*, published in 1991 for Game Boy and the Nintendo Entertainment System (NES). While the titular character's appeal was enough to drive sales, critics gave this action-puzzler only middling scores. Tajiri did other games for the Super Nintendo Entertainment System (SNES), including another collaboration with Nintendo called *Mario & Wario*, but it was never released outside of Japan. He also did *Pulseman* for the Sega Genesis in 1994, a side-scrolling platform game.

These efforts were enough to get him an audience and a contract with Nintendo, but Tajiri was unable to articulate his idea to their satisfaction. Miyamoto was intrigued by

2 Larimer, Tim. "The Ultimate Game Freak." *Time Asia*. November 22, 1999. http://www.cnn.com/ASIANOW/time/magazine/99/1122/pokemon6.fullinterview1.html (accessed September 11, 2015).

his pitch, however, and agreed to help the younger man develop his idea into a full game design. It was a splendid arrangement for Tajiri, who idolized Nintendo's star designer. "Since I was a teenager playing *Donkey Kong*," said Tajiri, "he's always been my role model. He's a mentor for my heart."[2] Tajiri acknowledged the maestro in his game by naming a character after him.

Even with Miyamoto's help, it took Tajiri an arduous 6 years to complete the first *Pokémon* game (see Figure 35.3). In the process, he nearly lost his studio, and

Figure 35.3 The original Game Boy version. At the start of the game, your character doesn't have a Pokémon to protect him.

five of his employees quit when they learned of the dire financial situation. Meanwhile, the Game Boy was marched steadily toward obsolescence. "When I finished *Pokémon*, I thought Nintendo would reject it," said Tajiri. "I was like a baseball player sliding into second base knowing he's going to be out."[3]

Published in Japan in 1996 and 2 years later in America, the game came in two flavors, each with a different assortment of *Pokémon* creatures. The player's task was to travel around the game world catching and training wild *Pokémon*, eventually assembling enough to take on an organized crime group using the creatures for evil. To catch a *Pokémon*, players first had to defeat it in turn-based combat, using a variety of moves unique to each species. During the battle, players can try throwing a Poke Ball at the opponent in an attempt to catch it. The player's *Pokémon* gains experience in combat and eventually levels up—an element derived from role-playing games.

Naturally, fans wanted to have both cartridges and thus access to more of the adorable little creatures, a rather obvious tactic to double sales. But Tajiri had another card up his sleeve: Mew, a secret creature. You couldn't purchase him; the only way to catch him—and thus complete your collection—was to trade with your friends using the Game Link Cable. Once word of his existence got out, everyone wanted to catch him—so they convinced their friends to buy the game, too. Sales began to soar (see Figure 35.4a and b).

When Nintendo finally realized it had a genuine hit on its hands, they moved quickly to capitalize on its popularity. A *Pokémon* anime series began airing on April 1, 1997, and has remained in production to this day. There's also a popular trading card game

---

[3] Chua-Eoan, Howard, and Tim Larimer. "Beware of the Pokemania." *Time.* November 14, 1999. http://content.time.com /time/magazine/article/0,9171,34342-3,00.html (accessed September 11, 2015).

(a)

(b)

Figure 35.4   Your first Pokémon is a hand-me-down from Dr. Oak. Once you've taken control of him (a), it's time to test him out in battle (b).

based on the franchise, and, of course, a myriad of toys and other merchandise. Howard Chua-Eoan and Tim Larimer of *Time* called it "Pokemania":

[It's] a multimedia and interactive barrage like no other before it, with children mesmerized into cataloging a menagerie of multiplicative monsters, with trading cards linked to games linked to television shows linked to toys linked to websites linked to candy linked back to where you started—a pestilential Ponzi scheme.[3]

Much like Electronic Arts' *Madden* series, *Pokémon* proved to be a source of perennial profits for Nintendo. To date, there have been six "generations" of the game, usually released in pairs (Diamond and Pearl; Black and White, etc.) and introducing a hundred or more new *Pokémon* to catch. There are also spin-off series galore, covering many different genres (pinball, puzzle games, action adventure, virtual pet, and more). The main series remains a staple of

Nintendo's handheld library, even if the original inspiration for the game—the Game Link Cable—is a distant memory in the age of Wi-Fi.

35.1 Playing *Pokémon* Today

Even though there are plenty of options for emulating a Game Boy on a modern PC, you'd be missing much of the point. I'd recommend tracking down a couple of vintage Game Boys and the requisite Game Link Cable—and of course two copies of the game—to enjoy with a friend. That said, there are versions of the game for every Nintendo handheld, and though each has its fans, arguably the core gameplay hasn't changed much.

Chapter 36

Ultima Online: Persistence Pays Off

Richard Garriott's *Ultima* series practically defined the computer role-playing game (CRPG) of the 1980s, and many aficionados still consider *Ultima VII: The Black Gate* (1997) as the greatest triumph of the genre. But "Lord British" was more than just a gifted designer. As a developer and publisher, his admittedly risky tendency to embrace the latest graphics and sound standards spurred innovation in gaming hardware, and his (in)famous insistence on quality packaging and inserts helped lift the profile of video games as a medium. Anyone who loathes the modern industry's reliance on incremental sequels, skimpy manuals, and me-too productions would find a staunch ally in Garriott. He wanted each new *Ultima* game to represent nothing short of a paradigm shift for computer games.

As we saw in Chapter 17, Garriott's sterling reputation nosedived with *Ultima VIII: Pagan* (1994). It wasn't all his fault; the early 1990s were a tumultuous time for the PC industry. His publishing and development company, Origin, suffered extreme growing pains as they struggled with swelling team sizes, escalating floppy disk costs, and the rapid disintegration of the Apple and Commodore 64 markets. When he applied for a loan to save his company, the application was promptly rejected—a real-estate bubble had burst in Texas, where their headquarters were located.

Out of sheer desperation, Garriott turned to Electronic Arts (EA), which acquired his company in 1992 in a stock-exchange deal. There was bad blood between the two industry giants; EA had sued Origin in a dispute over a distribution agreement they'd made back in 1984. EA argued that it had exclusive rights, and Origin "violated it in a very big and costly way," said EA founder Trip Hawkins.[1] Apparently, the furor was over a game called *Deathlord*, a 1987 CRPG that Garriott felt was a rip-off of his *Ultima* series. Garriott made good on his threat to leave EA's affiliate program if the publisher didn't pull it. EA refused, and Origin apparently paid a high price for it later

---

[1] Hawkins, Trip. "Escapist." *To the Editor.* 2007. http://www.escapistmagazine.com/forums/read/6.0 (accessed April 24, 2007).

Figure 36.1   *Ultima Online* was the first truly massive online role-playing game. (Scan courtesy of James Dunn.)

in the form of a crippling out-of-court settlement.[2,3]

Warren Spector, who'd joined Origin in 1989, said that at first the acquisition was good for both companies. "EA brought some much needed structure to our product greenlight and development processes. And we certainly got bigger budgets. We were able to do more and cooler things than we'd been able to do before." But the move from the "Rebellion" to the "Empire," as some Origin employees took to describing the shift in leadership, was not without cost. "EA gave us a lot of rope—enough to hang ourselves, as it turned out," said Spector.[4] Designers at Origin were accustomed to taking as long as they needed to complete a game. Now, they were being held to

strict deadlines. This resulted in several rushed games, including the aforementioned *Ultima VII*. Vicious infighting became the norm, and several promising projects were canceled as key personnel either quit or were fired.

EA was mainly interested in the *Ultima* series, and for obvious reasons: it still enjoyed a great reputation, and hordes of fans could be counted on to buy whatever product carried the label. As always, Garriott was uninterested in the type of quick "cash-in" sequels the publisher demanded, and instead went to work on a bold new venture that once again promised to revolutionize the industry: a massively multiplayer online role-playing game, or MMORPG (see Figure 36.1).

Now that we're so accustomed to MMORPGs, it's hard to imagine a time when the very idea seemed preposterous. True, multi-user dungeons (MUDs) had been around since the late 1970s, but their reliance on humble character set graphics—which made

---

[2] CGW. "Electronic Arts and Origin Pool Resources in 'Ultimate' Acquisition." *Computer Gaming World*, November 1992: 176.

[3] I was unable to find more about this lawsuit or the amount of the settlement. On a side note, "Scorpia" of *Computer Gaming World* wrote a very harsh review of the "mediocre" *Deathlord*, prompting an angry and indignant rebuttal in the October 1988 issue from its designer, Al Escudero.

[4] Verney, Allen. "The Conquest of Origin." *The Escapist*. October 11, 2005. http://www.escapistmagazine.com/articles/view /video-games/issues/issue_14/87-The-Conquest-of-Origin (accessed September 1, 2015).

them suitable even for slow, dial-up modems—was a fatal flaw in the eyes of PC gamers of the 90s. A logical workaround to this problem was a client program, which would contain the fancy audiovisuals and could be installed on an individual's PC. As with the early MUD technology, only tiny packets of information (such as player coordinates) would need to be routinely sent back and forth across the network.

One of the earliest examples of such a game is *Habitat*, which debuted in 1987 exclusively for the Commodore 64. Designed by Lucasfilm Games, it ran for a brief period on Quantum Link, the service that later became AOL. It offered third-person perspective in a two-dimensional (2D) world and focused on social activities. Players could write books, visit theaters, or even get married. The developers watched how the players performed and expanded the game accordingly, grafting on new features as they saw fit. It didn't offer RPG elements such as leveling or skills, and access was limited to off-peak hours, but it did pioneer many key innovations. The license changed hands a few times after the project shut down in 1988, reappearing on Japanese and American networks in various incarnations.

A more successful effort was Beyond Software's *Neverwinter Nights*, a game hosted on AOL between 1991 and 1997. This popular online RPG was based on SSI's Gold Box engine of *Pool of Radiance* (see Chapter 25). The addictive gameplay kept customers online, who had to pay by the hour for access. The game ended shortly after AOL switched to a flat-fee rate in 1996, turning games like *Neverwinter Nights* from money makers into money pits. AOL's ideal customer was now someone who made only minimal use of the service, logging on once in a while to check e-mail, not playing *Neverwinter Nights* from dusk to dawn. The game was taken down soon after (see Figure 36.2).

By the late 1990s, it was obvious to most that the Internet was the future of online gaming. The key advantage it offered gamers and publishers was independence from for-profit corporations like AOL, Genie, or CompuServe.

It's here that Archetype Interactive's *Meridian 59* enters the picture, a pioneering MMORPG developed by Archetype Interactive. Recognizing its potential, Trip Hawkins acquired it for his new 3DO venture in 1996, which he'd formed after leaving EA. *Meridian 59* was billed as the "first-ever Internet-based 3D MUD," and lived up to the hype. Here, we have all the features that are now a staple of the genre: three-dimensional (3D) graphics, RPG-style combat, player guilds, mail systems, and regular "expansions," or updates to the content or interface. Developed mainly

Figure 36.2 *Neverwinter Nights* (not to be confused with BioWare's title) was a pioneering game hosted on AOL.

by brothers Andrew and Chris Kirmse, it featured graphics comparable to *Doom*—a major step up from its predecessors. After buying the $50 game, players were charged a $10 monthly fee. It failed to generate the profits 3DO hoped for, though, and they pulled the plug in 2000. However, it retained enough fan support to survive despite this, and continues today. Andrew wrote a candid retrospective in 2000 that aptly summed up its legacy (see Figure 36.3):

Figure 36.3   *Meridian 59* had great graphics. It was never as successful as *Ultima Online*, but retains a small but dedicated group of players.

Though Meridian had many predecessors, such as *Scepter of Goth*, *Legends of Kesmai*, *Neverwinter Nights*, and Internet MUDs, it was the first Internet game from a major publisher, the first time that a massively multiplayer RPG was considered a "real" game and covered in the major game magazines. It was published over a year before *Ultima Online*; apparently the appearance of the *Meridian* alpha test is one of the factors that caused Origin to shift its attention and staff from *Ultima IX* to *Ultima Online*.[5]

Despite their bold innovations, none of these games was the killer app their developers hoped for. Most PC gamers simply lacked the awareness, interest, or money to play them. Thus, Garriott's decision to risk his *Ultima* franchise was a bold gamble indeed. The executives at EA were not at all enthusiastic. Even with the might of Garriott's *Ultima* franchise behind it, could it possibly succeed where so many others had failed? "*Ultima Online* was kind of a red-headed stepchild during its development," said Garriott. "Nobody at EA really understood what *Ultima Online* was all about."[6] EA demanded that Garriott focus his attention on developing yet another single-player *Ultima*.

Raph Koster filled the gap as the lead designer of *Ultima Online* (*UO*). Koster was no stranger to online game development; he'd implemented the award-winning *LegendMUD* a few years earlier. That game's celebrated attention to historical detail and its innovative character development system made Koster a natural fit for the position. Much like Garriott, Koster had bold ambitions and was not content merely to replicate

[5] Kirsme, Andrew. "History of Meridian 59." *Meridian59.com*. May 2000. http://meridian59.com (accessed September 3, 2015).

[6] Rausch, Allen. "From Origin to Destination." *Gamespy*. May 7, 2004. http://pc.gamespy.com/pc/tabula-rasa/512497p1.html (accessed September 2, 2015).

what had been done before. In particular, Koster wanted to find a way to capture the franchise's emphasis on virtue:

> We wanted to challenge players to act ethically, in the spirit of the *Ultimas* previous, without making it a set of quests that would be "gamed" and up on a cheat website within a couple of weeks—and we didn't want that to happen not because it meant extra work making new quests all the time, but because it meant that ethics themselves were being "gamed" and were therefore meaningless.[7]

Koster also wanted to do away with leveling, and didn't like the idea of "safe zones," where players would be immune from attacks by other players. These last two design decisions would have drastic consequences.

Less controversial innovations came by way of *Ultima VII: The Black Gate*, particularly its highly interactive game world. As with that game, *UO* players could do much more than just kill monsters. New players could opt for two basic templates for their characters: adventurer and merchant. The former of these was made up of the traditional RPG classes, such as warriors and mages. The latter was concerned with the economy and trades, such as tailors and fishermen. More advanced players could distribute their points as they saw fit. It was an impressively flexible system. An inflation mechanic for items determined the prices the in-game merchants charged for items, encouraging distant trade. Skills were improved by a brute force approach, improving with each successful use. *UO* had the 2D, isometric perspective of *Ultima VII*, albeit with better audiovisuals.

EA's attitude toward *UO* flipped from cold to hot after the game's first beta test on August 9, 1997. Origin's budget was so low at this point that they had to charge volunteer beta testers $5 for the privilege. "Within two days we had fifty thousand people," said *UO*'s director Starr Long, who directed the game. "They *paid* for the beta."[8] The beta wasn't without its problems. Most notorious of all was the assassination of Lord British himself by "Rainz," a 23-year-old software consultant from Indianapolis. Here's the story according to Rainz:

> The servers had just been taken down to prepare for the huge influx of players for the speech Lord British and Lord Blackthorne were giving throughout Britannia. When the servers came back up ... LB, Blackthorne, and their jesters were up on a bridge orating to the masses ... Luckily my character was a good thief who had high "stealing" skill. I desperately searched the backpacks of those around me and eventually came upon a fire field scroll. After that it was pretty simple, I just cast the scroll on the bridge and waited to see what would happen. Either LB or Blackthorne made

---

[7] Koster, Raph. "Ultima Online Postmortem." *Raph Koster's Website.* June 2000. http://www.raphkoster.com/gaming/post mortem.shtml (accessed September 3, 2015).

[8] Koster, Raph, Rich Vogel, and Starr M. Long. "Classic Game Postmortem: Ultima Online." *GDC Vault.* October 2012. http:// www.gdcvault.com/play/1016629/Classic-Game-Postmortem-Ultima (accessed September 3, 2015).

the comment "hehe nice try," can't recall exactly who. It was a humorous sight and I expected to be struck down by lightning or have some other evil fate befall me. Instead I heard a loud death grunt as British slumped to his death. After that it was just pure mayhem.[9]

Rainz was banned for his efforts, but he was just one of thousands of malicious players, whose malevolent antics earned them the name "pkillers" (or "griefers" in modern parlance). While some (and obviously the pkillers themselves) enjoyed this type of gameplay, it turned away players of a less hostile disposition. Origin tried various tactics, including a "karma" system and bounties, but eventually created a mirror world where players could explore unmolested.

Regardless of the "pkiller" phenomenon, *UO* became the first truly "massive" online RPG (see Figure 36.4). Richard Bartle, the creator of MUD we met in Chapter 5, wrote about the game's success in his book *Designing Virtual Worlds*:

> When *Ultima Online* garnered 50,000 subscribers within 3 months, people took notice. When it broke 100,000 within a year, jaws dropped. Nevermind the substantial income from retail sales: 100,000 people were *each* paying $9.95 *per month* having already bought the game—and none of that money was going to retailers! OSI was directly taking 12 million dollars a year from that one virtual world![10]

This sudden success broke more than records—it broke the servers the game was running on. According to Koster, they had designed the game with 300 players in mind, going by *Meridian 59*'s figures. "We expected to do better," said Koster, "but not by an order of magnitude."[7] Normally, soaring demand that exceeded a developer's expectations would've been a cause for celebration; for Koster and the *UO* team, it caused consternation. The unexpected influx led to massive lag and server shutdowns, and early reviews bashed it on this account.

Eventually, *UO* was able to overcome these growing pains, and when the dust settled, players found that it lived up to the hype—this was no mere game, but a world you could live in. Advanced features kept players invested in the long term. Players could build their own houses once they had accumulated sufficient capital for a deed. Houses were primarily places to store one's possessions but also served as stores for selling crafted items. Unfortunately, abandoned houses tended to get routinely deleted by the system, so it was important to log in every few days to "refresh" one's house.

Players could also join 1 of 13 professional guilds, arranged by profession (Thieves' Guild, Fellowship of Blacksmiths, etc.), as well as player-run guilds. Occasionally, these player guilds would engage in "guild wars," which allowed members to kill certain other players without fear of losing karma.

---

[9] Bannister, Paul. "Ultima Online: Interview with Rainz, The Man Who Killed Lord British." *Noctalis*. August 19, 1997. http://noctalis.com/dis/uo/blast02a.shtml (accessed September 3, 2015).

[10] Bartle, Richard A. *Designing Virtual Worlds*. Indianapolis: New Riders Publishing, 2004: 21.

Figure 36.4 *Ultima Online* featured a highly configurable interface.

All in all, *UO* was a staggeringly ambitious game that offered a multitude of options from the beginning, but it was only a small fraction of the game it has become today. EA churned out several expansions between 1998 and 2007, many of which significantly altered the game world and the gameplay. *Ultima Online: Renaissance*, released on April 3, 2000, doubled the size of the world by offering a "mirror image" world called Trammel (see Figure 36.5), which forbade pkilling. While some players rejoiced, others were displeased, feeling that the change threatened the economy. The problem was that "easy prey" could now easily

Figure 36.5 The land of Trammel was a controversial addition to the game.

level up and work on skills and crafts, since they didn't have to worry about pkills. With the risk factor reduced if not eliminated, the markets were soon saturated with product and inflation soared.

Despite these and later expansions, *UO* lost a large chunk of its player base to 989 Studios' *EverQuest*, which went online in 1999. *EverQuest* had several advantages over its rival. For one, it offered 3D-accelerated graphics, which made *UO* look antiquated in comparison. Player-versus-player (PVP) combat was limited to a designated server from the start, which made it easier (and less frustrating) for less aggressive players to flourish on the main servers—the emphasis there was on cooperating rather than competing directly with other players. There were several means in place to ensure cooperation, most notably monsters that were difficult if not impossible to beat alone. It was also less prone to lag than *UO*, even with dial-up modems. It did, however, punish death more severely: dying costs experience points as well as a tedious run to one's corpse. *EverQuest* surpassed *UO*'s userbase in 6 months, reaching more than 400,000 users in 2004.[10]

UO's legacy is important for the game industry, and its designers' "mistakes" are just as enlightening as their successes. As both Garriott and Koster have pointed out, *UO* boasted a far more interactive and intriguing game world than most MMOs even today, and its emphasis on varied gameplay styles and character diversity was ahead of its time. Perhaps this was its downfall. As Koster noted cynically, "More people are willing to do the same repetitive activity over and over again for the sake of getting a red polka dotted item to replace the green striped one, than are willing to engage in a broader range of activity."[7] The sheer range of possibilities was, on the one hand, empowering, but, on the other, intimidating to new players. When a new game came along with a much smoother learning curve, it not only was easier to play but also was intended for players to recruit their friends into the game. *EverQuest* would receive similar treatment after Blizzard's *World of Warcraft*, but I'll save that story for Chapter 47.

Garriott returned to the scene in 2007 with *Tabula Rasa*, a shooter/MMORPG hybrid with a sci-fi setting. Garriott's name and a series of interviews caught the attention of the media, and anticipation built to a fever pitch going into its release date on November 2, 2007. Despite some intriguing ideas such as "morality quests" and the ability to clone one's character to try out new professions, the game failed miserably, and closed down for good on February 28, 2009. Garriott placed the blame on NCSoft:

> There's really two games that I have shipped that shipped as less than I could have hoped or, I believe, less than I could have done: *Ultima 8* and *Tabula Rasa*. In both of those games it was immediately after selling a company to a larger company who had very strong opinions about how and why I should do the games that I was working on in a particular way.[11]

[11] Purchese, Robert. "Garriott: What Went Wrong with Tabula Rasa." *Eurogamer.net*. December 12, 2011. http://www
.eurogamer.net/articles/2011-12-12-garriott-what-went-wrong-with-tabula-rasa (accessed September 4, 2015).

Garriott now has a chance to prove this was the case with his *Shroud of the Avatar* game, whose Kickstarter fund drive raised nearly $2 million in 2013. It promises to offer the best of the single-player as well as the online experience, and will certainly be an impressive achievement if the team is able to deliver on all it has promised. In a nice symmetry with *UO*, future players of *Shroud of the Avatar* are also being asked to pay to help them beta test it—but this time in the form of an "Early Access" game on Steam. As of this writing, the expected release date of "Episode 1" is July 2016.

36.1 Playing *UO* Today

Playing *UO* is as simple as going to http://uo.com and setting up an account. You can choose from two clients: Enhanced or Classic. As their names suggest, the former offers an updated interface with better graphics, but many still prefer the Classic interface. There are usually free trials available. Alternatively, you can go to http://www.uoforever .com and play the classic game for free. This is the best option for fans of PVP, since there's no safe zone ("Trammel"). Keep in mind that this project is supported by donations, so be sure to chip in if you intend to stay awhile.

Chapter 37

Super Mario 64: No Disc, No Problem

The mid-1990s were a crucial turning point for the console side of the industry, which had to deal with two major innovations originating on the PC side: three-dimensional (3D) graphics and CD-ROM. Consoles had traditionally offered a vastly cheaper alternative to PC gaming, and its typically younger demographic was quite happy with two-dimensional (2D) masterpieces like *Sonic the Hedgehog* and *Super Mario Bros*. However, now that demographic was broadening to include older gamers, especially after the *Madden* series took off on the Genesis. Though their marketing campaigns suggested otherwise, Nintendo and Sega's rivalry was, if not friendly, at least not as ugly as what was about to come.

The real trouble started when rumors surfaced of an upcoming console from Sony, which not only would use the vastly more economical CD-ROM for storage but would have hardware optimized for 3D graphics. Sony had the deep pockets, clout, and technological expertise to seriously threaten both Nintendo and Sega.

Sega had jumped on the CD-ROM back in 1992 (1991 in Japan) with its Sega CD add-on, but neither that nor the later 32X add-on gained much traction. Desperate, Sega rushed its ill-fated Saturn console into production in 1995 (1994 in Japan), trying to beat Sony to the punch. Ultimately, neither the Saturn nor their last console, the Dreamcast in 1999 (1998 in Japan), were enough to threaten the Sony juggernaut.

Nintendo decided once again to play it cool, waiting a full 2 years after the PlayStation's Japanese launch to enter the next generation, but the long-awaited system had many scratching their heads. Sure, Nintendo had the trump card: superstar designer Shigeru Miyamoto. As always, the company believed great games, not great hardware, sold systems, and Miyamoto made the best. However, the Nintendo 64 was hardly a technological wonder. Incredibly, it still relied on old-fashioned cartridges for storage (see Figure 37.1). These cartridges could hold, at most, 64 megabytes, and cost more than CD-ROM discs, which could store over 650 megabytes or more. On the positive side, however, cartridges didn't suffer from the long loading times associated with discs. Other disc-based consoles like the 3DO, Philips' CD-I, Commodore's CDTV and CD32, and of course Sega's various attempts had all failed, and if Miyamoto delivers another killer app, the PlayStation might soon be joining them.

In terms of 3D graphics, the Nintendo 64 had more than enough power to rival the others (see Figure 37.2). However, the type of 3D platforming gameplay Miyamoto and his team envisioned for the next *Mario* title hadn't been invented yet. Adding a new dimension to a game like *Super Mario Bros.* wasn't just a matter of graphics; the real challenge was

Figure 37.1   Nintendo's decision to release another cartridge-based console was unpopular with third-party developers. *Super Mario 64* and other exquisite first-party titles compensated for the lack of external support.

Figure 37.2   Mario has made the transition to 3D in spectacular fashion.

the interface. Could older gamers accustomed to 2D *Mario* games—much less children—learn to move a character in three dimensions, particularly in situations that required precision?

Miyamoto and his team spent months just selecting the best camera view and layout. This hadn't been an issue with 2D platformers, since the screen could simply scroll left and right (or occasionally up and down) as the character moved along the X (horizontal) and Z (vertical) axes. The third dimension meant that characters could move along the Z axis; toward and away from the camera. This feature made the game worlds feel much more realistic and immersive, but at a cost. The groundbreaking 3D game *Alone in the Dark* (1992), for instance, was slow and difficult to navigate. That game was set up as a series of prerendered rooms or scenes, each with a "fixed camera." This arrangement wouldn't accommodate a fast-paced game like *Super Mario Bros.*, where fast movement and accurate collision detection were critical. Furthermore, gamers now expected the scenery as well as the characters to be rendered on the fly as they were in first-person shooters.

A more specific consideration is that the third dimension made jumps much harder to estimate; players might need to study the situation from several angles to properly aim and time a difficult leap. All of this hadn't been a problem with first-person 3D games such as id's *Doom* (Chapter 29), where the camera behaved as if it *were* the character, like a disembodied eye. Precision jumping sequences called for third-person perspective; players needed to be able to see the character and ledge from various angles. However, that required a dynamic camera that players could adjust as needed. To that end, the

Nintendo 64's controller was equipped with an analog stick and buttons designated specifically for controlling the camera.

Indeed, *Super Mario 64*'s interface was perhaps its greatest achievement. The integration of the analog stick was particularly impressive. Depending on how hard players pushed it in one direction, Mario would either tiptoe, walk, or run. Although the camera would automatically switch to the "recommended view," players were "cinematographers" as the manual put it, utilizing the con-

Figure 37.3 Princess Toadstool needs Mario's help once again.

troller's four "c" buttons. Mario was followed by the "Lakitu Bros.," a camera crew that flew around on a cloud. The player could move the camera closer or further (zoom) and around to get a better view of the scene. Miyamoto enjoyed just moving Mario around in 3D so much that at one point he felt "this didn't really have to be a game."[1]

Fortunately, the finished game was much more than a tech demo (see Figure 37.3). Mario's quest was to collect Power Stars, which had been stolen by Mario's famous nemesis, Bowser. Mario sought them within a set of magical paintings, which were self-contained worlds full of puzzles and monsters. It was an appropriate story and metaphor for the new style of gameplay. The worlds were diverse, bringing welcomed variety to both the aesthetics and challenges of the game. They also gave Mario a chance to show off his many abilities, such as swimming, climbing, flying, and even firing himself from cannons. Mario also had a bevy of jumps and leaps available, such as wall kicks, long jumps, and side and back somersaults—in short, the skills of a master acrobat. In addition to his classic squashing technique to destroy enemies, Mario could now punch and kick them as well. The game wisely introduced these techniques gradually to avoid bewildering novices (see Figure 37.4).

In stark contrast to the PlayStation, which launched with eight titles spanning the genres, the Nintendo 64 had only two games in its lineup. It's a good thing, then, that one of those was *Super Mario 64*. Critics were unanimous in their praise of the game's imaginative worlds and controls, with IGN's Doug Perry going so far as to call it "the greatest videogame to date, and one which all games, regardless of genre, will be judged."[2] It was precisely the killer app Nintendo needed for a successful launch of its new console: in just 4 months, more than half-a-million Americans had bought the

---

[1] Satoru, Iwata. "Iwata Asks: Super Mario Galaxy." *Nintendo.com.* 2007. http://iwataasks.nintendo.com/interviews/#/wii/super_mario_galaxy/3/1 (accessed September 4, 2015).

[2] Perry, Doug. "The Greatest 3D World Ever Created." *IGN.* September 25, 1996. http://www.ign.com/articles/1996/09/26/super-mario-64 (accessed September 4, 2015).

Figure 37.4   The Lakitu Bros. serve as camera operators in *Super Mario 64*. It's a nice way to connect the gameplay mechanics to the storyline.

Figure 37.5   The paintings in the castle are portals to other areas.

console and the game (see Figure 37.5). Eventually, Nintendo sold more than 11 million copies, and later editions are still top sellers.[3]

There were plans to release a sequel to *Super Mario 64*, but they were canceled along with the Nintendo 64DD add-on—a colossal failure. Instead, fans had to wait for *Super Mario Sunshine* in 2002, a title for the GameCube. *Super Mario Galaxy* was a hit title for the Wii console in 2007, whose sequel followed in 2010. The latest is *Super Mario 3D World* for the Wii U, published in 2013, but despite stellar reviews, it didn't turn out to be the system-seller Nintendo needed.

For now, though, let's return to those heady months after the release of *Super Mario 64*, when the future of the company looked as bright as the colors of its flagship title, and Nintendo's vaults were as unassailable as the long lost tombs of ancient pharaohs.

37.1 Playing *Super Mario 64* Today

It's best to play *Super Mario 64* on a Nintendo 64, since it's optimized for that system's unique controller. These systems are much easier and cheaper to acquire than a Nintendo Entertainment System (NES) or a Super Nintendo Entertainment System (SNES), and a great place to start your vintage console collection. Otherwise, you can pick up an aftermarket USB Nintendo 64 controller from a variety of manufacturers and play it via an emulator such as *Project 64*.

Nintendo released versions of the game for several later systems, including the Wii, Wii U, and DS. Check the virtual console for the latest pricing information.

---

[3] Buchanan, Levi. "Nintendo 64 Week: Day One." *IGN*. September 29, 2008. http://www.ign.com/articles/2008/09/29/nintendo-64-week-day-one (accessed September 4, 2015).

Chapter 38

Tomb Raider: A 3D Platformer with Legs

As Miyamoto and his team at Nintendo were hard at work on *Super Mario 64*, Core Design, based in Britain, was taking the concept of three-dimensional (3D) platforming in a very different direction. Core Design had been founded back in 1988 by former members of Gremlin Graphics.

They'd done a two-dimensional platformer called *Rick Dangerous* in 1989, whose titular character and level design were inspired by the film *Raiders of the Lost Ark*. In addition to the "Guulu" natives Rick could dispatch with his six-shooter, dynamite, or his "big stick," there were plenty of clever puzzles to challenge the brain as well as the fingers. A year later, the company moved into publishing, and were the earliest British team to make hit platform games for the Sega Genesis, Sega CD, and Sega 32X.[1] These titles included *Chuck Rock* (1991), *Bubba 'N' Stix* (1994), and *Asterix and the Great Rescue* (1994).

When Core began work on a 3D platformer, the original design called for another Rick Dangerous–like character in the lead role, and artist Toby Gard created another Indiana Jones–inspired character. However, Core's cofounder, Jeremy Heath-Smith, was wary of lawsuits and bored with male characters. Why not make the lead character a girl, instead? The idea might sound perfectly natural today, but it was a bold move at the time. Would male gamers be comfortable playing as a woman?

Gard's inspirations for Lara Croft—or Laura Cruz, as he originally wanted to call her—are not altogether clear (see Figure 38.1). Some sources claim it was Gard's younger sister, Frances. It's not hard to imagine. Like Lara, Frances had a long braided ponytail and chased after adventure—although she preferred shooting cameras to pistols. Gard remained adamant that his creation would not be a "page 3" girl, that is, a scantily clad pin-up like the ones featured in *The Sun*, a British tabloid.[2] According to Gard, "Lara was based on elements of Indiana Jones, Tank Girl, and … my sister. Maybe subconsciously she was my sister. Anyway, she was supposed to be this strong woman, this upper-class

---

[1] Moss, Richard. "It Felt Like Robbery: Tomb Raider and the Fall of Core Design." *Ars Technica*. March 31, 2015. http://arstechnica.com/gaming/2015/03/it-felt-like-robbery-tomb-raider-and-the-fall-of-core-design/ (accessed September 7, 2015).

[2] Davis, Johnny. "Toby Gard: Let the Battle Begin." *The Independent*. September 7, 2015. http://www.independent.co.uk/news/science/toby-gard-let-the-battle-begin-6171048.html (accessed September 7, 2015).

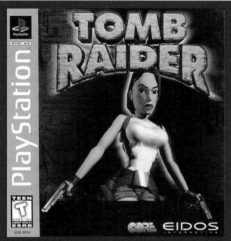

Figure 38.1   *Tomb Raider* introduced the world to Lara Croft, one of the industry's most celebrated characters.

adventurer." Croft was certainly no helpless princess—she could run, jump, dive, roll, swim, climb, and accurately aim and fire two pistols at once.

So how did this strong female character (d)evolve into a busty sex object? The story goes that one day when Gard was working on Lara, his finger slipped when he was adjusting her breast size. Instead of a 50% breast size, he selected 150%. The rest of the team stopped him before he could change the size back to normal.[3] Regardless of Gard's intention, the resulting "sexy" Lara would titillate gamers like

Figure 38.2   The impressive opening cinematics establish Lara as a highly skilled acrobat, climber, and markswoman.

no video game character had before—and no one would ever confuse her with Mario or Sonic (see Figure 38.2).

Lara leapt onto the scene in November of 1996, 6 weeks after *Super Mario 64*, and promptly gave the plumber a run for his money. Sony couldn't have been happier; now, the PlayStation had a wildly popular

"mascot" who could distinguish its platform from the likes of Mario and Sonic. She certainly caught the eye of the mainstream media, who plastered her image on the cover of both *Time* and *Newsweek*. It was clear that Lara Croft was no "safe" character intended for young children; she represented both danger and sex appeal. She earned hundreds of millions for Core Design, in sales as well as lucrative licensing deals.

Many critics expected a backlash. *IGN*'s review of the game read, "*Tomb Raider* is bound to stir up lots of trouble with the feminists. Lara Croft's unrealistic proportions can only lead to further gender stereotyping and objectification of women."[4] With these

---

[3] McLaughlin, Rus. "IGN Presents: The History of Tomb Raider." *IGN*. February 29, 2008. http://www.ign.com/articles /2008/03/01/ign-presents-the-history-of-tomb-raider (accessed September 7, 2015).

[4] IGN Staff. "Tomb Raider." *IGN*. December 13, 1996. http://www.ign.com/articles/1996/12/14/tomb-raider-5 (accessed September 7, 2015).

disclaimers out of the way, the staff went on to call it "one of the best games of 1996." A review in *The Economist* began with the question, "WHAT man could resist a creature like Lara Croft? This ravishing British heiress divides her time between acrobatic work-outs in her stately home and dangerous expeditions to exotic ruins. She wears shorts everywhere, which show off her sprinter's legs, and a tiny waist draws attention to her gravity-defying bust. Then there is the small matter of the twin automatic pistols she straps to her bare thighs."[5]

Was Lara Croft merely a sex object? Some argued that she did more to dispel sexist stereotypes than reinforce them. In an interview with *Forbes* magazine, Eidos spokes-man Gary Keith argued that "it used to be that when we played videogames, it wasn't cool to be a girl," and gave Lara credit for successfully challenging this assumption.[6] Although the game was ostensibly targeted at 18- to 35-year-old males, plenty of women enjoyed the game as well. "There was something refreshing about looking at the screen and seeing myself as a woman," said "Game Grrl" Nikki Douglas.[7]

Games scholar Espen Aarseth claimed it was all much ado about nothing: "When I play, I don't even see her body, but see through it and past it ... The dimensions of Lara Croft's body, already analyzed to death by film theorists, are irrelevant to me as a player, because a different-looking body would not make me play any differently."[8]

One man who would've vehemently disagreed with Aarseth was Lara's creator, Gard. He quit the company just 2 months after the game's publication. He was disgusted with the way Core's parent company, Eidos, was exploiting his creation with racy market-ing images. The trend continued, however, and by 1999 Lara was "posing" for *Playboy Magazine* and her in-game avatar became increasingly sexualized.

Although the game was better known on the Sony PlayStation and PC (see Figure 38.3a and b), it actually debuted on the short-lived Sega Saturn, where it was one of the system's bestsellers. The later versions had superior audiovisuals, but all had third-person perspective and a camera that followed along behind Lara (or over her shoulder). While the game had its share of precision jumping sequences, Lara's ability to grip onto ledges with her fingers made them easier to master, and more visually impressive. Lara used her pistols to shoot beasts or human enemies, but most of the gameplay was focused on avoiding traps and solving puzzles. Lara could push or pull objects, throw switches, and collect various items to use later. The game was a great deal more violent than *Super Mario 64*, with several grisly ways for Lara to meet her end, including falling onto spikes.

Perhaps the most important feature was superb control and response. There was no free roaming camera, but players could force the camera immediately behind Lara and then use the direction buttons to look around. This feature came in handy whenever the

---

[5] Staff. "Babes with Guns: Britain's Videogame Industry." *The Economist*, February 22, 1997: 74.

[6] Kafka, Peter. "Gender Benders." *Forbes*, January 12, 1998: 39.

[7] Kennedy, Helen W. "Lara Croft: Feminist Icon or Cyberbimbo?" *Game Studies*, 2002.

[8] Wardrip-Fruin, Noah, and Pat Harrigan. *First Person: New Media as Story, Performance, and Game*. Boston: MIT Press, 2006.

(a)

(b)

built-in camera was stuck at an awkward angle.

Another feature worth mentioning is the in-game tutorial system. Rather than thrust players directly into the adventure, *Tomb Raider* let players safely experiment with the controls in a special level called "Lara's Home." Later *Tomb Raider* games elaborated on the narrative possibilities of these in-game tutorials, filling players in on the backstory as they learned the ropes.

Beyond its radical differences in character and themes, *Tomb Raider* stood apart from *Super Mario 64* in another way: it wasn't exclusive to any single platform. Indeed, it was a best-selling and definitive title for both the Sony PlayStation and the PC. Later *Tomb Raider* titles appeared for Microsoft's Xbox as well as Nintendo's GameCube and Wii systems. These many games ranged widely in quality, and for

Figure 38.3 Shown here are the PlayStation (a) and PC (b) versions of *Tomb Raider*.

many years, it was commonly assumed Lara's best days were behind her. However, Crystal Dynamics' *Tomb Raider* (2012) and *Rise of the Tomb Raider* (2015) have returned her to the front page of the gaming press.

Lara's celebrity status ensured a future for the franchise, and to date, she's starred in dozens of games and two movies—*Lara Croft: Tomb Raider* (2001) and *Lara Croft Tomb Raider: The Cradle of Life* (2003), with Angelina Jolie in the titular role. To say that Lara made better Hollywood material than Mario is an understatement. Even Roger Ebert, well known for his curmudgeonly attitude toward video games, awarded it three stars—"Only a churl could find fault," wrote the dazzled critic.[9] When the question of whether she adequately filled Lara's bra came up, Jolie responded candidly: "We didn't want to make them as big as in the game, but at the same time we didn't want to take away from her the things that are, you know, her trademarks"[10] (see Figure 38.4).

---

[9] Ebert, Roger. "Lara Croft: Tomb Raider." *Roger Ebert.com*. June 15, 2001. http://www.rogerebert.com/reviews/lara-croft -tomb-raider-2001 (accessed September 7, 2015).

[10] Miller, Prarie. "Angelina Jolie on Filling Lara Croft's Shoes and D-Size Cups." *NY Rock*. June 2001. http://www.nyrock.com /interviews/2001/jolie_int.asp (accessed September 7, 2015).

As for Tony Gard, Lara's creator, Crystal Dynamics wooed him back to the franchise as a story consultant for *Tomb Raider: Anniversary*, a 2007 remake of the original. He was more heavily involved in *Tomb Raider: Legend* (2006) and *Tomb Raider: Underworld* (2008). Notably, these games feature a Lara with more realistic bodily proportions. While arguably as sexy as ever, Lara is no longer a sexualized pin-up girl. Indeed, the latest *Tomb Raider* games feature exactly the sort of strong and capable character that Gard envisioned from the start.

38.1 Playing *Tomb Raider* Today

The first (and probably roughest) version of *Tomb Raider* you can play is the one for

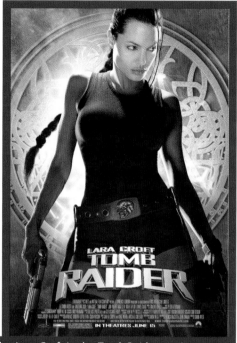

Figure 38.4 Angelina Jolie was chosen to play Lara Croft in the *Tomb Raider* movies.

the Sega Saturn. Finding a working Saturn for a cheap price may not be easy, however, since their run was very limited. If you'd rather try emulation, Yabause and SSF are both viable options. You might prefer the more popular PlayStation incarnation, though. Used PlayStations are cheap and plentiful, and you shouldn't have any issues finding a used *Tomb Raider* disc for it. The PC version is the easiest to acquire; simply go to Steam and look for *Tomb Raider I*. If you're not up for "retro" graphics, try *Tomb Raider: Anniversary*, which updates the original in a number of significant ways.

Chapter 39

Final Fantasy VII: The Legend of the Square Disc

January 31, 1997, is a date that will live in infamy, at least among the Nintendo faithful. For on that day, Square terminated its decade-long relationship with Nintendo by publishing its seventh *Final Fantasy* game exclusively for the Sony PlayStation. Fans of the epic Japanese role-playing series had grown up playing it on their Nintendo Entertainment System (NES) and Super Nintendo Entertainment System (SNES), and they fully expected to play the next on their Nintendo 64. The overwhelming acclaim the game received from critics was the salt in the wound—this was the best *Final Fantasy* ever, and you needed to buy a PlayStation to play it.

Nintendo had hoped its groundbreaking *Super Mario 64* would turn the tide against Sony, but *Final Fantasy VII* (Figure 39.1) showed them the error of their ways. In particular, it showed that discs, not cartridges, were the future of consoles. Nintendo had assumed the long loading times associated with discs would trump their substantial advantages in storage capacity and cost. Square's developers, however, had overcome these challenges, providing a nearly seamless experience that made loading times all but moot. Above all else, though, the design team revealed the PlayStation's capabilities as a storytelling platform. Its sophisticated three-dimensional (3D) graphics, computer-generated imagery (CGI) cut scenes, and lovely prerendered backgrounds were all stunning for the era, but its lasting appeal is owed to its involving story, memorable characters, and compelling gameplay. Widely regarded as one of the best games of all time, *Final Fantasy VII* was a major step forward, not just for the genre, but for the industry as a whole.

Square allocated $45 million for the game's development, an unprecedented sum for the era.[1] The bulk of the money was lavished on cinematic CGI cut scenes, which complemented the already impressive in-game graphics. Those featured 3D polygonal characters shown against prerendered backgrounds; quite a leap forward from the two-dimensional (2D) tile-based graphics of the previous games. The finished game would span not one but *three* CD-ROMs.

During most of the game's development, Square assumed Nintendo's upcoming console would follow Sega and Sony's lead in relying on CD-ROMs for storage. However,

---

[1] Maragos, Nich. "38. Final Fantasy VII." *1up.com*. n.d. http://www.1up.com/features/essential-50-final-fantasy-vii (accessed September 8, 2015).

Figure 39.1 *Final Fantasy VII* shipped on not one but three discs.

Figure 39.2 There was nothing at all subtle about this infamous magazine advertisement.

a last-minute decision to stick with cartridges left the developer with an awful choice: strip out huge chunks of the game, or switch sides to join the competition. It's fun to consider what might have happened if they'd thrown their lot in with Sega and their Saturn console, but it's not hard to see why they chose Sony instead. Sega had tarnished their reputation with a series of ill-conceived add-ons and rushed the Saturn into production before it was ready. The clincher, though, was that the PlayStation was a hundred dollars cheaper. Nintendo's president, Yamauchi, was incensed at the news. He vowed that a *Final Fantasy* game would never again befoul one of Nintendo's consoles.[2]

The news that the new *Final Fantasy* game would be exclusive to the PlayStation was bigger news in Japan than in the United States, where it was still widely assumed that console gamers simply weren't interested in the genre. Only a handful of *Final Fantasy* games had made

their way to America. Before *Final Fantasy VII*, the last import had been the sixth game in Japan, released here as *Final Fantasy III* for the SNES in 1994. Despite Nintendo's heavy-handed censorship policies for the American localization, it received rave reviews and was a modest bestseller. However, the series still hadn't caught on like it had in Japan, a situation that Square and Sony were determined to rectify. To that end, Sony created three 30-s television spots showing off the game's CGI cinematics, airing them on all the major American networks.

In a move reminiscent of Sega's "Nintendon't" campaign, Sony published a series of brutal magazine ads designed to promote both the game and the PlayStation at Nintendo's expense. One infamous ad read, "Someone please get the guys who make cartridge games a cigarette and a blindfold" above a compelling still from one of the game's cut scenes (see Figure 39.2). Just in case anyone missed the ad campaign, Sony bundled a demo of the game with its console. Most of the game's marketing focused on the enormous size and cost of the production.

---

[2] McLaughlin, Rus. "IGN Presents: The History of Final Fantasy VII." *IGN*. April 30, 2008. http://www.ign.com/articles/2008/05/01/ign-presents-the-history-of-final-fantasy-vii (accessed September 8, 2015).

Needless to say, *Final Fantasy VII* was a terrific bestseller. No one was surprised it sold briskly in Japan, where the series was already a pop culture phenomenon. The real shocker was how well it did in America—1.6 million copies (6 million worldwide) were sold in 2 years.[3] If nothing else, the game proved there was most definitely a market for Japanese role-playing games (JRPGs) in America, and many more would follow.

Although the game's audiovisuals may seem dated today, modern gamers can still appreciate the story and richly developed characters (Figure 39.3a and b). *Final Fantasy VII* is set in what can perhaps best be described as an alternative future of fantasy and sci-fi; factories and robots mesh with magic and swordplay. The planet Gaia is being slowly destroyed by the giant corporation named Shinra,

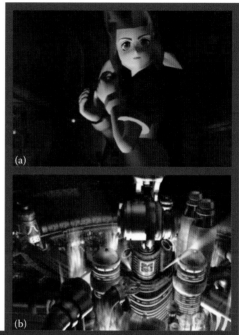

Figure 39.3 The opening cinematic shows off what the engine is capable of: emotionally expressive characters (a) and a massive, highly detailed game world (b).

which is hell-bent on acquiring a mystical energy called Mako. Cloud Strife, a spiky-haired youth carrying an enormous blade (see Figures 39.4 and 39.5), is a hesitant mercenary assisting a group of eco-terrorists named AVALANCHE, committed to destroying the Mako reactors. They are opposed by SOLDIER, Shinra's elite squadron of fighters.

Eventually, Cloud finds himself embroiled not only with AVALANCHE but also with a sweet "flower girl" named Aeris. He agrees to be her bodyguard, but players decided how to handle her as a love interest. Aeris is being pursued by SOLDIER, who may be interested in what she believes to be useless white materia. The story was quite intricate and expertly paced,

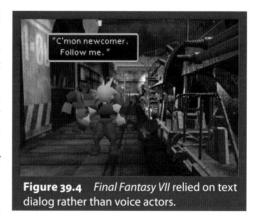

Figure 39.4 *Final Fantasy VII* relied on text dialog rather than voice actors.

---

[3] Business Editors, a. H. "Square soft's Final Fantasy VII joins top-selling videogames in PlayStation's 'greatest hits' series…" *Business Wire*, June 29, 1999: 1.

Figure 39.5   The first of many, many combats.

and it would be a shame to give away the many surprises here. Suffice it to say, it's easy to get attached to the characters and care about what happens to them, and the narrative turns out to be much darker and sophisticated than you'd expect.

Sakaguchi said that the idea for this story had been with him since his mother passed away during the development of *Final Fantasy III*: "I ha[d] been thinking about the theme of life. Life exists in many things, and I was curious about what would happen if I attempted to analyze life in a mathematical and logical way. Maybe this was my approach in overcoming the grief I was experiencing."[4] *Final Fantasy VII*'s powerful engine finally gave Sakaguchi the tools he needed to adequately explore this concept.

The staggering success of *Final Fantasy VII* made sequels practically inevitable, and indeed, today one could easily write another book covering the many sequels, spin-offs, crossovers, and feature films that followed in its wake. Its ultimate legacy extends beyond the franchise itself. It played a large part in bringing the JRPG to America, but also helped establish the PlayStation as a global gaming platform. Finally, its rich, cinematic narrative and story demonstrated the potential of console games as a respectable cultural medium.

39.1 Playing *Final Fantasy VII* Today

There are several viable options for playing this epic JRPG today. Assuming you don't have a vintage PlayStation lying around, I recommend the Windows version on Steam. There are also versions for iOS, PSP, Vita, and PS3.

Square Enix announced they were working on a remake of the game at Sony's E3 press conference. It is planned to be released in separate parts, exclusively on the PS4. We will likely learn more at E3 2016 in June.

---

4   PlayStation Underground. "Hironobu Sakaguchi Interview." *The Final Fantasy VII Citadel.* 1997. http://www.ff7citadel.com /press/int_sakaguchi.shtml (accessed September 8, 2015).

Chapter 40

Metal Gear Solid: Lights, Camera, Inaction!

With more than 41.2 million copies sold to date, Hideo Kojima's *Metal Gear* is easily one of the most successful video game franchises (see Figure 40.1).[1] The 2011 Gamer's Edition of the *Guinness World Records* declared the series' chief protagonist, Solid Snake, the fourth most popular video game character of all time.[2,3] As of this writing, *Metal Gear Solid V: The Phantom Pain*, which Kojima insists is the last game of the saga, is receiving perfect scores by all the top video game sites, and topping PC, PS4, and Xbox One sales charts. In the fourth game, Snake said, "I'm no hero. Never was, never will be." Millions of his fans would strongly disagree!

As we've seen with so many of video game's biggest franchises, its creator had a very hard time getting anyone to take his idea for a "stealth" game seriously. Everyone else believed that gamers wanted to search and destroy, not hide and sneak. "I had such a hard time convincing people," said Kojima (see Figure 40.2). "I had so many things going against me ... For one, my first game had been cancelled, so I hadn't released anything yet. Then I was working in a large creative group, and I was the youngest. Finally, the type of game I wanted to make didn't exist."[4]

Kojima must not have been aware of Silas Warner's *Castle Wolfenstein*, which we touched on briefly back in Chapter 29, or Sega's *005*, two games from 1981 that are clear progenitors. In any case, these games had long faded from the scene by the time the first *Metal Gear* game appeared on the Nintendo Entertainment System (NES) in the summer of 1987. It was especially popular in the United States, where it sold more than a million copies.

---

[1] Konami. "Konami to Exhibit at World's Premier Game Show." *Konami Digital Entertainment*. June 15, 2015. http://www.konami-digital-entertainment.co.jp/en/news/release/2015/0615/ (accessed September 9, 2015).

[2] Field, Damian. "Top 50 Video Game Characters of All Time Announced." *Gamasutra*. February 16, 2011. http://www.gamasutra.com/view/pressreleases/68759/TOP_50_VIDEO_GAME_CHARACTERS_OF_ALL_TIME_ANNOUNCED_inGUINNESS_WORLD_RECORDS_2011_GAMERrsquoS_EDITION.php (accessed September 9, 2015).

[3] This ranking put him just behind *Halo*'s Master Chief and just above *Final Fantasy*'s Cloud Strife in terms of popularity. Mario and Link took the top two spots.

[4] Parkin, Simon. "Hideo Kojima: Video Game Drop-Out Interview." *The Guardian*. May 23, 2012. http://www.theguardian.com/technology/gamesblog/2012/may/23/hideo-kojima-interview-part-1 (accessed September 9, 2015).

Figure 40.1   The cover of *Metal Gear Solid*, much like its protagonist, was inconspicuous.

The story of *Metal Gear* goes further back, however. Kojima had been hired by Konami to develop games for MSX, a standard for home computers developed by Microsoft and Japan's ASCII Corporation. Microsoft hoped to instigate another "IBM Compatible" situation, where rival manufacturers like Sony, Hitachi, and Toshiba would compete to build better and cheaper computers that could run compatible software. MSX gained some traction, mostly in Japan and South Korea,

Figure 40.2   Hideo Kojima at the 2010 Japan Expo. (Photo courtesy of Georges Seguin.)

but fell far short of Microsoft's hopes for a true global standard.

There was a silver lining for Kojima, however. The MSX may have lacked the prestige and market share of Nintendo's Famicom system, but that also meant less competition—and less scrutiny. Kojima was also excited about its power; it enabled "animations that wouldn't have been possible

on the Famicom."[4] Indeed, when Konami ported the game to that system, they made some glaring omissions—including the titular Metal Gear end boss!

The title did well enough, however, that Konami ordered a sequel—this time exclusively for the Famicom. Since Kojima was still assigned to the MSX division, though, he didn't know anything about it until after the fact. "I was quite new at the company and had no influence," said Kojima.[4] The resulting game, *Snake's Revenge* (1990), was by most accounts a shoddy and shameless cash-grab and is not considered part of the *Metal Gear* canon. Kojima, meanwhile, did his own proper sequel called *Metal Gear 2: Solid Snake* for the MSX2.

The *Metal Gear* series stayed in the shadows throughout the 16-bit era as Kojima worked on two intriguing graphic adventure games, *Snatcher* in 1988 (released in 1994 for the Sega CD) and *Policenauts* in 1994, which sadly never left Japan. Some sources claim that around this time Kojima was planning a third *Metal Gear* for the 3DO, though support for that system dried up before he finalized them. In any event, around 1995, news and hype began to build about a new *Metal Gear* game in the works for Sony's PlayStation. Two years later, Konami showed off a video of the game-in-progress at E3. Much was made of the realism of the game's weapons and impressive cinematics, but its "stealth" gameplay was what had people most intrigued: "Thousands of visitors stormed E3 1997 and while many of them went to play *Final Fantasy VII*, all of them left talking about *Metal Gear Solid*"[5] (see Figure 40.3).

I'll instruct you by codec after you reach your target.

Figure 40.3 The game opens with a fantastic cinematic worthy of a Tom Clancy film.

The "tactical espionage action" game viewers saw that day promised a vastly different experience from *Final Fantasy VII* or pretty much any other game, for that matter. For one thing, the weapons were as accurate as the designers could make them; Konami had them dress up in military fatigues and even had them train with a real-life American SWAT team.[6]

By this point, Kojima had risen up the ranks at Konami to the point where he could do things his way—and work with people of his choosing. One of his best people was a young artist named Yoji Shinkawa, who sculpted models of vehicles and other components out of plastic and clay. "He used so many chemicals he had to work from home," said Kojima. "I would visit his apartment every day to check that he was okay."[4]

Kojima chose to add the word *solid* to the title not only to acknowledge the character Solid Snake but also to emphasize the power of the game's three-dimensional (3D) engine. Unlike *Final Fantasy VII*, which used prerendered backgrounds, everything in *Metal Gear Solid* was rendered in 3D—"right down to the littlest details, like items residing on desks and maggots festering on rotting corpses ... There's no 2D trickery here," wrote *GameSpot*'s Jeff Gerstmann.[7] Another major improvement was using real voice actors, not just text. Solid Snake was voiced by David Hayter, who continued to lend his talents to the role until the fifth game, where he was replaced by Keifer Sutherland. "English voice work in *Metal Gear Solid* is surprisingly good," wrote Gerstmann. "What they're actually saying may be a bit hokey and clichéd at times, but at least they deliver the dialogue with the right amount of conviction."

The story concerned a retired soldier, Solid Snake, who is called back to duty to stop FOX HOUND, a group of terrorists who have taken over a nuclear missiles facility on

[5] Gallagher, James. "PlayStation at E3: 1997." *PlayStation.Blog.* June 3, 2010. http://blog.eu.playstation.com/2010/06/03 /playstation-at-e3-1997/ (accessed September 9, 2015).

[6] Bartholow, Peter. "Metal Gear Solid Casts Its Spell." *GameSpot.* September 6, 1997. http://www.gamespot.com/articles/metal -gear-solid-casts-its-spell/1100-2467579/ (accessed September 9, 2015).

[7] Gerstmann, Jeff. "Metal Gear Solid Review." *GameSpot.* September 25, 1998. http://www.gamespot.com/reviews/metal -gear-solid-review/1900-2546002/ (accessed September 9, 2015).

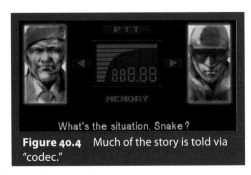

Figure 40.4   Much of the story is told via "codec."

Shadow Moses Island. Snake's job is to sneak into the site, rescue two hostages, eliminate the terrorists, and stop a nuclear missile strike. Snake must go it alone, but his "Codec" (Figure 40.4) allows him to radio for help with puzzles or other problems—and is also used to flesh out the story.

The game's claim to fame, of course, is its stealthy gameplay. Snake could stick to walls, peer around corners, crawl under things, or make noises to distract enemies (see Figure 40.5). If Snake happened to get spotted, the enemy would call for reinforcements to attack him—who will usually easily kill snake with their superior firepower. Snake's best hope at that point was to get back out of sight and stay there, eventually returning the game to "Infiltration mode." A helpful radar system helped Snake to stay out of the fields of vision of soldiers and surveillance cameras, and TERM.G goggles provided night vision. Though stealth was Snake's best ally, he could find and use many different weapons, including a SOCOM pistol, a FA-MAS rifle, C4, grenades, a PSG1 sniper rifle, or even a NIKITA remote-controlled missile. Snake also liked cigarettes, which occasionally proved useful.

Everyone seemed to assume the game would be a smashing success—everyone, that is, but Kojima and his team. "Neither me nor anyone else expected *Metal Gear Solid* to sell at all," claimed Kojima. "That was fortunate, because I didn't have to worry about sales. So pretty much all I did was put in that game all the things I really like."[8] When news arrived that it was flying off the shelves in America, Kojima was more surprised than anyone.

The game's rousing success put Kojima in the spotlight, and his celebrity status grew as work on the inevitable *Metal Gear Solid 2* began. When it was done, many wondered if the fame had gone to his head. While it received glowing reviews in much of the gaming press, many gamers were turned off by the convoluted storyline. The real controversy, though, was that you spent most of the game playing a whiny, annoying character named Raiden instead of Solid Snake. The disappointment over these elements might well have diminished some gamers' enthusiasm for the inevitable third entry in 2004, though many fans now consider it the best in the series. 2008's *Metal Gear Solid 4: Guns of the Patriots* was another rousing success for Konami, earning the highest scores on major gaming sites, though some found the storyline confusing.

Indeed, if there's been one persistent criticism of the series, it's Kojima's tendency for contorted storytelling techniques, often in the form of extended, exposition-laden cut scenes. The net is full of "concise" guides to help newcomers get acquainted with the many intertwining (or downright contradictory) story arcs. "*Metal Gear*'s story is a mess," wrote Luke Plunkett for *Kotaku*. "Hideo Kojima might make great stealth games, but boy,

8   Makuch, Eddie. "Kojima Didn't Think Metal Gear Solid Would Be a Hit." *GameSpot*. March 14, 2014. http://www.gamespot .com/articles/kojima-didn-t-think-metal-gear-solid-would-be-a-hit/1100-6418318/ (accessed September 9, 2015).

the dude also needs an editor."[9] Edward Smith of the *International Business Times* called him a "terrible writer," and claimed that the industry, "hungry for auteurs," has "elevated Kojima to the status of a leading light ... We take sexism, stupidity, plagiarism, and trash and rebrand them as stylish, personal, homage, and Japanese. We incrementally and imperceptibly lower the bar for this already

Texture/Pixel Artist
Ikuya Nakamura

Figure 40.5   When Snake is backed against a wall, the camera zooms back to give you a look down the corridor.

struggling culture."[10] No levelheaded critic could dismiss the occasional mangled translation, inappropriate gag, or self-indulgent cut scene. Yet even Homer nodded, and there are plenty of profound moments in each game to compensate for Kojima's faults. My favorite quote from Snake is "building the future and keeping the past alive are one and the same thing," from *Metal Gear Solid 2.*

Others have more tolerance or even an appreciation for Kojima's awkward humor or outright zaniness, such as the recurring diarrhea jokes, ogling of female characters, or the conversation Snake has with a talking cat in *Metal Gear Solid: Peace Walker* (2010). A trademark gag is the cardboard box "disguise," which Snake dons to sneak around ... in plain sight of enemies.

If there's one thing that fans can agree on, it's the meticulous attention to detail, the epic boss fights, Snake's cool devices, and, above all, the willingness of its designers to push the boundaries of the medium.

40.1 Playing *Metal Gear Solid* Today

There are several ways to play *Metal Gear Solid* today beyond playing it on a vintage Sony PlayStation. Konami offers the game as part of its *Metal Gear Solid the Legacy Collection* for PS3, and there's the *Metal Gear Solid HD Collection* for the Xbox 360, PS3, and Vita. The latter, as the title implies, updates the graphics for modern displays. Windows users have fewer options; you could search out one of Microsoft's *Metal Gear Solid* copies from 2000, but anticipate compatibility issues. If I were you, I'd just track down a vintage PlayStation; they're cheap and fun to collect for anyway.

---

[9] Plunkett, Luke. "A Concise Guide to Metal Gear's Overblown Story." *Kotaku.* March 11, 2014. http://kotaku.com/a-concise-guide-to-metal-gears-overblown-story-1541752116? (accessed September 9, 2015).

[10] Smith, Edward. "Metal Gear Solid 5: It Is Time to Admit Hideo Kojima Is a Terrible Writer." *International Business Times.* August 27, 2015. http://www.ibtimes.co.uk/metal-gear-solid-5-it-time-admit-hideo-kojima-terrible-writer-1517034 (accessed September 9, 2015).

Chapter 41

Ocarina of Time: Miyamoto's Finest Hour

The 1998 holiday season was a tough time for Nintendo. Their Nintendo 64 console had taken a beating in the gaming press for its outmoded cartridge technology, and Sony's PlayStation was rocking the charts thanks to groundbreaking hits like *Tomb Raider*, *Final Fantasy VII*, and *Metal Gear Solid*. However, the Nintendo 64 had its share of hits, too. Besides *Super Mario 64*, which we covered in Chapter 37, there was Rare's *GoldenEye 007* (1997), an undisputed masterpiece that introduced millions of console gamers to the first-person shooter genre. Nintendo had also updated its *Star Fox* and *Mario Kart* series to support the console. Despite the success of these titles, Nintendo was still losing ground to Sony, whose lower royalties and CD-ROM support gave them an edge with third-party developers. In September of 1997, the PlayStation had more than 300 games, and the Nintendo 64 only had 45. It appeared as though the Nintendo 64 might soon be joining the Sega Saturn in the "Where are they now?" file.

Nintendo's lack of third-party support was a dire matter, even if their in-house development team was second to none. If anyone knew how dangerous it was to go alone, it was Miyamoto. If *The Legend of Zelda: Ocarina of Time* was anything short of flawless, the Nintendo 64 was done, and most likely Nintendo's future as a console maker.

If *The Legend of Zelda: Ocarina of Time* was not without flaw, it was without peer. It was the greatest game of Shigeru Miyamoto's career, if not of all time (see Figure 41.1).

Its arrival on November 21, 1998, just in time for the vital Christmas season, received an immaculate critical reception by all the major game sites. "To call it anything else [than perfect] would be a bald-faced lie," wrote Gerstmann for *GameSpot*.[1] IGN's Peer Schneider called it "the biggest game of the decade" and gave it his highest recommendation. "If you're making games and you haven't played this game, then you're like a director who has never seen *Citizen Kane* or a musician who has never heard of Mozart."[2] Gaming magazines weren't the only sources of such veneration. After playing it for 4 hours, *Time* magazine's Joshua Quittner declared that it would change the world:

---

[1] Gerstmann, Jeff. "The Legend of Zelda: Ocarina of Time, Reviews" *GameSpot*. November 23, 1998. http://www.gamespot .com/reviews/legend-of-zelda-ocarina-of-time-the-review/1900-2543677/ (accessed September 10, 2015).

[2] Schneider, Peer. "The Legend of Zelda: Ocarina of Time, Reviews" *IGN*. November 25, 1998. http://www.ign.com/articles /1998/11/26/the-legend-of-zelda-ocarina-of-time-review (accessed September 10, 2015).

Figure 41.1   Within this unassuming cartridge lies Miyamoto's greatest masterpiece.

Figure 41.2   Even without the luxury of discs for storage, *Ocarina of Time* managed impressive, even beautiful cinematics.

To those of you who have never played a video game, or even seen one, my rapture will sound goofy. But trust me. In some ways *Zelda* is every bit as compelling as the best painting I've ever seen, or even the best movie. The experience of a good video game is transcendent; *Zelda* is a great video game.[3]

Nintendo had already sold a quarter of a million copies in preorders; within 6 weeks, they'd sold 2.5 million at a staggering $70 per cartridge. The game even triggered an intense demand for real ocarinas, a formerly obscure musical instrument.[4] More importantly, *Ocarina of Time* was luring gamers away from the PlayStation, even with hits like *Crash Bandicoot: Warped* to contend with. "Clever as it is," wrote Quittner, "*Crash* now feels to me—after playing *Zelda* and getting lost in what Miyamoto calls the 'miniature garden'—flat and outdated."

A 2009 retrospective by IGN concluded that *Ocarina of Time* "is the only game made in the last 20 years that genuinely deserves to be called a masterwork," arguing that it "survives the march of time in ways that other landmark games such as *Tomb Raider* do not because of the way its pieces fit together—even the pieces that are not revolutionary."[5] But you get the idea; almost everyone who played the game cherished the experience (see Figure 41.2). It eventually sold nearly 8 million units and is still a top seller on Nintendo's virtual console. Needless to say, it was exactly the shot in the arm the struggling Nintendo 64 console needed to fend off Sony.

---

[3]   Quittner, Joshua. "Foolishly Perfect." *Time*, November 23, 1998: 148.

[4]   King, Sharon. "Can You Play 'Feelings' on the Ocarina?" *New York Times*, February 15, 1999: C4.

[5]   Buchanan, Levi. "Is Legend of Zelda: Ocarina of Time Overrated?" *IGN*. February 11, 2009. http://www.ign.com/articles/2009/02/12/is-legend-of-zelda-ocarina-of-time-overrated (accessed September 10, 2015).

Miyamoto had begun designing *Ocarina of Time* as he was working on *Super Mario 64*.[6] It was originally intended to take advantage of an add-on called the 64DD, which added a proprietary disk drive and Internet connection for access to a dedicated e-commerce site. Never released outside of Japan, the 64DD had the potential to rectify many

Figure 41.3   An action shot demonstrating the innovative "Z-Targeting" system.

of the perceived faults of the Nintendo 64, especially the limited storage capacity of its cartridges. However, Nintendo canceled it shortly after a repeatedly delayed and ultimately lackluster launch in 1999.

Miyamoto must have had his own doubts about the 64DD, but he kept them to himself. He did, however, prepare for a worst-case scenario in which memory constraints would force him into a design similar to *Super Mario 64*, with separated zones instead of the open-world environment the game became known for.[7] Fortunately, Nintendo allowed him to publish it on a 32-megabyte cartridge.

Ocarina of Time adapted the series for the three-dimensional (3D) era, adopting many of the techniques worked out for *Super Mario 64*. However, it introduced "Z-Targeting," which let Link lock on to a target and perform strafing and other maneuvers without having to wrestle with the camera (see Figure 41.3). Another nice feature was that the function of the controller's buttons, which were always displayed on screen, changed depending on the context—a versatile but intuitive control scheme. It also incorporated many clever puzzles, with several based on the titular musical instrument. The boss battles were more than just audiovisual spectacles; each required a unique strategy and granted a special boon if defeated.

Perhaps the most impressive aspect of the game was its vivid, picturesque game world. There was so much to do and explore that players quickly forgot about the supposed crippling limitations of the cartridge format. An exquisite soundtrack by Koji Kondo added to the already considerable ambience. Instead of hours of prerendered footage, the game relied on real-time rendered cut scenes to advance the story. Text was used instead of digitized recordings of voice actors, but characters generally had sound effects, such as a grunt, sigh, or yawn, to lend them personality (see Figure 41.4). It's easy to forget that the characters aren't actually talking; your imagination fills the void.

---

[6] Staff. "Miyamoto Speaks." *Nintendo Power*, October 1989: 65–67.

[7] Watts, Martin. "Translated 1997 Interview with Miyamoto Reveals Nintendo 64 Insights." *Nintendo Life*. April 13, 2013. http://www.nintendolife.com/news/2013/04/translated_1997_interview_with_miyamoto_and_itoi_reveals_nintendo_64 _insights (accessed September 10, 2015).

Figure 41.4   The artists did a good job conveying emotion on the character's faces.

This last point brings me to what I think is the game's true appeal, or at least what allows it to hold up so well after all these years. Unlike so many other early 3D games, whose developers made a virtue out of leaving as little to the imagination as possible, *Ocarina of Time* did the opposite. It is possible for an orchestra of a hundred musicians to move the soul. The same can be said of a boy and his 12-hole ocarina (see Figure 41.5). If Miyamoto has taught us anything with his great masterpiece, *Ocarina of Time*, it's that skill, talent, and soul will always be a match for pomp and circumstance.

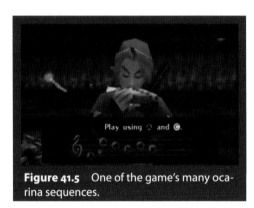

Figure 41.5   One of the game's many ocarina sequences.

There have been several hit *Zelda* games after *Ocarina of Time*, and while several are certainly noteworthy, so far none have managed to eclipse it. According to Miyamoto, a new *Zelda* game is currently in the works for the Wii U, apparently scheduled for release some time in 2016. Miyamoto's role seems to be limited at the moment to consulting on the project. Much like the Nintendo 64, the Wii U is currently struggling for recognition, and a bold new *Zelda* title might be just the thing to revitalize the platform.

41.1 Playing *Ocarina of Time* Today

As with *Super Mario 64*, I recommend picking up a used Nintendo 64 and the cartridge. The systems and games are cheap and fun to collect—yet not old enough to be thought of as "collector's items" to most people. Otherwise, the aforementioned Nintendo eShop makes it easy to acquire the game for Wii, Wii U, DS, or 3DS.

Part V
The Laggards

This section brings us up to modern times. Video games have come a long way since the days of *Spacewar!* and *Pong*, and though outmoded stereotypes of nerdy gamers persist, more people are playing them than ever before. I knew something had changed when my self-described "computer illiterate" grandparents and in-laws bought PCs so they could play *Bejeweled*, *Bookworm*, and the ever-popular *Tetris*. Riding the bus and walking the hallways of my college campus, I see all manner of people playing games on their mobile phones or dedicated handhelds, all but oblivious to the outside world—and certainly not concerned with what I or anyone else thinks about it. "Game Studies" programs at colleges and universities are sprouting like mushrooms. Someone asking the question "Can a video game make you cry?" today would sound more ignorant than profound.

Furthermore, the industry has matured. On the negative side, that means fewer groundbreaking hits like *Doom* or *Super Mario 64*. Indeed, most of the games coming from major publishers are sequels to existing franchises, offering only incremental improvements to well-established gameplay mechanics. Given the exorbitant costs required to make a modern "AAA" title, it's not hard to imagine why publishers prefer to play it safe.

On the positive side, there is now robust "indie" development taking place. Small teams or even individuals are able to develop, publish, and occasionally strike it rich with a breakthrough like *Minecraft* or *Angry Birds.* The mobile phone market and the insatiable demand for "apps" drove much of this development, but there's also a growing demand for lean indie titles on consoles and PCs. Each of the major consoles has its version of an online store where such games are available, and the number of new indie titles appearing on Steam each month is staggering. Admittedly, many of these games are mediocre or downright awful, but there's never been a better time for a talented and dedicated developer to get her work noticed. Furthermore, crowdfunding options like Kickstarter, Indiegogo, and the upcoming Gambitious let gamers, not executives, decide which projects get funded.

I'm usually reticent to predict the future. After all, we've seen time and time again in this book how disruptive real innovations can be—they tend to come out of nowhere, and often to the surprise and dismay of so-called expert analysts. As of this writing, much ink (or, at least e-ink) is being spilled concerning the impending revolution of Augmented Reality Gaming (ARG) and VR headsets like the Oculus Rift or Project Morpheus. It's easy to imagine some truly wonderful potential applications for both, but, as they say, seeing is believing. I wouldn't be surprised if some hopelessly brilliant, "Why didn't I think of that?" application for a smart watch takes off instead.

One thing I can say with confidence is that video games are here to stay, even if they evolve far beyond what is imaginable today.

Chapter 42

Dance Dance Revolution: Konami Shakes Its Money Maker

Don't you hate going to concerts where the musicians just stand around on stage, eyes shut, playing their instruments like robots?[1] What a difference it makes when the performers start dancing and jumping around on stage! Indeed, the hottest pop artists are as well known for their signature dance moves as their pipes. Michael Jackson, Elvis Presley, Madonna, and even Miley Cyrus knew the performance value of a good dance routine.

Until *Dance Dance Revolution* (*DDR*) hit the streets in 1998, watching someone play video games was, if possible, even less interesting than the most stationary concert. There's just no real way to make pushing buttons on a controller or pushing a mouse around look exciting. Even in Korea, where esports are a cultural phenomenon, the spectacle is the game on the screen, not what the player themselves are physically doing at their keyboards. Imagine how dreary it would be to watch a *Starcraft* tournament if all you saw was the players' hands!

The problem is that gaming is mostly a sedentary activity, an aspect that contributes to the persistent stereotype of gamers as pasty, scrawny, or obese teens with less social grace than an Infocom parser. Whenever a so-called gamer is cast in a television show, whether it be *Law & Order*, *X-Files*, *Bones*, or *CSI: Miami*, chances are that he (very seldom *she*) is a whiny wimp with no interest or ability in sports, athletics, or personal hygiene.

Enter *DDR* (Figure 42.1). Standing over 8-feet high, with an impressive speaker system and its own elevated stage, this was an arcade machine like no other. Whoever dared to set foot on that platform would not just see a spectacle on a screen; he or she would *be* the spectacle, much to the delight (or perhaps horror) of everyone else in the arcade. This was no game for the shy, inhibited young men who typically frequented arcades. Indeed, as these types made their way to their favorite fighting, sports, or driving game, it might very well be their bored girlfriends who drifted over to the beckoning *DDR* machine (see Figure 42.2).

---

[1] Unless, of course, the band in question is Kraftwerk. Then it's super cool.

Sometimes described as "karaoke for the feet," *DDR* was another example of that classic design paradigm of "easy to learn, hard to master." The stage was divided into sections, each with four squares arranged in a plus-shape. As a pop song bumped and thumped on the speakers, arrows whizzed by on the screen, indicating which platform/s to step on. A wacky DJ cheered or jeered accordingly as you tried to match the sequence with your feet.

Miguel Balauag, a student at Stanford University, was an arcade-goer in the late 1990s. He soon took notice of the new *DDR* machines and paints a vivid picture of players trying it for the first time:

Figure 42.1   A first-generation *DDR* machine. It certainly got your attention.

Usually they were with a group of friends, and one of them would finally work up the courage to play. She (as it usually was) would have to persuade one of her friends to join her, and they would laugh at themselves throughout the entire song. One time, the friends took a picture of the two players while they posed. *Dance Dance Revolution* was clearly not a typical arcade experience.[2]

DDR was already a hit in Japan by the time it hit America in 1999, but few expected the $15,000 machines to sell in the triple digits.[3] But soon, communities were forming around the game, and expert players spent hours each week (and often a sizable portion of their income) practicing and incorporating their own impressive flourishes.

Details concerning *DDR*'s design and development at Konami are not easy to come by. It seems likely the team was inspired by earlier music-themed games, including SCEI's *PaRappa the Rapper* (1996), their own *Beatmania* rhythm game in 1997, and Metro Graphics' *Bust a Groove* (aka *Bust-A-Move*) in 1998. Each of these games was more popular in Japan than elsewhere, probably because they lacked the exhibitionist qualities

---

[2] Balauag, Michael. "Dance Dance Revolution: A True Revolution." *How They Got Game*. 2004. http://web.stanford.edu/group/htgg/cgi-bin/drupal/?q=node/689 (accessed September 13, 2015).

[3] Tran, Khanh T.L. "'Karaoke for Feet'—In the Latest Arcade Craze, Players Show a Machine Their Fanciest Footwork." *Wall Street Journal, Eastern Edition*, August 16, 2000: B1.

of *DDR*. *Beatmania*, for instance, had a similar setup of rapidly scrolling symbols, but players were merely tapping buttons or rotating a turntable, not dancing. It's mesmerizing to see a talented player at these machines, hands flying in a blur of speed, but admittedly not as sexy as *DDR* aficionados at work. *Bust a Groove* was all about dancing, but players merely controlled the dancers on-screen rather than dance themselves. If there was anything truly revolutionary about *DDR*, it was that shift from on-screen to on-stage performance, a shift that made it as fun to watch as to play.

DDR soon made its way to the Play Station and Dreamcast consoles, where they made for excellent party games. Still, they're hardly a substitute for an arcade machine and an appreciable crowd. They're definitely a good way to practice

Figure 42.2   A couple of cosplay dancers enjoying a later version of the game at FanimeCon 2014. (Photo courtesy of Michael Ocampo.)

and fun way to exercise, however—an aspect that touched off a wave of "exergames" designed precisely for that purpose. *DDR* and similar games were soon showing up for P.E. classes around the country.

The music for *DDR* is mostly licensed from other artists, though some are produced by composers working for Konami. Naturally, the soundtrack has varied over the years, and the constant demand for new tunes led to a lucrative aftermarket for new songs—which could be installed in arcade machines with a new mix kit. To date, Konami has developed 14 iterations and three different "generations" of arcade machines, the latest introduced in 2013.

DDR's success led to a surge of similarly inspired products, most notably RedOctane's *Guitar Hero* (2005) and MTV Games' *Rock Band* (2007). These games focused on making players feel like rock or pop stars and were more appealing to players who'd rather play guitar or play the drums than dance. Ubisoft's *Rocksmith* evolved the concept into a set of music lesson, promising a fun and easy way to learn to play an actual guitar.

Whether to use *DDR* or these later games to learn, show off, exercise, or simply goof around is up to you. But please, don't do it from the couch.

42.1 Playing *DDR* Today

There's really no question about this one. If you want to play *DDR*, you need to do it in an arcade, preferably with a group of friends along to support you. The site http://www .ddrfreak.com tracks machine locations around the country. There are several different options for PS3, Wii, and the Xbox 360, but oddly enough, none for modern consoles. Ubisoft's *Just Dance* and Harmonix's *Dance Central* are reasonable alternatives. Be sure to check what songs are available before making a purchase, however.

Chapter 43

Grand Theft Auto III: The Industry's Bad Boy

Rockstar Games' *Grand Theft Auto* (*GTA*) is another of the industry's largest and most successful franchises (see Figure 43.1). Despite what you may read online, *GTA* wasn't the first game with open-ended or "sandbox"-style gameplay, in which players are basically left to explore and interact with a virtual world as they see fit. Indeed, Gary Penn, one of the game's developers, cites *Elite* (see Chapter 13) as a key influence, going so far as to call *GTA* "*Elite* in a city."[1] Likewise, it was hardly the first game that let players commit atrocities and, contrary to popular opinion, is hardly the worst offender in that regard.

What really made the series influential was the unprecedented realism of the fully realized three-dimensional (3D) world, introduced in the third game (2001). Each subsequent installment has raised the bar set by its predecessor, wowing everyone with the best politically incorrect audiovisuals money can buy.

The first *GTA* was created by DMA Design, a developer based in Scotland who became Rockstar North in 1999. When *GTA* was published in 1997, DMA was best known for an adorable series of puzzle games called *Lemmings* (Figure 43.2), which debuted in 1991 for Commodore's Amiga computer. Even those cutesy games had violent content—the lemmings could die in countless gruesome ways, and you could make them explode in a shower of blood.

After *Lemmings*, DMA landed what seemed like a golden opportunity to develop an exclusive launch title for the Nintendo 64. The game they produced, *Body Harvest*, was an innovative 3D title that foreshadowed much of what was to come with *GTA III*, with open-ended gameplay and the ability to commandeer vehicles. Miyamoto and others at Nintendo objected to the game's blood and gore, however, and it wasn't published until 1998.[2]

Even those who played *Body Harvest* (Figure 43.3) weren't prepared for DMA's "mission-based crime sim," *GTA*. Unlike the later games, which were rightfully celebrated

---

[1] Donovan, Tristan. "The Replay Interviews: Gary Penn." *Gamastura*. January 31, 2011. http://www.gamasutra.com/view/feature/134644/the_replay_interviews_gary_penn.php (accessed September 13, 2015).

[2] McLaughlin, Rus. "IGN PRESENTS: THE HISTORY OF GRAND THEFT AUTO." *IGN*. March 28, 2008. http://www.ign.com/articles/2008/03/28/ign-presents-the-history-of-grand-theft-auto (accessed September 13, 2015).

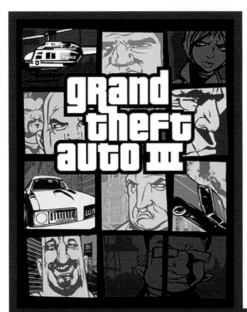

for their graphics, the original game had only a humble top-down perspective, with two-dimensional (2D) graphics that could easily be mistaken for those of the aforementioned Amiga. It was originally called *Race'n'Chase*, and conceived as a multiplayer "racing and crashing game."[3] From the start, the player was intended to commit crimes—one of the missions was a bank robbery, and the design document mentioned carjacking. Pedestrians—including schoolchildren—would wander all around, and could be run over, though it's not clear if this would be rewarded or punished.

The project came close to being canceled, but not because of any moral scruples. The problem was a faulty prototype.

Figure 43.1   The third *Grand Theft Auto* was as controversial as it was innovative. It easily outsold its predecessors and remains one of the industry's best-selling franchises.

"It crashed all the fucking time," said Penn, "and the car handling was appalling ... It was awful."[1] Indeed, the 2D engine was actually a concession to the programmers' inability to do it in 3D, which they attempted four times before giving up.

Even in 2D, the code was so messy that one day when Penn sat down to play, he noticed the police had gone psycho. Their pathfinding routines had gone berserk, and they seemed to be trying to drive right through his car. It was crap. It was madness. But for the first time since he'd started working on the damn thing, he was actually having fun.

Just to make sure he wasn't losing his mind, Penn consulted his fellow designers. "Everybody went, 'Hey, this is actually pretty cool. There's something in this; this is working.'"[1] Instead of toning down the craziness, Penn and the team tried their best to ratchet it up.

Despite their best efforts, the published game was by no means free of bugs. Critics also complained about the sloppy camera and wonky controls. However, the premise of role playing a low-level thug was interesting, if grim. Players marveled at the "freedom" to run over pedestrians, maim or kill Hare Krishnas, pimp prostitutes, steal cars, and, in general, live out their most violent anarchic fantasies (see Figure 43.4).

[3] Ransom-Wiley. "Race'n'Chase: Original GTA Design Docs Posted." *Engadget*. March 22, 2011. http://www.engadget.com/2011/03/22/race-n-chase-original-gta-design-docs-posted/ (accessed September 13, 2015).

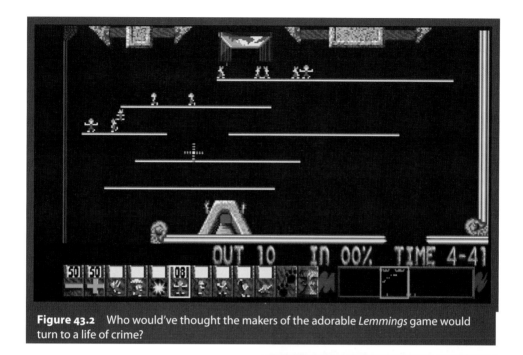

Figure 43.2 Who would've thought the makers of the adorable *Lemmings* game would turn to a life of crime?

Another popular feature that became a staple of the series was an in-game radio with seven fictional stations. Later, licensed tracks would become a defining quality of the series, but for this game, all the music was composed in-house by Colin Anderson, Craig Conner, and Grant Middleton, who by all accounts did a fan-

Figure 43.3 *Body Harvest* was a bit too bloody for Nintendo. (Photo courtesy of David Fuchs.)

tastic job. I particularly liked the theme song, "Da Shootaz," the lyrics of which described the gameplay and set the tone for the rest of the game—fight the power (of the police).

The game became a cult classic, and a sequel appeared in 1999 for Dreamcast, PlayStation, and Windows. It was really just more of the same, with slightly improved graphics and controls.

Meanwhile, other employees at DMA were finishing up *Space Station Silicon Valley* (*SSSV*), a 3D platformer game for the Nintendo 64. Leslie Benzies, lead programmer on that project, took over as producer for *GTA III*.

Sony's PlayStation 2 debuted to great fanfare on March 4, 2000, and was the obvious choice for the new *GTA*. However, it was a notoriously difficult machine to program for. Cory Bloyd of Munkeyfun Studio noted that it took some development teams over a month just to get a single triangle to appear on screen.[4] To ease

Figure 43.4   The first two *Grand Theft Auto* games were top-down 2D games.

the pain, a British team named Criterion Software had released a 3D API named RenderWare that made the process much easier, even if DMA's programmers had to rewrite large chunks of the code to accommodate their purposes.[5] Even with this tool in hand, Benzies was anything but confident. "Being able to actually make [*GTA III*] was a shock to us ... A lot

Figure 43.5   An official screenshot from the PlayStation 2 version of the game.

of people in the studio said we couldn't do it." It was one thing to make a standard first-person shooter with linear levels; a game with a sprawling open world was a different matter entirely (see Figure 43.5).

The transition from 2D to 3D was far from a straightforward process. Dan Houser, cofounder of Rockstar Games (who bought out DMA Design in 1999), said that there were "vast numbers of problems we had not really thought about," such as recording 8000 lines of dialog for the people walking on the streets, and figuring out motion capture routines for the cut scenes. "So many things about the game technically and design-wise had never been done before," said Houser.[6]

[4] Mudgal, Kartik. "Developer explains what it's like developing for each console: PS3 being the hardest." *Gaming Bolt.* July 31, 2012. http://gamingbolt.com/developer-explains-what-its-like-developing-for-each-console-ps3-being-the-hardest (accessed September 13, 2015).

[5] French, Michael. "Inside Rockstar North—Part 3: The Tech." *Develop-Online.* October 5, 2013. http://www.develop-online .net/studio-profile/inside-rockstar-north-part-3-the-tech/0184140 (accessed September 13, 2015).

[6] Miller, Greg. "DAN HOUSER TALKS GRAND THEFT AUTO III." *IGN.* October 11, 2011. http://www.ign.com/articles/2011/10/18 /dan-houser-talks-grand-theft-auto-iii (accessed September 13, 2015).

Then, September 11th happened. Rockstar's headquarters was within walking distance of the World Trade Center, and even the so-called bad boys of the game industry weren't insensitive to the tragedy. Houser pushed the game's release back 3 weeks, giving the team time to scrub material that might hit too close to home, such as a homeless anarchist named Darkel.²

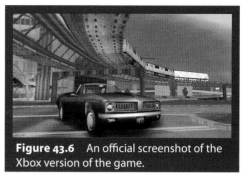

Figure 43.6 An official screenshot of the Xbox version of the game.

When the game finally appeared in shelves on October 22, 2001, it soon became apparent that the third time had been the charm. All the top gaming sites raved about it, especially its huge, realistic game world, voice acting, and soundtrack while cautioning all players to take its mature rating seriously. "As far as videogame content goes," wrote Doug Perry of *IGN*, "it's about as far from *Super Mario 64* as you can get."⁷ Indeed; Mario was lucky to get a kiss from Princess Peach!

The player is again cast as an anonymous thug trying to move up the mob ladder. The setting was Liberty City, "the worst place in America" according to the manual. It was one of the three cities from the first game, and based on New York City. The plot was more involved this time, though, with double crosses, revenge, and love triangles, all told through copious cut scenes and forming the basis of the missions. Players chose how involved they wanted to get in these machinations, if at all. Indeed, you could make your living driving a taxi, ambulance, or fire truck.

Like the previous games, *GTA III* had plenty of driving sequences, but it took a lot of practice to avoid wrecking the vehicles. It took much more skill (and patience) to stay within the law, stopping at traffic signals, and obeying the speed limit, than to drive like a maniac—no doubt part of the design (see Figure 43.6).

GTA III sold more than 13 million copies,⁸ a figure that made sequels and spin-offs all but inevitable. Accordingly, there are now 11 stand-alone games and four expansions in the series. The latest was *Grand Theft Auto V*, released in 2013, which was accompanied 2 weeks later by *Grand Theft Auto Online*, which supported up to 30 people in multiplayer mode. The former received rave reviews, while the latter was panned for its many glitches and server issues.

Each game in the series has been controversial. Much was made of picking up prostitutes in *GTA III*, especially the fact that players could murder them afterward to take back their money. However, that was nothing compared to the ire over "Hot Coffee,"

---

⁷ Perry, Doug. "Grand Theft Auto III." *IGN*. October 22, 2001. http://www.ign.com/articles/2001/10/22/grand-theft-auto-iii-3 (accessed September 13, 2015).

⁸ VGChartz. "Grand Theft Auto 3." *BGChartz*. 2015. http://www.vgchartz.com/game/891/grand-theft-auto-iii/ (accessed September 13, 2015).

an unauthorized mod for *GTA: San Andreas* that enabled an otherwise inaccessible sequence. It was widely and wrongly believed that this mod showed graphic sexual intercourse. The reality was much less titillating—the characters didn't even remove their clothes—but it was still certainly in very poor taste. With or without this mod, the *GTA* series is clearly not for everyone; it is often crude and obscene, and all but the crassest players will encounter situations they find morally objectionable in these games.

According to Benzies, his team never intentionally went for shock value, insisting instead that they merely wished to show what life was really like in "the Old West or the criminal underworld or cocaine-flooded Miami." He attributed the media furor to a ploy to sell more newspapers, and that now "people know that games are no longer all about eating dots or blowing up spaceships; that they can be dark and edgy and challenging."[9] Whether one considers *GTA* "dark and edgy and challenging" or simply "disgusting" is a matter of taste, but there's no denying its role in establishing (and defending) a market for "mature" games.

GTA III's success inspired many other developers to make a sandbox game. Examples include Sony's *The Getaway* (2002) for the PS2, which painstakingly modeled a portion of the city of London for its gangster-themed setting. Then there's Electronic Arts' *The Godfather: The Game* (2006), THQ's *Saints Row* series (2006–), Realtime Worlds' *Crackdown* (2007), and Electronic Arts' *Mercenaries 2: World in Flames* (2008), a third-person shooter set in Venezuela with destructible environments. *GTA III*'s influence is also evident in games as diverse as the later *Far Cry* games, the *Batman: Arkham* series, *Fallout 3*, and even BioWare's *Dragon Age* series.

43.1 Playing *GTA III* Today

GTA III is available for download on Steam for PC and Mac, or you could get it directly from the Rockstar Warehouse (http://www.rockstarwarehouse.com). There are also versions for iOS and Android devices. There are rumors that Rockstar and Take-Two are planning a remastered HD collection for modern systems, but nothing concrete yet. Until then, you can look for the original Xbox or PS2 versions if you prefer to play on a console.

---

[9] Rosenberg, Adam. "Exploring Grand Theft Auto: Vice City's lasting impact on society with Rockstar's Leslie Benzies." *Digital Trends.* December 13, 2012. http://www.digitaltrends.com/gaming/exploring-grand-theft-auto-vice-citys-lasting -impact-on-gamer-culture-with-rockstars-leslie-benzies/(accessed September 13, 2015).

Chapter 44

Halo: Combat Evolved: Spartans Never Die

Bungie's *Halo: Combat Evolved* is, without question, one of the best and most influential first-person shooter (FPS) games ever designed (see Figure 44.1). Its impact is three-fold. First, it helped popularize the FPS genre on consoles. Second, it was not merely "as good as" successful PC FPSs like *Doom* or *Quake*; *Halo*'s ambitious story arcs, characters, and cinematics pushed the genre forward as a storytelling medium. Finally, it gave Americans a sound reason to purchase Microsoft's Xbox console. This might seem like a minor point, at first, but the Xbox represented a viable alternative to Japanese-controlled platforms. Furthermore, its PC-like architecture was much more familiar to former Windows developers than the competition, making it easier to bring their PC games to console.

Bungie's story begins in 1991 with a freeware game for Macintosh called *Gnop!*. It was a humble clone of *Pong* programmed by Alex Seropian, a math major at the University of Chicago. Afterward, Seropian decided to try something more ambitious and managed to sell 2500 copies of a top-down tank game called *Operation Desert Storm*.[1] These were lean years for sure, but Seropian was convinced he had a future in this business.

Things began to look up after the publication of *Pathways into Darkness* in 1993, Bungie's first attempt at a FPS. Its three-dimensional (3D) engine was created by Jason Jones, a programmer Seropian had met in an artificial intelligence class and hired as Bungie's first employee (see Figure 44.2).[2] Inspired by *Wolfenstein 3D*, *Pathways into Darkness* was the first Mac game with real-time texture mapping, and earned Jones a reputation as a "programmer extraordinaire" at the Macworld Expo that year.[3]

The real breakthrough came a year later, when Bungie rolled out its follow-up game, *Marathon*. This was a state-of-the-art FPS game, with support for networked multiplayer,

---

[1] Bungie, Inc. "Bungie History." *Bungie.net.* 2015. https://halo.bungie.net/inside/history.aspx?link=HistoryOfBungie_p1 (accessed September 13, 2015).

[2] Mahin, Bill. "Monsters in a Box." *Chicago Reader.* March 23, 2000. http://www.chicagoreader.com/chicago/monsters-in-a-box/Content?oid=901762 (accessed September 13, 2015).

[3] Deniz, Tuncer. "IMG's The Making of Pathways into Darkness." *Pathways Into Darkness.* December 1993. https://halo.bungie.net/inside/history.aspx?link=HistoryOfBungie_p1 (accessed September 13, 2015).

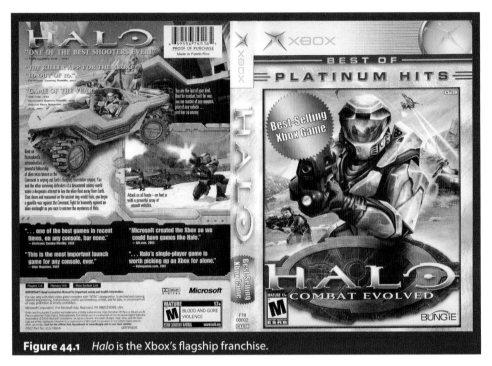

Figure 44.1   *Halo* is the Xbox's flagship franchise.

great graphics, and, according to Guinness World Records, the "first commercial FPS to allow players to use the mouse to freely look around a 3D environment."[4] "It's an optical illusion," admitted Jones later. "All the characters are bitmaps; you could only draw trapezoids. When you look up and down in *Marathon*, it's actually just distorting the geometry." Trick or not, *Marathon* was the game that "changed Bungie from boutique developer to leading Mac publisher, almost overnight."[1]

The new funds helped Bungie to expand into multiplatform publishing. Their first PC offering was a port of *Marathon 2* in 1996. Their next project, *Myth*, was a real-time "tactics" game, which omitted the resource management aspects of games like *Warcraft: Orcs & Humans*. Both *Myth* and its first sequel, published in 1998, were well-received, award-winning productions.

At the MacWorld Expo in the summer of 1999, the consummate showman, Steve Jobs, made a stunning announcement. "We're starting to see some great games come back to the Mac, but *this* is one of the coolest I've ever seen: *Halo*."[5] After assuring the audience that everything was running on a real Mac, Jones gave the audience the world's first glimpse of *Halo*, opening with the now-iconic theme music. This

---

4   Guinness World Records. "First Use of Freelook in a FPS." *Guiness World Records.* 2015. http://www.guinnessworldrecords .com/world-records/first-use-of-freelook-in-a-fps (accessed September 13, 2015).

5   Forum Extreme. "Halo Macworld 1999: First Halo Announcement & Trailer." *YouTube.* November 20, 2008. https://www .youtube.com/watch?v=y2obYHzJ3n8 (accessed September 13, 2015).

was followed by footage of human and alien characters racing across the varied terrain in a variety of the game's now-familiar ground and air combat vehicles.

A strict nondisclosure agreement prevented journalists from discussing what they'd seen, but tantalizing details soon emerged about this "third-person action game." A screenshot surfaced, revealing a chain gun–wielding soldier in futuristic armor against a photo-realistic sunset. An ATV (no doubt a prototype of a Warthog) is perched on a nearby hill. A few months later, Bungie released more details, including the basic story—humans on a mysterious circular structure making a last-ditched stand against the alien Covenant. Much was made of the promised multiplayer mayhem, especially the possibilities of the game's many vehicles and realistic physics: "Bullet casings drift through water at a slower rate than through the air," wrote Daniel Morris of *PC Gamer.*[6]

Figure 44.2   Alex Seropian and Jason Jones.

Rumors and speculation continued throughout the year and into the next, but one in particular stood out: Microsoft was said to be in talks to acquire Bungie.[7] This spectacular rumor was confirmed at E3 weeks later, along with another bombshell: *Halo,* which Jobs had declared a major coup for the Mac, would be exclusive to Microsoft's Xbox console!

As Bill Loguidice and I discussed in our sister book, *Vintage Game Consoles,* many had doubts about the Xbox. In particular, reviewers questioned whether Microsoft or any American company really understood console gaming and saw little reason to think the Xbox would fare better than the 3DO or Apple's Pippin. Meanwhile, the many Mac fans who'd salivated over the footage Jones had shown a few years ago were now informed the game would lack online multiplayer, and was being retrofitted as a standard FPS rather than the intriguing "third-person" game promised earlier. "We had to throw away everything we had to take advantage of the power of Xbox," said

6   Morris, Daniel. "PC Gamer Halo Scoop." *PC Gamer*, October 1999: 40.

7   IGN Staff. "Rumors, Rumors, Everwhere, But None to Drink." *IGN.* June 15, 2000. http://www.ign.com/articles/2000/06/16 /rumors-rumors-everywhere-but-none-to-drink (accessed September 13, 2015).

Jones, who had nothing but nice things to say about the console.[8] *Halo* fans would have to wait a year to play it over Xbox Live.

Of course, with or without Xbox Live support, everyone could see that *Halo* was a fantastic game well worth the cost of buying an Xbox. It was the first game of its console generation to sell more than a million copies: "Statistically, this means that more than six copies ... have been sold

Figure 44.3   Master Chief's first mission was to calibrate his suit, which was a nice pretext for a tutorial.

every minute of every day since its launch on November 15, 2001," reported Microsoft.[9] Major game sites awarded it their highest scores. *IGN*'s Aaron Boulding called it a "can't miss, no-brainer, sure thing, five star, triple A game," adding that "Microsoft created the Xbox so we could have games like *Halo*."[10]

According to Joe Fielder for *GameSpot*, "Not only is this easily the best of the Xbox launch games, but it's easily one of the best shooters ever, on any platform," which must've struck many FPS fans as sheer blasphemy.[11] FPS had been born on PCs, and with the lone exception of Rare's splendid *GoldenEye* (1997) for the Nintendo 64, hadn't done well on consoles. The main problem was the controls. FPS gamers were long accustomed to moving with the left hand on the keyboard (WASD) and aiming and firing with the mouse in their right hand. It was hard to imagine achieving a similar level of precision and comfort with a game controller. The Xbox's controller featured two analog sticks, one for each thumb, and trigger buttons for firing. While the debate still rages about whether keyboard and mouse is preferable, most players found this solution adequate if not superior (see Figure 44.3).

Halo: Combat Evolved was exactly the killer app that Microsoft needed to get its Xbox taken seriously. The first sequel, *Halo 2*, appeared in 2004, and was easily one of the most highly anticipated titles in Xbox history. More than a million and a half copies were pre-ordered, and major news stations covered the immense lines of eager gamers desperate

[8] Tyoama, Kevin. "Holy Halo." *Next Generation Magazine*, May 2001: 60–64.

[9] Microsoft. "Halo: Combat Evolved" for Xbox Tops 1 Million Mark in Record Time." *Microsoft News Center.* April 8, 2002.   http://news.microsoft.com/2002/04/08/halo-combat-evolved-for-xbox-tops-1-million-mark-in-record-time/ (accessed September 13, 2015).

[10] Boulding, Aaron. "Halo Review." *IGN.* November 9, 2001. http://www.ign.com/articles/2001/11/10/halo-review (accessed September 13, 2015).

[11] Fielder, Joe. "Halo Review." *GameSpot.* November 9, 2001. http://www.gamespot.com/reviews/halo-review/1900-2823816/ (accessed September 13, 2015).

Figure 44.4 Shown here is the *Halo: Master Chief Collection*: (a) the "Classic Mode" and (b) the remastered version of the same scene.

to be among the first to buy it. From that point on, no one ever questioned whether console gamers could appreciate FPSs.

To date, there have been five official *Halo* games and four spin-off games. *Halo 3*, published in 2007 for the Xbox 360, was the last made solely by Bungie. The franchise was handed over to 343 Industries, named after the 343 Guilty Spark character. A few

Bungie employees left to join their ranks, including Frank O'Connor, who assumed the title of Franchise Director.

The latest in the main series is *Halo 5: Guardians*, slated for release on October 27, 2015. It will be exclusive to the Xbox One. As of this writing, there is concern about the game's lack of support for local multiplayer, but otherwise seems all but certain to be another best-selling entry in the venerable franchise.

44.1 Playing *Halo: Combat Evolved* Today

If you have an Xbox One, you can't go wrong with *Halo: The Master Chief Collection* (Figure 44.4a and b), which lets you switch between remastered and vintage Xbox graphics modes. It also includes *Halo 2, 3,* and *4*. Otherwise, used Xboxes are cheap and plentiful, and you shouldn't have a tough time finding the disc. There have been ports of the original game for PC and Macintosh available since 2003, but be prepared for compatibility issues running them on modern machines.

Chapter 45

Call of Duty: Wars with Friends

Call of Duty (Figure 45.1) is one of the industry's best known franchises, with global life-time sales exceeding $10 billion. According to CEO Bobby Kotick of Activision Blizzard, publisher of the series, these revenues "far exceed box office receipts for such household movie franchises as *Hunger Games*, *Transformers*, *Iron Man*, and *Avengers* combined."[1] This first-person shooter (FPS) series debuted in October of 2003 exclusively for PC, but has since become a multiplatform, global juggernaut. Many fans play it for its cinematic single-player campaigns, but it's also a prominent eSport. The 2015 *Call of Duty* World Championship was a 3-day international event, with 32 teams competing for $1 million worth of prizes.[2] To date, there have been 15 games bearing the *Call of Duty* title, including the spin-off series *Black Ops*, *Modern Warfare*, *Ghosts*, and *Advanced Warfare*.

Confederate general Robert E. Lee once said, "It is well that war is so terrible, or we should grow too fond of it." The success of *Call of Duty* seems to bear this out. Though many of us would not want to admit it, there is something primordially enjoyable about the idea of combat, especially if we aren't actually being shot at. The genius of the *Call of Duty* series is to carefully walk the line between arcade and simulation, Hollywood, and history. It's not that the terrible consequences of war are never shown; there are plenty of poignant moments in each campaign. However, the focus is on those aspects Lee feared would make us fond of war—namely, the camaraderie, adventure, and glory. In the words of Peter Gabriel, these are games without frontiers, war without tears.

The story of *Call of Duty* begins with *Medal of Honor*, a game developed by DreamWorks Interactive and published by Electronic Arts (EA) for the Sony PlayStation in 1999. DreamWorks Interactive was a collaboration between Microsoft and DreamWorks SKG, a film studio cofounded by director Steven Spielberg along with Jeffrey Katzenberg and David Geffen. In 1998, Spielberg's *Saving Private Ryan* grossed $481 million at the box office and created a demand for more World War II–themed movies and TV shows. However, when Spielberg pushed for a World War II video game, the developers

---

[1] Business Wire. "Call of Duty: Advanced Warfare Is the Biggest Entertainment Launch of the Year." *BusinessWire*. November 20, 2014. http://www.businesswire.com/news/home/20141120005311/en/Call-Duty-Advanced-Warfare-Biggest -Entertainment-Launch#.VfchG_IVhBc (accessed September 14, 2015).

[2] Stuart, Keith. "Call of Duty World Championship 2015: Denial claims victory in thrilling finale." *The Guardian*. March 29, 2015. http://www.theguardian.com/technology/2015/mar/30/call-of-duty-world-championship-2015-denial-claims-victory -in-thrilling-finale (accessed September 14, 2015).

at DreamWorks Interactive told him it was a "poor setting for a game."[3] Spielberg persisted, however, and *Medal of Honor* went into production. Before it was finished, however, the disappointing sales of the studio's *Jurassic Park*–themed games convinced Spielberg to sell out to EA. "Had we not sold, we would have been able to stay in business just based on the success of *Medal of Honor*," said Spielberg, who called it one of the "dumbest things I ever did."[4]

Figure 45.1   Standing out in the open is the quickest way to die in *Call of Duty*.

Unlike most of the FPS games on the market at that time, *Medal of Honor* eschewed fantasy and sci-fi for modern history, incorporating actual World War II weapons like the M1 Garand and Mark II Frag Grenade. It was quickly recognized as one of the best FPS available for the PlayStation, and more than a match for Rare's *GoldenEye* on the Nintendo 64. The ambience, well-designed gameplay, and intuitive control scheme were the talk of the industry. A grand new series had begun.

Eager to expand *Medal of Honor* into a multiplatform franchise, EA tapped id Software to make one for the PC, who in turn sent them to an Oklahoma-based team called 2015, Inc., who made games with id's proprietary 3D engine. They'd only released one product: an expansion pack for Ritual Entertainment's *SiN* game called *Wages of Sin* (1999).

2015 proved up to the challenge; *Medal of Honor: Allied Assault* (2002) was a critically acclaimed masterpiece. Reviewers raved about its portrayal of the storming of Normandy beach, calling it "the most intense and well-executed set piece in shooter history."[5]

In a move reminiscent of David Crane and company's exodus from Atari to form Activision, Grant Collier and Vince Zampella decided that they'd be better off on their own. They called their new studio Infinity Ward and moved from Tulsa to Santa Monica. Their colleague Jason West joined soon after, and then most of the rest of the *Allied Assault* team followed.

---

[3] Campbell, Colin. "HOW STEVEN SPIELBERG INSPIRED TODAY'S TOP SHOOTERS." *IGN*. May 29, 2012. http://www.ign.com /articles/2012/05/30/how-steven-spielberg-inspired-todays-top-shooters (accessed September 14, 2015).

[4] French, Michael. "Spielberg: Selling to EA was 'the smartest and dumbest thing I ever did'." *Develop*. May 14, 2009. http://www.develop-online.net/news/spielberg-selling-to-ea-was-the-smartest-and-dumbest-thing-i-ever-did/0104595 (accessed September 14, 2015).

[5] Wolpaw, Erik. "Medal of Honor: Allied Assault Review." *GameSpot*. January 23, 2002. http://www.gamespot.com/reviews /medal-of-honor-allied-assault-review/1900-2841761/ (accessed September 14, 2015).

Kotick of Activision was happy to support the new venture. Not only was the team battle tested, so to speak, but it was a great chance to stick it to EA, his company's greatest rival. Infinity Ward began work on *Call of Duty*, which they announced in the spring of 2003. From the start, Activision had bigger plans than just a single game—*Call of Duty* was a new brand.[6] The team licensed the

Figure 45.2   There are plenty of great narrative moments in the game. These Russian soldiers can either fight or be shot dead by their own countrymen!

same three-dimensional engine they'd used for *Allied Assault*, but this time pushed it to its limit.

Call of Duty was released in 2003, and reviewers lavished it with praise, especially for the way the player's characters cohered with AI-controlled characters as a unit. Not only was this more realistic from a historical point of view, it also made the game feel immersive. Another nod to realism was the need for cover; players who foolishly rushed out onto the battlefield, guns blazing, quickly learned better. There was even a "shellshock" feature; getting too near an explosion temporarily distorted the character's vision, sound, and movement. The expansiveness of the campaign was also noteworthy. Instead of just showing the war from one side, the game had separate campaigns for the Americans, the British, and the Soviets. It sold more than 4.5 million copies and solidified Infinity Ward's reputation as a triple-A developer (see Figure 45.2).

Meanwhile, Microsoft had a problem. It was set to launch its next-generation console, the Xbox 360, but its flagship developer, Bungie, was nowhere near finished with their next *Halo* game. When an offer came down to have Infinity Ward add a *Call of Duty* game to support the launch, Collier was "ecstatic."[7] They only had 2 years to make it happen, so they hired 50 new employees and scrambled to learn what they could about the new console.

Their efforts paid off. *Call of Duty 2* was easily the best of the Xbox 360's launch titles—indeed, 85% of new Xbox owners picked up a copy.[7] Critics marveled at the meticulous detail of the environments, the special effects, and the almost visceral feeling of immersion one experienced playing it. Once you were done with the epic campaign, it was time to head to Xbox Live and try out the multiplayer (or up to four players in split-screen mode).

6 Fahs, Travis. "IGN PRESENTS: THE HISTORY OF CALL OF DUTY." *IGN*. November 6, 2009. http://www.ign.com/articles/2009/11/06/ign-presents-the-history-of-call-of-duty (accessed September 14, 2015).

7 Takahashi, Dean. "The Making and Unmaking of Infinity Ward." *Venturebeat*. Marcy 7, 2010. http://venturebeat.com/2010/03/07/the-making-and-unmaking-of-infinity-ward/ (accessed September 14, 2015).

Needless to say, Activision was eager to exploit its hot new brand for all it was worth, and commissioned other developers to relieve the pressure. The arrangement occasionally led to drama and even litigation at times, but Infinity Ward continued to grind out best-selling *Call of Duty* titles despite Collier's departure in 2009 and the firing of Zampella and West the following year. This pair wasted little

Figure 45.3   This eerie scene is an effective reminder of the terrible destruction of war.

time founding a new company, Respawn Entertainment, which released its first game, *Titanfall*, in 2014.

The *Call of Duty* series has seen its ups and downs over the years, and much like the *Madden* series, longtime fans like to complain of a lack of innovation or originality in the newer entries (while continuing to buy them). The term *brand fatigue* seems to describe it well. Many fans who lived for *Call of Duty*'s multiplayer have long since migrated to Digital Illusion CE's *Battlefield* series. Still, both series have much to offer, and there are still plenty of us who prefer the cinematic campaigns of *Call of Duty* to multiplayer mayhem (see Figure 45.3).

45.1 Playing *Call of Duty* Today

The original *Call of Duty* is available on Steam for PC. Activision published *Call of Duty: Classic* for the Xbox 360 and PS3 in 2009, which upscaled the graphics to HD. There are rumors of a remastered edition for Xbox One and PS4, but there were no official announcements at the time of this writing.

Chapter 46

Half-Life 2

Half-Life 2 (Figure 46.1) is widely regarded as the finest first-person shooter (FPS) ever made and deserves a spot near the top of any credible "best ever" list of video games. It's been over a decade since its publication on November 16, 2004, and I've played many hundreds of games since my first journey with Dr. Gordon Freeman. Yet, none of them has managed to surpass the enjoyment of that first hoverboat ride, the thrill of using the Gravity Gun, or the terror I felt at Ravenholm. From its iconic opening scenes at City 17 to the epic confrontation at the Citadel, I was hooked.

Half-Life 2 was widely celebrated at the time for its story, a fact made all the more remarkable for a game without cut scenes. Instead, players experienced that story through Gordon's eyes and ears, seeing events unfold or hearing about them from other characters. Identifying with Gordon was easy—he was no super soldier, after all, but a bespectacled physicist; more Walter White than Dwayne Johnson.

The game sold more than 12 million copies and helped make Valve's Steam service a bastion of PC gaming.[1] In an industry in which even mediocre games have sequels in the double digits, fans have longed for a *Half-Life 3* so long that the phrase "Half-Life 3 Confirmed" has become a meme.

Valve Corporation was founded on August 24, 1996, by two millionaires who had earned their fortunes at Microsoft: Gabe Newell and Mike Harrington. Their debut game was the original *Half-Life*, which was published by Sierra On-Line on November 8, 1998. Built with a modified version of id's *Quake* engine, *Half-Life* became an instant classic. All reviewers praised the AI, which was leaps and bounds ahead of most games. The enemies would split up to attempt to flank you, and would even yell "fire in the hole!" at their comrades as they scurried away from your grenades.

The game also did away with discrete levels, a convention born of necessity that had hung on despite advances in technology. Gone also were the intrusive cut scenes that other designers relied on so heavily for exposition (see Figure 46.2).

It wasn't perfect; the loading times between areas turned off some, and some parts of the game were more frustrating than challenging. But these nitpicks didn't stop prominent reviewers from declaring it "the best shooter since the original *Doom*."[2]

---

[1] Chiang, Oliver. "The Master of Online Mayhem." *Forbes*. February 9, 2011. http://www.forbes.com/forbes/2011/0228/technology-gabe-newell-videogames-valve-online-mayhem.html (accessed September 14, 2015).

[2] Green, Jeff. "Half-Life." *Comptuer Gaming World*, April 14, 2010: 168, 169.

Figure 46.1 *Half-Life 2*, a solid contender for the best game ever made.

Instead of rushing a sequel into production, Newell told his team to take as much time and money as they needed to make a truly revolutionary title. "There's going to be no producer making bad decisions about what has to happen on this project," Newell assured them. "The only pressure we have is to build a worthy sequel to *Half-Life*."[3] As the development dragged on, Newell's friend and Valve's cofounder, Harrington, left the company.

A company named GearBox Software was assigned to pick up the slack with two expansions for *Half-Life*. Valve also fostered an active modding community by releasing *Half-Life*'s software development kit and lending their support to the more promising projects. Far and away the most successful was one called *Counter-Strike*. Valve hired its developers, Minh Le and Jess Cliffe, and released it as a stand-alone commercial version in 2000.

At the Game Developers Conference in 2002, Valve had a major announcement, but it wasn't a new game. Instead it was Steam, a digital distribution service. Presented as a benign way to expedite patches, gamers soon learned of a corporate agenda: Steam was an online authentication service—a scheme to thwart pirates and cheaters. Gamers would have no choice but to use it if they wanted to play Valve's games. Many feared that a shutdown or glitch with Steam's servers would mean they wouldn't be able to play their legitimate copies, and others had concerns about privacy.

---

[3] Keighley, Geoff. "The Final Hours of Half-Life 2." *GameSpot*. November 12, 2004. http://www.gamespot.com/articles/the-final-hours-of-half-life-2/1100-6112889/ (accessed September 14, 2015).

Figure 46.2   The first *Half-Life* opens with a terrifying long descent into a secret base. If you stay alert, you'll notice signs of trouble.

It wasn't until November of 2004 that *Half-Life* fans finally got the full-fledged sequel they'd been waiting for (see Figures 46.3 and 46.4). Valve had promised it would be out a year earlier, but got bogged down in a legal battle with their publisher, Vivendi Universal, over Steam. As if that weren't bad enough, Newell realized Valve's servers had been hacked, and confidential information—including source code and a playable version of the game—had been leaked. This situation certainly didn't inspire confidence among those already worried about privacy.[4] "It just felt like each day was getting worse," said Newell. "First the source code. Then the game. And then people started using the game to compose ... screenshots of Dr. Kleiner performing oral sex on Alyx. It's basically your worst nightmare."[3]

When the game finally shipped, reviewers were ecstatic about the game, but not nearly as excited about having to register it on Steam. Jeff Green of *Computer Gaming World* deducted a half point from his review on account of it, calling it an "obtrusive, user-hostile abomination":[5]

4   Dunn, Jeff. "Full Steam Ahead: The History of Valve." *Games Radar.* October 4, 2013. http://www.gamesradar.com/history -of-valve/ (accessed Septemebr 14, 2015).

5   Green, Jeff. "Half-Life 2." *Computer Gaming World,* February, 2005: 78–79.

Because your *Half-Life 2* copy is linked to your Steam account, it severely restricts your ability to trade, resell, or buy the game used. Valve's attempts to limit these practices by forcing you to register with its online program just to play, adding unnecessary clutter to your PC's startup, are just lame.

Figure 46.3   Gordon will find many willing allies along the way. But can he really trust them?

I was one of many who picked up a used copy of the game everyone was raving about. For $30, I thought I was getting a great deal. When I got home and tried to install it, though, I learned that the code had been used already, and I'd have to pay full retail price ($60, if memory serves) to play it! It was my first encounter with Steam, and I felt

Figure 46.4   The Gravity Gun is one of the coolest weapons of any FPS game.

burned. Like most PC gamers, though, I eventually warmed up to the service, especially after it began offering its extremely popular sales program, achievements, and other nifty features.

Half-Life 2 was built using Source, an engine Valve had developed in 2004. It allowed for better audiovisuals and physics than the earlier GoldSrc engine. Five months earlier, Valve used it to remake the first game (*Half-Life: Source*).

Valve released two "episodes," or expansions to *Half-Life 2*, the first in 2006 and the second in 2007. These continued the story, added some enhancements, and were generally well received. A long-awaited third episode has yet to materialize and the source of almost as much rumor and speculation as *Half-Life 3*.

I'll end this chapter with *Portal*, a fiendishly clever puzzle platform game Valve released in 2007. Instead of a gun or crowbar, the player's character (Chell) wields a portal gun, which when fired at an appropriate surface becomes an orange or blue portal. Objects that enter one of these portals exit out the other. From this basic mechanic, the developers derive a fascinating series of puzzles. A sinister AI called GLaDOS monitors the action and taunts the player. *Portal 2*, released in 2011, greatly expanded and refined these concepts into what is truly a masterpiece of the genre.

46.1 Playing *Half-Life 2* Today

Contrary to what many feared back in 2004, *Half-Life 2* is still available on Steam for PC and Mac. There are also versions for PS3 and the Xbox 360.

Chapter 47

World of Warcraft: An MMORPG for the Masses

World of Warcraft (*WoW*) MMORPG's servers were opened to the public on November 23, 2004, and over a decade later, it's still the #1 game in its category. As of this writing, the game has 5.6 million subscribers,[1] down from its peak of 12 million in October of 2010.[2] Even after this precipitous drop, *WoW* is still one of Activision's biggest sources of revenue, and an upcoming expansion called *Legion* will, if history is any indication, send at least a few millions of those former subscribers back to Azeroth (Figure 47.1) (assuming they can still remember their passwords!).

That *WoW* has maintained its dominance in the field despite competition from so-called *WoW* Killers like Funcom's *Age of Conan: Hyborian Adventures* (2008), BioWare Austin's *Star Wars: The Old Republic* (2011), and ArenaNet's *Guild Wars 2* (2012) says something about its staying power. Modern gamers have a wealth of MMORPGs to choose from, including one based on such hallowed properties as J.R.R. Tolkien and *Dungeons & Dragons*. What keeps people and so many gamers of every walk of life logged in every week (if not every day) just to "do their dailies," run a raid with their guild, or level up yet another "alt" character?

Back in 2004, *WoW*'s rise to prominence was hardly a done deal. Sony's *EverQuest* had handily pushed *Ultima Online* off the throne in 1999, mostly by making life easier for novices and updating the graphics. Of course, 5 years later, those graphics weren't nearly as impressive, so Sony released *EverQuest II* on November 8, most likely hoping to stem the flow of emigration from Norrath to Azeroth.

As we saw in Chapters 33 and 34, Blizzard was already a major player in the online gaming world thanks to their Battle.net server. They'd been the first company to really generate profits with an online model, and their hugely successful games earned them the respect, if not the veneration, of the rest of the industry. Much as *EverQuest* (Figure 47.2) had done back in 1999, *WoW* soon became *the* MMORPG, rapidly seizing market share but also swelling that market to unprecedented numbers: By September 19, 2008,

---

[1] Tassi, Paul. "'World of Warcraft' Has Lost 44% of Its Subscribers in Six Months, But That's Okay." *Forbes*. August 2, 2015. http://www.forbes.com/sites/insertcoin/2015/08/05/world-of-warcraft-has-lost-44-of-its-subscribers-in-six-months-but-thats-okay/ (accessed September 15, 2015).

[2] Peckham, Matt. "The Inexorable Decline of World of Warcraft." *Time*. May 9, 2013. http://techland.time.com/2013/05/09/the-inexorable-decline-of-world-of-warcraft/ (accessed September 15, 2015).

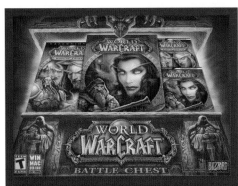

Blizzard announced that the game had reached 10 *million* subscribers, a remarkable figure when we consider that just 10 years previously, *Ultima Online* had become the first to hit 100,000.[3]

The industry first became aware of *WoW* at a London trade show in 2001. Bill Roper, who gave the presentation, described a game with "faster, more action-oriented combat, a polished

Figure 47.1   I'm not sure whether to call this one a game or a "lifestyle." I've certainly spent a good portion of my life questing and adventuring in Azeroth!

interface, and an accessible format to reach a wider audience than games in the genres typically do."[4] Online play wouldn't be a "value add" as it had been with *Diablo*; players would have to buy the game and then pay a monthly subscription for access. Roper said the game

Figure 47.2   Before there was *World of Warcraft*, there was *EverQuest*. Some gamers still prefer it, but many abandoned their accounts, never to return.

had already been a full year in development, and that beta testing might take another. In reality, it'd be another 3 years, but the wait was worth it.

Sam Didier, Blizzard's art director, said that the inspiration for *WoW* came during the development of *Warcraft III*. "At one time, we had a behind-the-character camera in *Warcraft III*, much like you see in *WoW* now. We were thinking of a slightly different, RTS-slash-RPG vibe for the game."[5] Many of Blizzard's designers were avid fans of *EverQuest*, including Rob Pardo, vice president of game design. In fact, his role as leader of a prominent guild on that game helped get him the job. There were many ideas floating about possible settings for the game, but the team eventually settled on their already-established *Warcraft* universe.

---

[3] Bartle, Richard A. "From MUDs to MMORPGs: The History of Virtual Worlds." In *International Handbook of Internet Research*, by Jeremy Hunsinger, Lisbeth Klastrup, and Matthew M. Allen, 23–39. New York: Springer Science & Business Media, 2010.

[4] Parker, Sam. "ECTS 2001: World of Warcraft Announced." *GameSpot*. September 2, 2001. http://www.gamespot.com /articles/ects-2001-world-of-warcraft-announced/1100-2810134/ (accessed September 15, 2015).

[5] Fahey, Rob. "The Making of World of Warcraft." *Eurogamer.net*. Number 8, 2009. http://www.eurogamer.net/articles/the -making-of-world-of-warcraft-article (accessed September 15, 2015).

One of the game's most distinctive features is its cartoonish aesthetic, which was chosen largely as a concession to the game engine. "Any game will age," said Chris Metzen, vice president of creative development, "but there's something timeliness and Disney-ish about *WoW*'s look."[5] A more realistic-looking game would have aged much less gracefully.

Besides impressive audiovisuals and an intuitive interface, the developers had clearly benefited from a careful study of the competition. Although there are many aspects of the game we could talk about, perhaps the most significant is its careful balance between PVP (player versus player) and PVE (player versus environment). Although, like *EverQuest, WoW* offered dedicated servers for PVP, the rules for PVP on regular servers were relaxed. Players who wanted to fight other players had several options at their disposal, from harmless duels to battlegrounds, where members of the two opposing factions (allies and hordes) clashed in battle. However, at any time, players could flag their characters for PVP, making it possible for any other flagged character to attack them. The game encouraged PVP mostly in the battlegrounds, where players could compete for special titles and equipment (see Figure 47.3).

PVE is probably where *WoW* shines the most, however, ensuring that even the most antisocial player has plenty of fun things to do (see Figure 47.4). This is most evident in the quest structure; there were hundreds of possible quests to fulfill, many of which were easy enough for a solo player to complete. Indeed, I've known many players who never joined a guild or even a group; they only played alone, and liked it just fine that way. According to Metzen, *WoW*'s focus on quests was a response to the problem of getting lost in other MMOs. "You would simply head out, and if you found yourself in a place that

Figure 47.3   There are many races and classes to choose from, and each combination offers a unique experience.

Figure 47.4   Loot, loot, and more loot. The quest for a higher item level never ends.

was above your level, you got clobbered."[5] Quest givers were identified with gold exclamation points over their heads, an effective (if comical) design.

There were also quests for groups, which usually involved entering an "instance." This concept of "instances" is particularly important, since the problem it solved was one of the main complaints about *EverQuest*. The nature of MMORPGs makes it hard for one person or even one group to complete certain objectives, such as defeating a particularly powerful foe. By the time the group arrives on the scene, another group has already killed the beast. To make matters worse, some players may opt to "kill steal" or "boss camp," meaning to either swoop in at the last minute to finish off and loot a monster (and thus gaining the treasure and experience), or simply hanging around where the monster reappears after death, selfishly killing it again and again before anyone else can respond. This type of malignant player, called a "griefer," is too common on MMOs and is the reason many otherwise satisfied players cancel their subscriptions.

The "instance" solved many of these problems by making certain areas of the game unique to an individual player or group. When a group entered an instance together, a special version of that instance was created just for them; no other players were allowed inside. Blizzard later added a "looking for group" tool to help players find groups for instances, and eventually a "looking for raid" tool for bringing together larger groups for "raiding," or larger, 10- to 40-person instances with much tougher bosses and better loot.

Not many would claim *WoW* was perfect then or now, but for many, it had just the right balance of complexity. It was remarkably easy to create a character and get started in the game, and new abilities were added gradually, smoothing out the learning curve. Expansions were much less frequent than we've seen in past MMORPGs, which made

Figure 47.5   The *Mists of Pandaria* expansion added an Asian-themed land, a panda race, and a monk class. Apparently, someone at Blizzard had watched *Kung Fu Panda* a few too many times.

their eventual releases into major events that brought in new players as well as encourage old ones to return. To date, there have been five of these: *The Burning Crusade* (2007), *Wrath of the Lich King* (2008), *Cataclysm* (2010), *Mists of Pandaria* (2012) (Figure 47.5), and *Warlords of Draenor* (2014). In addition to these commercial expansions, Blizzard has regularly issued mandatory patches, which added content and tweaked or made major revisions to the game mechanics.

The future of *WoW* seems bright, especially now that the next expansion, *Legion*, is just around the corner. Even if it's half the size it was at its peak, *WoW*'s player base is still large enough to make it easy to find and join a group for instancing or raids, and there are always plenty of solo-player activities to do whenever you log in. For longtime players such as myself, *WoW* is not so much a game as a favorite destination—a splendid vacation from reality that's always just a few clicks away.

47.1 Playing *WoW* Today

Simply go to http://us.battle.net to begin a free trial of the game; you can level a character up to 20 before taking out a subscription. There are clients for Mac or PC. There have long been rumors of a client for consoles, but I wouldn't hold my breath.

Chapter 48

Wii Sports: Let Grandpa Teach You

As 2006 drew to a close, Nintendo's dominance as a console maker seemed like a distant memory. Its Nintendo 64 had barely held its own against Sony's PlayStation, thanks in large part to *Super Mario 64* and *Ocarina of Time*. Its next console, the GameCube, languished in third place behind the PlayStation 2 and a new contender, Microsoft's Xbox. When news arrived in 2005 about Nintendo's "Revolution" console, it was easy to be cynical. While Sony and Microsoft were touting the awesome technology of their upcoming PS3 and Xbox 360, respectively, Nintendo was once again sticking to its philosophy of doing more with less. "It's not all about having 'turbo power,'" said Nintendo president Iwata. "It's about what you do with it."[1]

To many, "Revolution" seemed more like a desperate attempt to catch up to the innovations of previous generations. While perhaps "revolutionary" for a Nintendo console, full-capacity optical discs, an online gaming service, and backward compatibility were hardly new. As always, Nintendo played up its ever-popular *Mario* and *Zelda* franchises, but even these venerable titles no longer commanded the near-universal devotion they once enjoyed.

The only aspect of the system that truly had the potential to be revolutionary—or catastrophically awful—was the controller. Nintendo was tightlipped about the details, but rumors swirled about a newfangled, wireless device with gyroscopes. Others imagined a stylus technology similar to the DS. What was finally revealed at the Tokyo Game Show in 2005 was a white stick that looked like a TV remote. A secondary attachment called a "Nunchaku," which connected to the stick with a short cable, added an analog stick and a couple of trigger buttons. The contraption looked more like a medical device than a gamepad.

According to Miyamoto, neither the controller nor the system was intended to appeal to mainstream gamers: "We want something that anyone, regardless of age or gender, can pick up and play. We want a controller that somebody's mother will look at and not

---

[1] Thorsen, Tor, and Tim Surette. "Nintendo's Revolution Is Nigh." *GameSpot*. May 17, 2005. http://www.gamespot.com /articles/nintendos-revolution-is-nigh/1100-6125078/ (accessed September 15, 2015).

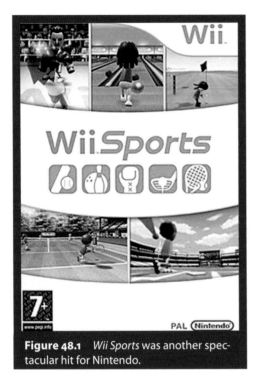

Figure 48.1 *Wii Sports* was another spectacular hit for Nintendo.

be afraid."[2] Later, Nintendo announced that even the name of its console would reflect this desire for inclusivity:

Wii sounds like "we," which emphasizes this console is for everyone. Wii can easily be remembered by people around the world, no matter what language they speak. No confusion. No need to abbreviate. Just Wii.[3]

Naturally, the Wii puns flowed freely: "Mum, I finished my homework. Can I play with my Wii some more?" At this point, it was even some Nintendo stalwarts who must have been rethinking their commitment to the brand.

But then there was *Wii Sports.* Suddenly, everything made sense (see Figure 48.1).

Wii Sports was not a single game, but rather a collection of casual games: baseball, boxing, golf, tennis, and my favorite, bowling. Each revealed the genius of the Wii's unusual controller; the motions you made with it were the same ones you'd make actually engaging in the sport, and were reflected by the onscreen character (a customizable "Mii"). The simulation wasn't perfect, and the graphics, while charming and quite serviceable, were hardly next gen. "If you're the hardcore type who wants a deeper sports game, you will find *Wii Sports'* overall depth sorely lacking," wrote one reviewer.[4]

But *Wii Sports*, like the system it was designed for, was never intended for them. Nintendo had reckoned—and reckoned correctly—that there was a much, much larger market for videogames than anyone had realized. That market was the laggards. Many had never played a videogame before. But now these men, women, moms, dads, grandmas, grandpas, boys, and girls looked at the Wii's controller, and they were not afraid.

[2] MacDonald, Mark. "Revolution Controller Revealed." *1up.com.* September 15, 2005. http://www.1up.com/news/revolution -controller-revealed (accessed September 15, 2015).

[3] Cole, Vladimir. "Nintendo 'Revolution' Now Called Wii." *Endgaget.* April 27, 2006. http://www.engadget.com/2006/04/27 /nintendo-revolution-now-called-wii/ (accessed September 15, 2015).

[4] Casamassina, Matt. "Wii Sports Review." *IGN.* November 13, 2006. http://www.ign.com/articles/2006/11/14/wii-sports -review (accessed September 15, 2015).

Wii Sports sold nearly 83 million copies, making it the second best-selling game of all time—placing it, appropriately enough, just behind *Tetris*.[5] But *Tetris* was ultimately a solitary game. *Wii Sports* was more fun with a group, and just about anybody could play it with you. The mainstream press marveled as the units even made their way into retirement homes,

Figure 48.2 These players are enjoying a bout of boxing. (Photo courtesy of David Murphy.)

where geriatrics formed their own virtual bowling leagues. A 72-year-old named Flora Dierbach observed that "a lot of grandparents are being taught by their grandkids. But, now, some grandparents are instead teaching their grandkids."[6] It was also a hit on college campuses, where it established itself as the ultimate party game (see Figure 48.2).

Figure 48.3 Katsuya Eguchi. (From http://gamasutra.com/view/feature/214472/diversity _communication_and_.php?print=1.)

Wii Sports was produced by Katsuya Eguchi (Figure 48.3), a 41-year-old who'd joined the company back in 1986. He'd helped design some of their biggest titles, including *Super Mario Bros. 3*, *Star Fox*, *Super Mario World*, and *Animal Crossing*. His basic design philosophy for *Wii Sports* was to keep it simple: "Not every game has to be like an encyclopedia. There is nothing wrong with magazines and comics." He also wanted to make a game that people would enjoy watching others play as much as playing themselves.[7] Clearly, he and his team succeeded on both counts (see Figure 48.4).

The Wii was the right system, with the right game, at the right time. A year later, Apple would launch the first incarnation of its iPhone, popularizing the "smartphone" and "apps" for every conceivable purpose, including, of course, all the casual games you

[5] IR Information. "Top Selling Software Sales Units." *Nintendo.co.jp*. March 31, 2015. http://www.nintendo.co.jp/ir/en/sales /software/wii.html (accessed September 15, 2015).

[6] Yam, Marcus. "Wii Invades Retirement Homes." *Daily Tech*. February 22, 2007. http://www.dailytech.com/Wii+Invades +Retirement+Home/article6191.htm (accessed September 15, 2015).

[7] Iwata, Satoru. "Iwata Asks: Wii Sports." *Nintendo*. n.d. http://iwataasks.nintendo.com/interviews/#/wii/wii_sports/0/0 (accessed September 15, 2015).

could ever want—no console required. The iPad and ensuing tablet bonanza saturated the market with cheap, capable devices with much larger screens—more than sufficient for casual games. Thus, it's hardly surprising that Nintendo was unable to duplicate the Wii's success with the Wii U.

Figure 48.4   The bowling game was by far my favorite part of *Wii Sports*. All the fun of bowling with no fear of athlete's foot!

Still, I wouldn't rule Nintendo out yet. As of this writing, the rumor mill is churning with speculations about the "Nintendo NX," apparently a hybrid console/handheld device that might also have smartphone capabilities. It's hard to imagine what a killer app for such a contraption might look like, but if anybody does, I'm betting it's Nintendo.

48.1 Playing *Wii Sports* Today

The cheapest solution is to buy a used Wii, which will probably come with a copy of the game. If not, it's one of the cheapest you'll find for the system. The Wii U is backward compatible with the disc, but you'll need some original Wii Remotes.

Chapter 49

Angry Birds: Slingshot to the Top

Rovio Entertainment's *Angry Birds* is a textbook case of what Clayton M. Christensen defines as a "disruptive innovation":

> Generally disruptive innovations were technologically straightforward, consisting of off-the-shelf components put together in a product architecture that was often simpler than previous approaches. They offered less of what customers in established markets wanted and so could rarely be initially employed there. They offered a different package of attributes valued only in emerging markets remote from, and unimportant to, the mainstream.[1]

There is little about *Angry Birds* that one might call original or technologically impressive. Indeed, "artillery games" have been around at least since the 1970s. These games had players in tanks, cannons, or catapults lobbing projectiles at each other, taking turns adjusting their angle and initial velocity until one of them connected with the other. Indeed, the Flash game *Crush the Castle* employed a similar flinging mechanic just a few months earlier. *Angry Birds* (Figure 49.1) was no technological breakthrough, either. As a bootleg cartridge demonstrated, it even runs smoothly on a Nintendo Entertainment System (NES).

But what *Angry Birds* had going for it was the "different package of attributes" Christensen was talking about. It was perfectly suited for its target platform, iOS, and took advantage of its touch screen to provide a wonderfully intuitive and tactile control scheme. Many iOS games then and now were still designed with console or PC paradigms; they were thus not optimized for the unique affordances provided by the iPhone or iPad. *Angry Birds* was built specifically for touch devices.

Furthermore, *Angry Birds* (Figure 49.2) was bursting with personality. Each type of bird had its own color, shape, and ability. The blue bird, for instance, split up into three birds when you tapped it. The white bird dropped exploding eggs, and the green bird would

---

[1]   Christensen, Clayton M. *The Innovator's Dilemma.* Boston: Harvard Business School Press, 1997.

Figure 49.1 *Angry Birds* was a killer app for iOS and Android.

Figure 49.2 *Angry Birds* made excellent use of the iPhone's touch screen. Pulling back the slingshot feels natural, and shooting the birds through the air is terrific fun.

swing back around like a boomerang. Learning the different functions of each bird was a key part of completing the game. That called for a considerable amount of strategy, as well as precision. However, the levels weren't so long or involved to make losing all that frustrating.

Finally, for a mere 99 cents, how could you go wrong? Nearly 2 billion people have downloaded one of the games, which have now become a huge franchise with its own toys, clothes, and cartoon series.[2] A feature film was released in May of 2016.

According to Mikael Hed, CEO of the Finnish company, *Angry Birds* started out as a single screenshot "of this angry bird character just trudging around on the ground."[3] He had solicited proposals for the studio's next game, and most were highly detailed—certainly more thought out than just this one image, submitted by Jaakko Iisalo. Something about it captured the team's imagination—but how to make a game out of it?

The answer came from an unlikely source—the newspaper. At the time, the swine flu pandemic was making headlines, and someone thought sickly green pigs would make great opponents for the birds.[4] It didn't make much sense, but neither do most cartoons.

[2] Gaudiosi, John. "Rovio Execs Explain What Angry Birds Toons Channel Opens Up To Its 1.7 Billion Gamers." *Forbes.* March 11, 2013. http://www.forbes.com/sites/johngaudiosi/2013/03/11/rovio-execs-explain-what-angry-birds-toons-channel-opens -up-to-its-1-7-billion-gamers/ (accessed September 15, 2015).

[3] Rigney, Ryan. "The Origins of Angry Birds." *PC World.* October 2, 2010. http://www.pcworld.com/article/206831/the _origins_of_angry_birds.html (accessed September 15, 2015).

[4] Mundy, Jon. "Interview: Rovio on the origin of Angry Birds, being inspired by swine flu, and why you may never see an Angry Birds 2." *Pocket Gamer.* October 13, 2010. http://www.pocketgamer.co.uk/r/Multiformat/Angry+Birds/news.asp ?c=24243 (accessed September 15, 2015).

Rovio estimated that iPhone users spent a combined 1 million hours per day helping the birds add injury to insult to those infernal pigs (see Figure 49.3).

Charles L. Mauro performed a cognitive analysis of the game in 2011 in an effort to understand and articulate its appeal. He concluded:

Figure 49.3   The designers were careful not to make the pigs look too scary or menacing.

> In the context of *Angry Birds*, success is bound up in slowing down that which could be fast, erasing that which is easily renewable, and making visual that which is mysterious and memorable.[5]

Mauro pointed out that although the game's design is only deceptively simple, it's actually quite clever. For instance, at several points, the action seems to lag; a pig might teeter for several seconds on an edge before falling off. This would get boring in most games, but Mauro claims (and I agree) that in *Angry Birds*, such moments are necessary—they give you time to relax as well as think about your strategy. Mauro makes several other cogent points; I highly recommend his essay.

To date, there have been 12 games in the *Angry Birds* series and three spin-off games. The latest, *Angry Birds 2*, was released in 2015. While its improved audiovisuals were well received, the "freemium" model of payment it introduced was not. The game was free to download, but after losing five lives, you had to wait half an hour for each bird to regenerate. Naturally, you could spend real money to speed up this process, but there were no options to simply buy the game outright.

The unprecedented success of *Angry Birds* ignited a gold rush of casual games for iOS and Android, but few achieved anywhere near the success of Rovio. *Flappy Bird* (2013) was an odd exception; its Vietnamese developer, Dong Nguyen, actually removed his game after its sudden international success made him an instant celebrity.[6] For every *Angry Birds* or *Flappy Bird*, of course, there are hundreds, if not thousands, of seemingly equally compelling games that are lucky to receive a dozen downloads. A 2012 study by App Promo found that 59% of apps don't even break even on their development costs.[7]

---

[5] Mauro, Charles L. "Why Angry Birds is so successful and popular: A cognitive teardown of the user experience." *PulseUX Blog.* February 6, 2011. http://www.mauronewmedia.com/blog/why-angry-birds-is-so-successful-a-cognitive-teardown -of-the-user-experience/ (accessed September 15, 2015).

[6] Russell, Brandon. "Flappy Bird Creator Says He's Pulling the Game for Good Tomorrow." *Techno Buffalo.* February 8, 2014. http://www.technobuffalo.com/2014/02/08/flappy-bird-getting-pulled-ios-google-play/ (accessed September 15, 2015).

[7] App Promo. "Wake Up Call—If You Spend It, They Will Come." *App Promo.* May 2, 2012. http://app-promo.com/wake-up -call-infographic/ (accessed September 15, 2015).

One can attribute the enviable success of *Angry Birds* to meticulous design, colorful characters, lucky timing, or some ineffable quality like personality or soul. I suspect it's some combination of each.

49.1 Playing *Angry Birds* Today

For obvious reasons, I suggest playing it on a touch-enabled device; a mouse, keyboard, or gamepad just isn't the same. Versions are available for just about every phone and tablet.

Chapter 50

Minecraft: Let Them Build It, and They Will Play

It is only fitting that the last and most recent game of this book is Markus "Notch" Persson's sandbox game *Minecraft*. Initially released on May 17, 2009, *Minecraft* brings us back almost full circle, to the days of the great innovators. The hackers of the Massachusetts Institute of Technology (MIT) loved building and tinkering with systems, from elaborate railroad models to sophisticated computer programs. Where some people saw only challenges to overcome, hackers found opportunities to create, and we have the whole universe of video games to thank for it. They would have loved *Minecraft*.

Persson (see Figure 50.1), a Swedish programmer and designer, became interested in game development at the tender age of seven, when his dad bought a Commodore 128. At the time, computer magazines were still printing programs in the form of source code, which Notch enjoyed typing into the computer. Naturally, this led to much learning about and experimentation with the code, and by eight, Persson had made his first game.[1] These skills served him well in his high school programming class, in which he made a version of *Pong* and impressed his teacher enough to skip the rest of the course.[2] He dropped out before finishing high school, moving from one tech-job to another. He was working at jAlbum, a maker of web-based photo albums, when he started development of *Minecraft* in his spare time. It took him about a week.[3] The game's iconic, blocky aesthetic was the product of necessity—he needed to finish the game fast to have enough money to fund his next side project.

Minecraft was inspired by an earlier block-based game called *Infiminer*, released in 2009. This "first-person competitive mining game" featured a procedurally generated world of blocks with an unmistakable resemblance to the later game. As the title suggests, it was focused on mining; players could dig down in search of valuable mineral

---

[1] Handy, Alex. "Interview: Markus 'Notch' Persson Talks Making Minecraft." *Gamasutra*. March 23, 2010. http://www.gamasutra.com/view/news/27719/Interview_Markus_Notch_Persson_Talks_Making_Minecraft.php (accessed September 15, 2015).

[2] Ewing, Adam, and Marie Mawad. "Minecraft founder Markus Persson: From 'indie' tech champion to potential billionaire on Microsoft deal." *Financial Post*. September 10, 2014. http://business.financialpost.com/fp-tech-desk/post-arcade/minecraft-founder-markus-persson-from-indie-tech-champion-to-potential-billionaire-on-microsoft-deal (accessed September 15, 2015).

[3] Peisner, David. "The Wizard of Minecraft." *RollingStone*. May 7, 2014. http://www.rollingstone.com/culture/news/the-wizard-of-minecraft-20140507 (accessed September 15, 2015).

deposits. A sandbox mode let players build structures.

Zachthronics, *Infiminer*'s developer, abandoned the project a month after its debut, but the source code was leaked and hackers moved in to pick up the slack. When Persson stumbled across the game, he "had a blast," but realized there was room for improvement. "Building was

Figure 50.1 Markus "Notch" Persson's *Minecraft* made him a billionaire, but not a happy man.

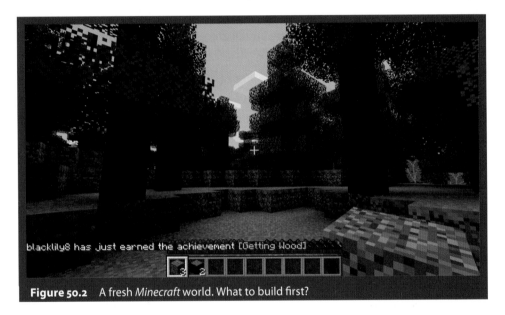

blacklily8 has just earned the achievement [Getting Wood]

Figure 50.2 A fresh *Minecraft* world. What to build first?

fun, but there wasn't enough variation, and the [aesthetics] were horrible. I thought a fantasy game in that style would work really well."[4] It was also riddled with bugs. Persson's new look was charming and more inviting, and, best yet, ran smoothly in a browser (see Figure 50.2).

As interest built in his project, Persson continued to add new features, including the all-important multiplayer and survival mode. This latter mode had zombies and skeletons who would come out at night; players had to work quickly to build an adequate shelter to defend against them. These additions made the game even more popular—so popular, in fact, they crashed Persson's server. Videos began appearing on YouTube, showing off

---

[4] Persson, Markus. "The Origins of Minecraft." *The Word of Notch.* October 30, 2009. http://notch.tumblr.com/post /227922045/the-origins-of-minecraft (accessed September 15, 2015).

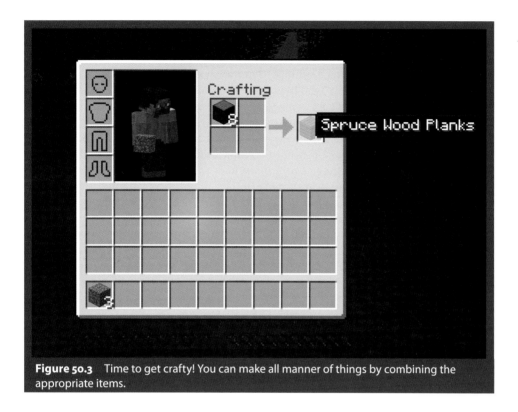

Figure 50.3 Time to get crafty! You can make all manner of things by combining the appropriate items.

elaborate structures people had built in the game, such as a replica of the *Enterprise* from *Star Trek*.[5] By 2010, Persson had thousands of players, including 6000 dedicated enough to pay his $13 early-bird fee to access the/indev/alpha, which featured the aforementioned survival mode.[6] Persson continued to graft on more features as the game moved from alpha into beta (see Figure 50.3). By January of 2011, he'd sold nearly a million copies, and was able to found his own company, Mojang, and hire his first employees.

The game was officially released on November 18, 2011, and won a number of prestigious awards. Persson then handed the reigns over to Jens Bergensten and went off to pursue other projects. Persson's departure didn't keep the game from receiving a steady flow of improvements and influxes of new fans.

---

[5] Mojang. "A Longer History." *Minecraft*. 2015. https://minecraft.net/game (accessed September 15, 2015).

[6] Handy, Alex. "Interview: Markus 'Notch' Persson Talks about Making Minecraft." *Gamasutra*. March 23, 2010. http://www.gamasutra.com/view/news/27719/Interview_Markus_Notch_Persson_Talks_Making_Minecraft.php (accessed September 15, 2015).

Persson made headlines again on September 15, 2014, when he sold Mojang to Microsoft for $2.5 billion.[7] Some figured Persson had simply sold out to the same sort of corporate influences he'd railed against earlier in his career. However, Persson blamed it on his discomfort with being a symbol. "I'm not an entrepreneur. I'm not a CEO. I'm a nerdy computer programmer who likes to have opinions on Twitter," said Persson. "I don't want to be … responsible for something huge that I don't understand, that I don't want to work on that keeps coming back to me."[8]

Fortunately for fans of the game, Microsoft opted for a mostly hands-off approach with Mojang and the *Minecraft* community. *Minecraft: Xbox One Edition* debuted on September 5, 2014, and a *Windows 10 Edition* beta was released on July 28, 2015. An education-themed version called *MinecraftEDU* has already been adopted by more than 2100 schools to teach "every subject from history to art to science."[9] So far, so good, but Microsoft will long remain a benevolent overlord.

As for Persson, the freshly minted billionaire seems miserable. He's often taken to Twitter to express his suffering: "Hanging out in Ibiza with a bunch of friends and partying with famous people, able to do whatever I want … I've never felt more isolated."[10] If the replies these Tweets have received are any indication, many find it hard to sympathize with his plight.

50.1 Playing *Minecraft* Today

Just go to http://minecraft.net/store to purchase versions Windows, Mac, Linux, PS3, Xbox 360, iOS, or Android. You can also get *Minecraft: Xbox One Edition* from the Xbox store or at most game retailers.

---

[7]   Peckham, Matt. "Minecraft Is Now Part of Microsoft, and It Only Cost $2.5 Billion." *Time*. September 15, 2014. http://time .com/3377886/microsoft-buys-mojang/ (accessed September 15, 2015).

[8]   Karmali, Luke. "NOTCH ON LEAVING MOJANG: 'IT'S ABOUT MY SANITY'." *IGN*. September 15, 2014. http://www.ign.com /articles/2014/09/15/notch-on-leaving-mojang-its-about-my-sanity (accessed September 15, 2015).

[9]   Gaudiosi, John. "The new way to learn? Brick by brick." *Fortune*. August 1, 2014. http://fortune.com/2014/08/01/minecraft -edu/ (accessed September 15, 2015).

[10]   Matyszczyk, Chris. "Billionaire who sold Minecraft to Microsoft is sad and lonely." *CNET*. August 30, 2015. http://www .cnet.com/news/billionaire-who-sold-minecraft-to-microsoft-is-sad-and-lonely/ (accessed September 15, 2015).

Afterword

I hope that you've enjoyed this whirlwind tour through 50 of the greatest and most influential video games of all time. I encourage you to try them all, even the ones you think you won't like. You'd be surprised how fast these games can grow on you.

I'd like to take a moment to reflect on some things I've learned in the course of researching and writing this book—some insights, I think, into what it takes to make a great game.

First, every great game gets made because somebody wants to play it badly enough to make it. I frequently encounter people who assume that a "good idea" is their ticket to glory in the games industry, but the reality is that every professional game designer already has a drawer full of them. If you take it upon yourself to learn how to make your idea into a working game, no matter how crude (*Minecraft*!), you're already far, far ahead of the pack.

Second, if just being able to play the game you envision isn't reward enough—in other words, if you're in it for the money, fame, or status, don't quit your day job. Sid Meier, Will Wright, Richard Garriott, and John Romero did not get to where they are today because they wanted to get rich and famous. Indeed, in many cases, they seemed hell-bent on ruining themselves and their companies! They set out to make the games they wanted to play, even if everyone else thought they were stupid.

Finally, "originality" is overrated. Some designers may pride themselves on doing something wonderful that's never been done before, but they're misguided for three reasons. For one, as I was writing this book, I came to the painful realization that the old saying is true—there's nothing new under the sun. You're never "first," but only early— and you don't want to be the schmuck that rings the doorbell when the hosts are still setting up for the party. If you want to make a better impression, try being "fashionably late," which brings me to my second point: Time spent polishing and playtesting a game is never wasted. Many are the games that flopped because they had too many bugs. How many games do you know that failed for the lack of them? Finally, no matter how much sense it makes to sell out, do not sell out. If the money didn't bring you into this business, don't let it take you out of it.

I end each of my "Matt Chat" episodes with a relevant quotation. Perhaps it would not be a bad way to end now, either. I leave you, then, with the words of the great Shigeru Miyamoto, words that I think aptly sum up my afterword, this entire book, and perhaps our very lives: "A delayed game is eventually good, but a rushed game, forever bad."

Index